Imprisoned

Sponsored by the Rosa Luxemburg Stiftung with funds of the Federal Ministry for Economic Cooperation and Development of the Federal Republic of Germany. This publication or parts of it can be used by others for free as long as they provide a proper reference to the original publication.

First published by Jacana Media (Pty) Ltd in 2018

10 Orange Street
Sunnyside
Auckland Park 2092
South Africa
+2711 628 3200
www.jacana.co.za

© Sylvia Neame, 2018

All rights reserved.

ISBN 978-1-4314-2734-5

Cover design by publicide
Editing by Alison Lowry
Proofreading by Megan Mance
Index by Megan Mance
Set in Ehrhardt MT 11/13pt
Printed by ABC Press, Cape Town
Job no. 003361

See a complete list of Jacana titles at www.jacana.co.za

Imprisoned

The experience of a prisoner under apartheid

Sylvia Neame

I sometimes have the feeling that I am not a real human being but rather some bird or other creature in deformed human form. (Rosa Luxemburg, letter, 2 May 1917, from Wronke – a fortress in Berlin)

Thus I am from my cell on all sides tied by invisible, fine threads to a thousand small and big creatures and I respond to all with disquiet, pain and self-reproach ... (Rosa Luxemburg, letter, 12 May 1918, from prison in Breslau)

I walked just now like an animal in a cage my usual 'stroll' along my wall, there and back, and my heart contracted convulsively from distress because I cannot leave here, oh, if only I could go from here! (Rosa Luxemburg, letter, 15 January 1917, from Wronke)

Acknowledgements

I wish to thank Gabriele Mohale, archivist at the History Papers Research Archive, University of the Witwatersrand, for the many occasions when she has come to my assistance in the course of preparing this manuscript for publication.

I am also deeply grateful to my late maternal grandmother, Maude Barlow, from whose scrapbook I extracted the newscuttings about my detentions and court appearances. I have much else to thank her for, not least her curiosity, her resilience and love of the arts, all of which she in one way or another passed onto me.

I am grateful to the Rosa Luxemburg Foundation for financial assistance for this publication. I am especially moved by this since the year 2018 is the centenary of Rosa Luxemburg's murder in Berlin, together with Karl Liebknecht, by right-wing elements.

English translations from Briefe aus dem Gefängnis, *published by Karl Dietz Verlag, Berlin, 1987.*

Contents

In the death cell in Pretoria 1
On the way from Pretoria to Barberton Prison 27
I join my fellow trialists 39
Introduction to the routine 44
The authorities' campaign of provocation 48
I am charged with using indecent language 59
We are classified as highly dangerous convicts 65
Night-time lock-up 68
Are we stoics? 74
Washing laundry 80
The doctor 82
I have a gaol visit 86
Our organisation, their disorganisation 88
The prison experience 93
An easing up begins 96
A prisoner breaks down 103
Behaviour of prison officials, including Matron Bester 111
I move from a single to a communal cell .116
Christmas 1965 124
New Year 139
Captain Broodryk turns up 142
Rehabilitation 149

Excursion to the local hospital	152
A visit from Judge Boshoff	161
I receive news of Kathy	170
We share information and letters	173
Flashbacks	181
Three chameleons join the tortoise in captivity	187
My appeal: the authorities play cat-and-mouse with me	195
A new phase in our washing duties	201
I win my appeal	204
Letting off steam	207
We meet the Rev. Canon Langley	212
The prison look	218
My second hospital outing	222
Condition of our prison clothing and other matters	228
I have a depression	233
I write as a form of therapy	240
Something of the life of black prisoners at Barberton	252
The prisons service	256
Prison symptoms	259
More diary entries	264
Ann writes poetry	273
Venetian blinds	276
Judge Ludorf visits	284
Ann complains about Matron Bester	288
Judge Hiemstra on a visit	292
Brigadier Viljoen	294
We win a battle	301
Early release – Amnesty 31 May?	304
Aucamp comes with a high prison official	313
The screws are on and Matron Bester breaks down	322

Further extracts from my diary 328
Our alcohol industry 334
Reclassification from 'C' to 'B' group 341
Viljoen and a conflict: Prisons/Security branch 344
Leslie Schermbrucker and Violet Weinberg join us 354
Mark Weinberg dies 359
The tortoise and I 365
Birdwatching 372
Preparing for the art exhibition 380
Objectivity, subjectivity – and Canon Langley 390
The prison board comes 395
Cultural concerns 400
The tempest 407
The psychologically complex question of escape 413
My own attempt at escape 418
The festive season, 1966 436
Gate-fever 440
The prison board on another visit 443
The prospect of release 450
The prisoner's problem of space and location 454
Author's note 465
Index of names 469

ABOVE: Photo, with article by Ann Cavill, **Sunday** Express, *17 May 1964, taken in order to provide Ahmed Kathrada with a photo before his sentencing in the Rivonia Trial.*

In the death cell in Pretoria

ON THE WAY IN LATE JULY 1965 from the North End Prison in Port Elizabeth to Barberton Maximum Security Prison in the Eastern Transvaal I was delivered by Colonel Aucamp early one afternoon into Pretoria Central Prison. Here I was taken to the (white women's) death cell upstairs. Aucamp, together with Lieutenant Britz from Pretoria Central as female escort, had fetched me by car from Port Elizabeth. We drove up to Pretoria, with overnight stops at gaols in Colesberg and Kroonstad.

Colonel Aucamp had a wide range of responsibilities in relation specifically to political prisoners. He was, it appeared, a kind of liaison between the security establishment and the prisons and, as we discovered later, apparently had direct access to Minister of Justice BJ Vorster. It was Aucamp who was to have a crucial influence on our lives in Barberton Prison.

In Barberton I was due to rejoin my comrades from the Communist Party trial which had taken place over something like six months in the magistrate's court in Johannesburg until we had finally been sentenced in April 1965. We had been incarcerated since early July 1964. While the female trialists were to go to Barberton, our male counterparts, which included members of the Central Committee, were to serve their sentences in Pretoria Central.

A couple of days after the end of our Johannesburg trial I had been taken alone, without any explanation, to Port Elizabeth. Indeed, I was not even told what our destination was. On the way down, in a small compartment at the front of a large prison van, with other prisoners in the large compartment at the back, I had come to the conclusion that I was being taken to some gaol in the south of the country in order to serve my sentence of two years (four years, with two running concurrently) in solitary confinement. As I was to find out after about ten days – in solitary – in the North End Prison, I had been taken down to Port Elizabeth in order to face a new trial in a court in the eastern Cape village of Humansdorp, 58 miles away. It was to turn out to be a frame-up, one of many in the eastern Cape. After three and a half months in Port Elizabeth, I had been sentenced to an extra four years' imprisonment. So by the time I reached

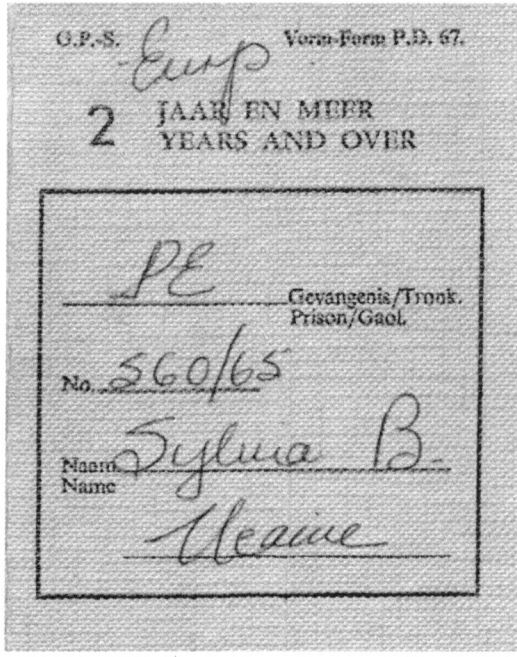

Pretoria Central in July 1965 I had six years to serve.

Pretoria Central was not unknown to me. I had spent one and a half months there in October–November 1963 as a 90-day detainee (without charge or access to a lawyer and no reading material except a Bible). My detention for interrogation at that time had to do with the Rivonia Trial

Above: This is the card I was given in Port Elizabeth.

In the death cell in Pretoria

which was due to start, with Nelson Mandela as accused number one. I had been involved with Ahmed Kathrada, one of the accused, and the Security Branch wanted to know more about him, including about a hide-out in Mountain View, one of the Johannesburg suburbs.

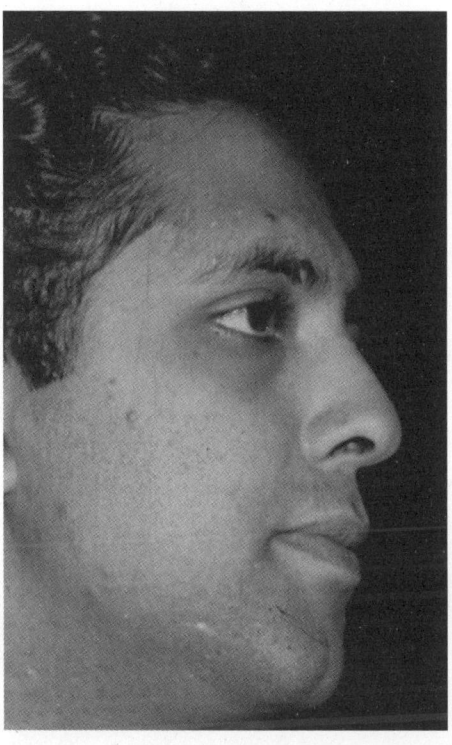

During that detention I had been in a cell right at the end of the hall upstairs, which had fifteen small single cells, seven on one side and eight on the other. All the other cells were empty. My only company were the huge rats that ran along wooden beams above the strong wire mesh that closed in my cell from the top, not far above my head. This hall opened up at the other end into a space that contained the white women's death cell from where a staircase went down to a door below, with access to a courtyard. At this time the death cell was unoccupied except for a short period when Ruth First was there.

Some seven months after my release from detention at the end of November 1963 I was taken once again to Pretoria Central. This was

Sylvia Neame

CASE NO. ....

ANNEXURE "A"

CHARGE SHEET

IN THE MAGISTRATE'S COURT FOR THE REGIONAL
DIVISION OF TRANSVAAL

HELD AT JOHANNESBURG.

THE STATE

versus

1. ABRAM FISCHER
2. IVAN FREDERICK SCHERMBRUCKER
3. ELI WEINBERG
4. ESTHER BARSEL
5. NORMAN LEVY
6. LEWIS BAKER
7. JEAN STRACHAN
8. ANNE NICHOLSON
9. CONSTANTINOS GAZIDES
10. PAUL HENRY TREWHELA
11. SYLVIA BRERETON NEAME
12. FLORENCE DUNCAN
13. MOLLIE IRENE DOYLE
14. HYMIE BARSEL

(hereinafter referred to as the accused).

COUNT 1:-

THAT the said accused are guilty of the offence of having contravened Section 11(c), read with Sections 3(1)(a)(i), 1, 2(1), 11(i) and 12 of Act No. 44 of 1950, as amended.

2.

for my second detention under the 90-day law, with again no access to a lawyer and my only reading a Bible. On this occasion there were several political detainees in single cells along one side of that same hall. As it turned out, they were to be my fellow trialists in the Communist Party trial later that year.

It was so cold that I did not sleep one minute during the two weeks I was there. It had snowed shortly before our arrest and the cells were unheated. We went on hunger strike as part of a campaign, directed against the 90-day detention law, demanding that we be charged or released.

After two weeks we were separated. I was taken to the police station in Fordsburg, Johannesburg, where I spent another one and a half months in solitary on a mattress on the concrete floor of a likewise unheated cell. This time round the cell was large and it had windows without glass, only wire mesh. The other detainees had been taken separately to various locations in and around Johannesburg.

After two months in detention, fifteen persons were charged for membership of the Communist Party. Accused number one was Bram Fischer and our trial became known as the 'First Bram Fischer Trial' or 'Bram Fischer and thirteen others'. Pixie Benjamin was to be discharged on our first day in court. She had been on hunger strike for over 50 days by this time, a really brave woman whose preparedness to risk her life in the fight against apartheid has almost been forgotten. During our awaiting trial period, which was to stretch into nine months, we were held at the Johannesburg Prison, known as the Fort.

It was about two o'clock in the afternoon on the way to Barberton that I was locked up in the death cell at Pretoria Central. It was to be expected, as I was a convicted prisoner, that I would have been instructed to take off my private clothes and put on a uniform. However, that was evidently too much work. I was given some food and told they would bring me some eating utensils. My cell door was closed and locked.

I waited for about fifteen minutes and then called the wardress – a young blonde, not bad looking, in the usual khaki uniform – through the broken spyhole of my cell door. I asked for eating utensils. She shrugged and mumbled that she would be bringing them. I waited another half an hour. When the next wardress passed my door, I called out again. She turned towards me, turned away and shrugged.

There was a young African woman in a cell not many feet from my cell door in the hall across the way from me. This was clearly used as the death cell for African women. Her door was open, just the grille locked. She stood there, quiet, resigned, looking outwards, hands behind her back. The wardress on duty with her sat on a chair in front of the cell. This prisoner, unlike me, was obviously awaiting execution. It was a gaol regulation that a prisoner sentenced to death should never for a moment be left alone in case they killed themselves.

I watched the woman through my spyhole for a bit and then had a look around my cell. Nothing much of interest, except a rather terrifying picture of Jesus on the door of my locker. Not a very comforting picture for a prisoner awaiting the rope and the trapdoor, I thought. There was a bed in one corner with a broken spring. This cell was larger than the death cell the African woman was in. It had two windows, very dusty, one looking over the stairway and the other looking out of the gaol towards a bowling green and a swimming bath, which would have been for the Prisons Department's staff.

I didn't much like being in the death cell because of its associations. When I was under my second 90 days in Pretoria the wardresses had teased us about Daisy de Melker's ghost, which they told us inhabited this part of the gaol. Daisy had been hanged in Pretoria in 1932 for poisoning two husbands and her son, and had become a notorious figure in South African prison mythology.

Margaret Rheeder, too, had been hanged in Pretoria Central – comparatively recently, in 1952 – and I was very conscious of the fact that I had taken much the same journey as she had when she came up to to be hanged. She had been in the same cell I had been in in Port Elizabeth and had been looked after by the same matron who had looked after me there, Matron Nel. Matron Nel had told me that Mrs Rheeder had torn her hair out in handfuls and screamed and sobbed when she was told that she had lost her appeal against her death sentence. She had been sentenced for murdering her husband with small doses of arsenic. She had been in such a state on the way up to Pretoria – she was taken under escort by train – that they had had to give her an injection to knock her out. Matron Nel told me that Matron Britz up at Pretoria Central hated taking women to be hanged, and she had particularly hated taking Mrs Rheeder. Somebody had described to me the blouse she wore, which was made in such a way that it could slip down in the process of hanging.

I had another link with Mrs Rheeder because not only had I been in the cell that she had been in in the Port Elizabeth gaol but when, after two months, a court had ordered that I should be taken out of isolation, the woman who was put in with me told me that she had known Mrs Rheeder personally. She used to sometimes sell her naphthalene.

No doubt, it had been a deliberate choice that she should join me. The two prisoners she had previously been with had been upset by her post-alcoholic hallucinations and it was probably thought that my new cell mate would be for me a harder burden to bear than solitary. Luckily, for me and for her, I seemed to make her feel more secure, as she told me, and after a few days she started settling down, although now and again she would see little men walking about in our cell.

Here in Pretoria Central, then, I was in Mrs Rheeder's death cell. I had a picture of her in my mind, one that I had gathered from things Matron Nel had told me – a blonde woman, quite attractive. The picture I had was that she had long hair but I may only have come to this conclusion in connection with Matron Nel's description of her tearing her hair out in handfuls when she heard she was definitely going to die.

I called to the blonde wardress again through the spyhole. 'Please could I have some eating utensils.' She turned and said with irritation, 'I haven't got more than two hands.' She then walked across to the wardress sitting in front of the African woman's death cell, and had a friendly chat. Typical Pretoria Central, I thought. Eventually, a knife and fork were brought but by this time my food looked so revolting, and in my tense state revolting-looking food was likely to make me vomit, that I decided rather to leave it.

I lay on my bed for a short time, staring at the ceiling. What an uncomfortable bed, a huge dip in the middle. I tried to do what I had done during my first 90 days when my stomach had gone into severe spasm and I had had a dreadful heaving but did not vomit. I probably hadn't had enough food in my stomach. I tried to put myself into a kind of stupor so that I could doze.

I wondered how I could survive on so little food. At some stage during my fabricated trial I had ceased to be able to eat, even the nice food Matron Nel often cooked and brought to court. I only managed half a slice of dry bread in the morning and a cup of what they called tea in a metal cup, this for over two months.

In the death cell my attempt to doze was constantly interrupted as I heard footsteps coming to a halt before my door. I would look up at the spyhole and there would be an eye looking in. Eventually, each time this happened I stuck my tongue out. I thought that would give the other prisoners – because this was obviously who they were – something to think about: a prisoner awaiting hanging who stuck her tongue out at her fellow human beings.

One of them asked me for tobacco. I said I had none. Another asked me who I was. I said I was a political prisoner.

'Polity … what is that?'

'I am against the government, against Verwoerd,' I answered.

A pause – obviously not understanding.

'I am against apartheid,' I said hopelessly.

'Oh, you are Congress,' she said. 'Congress'. (She was an African prisoner.)

'Yes, yes,' I said, catching onto that. 'Congress.'

'Oh,' she said. 'Shame. How long have you got?'

'Six years,' I said.

'Shame, that is a long time.'

'How long have you got?' I asked her.

'I go out May next year.'

'Oh, good,' I said, 'not so long. What are you in for?'

'Dagga and immorality. No tobacco?' she asked me hopefully.

'Sorry, none,' I said.

The shining dark object slipped away from the spyhole. I had this kind of conversation with several other prisoners. I stopped sticking my tongue out for I had established contact. I was no longer the condemned prisoner with bravado and contempt for my fellow human being. I was Sylvia Neame who had six years for 'Congress'! I was a person of some standing! I couldn't afford to stick my tongue out now!

I remembered that I might know one of the inmates in Pretoria. She had been at the Fort – in the African part of the gaol – and had then been moved after some trouble. I asked a prisoner who came to my spyhole if she was there, and she went to find her. I had a bit of a chat with her; she didn't have so long to go. I told her about my eastern Cape case. She made some sympathetic comment. I don't know what else I had expected but I felt let down. I don't quite know what I wanted. I think expressions of great horror. It seemed to have become rather a personal issue for me. It came down to something like this: not only was there my conviction of the good cause I was fighting for but a deep sense of how bad Du Preez was. There was little doubt that he had done evil things and, no doubt, was still doing them.

Sergeant Jonathan du Preez from the Security Branch had been the investigating officer not only in my case but in the cases of many people in the eastern Cape, including that of the trade unionist and ANC leader Vuyisile Mini, who had been hanged in November 1964, together with Wilson Khayinga and Zinakile Mkaba, not so long before my case began. Indeed, Mini was on occasion mentioned in the course of my trial. Du Preez had bragged to me that it was he who had got Mini hanged. He had also indicated that initially he had tried to get my case heard in a higher court, clearly suggesting that I, too, might have faced a death sentence. He claimed proudly that all in all he had managed to send sixteen people to their deaths.

Acccording to newspapers in the course of my trial, there had been simply hundreds of accused involved in court cases in the eastern Cape with so-called 'travelling/professional witnesses' going from trial to trial. Many of the accused had been sentenced to the maximum they could get in a magistrate's court, which was nine years; if less, this was usually because they had spent some time in prison before sentence. This had clearly been the policy deliberately adopted, with prosecution and magistrates following instructions from 'above', from the security establishment, which was becoming ever more powerful in an increasingly corrupt state.

Du Preez had also initially expected that I would be sentenced to nine years in the magistrate's court, as he'd indicated to me. The publicity surrounding my trial and the obvious problems in the state's evidence had clearly made this difficult. None the less, the hold of the Branch on magistrate and prosecutor had ensured that I was given a four-year sentence despite the glaring weaknesses in the state's case, not only weaknesses but clear indications that the evidence had been fabricated.

I remember how when the well-known anti-apartheid advocate David Soggot came down from Johannesburg to consult with me in the Port Elizabeth gaol – he was to represent me in the regional magistrate's court in Humansdorp – he at first did not believe me when I told him that I knew nothing of an ANC meeting in Grahamstown that I was alleged to have attended, that I had never heard of the 'New Plan' which, according to the charge sheet, I was supposed to have urged the meeting to adopt, and that some of the names of the people who were alleged to have attended I had never heard of before. However, Soggot soon became convinced that I had, indeed, not been at the meeting and that I was facing a frame-up. Black defendants had not been so lucky with their

lawyers, who had simply not believed them.

The 'New Plan', a state witness was to hold in the course of my case, was adopted after the banning of the ANC – the ANC, together with the Pan-Africanist Congress, had been banned in March 1960 – and was a policy for 'freedom for Africans by violence and sabotage'. As it happened, at the time of the meeting – it was alleged to have taken place in February 1961 – what later became known as the armed wing of the ANC, Umkhonto we Sizwe (the Spear of the Nation), had not yet been established. The alleged ANC policy of the 'New Plan' had evidently been invented by the Security Branch. Soggot later told me that he had been involved in several searing trials but he had never been so upset as he had been in the course of my trial.

Now, in the death cell in Pretoria, I saw Jonathan du Preez before me. There he was standing in the Humansdorp court in his smart pinstripe suit, hands nonchalantly in his pockets, with that slight swagger of his, pleased as Punch, a little boy proud of his work, proud of himself in general. One of the things that worried me about him was his tremendous naivety; he was corrupt, ambitious and yet like an irresponsible boy. The terrifying thing was that such a person should have the lives of people in his hands. The racist and authoritarian policy of apartheid had offered somebody with a psychotic love of power over other human beings a means of satisfying his ambition. As it happened, subsequent to my trial he was promoted from sergeant to lieutenant.

After I had been in the death cell for some hours, I noticed that I had no sanitary bucket. I called through my spyhole. There was no response. Eventually Lieutenant Britz came with my evening meal. She unlocked the door and then the grille, pushed my food in.

'I haven't a po,' I complained. And before she could back out and close the door I insisted, 'And I want to get out of these clothes, please. Could I have a uniform?'

'But you will be leaving tomorrow,' she answered. 'None the less,' I said, 'I want a uniform. These clothes are getting dirty. And I have to travel in them.' She was about to close the door. 'And I want a po.'

She got that clouded, vague, resentful, looking-at-a-prisoner look. I had had more than enough of it from her during my first 90 days. It was a look well known to prisoners. Almost every wardress I have ever come across has it. It is a sort of irritated shrug which says, You are a prisoner. You have no right to anything. And I'm busy.

I felt that feeling of helplessness I knew only too well. The door was going to be closed in my face and locked and I would be left without a po. Then I saw the expression in her eyes change; they were turned inwards, thinking, reconsidering. She turned to the wardress at her elbow. 'Gaan vat 'n po en 'n uniform.'

Ah, the Harold Strachan case, I thought. I had heard about it in Port Elizabeth. The po was brought to my door and Lieutenant Britz pushed it in – with her foot. A uniform came, too, one of the blue ones, instead of the dreary khaki.

'You'll have to wear your own shoes,' she said.

'All right,' I said magnanimously. At least I had got something.

'There is no globe in your cell,' she informed me.

'You mean I'm going to have no light tonight?' I asked anxiously.

'You will have no light. I have reported it to the men but they haven't come.'

'Can't you tell them to come now?'

'No, it is too late.'

Oh dear, I thought, I'm going to be in the death cell in the dark all evening and all night. Anyway, at least there was the other prisoner down the way and even if she went to sleep there would have to be a wardress there keeping watch. Or so I thought.

I suppose it must now have been about five o'clock. My cell was already almost dark. It was, in any case, a dark cell. To be able to read in it, I would probably need the light on even in the middle of the day.

Well, there was a long evening ahead of me. Luckily, I knew quite a few freedom songs. In addition, I had learned about 25 pop songs from one of the prisoners in Port Elizabeth. I would spend the next few hours singing, I thought. I put the blue uniform on. It was huge, came down to about the middle of my shins, very wide, too. It was size 38 – I am size 34. But at least I wouldn't ruin my own clothes, though I did feel a bit demoralised by the thought of what I must look like. Anyway, who cares? I asked myself.

I had also enquired from Lieutenant Britz as to when I was going to have some exercise. I was entitled to an hour a day and I had had none all day. And when was I going to have a bath? She responded that she didn't have time to give me exercise that day; I could have some the following day. And also a bath. I had made these requests all very fast, trying to fit them in before the shrug and the too busy sigh and the slamming of my door and the key turning in the lock.

Once she had left, I paced up and down from my door across to the window that looked out of the gaol. The floor was a dark grey, I supposed black really, but grey from the dust. There were little indentations in the floor from the metal feet of the bed ... and from my stiletto heels?

The panes of the large-ish window overlooking the staircase were covered in dust. They had been put in with putty that had not been painted. It looked soft. There were some short scratches in it – nail marks? I felt it with my fingers to see what it felt like. No, it was hard. There were some finger marks in the dust on the panes. I wondered whose they were and on which side of the panes they were, inside or outside? Inside, I supposed.

I looked through the other window overlooking the bowling green and the swimming bath. Not bad. At least there was a view, more than there was in the cells in the hall down the way. There the windows were very dusty and high up and behind thick wire and mesh, not really accessible; and some of the cells did not have windows at all.

In the death cell I examined the locker. Nothing inside it. Just a nasty, musty smell. There was a blue bedcover on my bed, rather grubby. The sheets looked as if they had been on that bed many months and slept in for at least a few weeks. They were grey and smelly and the blankets were dirty too.

Under the bed I tried to discover which spring was broken and I found that it was the same bed I had had during my first 90 days towards the end of 1963. It was now nearly August 1965. The spring had not yet been fixed. Of course it would never be repaired. Anyway, I felt a bit guilty about that spring for it had broken because I had sat on the bed about fifteen or sixteen hours a day while I read my Bible. And I had been informed by Lieutenant Britz (who was Matron Britz then, since promoted) that I was not allowed to sit on the bed. But I had told her

THE HOLY BIBLE

Revised Standard Version

CONTAINING THE

Old and New Testaments

Translated from the original tongues being the version set forth A.D. 1611

revised A.D. 1881–1885 and A.D. 1901

compared with the most ancient authorities and revised A.D. 1952

Sylvia Neame

LONDON
OXFORD UNIVERSITY PRESS
1962

I had a bad back, I couldn't sit on a hard stool, without any support, sixteen hours a day.

Under the bed in the death cell was a layer of dust. Revolting, I thought, and found myself breathing through my mouth instead of my nose as I am inclined to do when something revolts me. When I realised I was breathing all the dust straight into my lungs, I continued breathing normally. I had a look at the po; it didn't look too clean. And, of course, no disinfectant. A roll of toilet paper.

I went back to the spyhole to see what the other prisoner was doing. She was still standing there, just behind her grille, with her hands behind her back, looking outwards. I might have six years, I thought, four for something I hadn't done, but at least I wasn't going to die. Not yet, anyway, though one never knew what the Branch was going to be up to next. And they certainly seemed determined to give me a very bad time. I must say I didn't know why exactly the Branch had it in for me. I still do not know.

I imagined the woman before me in her blouse that was going to slip down as the trapdoor opened and she fell through into the room below, with the rope breaking her neck. I heard the thud that I was told one hears in other parts of the gaol as the prisoner drops through. And there were the faces of the ugly men in dark suits below, witnessing the execution. Ugh. There is something revolting about scientifically planned death.

I thought of Du Preez, so proud that he had sent sixteen men to their death. My God, didn't these people know what they were doing? I imagined Aucamp (in a dark suit) in that room below the trapdoor witnessing Vuyisile Mini's execution with an impassive face. During my first 90 days the rope had been constantly on my mind. The Branch had told me that they were going to hang my boyfriend, Kathrada. Well, they had not managed it.

I moved away from the spyhole and took the few steps to the locker where I again examined the gloomy picture of the Christ figure. Somebody seemed to have darkened the whole thing with pencil, making it look even gloomier.

Scratched on the wall between the window overlooking the stairs and the locker was a calendar with dates marked off. About 25 days in

March–April 1965 were crossed off. Nearby was another calendar July and August 1964, with nearly the full two months marked off. Were these calendars scratched onto the wall by condemned prisoners? More likely 90-day detainees. In almost any cell at that time, whether in a police station or a gaol, there were these little calendars.

I had another look inside the locker. It was too dark to see whether there was anything in it. But there had been nothing in it when I had looked earlier on so I supposed it was still empty, except perhaps for a cockroach or two. I remembered that there had been cockroaches in my cell down the hall, apart from the rats above my head. I hoped there were no rats in this cell. Probably not, as there was really no way in that I could see, except through my door, and that was locked, of course. I was pleased that the door was locked.

It was quite dark in my cell by now. Must have been about 6.30. I saw through my side window, the one over the stairway, a dusty image of a wardress in mufti coming up the stairs, in a bright green jersey, short boyish hair. She evidently had taken over from the wardress in front of the other condemned cell. I whistled through the spyhole, usefully the glass was broken. She came over. I had tried the bell in the cell earlier when I found I didn't have a po, and had found it was not working.

'Why isn't the bell working?' I asked. She looked friendly enough.

'Have a cigarette,' she said, preparing to push one through the spyhole.

'No. No, thanks. I don't smoke. Why isn't the bell working?'

'They've turned the bells off in the death cells because condemned prisoners ring the bell all day and night,' she replied, then added: 'When they get hysterical.'

'Oh, who for instance?'

'Mrs Rheeder,' she said.

She wandered off to the chair in front of the other cell.

'Hey,' I called after her. 'Tell the other prisoner if she gets bored during the night she must talk to me. I'll probably get bored too with no light in here and nothing to read.'

'Okay,' she said, 'I'll tell her.'

She moved over towards the woman, boyishly taking a puff from her cigarette, and then flicking the ash onto the black floor. She went up to the grille and passed her 'stompie' through to the girl who gave a few puffs and threw it down out of her cell. A light was on in the hall. I moved away from the spyhole and looked through the window over the stairs. It was dark there. I turned away, dark in my cell, too, but a small rectangle of light still at the window that looked out of the gaol onto the bowling green and swimming bath.

I decided it was time to sing the last few hours away before I climbed into the uncomfortable-looking bed. The bell downstairs rang. And the wardress in the green jersey went below. I started singing 'Nkosi sikelel' iAfrika' through the spyhole. My voice didn't seem to be carrying at all. So I went over to the window and projected my voice over the staircase. That was better. Good acoustics, I thought, though maybe it only sounds good to me in here. Maybe they can't hear me on the other side.

I ran through 'Nkosi' twice and then went over to the spyhole to see if I was having any effect on the other prisoner. No. She looked totally unaware of the fact that I was singing. Perhaps my voice didn't carry into the hall. It was quite possible. So I might as well sing to myself, I thought, and paced backwards and forwards in my cell from the door to the window looking outwards. I sang 'Shosholoza' and 'We Shall Overcome'. I remembered that John Harris had sung 'We Shall Overcome' as he walked to the gallows. Vuyisile Mini had also sung freedom songs as he walked to his death. 'Siyahamba'. I sang that five or six times. And so on.

In Port Elizabeth gaol when I was locked up in solitary I used to march up and down for hours singing freedom songs. I would sing out of the window of my cell as loudly as I could across the gaol. It is amazing how much time it can take up. And when I was feeling particularly tense and nervous, it helped me relax somewhat.

But it didn't stop me thinking. I remember this surprised me. Sometimes I would think about the songs I was singing, but most of the time my mind was turning over my court case. What had I been doing at the time I was supposed to have been at the meeting? In fact, I was already living in Cape Town at 138 Bree Street in the rented house of Gillian Jewell, that old Malay house, later pulled down by the apartheid government in the course of its policy of residential segregation. The ANC meeting had allegedly taken place in the eastern Cape, in Grahamstown. True, I had lived in Grahamstown (now Makhanda) while I attended Rhodes University but had left in November 1960, never to return, not even for the graduation ceremony which I think took place in early 1961.

Moreover, I was not a member of the Congress movement at the time but of the Liberal Party. I was active in the Liberal Party's organised sit-in campaign in Cape Town. We used to go into restaurants in mixed race groups, something not allowed in South Africa at the time. It was only in the course of 1962 that I joined the Congress of Democrats, the white alliance partner of the ANC.

As it happened, I was not simply accused of being a member of the Congress movement but of being a member specifically of the ANC. Membership by whites was impossible at that time. In fact, the policy was only changed in 1969 while the ANC was in exile. It would have been impossible for me as a white, more especially a young inexperienced one, to have attended an ANC meeting and, moreover, to have called for a radical change of policy. The whole charge was, in fact, absolutely ludicrous – in the witness box in the Humansdorp court I designated it utter nonsense.

None the less, I had known that I had to offer convincing evidence in my defence, perhaps above all in order to influence a higher court since it seemed that the magistrate, JL Cilliers, together with the prosecutor, PJ Kotze, was following the instructions of the security police. Apart from the efforts to remember my own movements at the time, there was a need to present the relevant political information which would expose how absurd the whole state case was.

Amongst other things, the defence managed to get Govan Mbeki as a witness. He was brought in a South African army Dakota by the Prisons Department to Humansdorp from Robben Island where he was serving a life sentence. Indeed, Govan gave me a look from the witness box which I knew meant, Love from Kathy. He came together with two young men who likewise were to give evidence for the defence. In one way or another, they thereby risked their lives. They were Winnard Mati and Terrance Makwabe from Cradock. One of them told my legal team

Robben Island men arrive

HUMANSDORP.—A South African Air Force Dakota touched down at Humansdorp at 10.30 today, bringing three witnesses from Robben Island to the Sylvia Neame trial.

The plane from Cape Town circled the town for about 20 minutes before landing. It was met by members of the Security Branch.

Sylvia Neame, 27, has pleaded not guilty to three counts of contravening the Suppression of Communism Act.

PRESS BARRED IN NEAME TRIAL

Herald Correspondent

HUMANSDORP.

THE Press is being excluded from the Regional Court at Humansdorp while Govan Mbeki, a prisoner on Robben Island, gives evidence in the trial of Sylvia

that he also had not been at the meeting but was serving years for this on Robben Island.

It was clearly important to offer as much evidence as I could as to my precise movements at that time. Who were the people I was seeing and who could possibly be alibi witnesses? As it happened, Gillian Jewell – she was a French teacher, having studied at the Sorbonne, and had been my French lecturer at Rhodes – appeared as a defence witness. Not only had we been living in the same house in Cape Town but we were both participating in the sit-in campaign.

Hadn't I perhaps written a letter or drawn money from a financial institution or signed into a hotel somewhere? And so on. What contradictions were there in the evidence of state witnesses that we had not noticed in court? My mind was in a continual whirl and there was nobody with whom I could talk in order to enable me to have some mental rest. True, I had my songs, which seemed to control my thinking a little.

Here in the death cell in Pretoria Central, my stopover before Barberton, I wasn't singing to stop the spinning because my mind wasn't spinning. I just wanted to pass the time in the dark until I felt tired enough to sleep, until I felt sleepy enough to forget about Daisy de Melker's ghost and Mrs Rheeder dropping through the open trapdoor.

I went to the window that looked towards the swimming bath. Occasionally somebody passed on the narrow tarred road that ran alongside the stone walls of the gaol beneath my window. Two women with headscarfs and carrying baskets passed just under my window while I was singing one of the pop songs I had learned from a fellow prisoner in Port Elizabeth gaol – a song that was sung by that well-known singer who was killed in an aeroplane crash on the way to Australia and whose name I cannot at the moment remember. It was a very popular song at the time and I had learned the words. The two women below obviously heard me for they looked around trying to discover where the voice was coming from. But they did not see me. Evidently, it did not strike them that the voice was coming from the gaol.

Down below in front of the main door of the female gaol, I saw the wardress in the green jersey with a young man, maybe her boyfriend.

'Who are you?' he called out, laughing, when he noticed me. 'Are you Daisy de Melker?'

'Yes!' I shouted. 'Daisy de Melker.'

It was dark in my cell. Probably about 7.30. The young wardress came up the stairs and went over to the other death cell. The woman was standing there as before, hands behind her back. She hardly appeared to change her position. I called through the spyhole and the wardress came over.

'When is she going to die?' I asked.

'She's been waiting for her appeal for months,' she said.

'How does she feel about it?' I asked.

'Oh, she says she is prepared to die if that is the will of God.'

'What did she do?' I asked.

'She and her boyfriend killed somebody. But she says she didn't do it. Her boyfriend did it – he's a gangster. And when she told her boyfriend that she was not prepared to do it, he stuck a knife into her.'

'Does she have a knife wound?'

'Yes, she does.'

'Do you believe her story?'

'Yes.'

'How does she feel about waiting?'

'Oh, she doesn't mind.'

'Oh,' I muttered. What else was there to say?

The wardress moved away from the spyhole. I went across to the staircase window. A wardress in mufti came and sat down on the top stair and the death cell wardress joined her. They chatted away. I started singing 'Nkosi sikelel' iAfrika' as loud as I could. They must have been about eight to twelve feet away from me but they didn't even turn round. Didn't voices carry from the death cell, I wondered.

I heard the condemned woman singing, very drearily, a song we had learned in the prison van that took us every day during our trial to the magistrate's court in central Johannesburg. Six of us had been in a tiny compartment in the front of the huge van. In the big space at the back were the African prisoners who were going to court and they used often to sing this song, 'Hya Kulamuzo, Hya Kulamuzo' and then other voices would sing, 'Salomani'. This woman had almost certainly been moved from the Fort to the Pretoria death cell. She must have been the young girl of nineteen we had heard about who had been sentenced to death while we were awaiting trial at the Fort.

Unusual for an African woman to sing so poorly. The voice stopped. I went to the spyhole. She had disappeared from her position near her grille. Heavens, she's going to sleep, I thought. The wardress had disappeared. Evidently, she was not going to stay at her post all night.

I was now alone. And I had to sleep in the bed in which Mrs Rheeder had probably slept. I took off my uniform and laid myself down in my underclothing as they had not given me a nightdress.

I was really in a kind of state of suspension in that death cell. I was there waiting, with no eye to the future. In Port Elizabeth the horror of those six years were with me. I remember standing in the front office of the gaol. The Officer-Commanding, a man called Van Wyk, was there, talking to me. Also present was the Matron-in-Charge, by name Matron Louw. Colonel van Wyk, with whom I had had a good relationship – indeed he had treated me sympathetically my whole stay in his prison – said at some point, 'You have a long time, Sylvia. I hope you are going to be a good prisoner.' He was kind, firm, treating me like a child.

The cold horror of those six years swept through me, six years during which I would be unable to be myself in any full sense. And I looked out of the large window of the office, which faced onto an extensive graveyard. I was quite alone with my six years, with the image of that cemetery outside and the road that ran between the cemetery and the female side of the gaol.

In Pretoria I was well on the way to Barberton in the Eastern Transvaal where I would join my comrades. They had already been there some months, three and a half in fact. But would I ever get there? I certainly didn't trust Aucamp. I might be kept in solitary somewhere. I might never be heard of again. Indeed, that was the feeling I had had initially when I arrived in Port Elizabeth. Not only had I been put into solitary but I had had no visitors. I was desperate for people outside to know where I was. I feared that I could just be put away forever and simply be lost to the world.

In the morning after a restless night in the death cell I saw Lieutenant Britz coming up the stone steps, helping herself by pushing up on the black metal hand rail, puffing a little, sighing. 'Here' (Lord), she muttered in her whining Afrikaans voice. There was a wardress with her. Well, I thought, Britz didn't know what I know and that was that a wardress hadn't been on duty all night in front of the cell of the condemned woman. A wardress was sitting there now ready for Britz to come up the stairs.

Britz unlocked the door of my cell. And then the grille.

'Morning, Lieutenant,' I said.

'Môre, Neame.'

I lifted with care the white enamel bucket with the lid and stepped out of my cell and put it down. I was following the gaol routine in a businesslike way. I took about five steps into the cell and swung round with what I considered was military precision and stood to attention. This was required of a prisoner and I thought I should underline that I was conscious that I was in the presence of the Matron-in-Charge who had just been made a lieutenant. I stood with feet apart, hands behind my back, eyes firmly ahead.

'All right, Neame.' She was pacified, pleased. For a moment I wondered if I'd found a possible ally but immediately dismissed the notion. Of course I hadn't. If she were given instructions to treat me badly, she would do just that. Be only too pleased to do so. But if I buttered her up at least that would discourage her from thinking about how to make my life unbearable, that is to take the initiative without instructions from Aucamp. 'You'll be getting your porridge, Neame.' My grille was locked. And then the door.

Lord, I must look a sight, I thought. Uniform nearly down to my ankles. I paced up and down the black floor of my cell, grey with dust, had a look out of the window. It was going to be a nice day. A slightly hazy blue sky. I sat on the dirty blue bedcover of my hurriedly made bed. Well, I wondered, will I see the others today or won't I? I felt the pain in my stomach and the familiar desire to vomit. I was frightened. What would they be up to next? Du Preez, on a visit to the gaol in Port Elizabeth, shortly before we had got on the road to Pretoria, had told me that the Prisons Department, that was undoubtedly Aucamp, together with the Security Branch, was determined to give me a bad time. After what had happened in Port Elizabeth and Humansdorp I believed him.

My door and grille were unlocked.

'Take your porridge, Neame.'

I fetched my porridge from outside the door and a mug of coffee. The porridge was cold and had a tight skin over the top. I pushed it partly aside with my spoon, and then added some sugar. No milk, of course. The coffee was cold, too, with a purplish, whitish, brownish look on top. I forced myself to take three spoons of porridge, trying not to vomit. And I drank about half the coffee. I smelled the dreary half-musty, half-sweet smell of my bedclothes. Ugh, I wanted to vomit. I stopped eating. That was all I could manage. I got up from the little table that was between the end of the bed and the wall. I had been sitting on the black metal raised piece at the end of my bed. I was stiff and aching. I hadn't slept much. But that was not unusual in the last three and a half months.

Locked up in isolation in the Port Elizabeth gaol, my mind had spun over my case all day, all night. Some nights I had not slept for even five minutes, my mind spinning and spinning. My pulse beating at great speed. In that cell with the parquet floor. My bed suspended somewhere in the middle. Those gloomy dirty frosted windows. So cold. And so dirty. The frosted windows smooth on the inside, bubbly on the outside. The black soot used to collect there. And when I touched the parquet floor a coating of black came off onto my fingers.

Originally I had thought this was from train smoke for all day and all night I heard trains nearby. Also the smell of the sea, which was a couple of hundred yards behind the gaol. Dirty industrial area sea. Towards the end of my stay in Port Elizabeth Matron Nel told me that the soot came from the smoke of a gaol chimney, which I could see from the window of my cell. And I did see it belching out black smoke.

That morning I passed a few hours in the death cell just sitting on my bed, staring into space, thinking. I thought about Du Preez, that product of white baasskap, of a sick society. I thought about the women in Barberton. About Aucamp. And I looked through my spyhole at the other prisoner. Sometimes I also looked down through the window over the concrete stairs but not often for there was not much to see there. And out of the window towards the bowling green and swimming bath. I saw a dog running along the edge of the bath. Up and down. Up and down. Stretching his head out over the water, trying to reach it. Nearly falling over. He didn't ever reach the water. Eventually, tail pointing high, he trotted off and out of sight. A black and white fox terrier. I could see the man with a gun at the barrier past the main door of the female gaol. He was in a little sentry box.

I did not know the time because I had no watch. The prison authorities remove one's watch with all the other personal things one has on arrival in a gaol. It must have been about nine or ten when Britz unlocked me for a bath and exercise. Taking my towel and soap, I went down the concrete stairs with the black metal railings in my long blue uniform and my navy high-heeled shoes. I knew the courtyard of Pretoria Central well. I had exercised there one hour a day for one and a half months during my first 90-day detention. I had exercised there during the two weeks of my second detention for about 45 minutes a day.

I walked out of the door at the bottom of the stairs onto slate-grey paving, just on the inside of the big wooden front door of the prison, which was to my right. I continued through another door to the left into the courtyard, up the grey paving stones to the white female bathroom section. There was always an unpleasant smell here. Warm, sweet, soiled smell. Revolting. The baths were always filthy. I looked at all five to find the cleanest. And then tried to clean it as much as possible before turning on the tap. There was hot water.

I had just about finished washing myself and was about to climb out of the bath when I heard Britz calling 'Neame, Neame!' I wrapped a towel around me and went to the window at the end of the bathroom section looking towards Britz's office.

'Neame, Colonel Aucamp has phoned. He will be here in a few minutes. Are you ready?'

'Yes, yes, Matron, I'm just getting dressed.'

I rushed back to the bathroom and climbed into my private clothes: a tartan suit, navy blue woollen blouse, and my navy blue high-heeled shoes. No make-up. No access to an eyebrow pencil. I must look awful, I thought. My face felt wet and shiny after the steam in the bathroom.

'Neame, Neame!'

I picked up my towel and blue uniform and rushed out of the bathroom section onto the grey paving.

'Neame, Colonel Aucamp is here!'

'I must fetch my things from my cell, Matron.'

'Yes, but hurry up. Colonel Aucamp is waiting.'

I ran up the concrete stairs into my cell, which was unlocked by the wardress who was escorting me. I looked around – unable to concentrate – for the things I should take with me. I picked up a few articles. And stood motionless, confused.

'Hurry up, Neame. Colonel Aucamp is waiting.' Lieutenant Britz was at the bottom of the stairs, shouting up.

'Yes, yes. I am hurrying up.'

I picked up my towel, leaving the blue uniform lying on the dingy, smelly bedcover. I had a quick look into the locker with the small picture of Christ on one side. And out and down the stairs, a wardress escorting me. 'Come to the office, Neame.'

I went to the office. Colonel Aucamp was there with Lieutenant Britz. I nodded and murmured, 'Good morning, Colonel.' I had better be nice to him, I thought; otherwise who knows what might happen to me. He didn't say anything. There may have been a slight gesture of his head. A fat, short man, very little of a thick neck. Strangely shaped head, flat on the top. Closely cut mousy hair, maybe going grey. Steely blue eyes which looked at me with a cold, withdrawn look, not wanting me to see what he was thinking ... and a look of lurking hatred.

'Neame, here is your watch and your rings and your money. Count your money to see that it is correct. And then sign here in the book.'

I did that. 'Aren't you escorting me, Lieutenant?'

'No, Neame.' She was being nice. 'I didn't have enough time to get ready.'

I picked up my brown tartan travel bag and my wickerwork handbag and stepped across the grey paving to the large wooden front door.

On the way from Pretoria to Barberton Prison

THE DOOR WAS UNLOCKED. I was out in the street. A young man drove the car. Aucamp sat beside him. My escort this time was a short, fair-haired, middle-aged woman – pleasant faced. I gathered during the drive that she was Aucamp's wife. I was surprised for she looked too pleasant and uncomplicated. Quite pretty too. I wondered how he had managed to win her. He did have an impact on one, I decided, however awful he might be. There was a certain intensity about him which could be attractive. Leaving the stone walls of Pretoria Central behind, Aucamp instructed the young man to drive to a garage where we filled up with petrol.

It must have taken us about five hours to Barberton. It became terribly hot. I had the charcoal jersey on that had been given to me by the wife of junior counsel, CP Briggs, at Port Elizabeth. A big change of climate from down there at the coast. In that gaol I had been really cold and often freezing at court.

I have a few memories of the journey to Barberton: Mrs Aucamp reading a women's magazine next to me on the back seat while I made an effort to see if there was anything interesting in it but didn't – she was reading a love story. Thereafter all I saw were some advertisements. On the left side of the road a strange white and grey building. Mrs Aucamp commented, 'I wonder what that is?' She spoke in Afrikaans and I responded in English, 'I think it's a church.' And as we passed by the front of the building I caught sight of a small graveyard on the side and I said, 'Yes, it must be. See that graveyard.'

I felt Mrs Aucamp go on the defensive as I spoke my first sentence.

There was also an element of aggression. The tensing of her body said, You are English and you think you are better than me. But you are not.

After that there was silence in the car. We stopped at a café for some tea. My empty stomach was making me feel terrible so I asked Aucamp if I could have something to eat. He shifted a little uneasily but was fairly detached.

'What do you want?'

'Anything. Even dry bread. Just something to put into my stomach.'

His wife said she would like a scone. So I got one too.

While we were sitting in the café Mrs Aucamp suddenly turned to me and asked, 'Are you one of the politicals?' She had obviously been turning over in her mind why I clearly had no shame that I was a prisoner. She had come to the conclusion that my self-confidence, of which, I must say, I was totally unaware, was not because I was English but because I was one of the politicals, a different category from the run-of-the-mill prisoner. At the same time, I kept my answers short. I was conscious that a prisoner, even a political prisoner, does not seek to engage in normal conversation with a free human being. That would somehow mean breaking the rules. To an extent one was required to acknowledge one's inferiority or, perhaps more to the point, one's socially excluded status.

As I ate my scone I could hardly take my eyes off the dangling flypaper hanging from a light shade, attached to a rather high ceiling. Many flies were stuck to the paper. I identified myself with the fate of these flies.

There were many wire baskets and pot plants in the café. When we had finished our tea and scone, Mrs Aucamp bouncily went over to the owner to discuss the pot plants. Aucamp stood around with his detached air. Outwardly relaxed. I felt this was a very self-conscious attitude and that he was especially conscious of it in front of me. It said, I haven't got it in for anybody. I am just doing my duty. And I am not ambitious.

I had, in fact, thought a great deal about Aucamp in Port Elizabeth, especially when I'd first arrived. I suspected that he had taken me down there in order that I should serve my sentence in solitary and this because I had annoyed him personally. I remember trying to explain this to David Soggot after I was allowed to see him. I said Aucamp got on all right with men, with this pally detached, 'I'm-on-the-level' manner, but that his relationship to women could be pathological.

He liked women. I remember how friendly he used to be to me. He would look at me with those friendly blue eyes and say, 'Sylvia this' and 'Sylvia that'. But if he felt a woman did not take to him or that she had an independence of mind which involved what he felt was an insufficient recognition of his special status, both socially and sexually, he turned cold and vicious and was determined to break her.

My fight against solitary confinement at the Port Elizabeth gaol had strengthened his feeling that I was not merely a political, but a personal enemy. Moreover, in the presence of the Officer-Commanding, Colonel van Wyk, I had treated him not only with considerable anger but with contempt.

Within ten days of my arrival in Port Elizabeth I had discovered that I had not been transported down there because of Aucamp at all, though undoubtedly he had given the instruction that I should be kept in solitary while I was there. That it had little to do with him became clear to me when I was served with the new charge. Moreover, later, after I had been sentenced in Humansdorp, Du Preez told me that my second charge had already been decided upon at the time of my arrest in July 1964, that is, even before I had been charged with membership of the Communist Party. In fact, he claimed that he had asked the Johannesburg Security Branch not to worry about keeping me for the communism trial as he had a good magistrate and prosecutor in Humansdorp and they would ensure that I got nine years.

> STAFF REPORTER 7 July 1965
>
> HUMANSDORP.—It appeared that the top A.N.C official in the Eastern Cape in 1963 was a police informer, and that the Rivonia arrests had taken place two weeks after he had visited there, said Mr. D. Soggot, defence counsel for Sylvia Neame, yesterday.
> The official whose name may

ABOVE: *From the* Rand Daily Mail, *7 July 1965.*

Du Preez told me other things, including that he had been sitting in a car outside Liliesleaf Farm in Rivonia when the arrests took place and that it was a person from the eastern Cape who had given Rivonia away. As it happened, in the course of my Humansdorp trial information had emerged in connection with one of the state witnesses which suggested that it was a man who had accompanied Govan Mbeki to Rivonia who had given the place away.

Crucial for my relationship with Aucamp, subsequent to the Port Elizabeth interlude, was that he suspected that Du Preez had talked too much and that at some stage I would attempt to use what he had told me not only against Du Preez himself, but more generally against the security establishment and the justice system. Moreover, the fact that

---

HAYMAN & ARONSOHN
SOLICITORS
INCORPORATING
CHARLES LEWIS & LAZAR

RUTH W. HAYMAN B.A., LL.B.

TELEPHONE 838-1496/7
RES. 42-3170

OUR REF. MISS HAYMAN/ZA
YOUR REF.

TELEGRAPHIC ADDRESS:
"LEWCHAS"
P.O. BOX 7390

205 NATIONAL MUTUAL BUILDINGS
COR. RISSIK & MARKET STREETS
JOHANNESBURG

10th May, 1965.

Graham Neame, Esq.,
Department of History,
Rhodes University,
P.O. Box 94,
GRAHAMSTOWN.

Dear Graham,

re: SYLVIA'S CASE.

The up to date news about Sylvia is that she is being charged in the Regional Court, Humansdorp, with being a member, furthering the aims, etc. of the A.N.C. and that the Trial is due to commence on the 18th May, 1965.

A preliminary statement has already been taken by Counsel from Sylvia who was interviewed at the Port Elizabeth Gaol and Advocate D. Soggot from the Johannesburg Bar will appear on her behalf on the 18th May, 1965. He flew to Port Elizabeth on Friday to take a more comprehensive statement from her.

From the preliminary statement, it is clear that Sylvia's defence is one of alibi and I have accordingly written to Attorneys in Cape Town to interview possible defence witnesses. I have also dropped a line to Caroline to let her know what is going on.

I will report progress to you from time to time.

Yours sincerely,

Ruth.

the point was being made in the English-speaking mass media that my trial in Humansdorp had some very worrying features could only have served to underline the possible threat I posed.

On the trip from Pretoria to Barberton, I have a picture of heat over orange trees. I had never been in this area before. The first time I had ever heard of Barberton was when I was awaiting trial at the Fort when somebody, a wardress or another prisoner, had said there was a female gaol there. I knew that Barberton was somewhere in the Transvaal but that was all.

As we travelled along the road in the ever increasing heat, it was as though we were leaving civilisation behind us. I was very hot in my charcoal jersey. I could feel my face was flushed. But I did not take off my jersey. I felt it was part of my identity. And I knew that for somebody in gaol, it is important to preserve one's sense of identity as far as possible for they took so much away.

They took away your clothes and gave you a uniform, often very ugly, as my one in Port Elizabeth was, and they gave you heavy brown clodhopper shoes, army shoes. And they took away your make-up. They took away your talc and your perfume. They took away your watch and your jewellery. They took away your underclothing and either gave you none or gave you underclothing that was so hideous that to wear it was degrading.

I remember at the Fort, after we had been sentenced, how I never lost the image of the underclothing I was wearing. I had no bra but I had long baggy woollen bloomers, with no elastic in the thighs so they hung down almost to my knees, under my worn khaki uniform. I remember particularly when the lawyer, Denis Kuny, came to visit us all. Denis had been a member of our legal team. This was the last contact for a long time that we were to have with the outside world. And I tried to pull my bloomers up so that they would not hang down below my uniform. And Denis, asked by one of us what we looked like, whether we looked awful – we were actually hoping for reassurance – lowered his eyes and said nothing. He told somebody later that he thought we looked like a rugby team.

Over our uniforms we had dark brown jerseys with a red stripe at the bottom ribbing. We had had to fight for those jerseys. The lieutenant at the Fort ran her gaol on military lines: this meant, amongst other things, that jerseys were issued on a particular date each year to prisoners, sometime in the second half of April, I think it was. Before this not even members of the Prisons Department's staff were allowed to wear jerseys openly. When it was cold they hid them under their jackets.

After we were sentenced, since there had been a sudden drop in temperature in Johannesburg and we were freezing, we started a campaign for jerseys and we were successful. The other prisoners got them too. And the staff. I remember when it was cold at the Fort when we first arrived there after we had been charged, and we asked a hard labour prisoner, Teresa, one day whether she wasn't freezing without a jersey, she had commented simply, 'The Lieutenant hasn't issued jerseys yet.' She accepted that. For her to be cold was a part of prison life. It was part of the punishment. The lack of the right to make a choice, too, was integral to the prison system. Choices were made by others.

That was the whole atmosphere at the Fort, in Port Elizabeth gaol, in the Roeland Street gaol in Cape Town, where I had once spent a weekend during the sit-in campaign, in every gaol I had been in. It was evidently part of the regime that a prisoner should be cold, hungry, in degrading clothes. At any rate, for me this was gaol. I had never heard of rehabilitation. I had never thought about a penal system in that sort of academic, sociological way. This degrading atmosphere was part of all the gaols I knew, and so I thought, This is what prison anywhere is meant to be. This is the experience called 'going to prison'.

Eventually we came down a steep pass to Barberton. It was very hot and very dry. The area looked drought stricken. Barberton was dominated on one side by huge bare dry hills, with steep, so steep, brown roads going up the side. Asked whether anyone had ever driven up that mountain, Aucamp responded that it was so steep that the car was almost vertical at times.

'That is the road to Swaziland,' he said.

My God, I thought, Swaziland! 'Are we near Swaziland?'

'The prison is over there,' Colonel Aucamp said, and he pointed towards the base of the huge bare hills.

As the car drove along the Barberton street towards the hills, I had a sudden desire to open the car door and throw myself out for I felt the walls of that prison closing in on me, closing in on me for six years. In that gaol at the foot of those hills. In that isolation and heat, far from anything I knew.

I was surprised at this reaction because I had expected to be focused on meeting the others again and discussing what had happened to me down in Port Elizabeth and seeing what Barberton Prison was like. A general exchange of information. But the years ahead of me had sunk deep down into my consciousness. There was the cold horror and that typical gaol feeling which is quite unique. It was the same horror I had felt when the magistrate of Humansdorp sentenced me to four years. I had been expecting to get off since I had concluded that he would not dare let another court see that record, that record that exposed it as a frame-up.

At the same time there was an element of resignation, the resignation of somebody caught up by something too powerful and corrupt to be able to do anything about it. The magistrate's face was yellow as he sentenced me. I remember that the prosecutor's face was yellow too. And I told Dave Soggot that the prosecutor was looking upset about the whole business because it had come to this. But then I saw that Du Preez looked yellow, too. And I realised this was caused by the lights which had been turned on as the proceedings continued into the late evening.

At the end of it all, in front of the press in that courtroom, Du Preez took my thumbprint. For me it was demeaning. His hand holding mine was like a block of wood, utterly insensitive. On his face was that usual look of self-satisfaction. He was displaying personal – and state – authority.

I did not throw myself out of the car. It was an impulse with effectively no practical meaning. We went through what appeared to be a farm gate, and I saw a board on the side of the brown gravel road, with the words SOUTH AFRICAN PRISONS DEPARTMENT. We passed a few buildings on the left, thereafter a grey-brown split-pole fence, with what looked like a golf course on the other side of it. The road curved round to the left and we drove into a grey gravel driveway. On the left was a large yellow building. The car pulled up near some steps going up into the building. On our right was a bed of flowers, mainly orange. Well, it looks quite nice, I thought.

I looked up towards the windows on the front of the building and saw five great cages over five windows. They must be in there, I thought. I had a picture of them in their uniforms with white aprons on in a large laundry section. There they were organising the laundry. The ironing was being done by black prisoners. I had gathered from Pretoria Central that it was essentially organisational work that was performed by white women prisoners though, true, at Kroonstad they sewed.

I imagined a large airy room – the sort of room one would see in an old building rather than a new one. This was because all the gaols I had been in were relatively old, except for the North End Prison in Port Elizabeth, which I think they said was built in 1954. Barberton Prison was built in 1958 on the basis of a new plan. There were several other gaols built in exactly the same way – Worcester, Pietersburg. At the same time, though it was one of the new gaols, Kroonstad was quite different, amongst other things because there was much more space.

The young driver and Colonel Aucamp stepped out of the car, then Mrs Aucamp; then the car door was opened for me. Somewhere on this trip I had asked Aucamp whether this was a rehabilitation centre and he had said, 'No, it is a hard labour prison. You people can't be rehabilitated. Politics is just a matter of opinion.' The same – I felt hypocritical – detached air. My luggage was taken out of the back of the car, my tartan travel bag and a white plastic bag with odds and ends in it. Up the stairs we went, through an open door and up to a grille. A wardress in khaki uniform unlocked it and we passed inside. The grille was locked behind us.

I was taken to a room on the left of a passage. A clean new prison this was. On the floor was yellowish-ochre linoleum or perhaps it was Masonite. There was a counter with brass bars, as in a post office, and next to this was a structure with two small windows, made of perspex, and round these windows was soundproof boarding. On the other side of the windows were two cubicles. So these must be two 'visiting rooms', used when prisoners received visits.

There was a table in the room. A young blonde matron in the usual khaki sat down there and took down a list of my possessions in a large book with columns. I stood beside the table, shifting from one foot to the other. It was extremely hot. I still had my jersey on. Colonel Aucamp had disappeared into a room on the other side of the passage. Several loud voices – male and female – came from it. With me was Mrs Aucamp and the young driver. The matron, who had been writing in the book, went out. I knew she was the rank of a matron because she had sergeant's stripes on her arm.

Mrs Aucamp had relaxed.

'Are you a university student?' she asked.

'Yes,' I said.

She went over to the counter to have a look. 'Is this for contact visits?' she asked the young man in Afrikaans. 'Do you think one can kiss anyone from here?' And she jumped up and held onto the bars, kicking up her legs behind her, laughing. She went through to join the others in the room across the passage. And the young man disappeared too. The matron came back and went on filling in particulars of my possessions in the large book.

About an hour must have passed. I went over to the window and had a look outside – grey gravel pathway, orange flowers, ugly pond. I went back to the table and stood wilting. An African woman prisoner with red headscarf and light brown coarse overalls came in. Short and plump. She had a cup of tea and put it down in front of me.

'For me?' I enquired, surprised.

'Yes,' she said.

Heavens, this is nice, I thought. I started drinking.

'You had better not let anyone see you drinking that,' the matron said.

'Oh, all right,' I said. And I was careful. Tea finished, I continued to stand in the heat. I let my mind drift, resigned. Suddenly I heard an incredible screech. Looking up, I saw a woman in uniform.

'In hierdie tronk staan jy met jou hande agter jou rug!'

Without a word, I shifted my hands behind my back, with not a look on my face.

'Jirre, wat kan ons doen met hierdie soort mens?' My God, what can one do with this kind of human being?

Then she went out. I wondered whether that yell was to impress Aucamp. At any rate, she must feel he would have nothing against it, I thought. The voices droned on in the room across the passage. I asked the young matron where my friends were. Looking nervous, she said I would see.

Another young wardress with a large bosom came to have a look at me. She stared at me, quite unembarrassed.

'Are you one of them?' she asked.

'Yes,' I said.

The young matron – as it happened, I had actually seen her at the Fort a few times while I was awaiting trial – commented, 'You have six years.' She was filling it in the book, I supposed. She gave me a searching look – probably to see how I felt about it. She didn't look happy. She seemed uneasy, apprehensive.

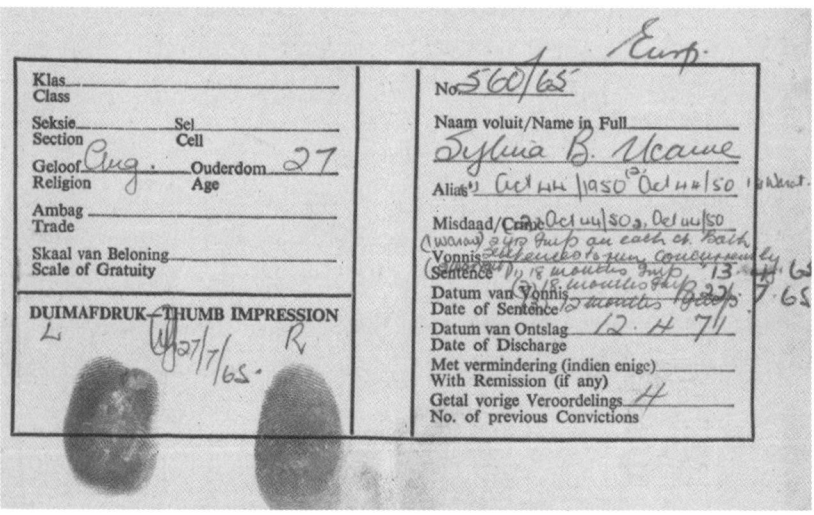

I saw the woman who had screamed at me walking down the corridor. She looked pleased with herself. 'I am going to get Middleton,' she said. She went a few yards down the passage and opened a door. 'Middleton!' she shouted. The sound of a grille unlocking.

'Are they down there working?' I asked the young matron. She looked uncertain and did not answer. Then I caught a glimpse of Jean going by with a wave. I could not see what she looked like, except that she had on one of the new blue uniforms. Well, that's a good sign, I thought. Blue uniforms probably meant 'rehabilitation' and all that.

The Lieutenant at the Fort had spoken about the new blue uniforms with great pride. She had spoken of them as though they were the bright blue banner in a great campaign that was to bring about change in the attitude of the South African Prisons Department to prisoners – a campaign she led. So maybe Barberton's okay, I thought.

'Neame, come with me.' It was the woman who had yelled at me. I followed her to the room across the passage. In my imagination I had seen the room as a friendly little common room where they were all having tea. I went in through the doorway. It was an office. There was a large desk which seemed to take up most of the room and behind which Aucamp was sitting. He was short, crouching over the desk, large blue eyes with an unfriendly glint in them looking directly at me.

'Well, Sylvia,' he said, 'I'm telling you this because I don't want you coming to me and saying that I talk behind your back.' A long pause with the unfriendly eyes looking at me. 'I have warned the other prisoners that you are a troublemaker and that they are not to listen to you.' There was a man in uniform standing on his left. Present too was the matron with the huge shouting voice; also Mrs Aucamp and the young driver.

'What do you mean, I am a troublemaker?'

A pause. 'You know what I mean. You are a troublemaker.' Another pause. 'Now, is there anything you want to say about Port Elizabeth?'

The man in uniform said, 'She can't say anything about Port Elizabeth. She is a prisoner.' He had a stupid, pompous half-smile on his face. 'What can she say about Port Elizabeth?' he repeated. 'She is a prisoner.'

He was a fat, ugly man. I smiled at him with a winning, condescending smile. I supposed he was the Officer-Commanding and the shouting woman must be the Matron-in-Charge. I felt Aucamp was looking at me suspiciously but couldn't be quite sure because his blue eyes glinted with subtle changes of expression, changes of expression which he was obviously trying to hide. I realised that a big worry for him was that Du Preez had perhaps told me too much.

I asked: 'What do you mean, do you have anything to say about Port Elizabeth? What about Port Elizabeth?'

'Anything in connection with Port Elizabeth?'

'I prefer not to say anything at this stage.'

Aucamp winced. 'All right, you can go,' he said. 'And don't let me have any trouble from you.'

Tired, hot, tense, I was eventually escorted down the passage to the door from behind which Jean had emerged earlier. The yelling woman opened this grey-painted door, then a grille and, once I was through, closed the door and locked the grille behind me.

I join my fellow trialists

I FOUND MYSELF STANDING in a large-ish space, facing my comrades from the Johannesburg trial. They seemed to be standing in some sort of line behind a table with chairs. The young wardress, the one with the big bosom who had greeted me with the words 'Are you one of them?' was hovering close by. I expected the others to shout friendly excited 'Hello's' and come running up to me but they stood in that apology for a line – they were supposed to be on parade, I imagined – and looked at me silently. There was a strange look in their eyes. At first I could not quite fathom what that strange look communicated. Weren't they pleased about my coming?

Their eyes were withdrawn, suspicious, a bit like the eyes of patients in a mental hospital. And there was almost an animal look of pain. I stood silently, hesitantly, looking at them. And then somebody – I can't remember who, it may have been Mollie – came forward in a rush and kissed me and the others did the same. They were responding to my coming but they were still withdrawn.

'Go to that cell,' the wardress said, 'and strip. I want to search you.'

I was used to this. I went to a small single cell on one side of the central space, and stripped. After a minute some of the others followed me.

'Heavens you've lost weight,' somebody commented.

'Yes, they have given me a terrible time,' I responded.

'Go to the bathroom and have a bath,' the wardress said.

'But I have just bathed,' I said, 'a few hours ago in Pretoria.'

'That doesn't matter; you have to bath again.'

I went to the bathroom in a small section on the other side of the central space. There was a sluice, a toilet and a bath.

Some of the others followed me.

'I have six years,' I said. 'It was a fabricated case, fabricated through and through.'

They looked at me. The wardress came in. 'You are all to get out of here,' she ordered. Their eyes turned on her suspiciously and I saw that there was also hostility and disdain. They went out and left me alone in the bathroom. I wondered why they all seemed so strange but I didn't give it much thought. I hurried up in the bath so that I could join them again. When I came out, they were all sitting around the table in the central space.

This central area had a grey polished concrete floor. Apart from the table, there were three or four narrow brown wooden lockers, about chest high, against the wall. And in a narrower area, leading off the central space, on the other side from the grille and door at the entrance to the section, there were to the right two concrete laundry basins with concrete graters and one that was smooth surfaced. Across the way from these were two white enamel washbasins.

The cell where I had stripped was to be my cell. It was about six and a half feet by nine feet. In it was a bed and a small mat on the yellow-ochre linoleum floor. That was all.

There were three single cells, all the same size. They had windows on the front side of the gaol, facing the golf course. These windows were covered with the large cages I had seen from the outside. Each single cell had a little window looking into the central space. The two outer single cells both had another large window in one of their side walls but these could not be opened. There were two communal cells, one on either side of the central space. The one facing the front had cages on its two large windows.

I joined the others at the table. There were seven of us – Stephanie Kemp, Mollie Anderson-Doyle, Jean Middleton, Flo Duncan, Ann Nicholson, Esther Barsel and myself. It was quite a squash at the table. Three on one side, two opposite and one at each end. The middle person on the side that had three people hardly had room to move her elbows.

By the time I got to the table, the others seemed almost to have finished eating. Most of them were drinking some liquid, possibly the gaol coffee. There was some soup for me. It did not look very nice. I tried to take a few spoonfuls but I was shaking so much I could hardly get the

I join my fellow trialists

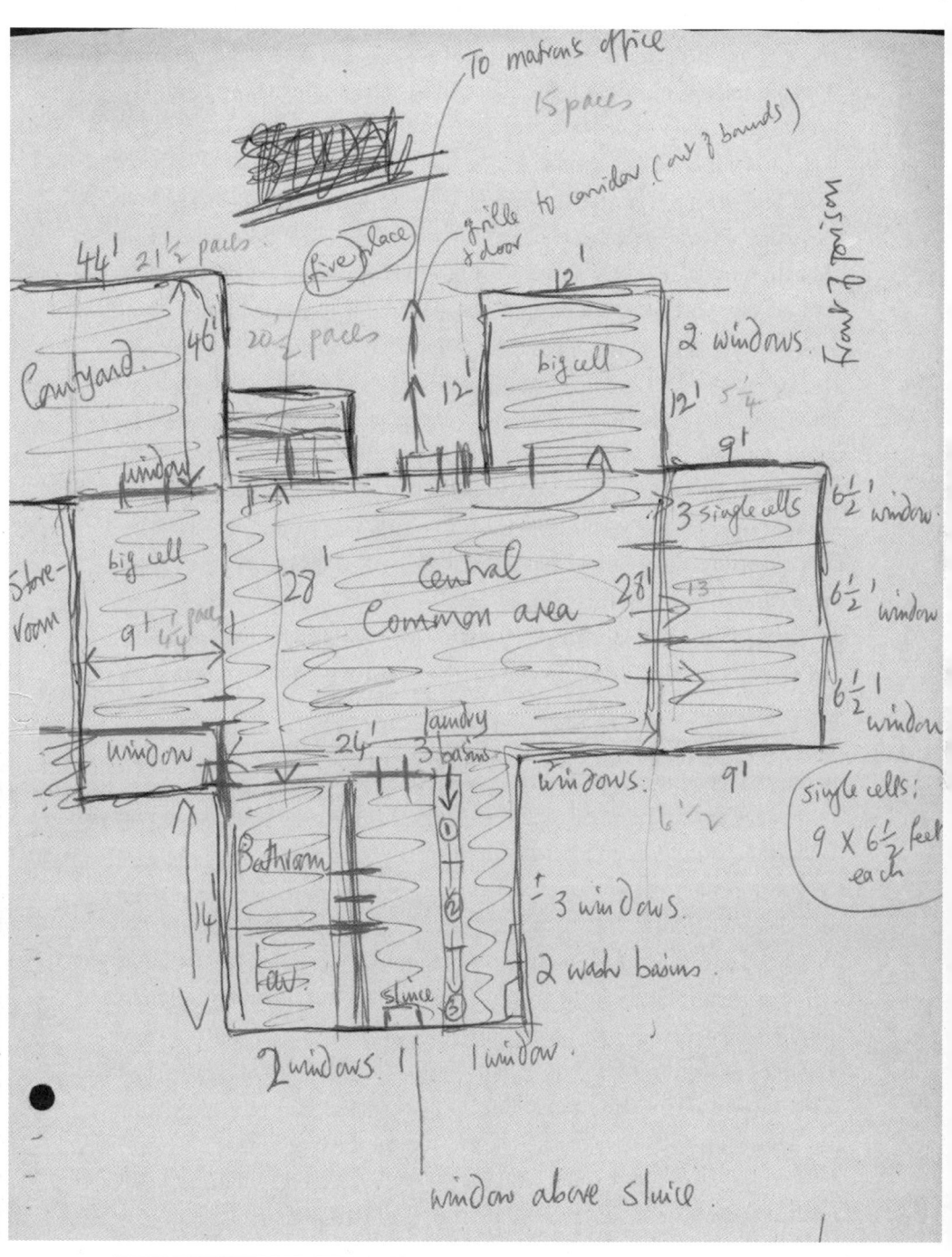

ABOVE: *Plan of our section in Barberton.*

spoon to my mouth. And, in any case, I wasn't very interested in eating. The plump wardress was standing right up against the table listening to every word. She was watching my face, watching my spoon shaking. She had a self-satisfied, pompous look on her young fresh face.

'I've got four years for something I didn't do,' I said. 'The people in the eastern Cape are having a terrible time. They have been arrested in their hundreds, and there appear to have been a lot of fabricated cases. One of my witnesses told Soggot that he had eight years for something he hadn't done. A big problem from the start was that even their lawyers had not believed them when they were told that the prosecution case was a lot of lies. The result was that not only did people get heavy sentences on fabricated cases but what was going on in the eastern Cape had not filtered through to the rest of the country, in particular to the mass media, let alone into the international arena. It was my case that alerted the journalists.'

I went on: 'You should have heard the witnesses in my case. Some of them had learned their evidence off by heart. Some of them were travelling witnesses, going from trial to trial, telling their lies. Of course, they had been bought or threatened or actually tortured. It was quite obvious in court that my case was a frame-up and yet that magistrate gave me four years. And he would have given me nine had he been able to do so. It was terrible, terrible.'

I could not find words to express the reality of my experience in Port Elizabeth. 'You just can't imagine how terrible it was.'

I did not get much response from the others. They seemed uneasy with the wardress standing there. And, of course, Aucamp had warned that I was a troublemaker and that they should not listen to me; listening to me or even indicating their disgust at what the authorities were doing would very possibly get them into further trouble. It soon became apparent to me that they had been having a really bad time in Barberton. That accounted for the strange look in the eyes.

'Hurry up with your food, Neame,' the wardress warned.

I tried to get a few more shaking spoonfuls into my mouth. 'Oh, I can't eat this,' I said, and pushed it away. 'I'll have some coffee.'

'You are really very thin,' somebody commented once again.

'They gave me a hell of a time. They kept me in solitary for quite a long time until I took them to the Supreme Court. And the food in Port Elizabeth was terrible. I've hardly eaten for three months. And then I was in Pretoria on the way through, and you know what the food's like there. You can't make out what you are eating. Is it fish or is it rather meat or only vegetables, mixed together in a kind of indistinguishable mash.'

The others washed the dishes in a laundry basin, while I finished off at the table. And then we stood on parade – in a line between the laundry basin area and our eating table. We were then locked up for the night by a wardress who came through the grille that led into the passage I had come down.

After we had been locked up in our cells and the wardress had gone out, locking the grille at the entrance to our section behind her and the door, I started telling the others further details of what I had experienced after I'd left them at the Fort several months before. I spoke through the little window that looked into the central space.

I had only just started when the door to the passage was thrown open and the Matron-in-Charge appeared. She began yelling at me. Some of it was screamed in such a crazy manner that I could not make it out. Her aim seemed to be to scream as loudly as she could, rather than communicate. The door slammed shut again.

'Good God,' I muttered, 'is the woman mad?'

There was silence from the other cells. I went and sat on my bed. I was exhausted. I put on my ticking nightdress and climbed into bed. A wardress came to look in our cells every half hour. Apart from the locked grille and the door at the entrance of the passage, we were locked in our cells, first behind a grille, and then a locked door.

I found myself relaxing at last after those nightmare months. I was back with the others. I felt I no longer had to maintain absolute vigilance, an iron will that would ensure the authorities would not catch me off guard. I did not have to watch and calculate their every move nor watch myself constantly in case I fell into a trap. Especially important was that if anything untoward happened to me, my comrades would be able to inform our people outside. It seemed I wasn't going to be put away for years with nobody knowing exactly where I was. And so that night, the first time in many months, I sank into an exhausted heavy sleep.

Introduction to the routine

I WOKE WITH A BELL RINGING. It was still dark in my cell. I looked up at the window with the cream horizontal bars. There was bright electric light shining on the cage and onto the window. Except for one clear pane of glass at the top of each window, the rest was frosted. I was used to getting up in the dark since the first bell in the North End Prison went at 5.30. I wondered what the time was here but decided not to risk asking someone. I did not want to be shattered by a scream at this time of the morning.

I put on my uniform, stockings and shoes, pulled up my bed. I waited in the dark, sometimes sitting on my bed, sometimes pacing up and down in the small area between the outside wall and the grille. A second bell rang. It must have been, I calculated, either fifteen or 30 minutes after the first. Still nobody came. Then I heard footsteps coming from somewhere and then a tramp on the gravel below my window. We were unlocked by the Matron-in-Charge accompanied by a wardress. I stood at attention inside my grille, feet slightly apart, hands behind my back, eyes forward. I ventured a muttered 'Good morning' but evidently the Matron was having none of that. She did not even look at me.

The large brass key went into the keyhole in my grille. It was deftly and militarily turned with a lot of metallic noise. She went on to the next cell. I waited on my mat at attention until I heard the grille at the entrance of our section close, the key turned, and the door slammed to.

God, I thought, what people! I stuck my head out of my cell to see what everyone else was doing. They were carrying their grey metal pos to the sluice or, with toothbrush and toothpaste, going to the basins. I took my po along to the sluice and emptied it, and then went to the basins to clean my teeth.

Introduction to the routine

'Parade, julle mense!' the large wardress shouted.

Everyone lined up in the same place as the day before. The Matron-in-Charge opened the door and unlocked the central grille. Porridge was brought in. Already on our table were marmalade, sugar and milk, which the others had divided up and put into separate little face-cream jars. The central grille was locked again and the door slammed.

'Julle kan eet,' the wardress said.

We took seats at the table. The wardress stood right behind one of our chairs.

'What is the time?' I asked.

'We are unlocked at about six,' someone said.

'What work do we do?' I asked.

'Laundry,' someone else said and pointed to several bags lying near the basins. 'We wash the jackets, pants and shirts of the African men prisoners.'

'They're a bit smelly,' I observed.

'What do you expect?' somebody said. 'They have to wear them for a week, doing hard labour, and I suppose, like the black prisoners in other gaols, they are allowed only one shower a week.'

The wardress shuffled uneasily. 'Kom, kom, julle mense, julle moenie praat nie. Julle moet eet. Dis laat, en julle moet begin was.' Come, come you people, you must not speak. You must eat. It is late and you must begin to wash.

The meal continued in silence. Porridge, with milk and sugar, brown bread and marmalade. The marmalade had to last the whole day. It was sufficient for two slices of bread. There was no butter.

When we were finished we washed our dishes and cutlery in one of the laundry basins. It was fairly deep and the dishes had to be lowered carefully. One of us washed and put everything on top of a locker that stood next to the basins. This was Jean's locker. In it were some of her clothes, clean bed linen, face-cream, toothbrush, etc. Water dripped from the wet dishes onto the top of the locker, warping it, and dripped down into her locker, wetting what was inside. Others dried the dishes.

After this was done, somebody made the fire with wood and coal in the little boiler room that was just outside our 'portaal', at the entrance to the courtyard. We called the central space 'portaal', the Afrikaans word. Another ran a dry cloth over all the floors of the cells and of the portaal and the bathroom section, did the dusting, shone up the brass. Three worked at the concrete laundry basins. Two with ridges had clearly been installed with the intention that they should be used for washing laundry. The third concrete basin, which was smooth faced, was meant to be for rinsing but it was also used for washing. A wooden washing board was put in it for the purpose.

So three of us stood elbow to elbow at the basins. We had to twist our bodies to clean a particularly dirty article, and we had to do a lot of this for we were washing in cold water (this was our choice in order to preserve our hands). We would then find ourselves pushing into the person next to us. It was very hot this first day. There were windows just behind us and the sun beat down on our backs. However, it was not as bad as it was in summer, particularly the summer when there was a terrible drought – 1966 – the worst drought South Africa had had in 60 years, we'd hear.

The men's jackets were of hard white canvas. The shorts were also of a hard material, probably canvas. The khaki shirts were made out of a softer fabric. The clothes were all very dirty. They stank of sweat and a dank, mouldy canvas smell. Many of the shirts were covered in black coal dust. Some of the shorts had blood on them. There were red stripes across the back, the red stripes sometimes becoming patches of blood where the prisoner had bled more profusely. There was a peculiar smelly yellow substance mixed with the blood, which at first I thought was pus but was told was actually sulphur ointment. The ointment was put on the open wounds of prisoners who had received lashes. About five pairs of shorts a week were in this condition.

Each week they sent in to us about 120 shirts, 90–110 jackets, 70–90 pairs of shorts. We began work at about 7 in the morning and worked through to about 11 or 11.15 when we were given a bit of exercise before lunch. When I first started washing my hands kept slipping onto the concrete ridges, and they would bleed. The tough material of the clothing also scraped against my hands, producing blisters and abrasions, but after some weeks I got the hang of it and did less damage to myself.

What I found particularly agonising was my back. The angle at which one had to stand at the basin was an uncomfortable one. To have to stand for five or six hours of any day at that angle produced indescribable aches and pains. At the best of times I have a painful back. And it was tough laundry, not ordinary cloth, and we could not let up for a minute without having a complaint from the wardress who stood right up next to us at the basins.

We were not allowed to speak at all while we worked. Even if I asked the person next to me, and we were literally rubbing elbows, to pass me a piece of soap because I had run out, the wardress would shout, 'Julle moenie praat nie! Julle kan nie werk en praat.' You must not speak. You cannot work and speak. And so we worked in silence, rubbing away at the shorts, shirts and jackets, putting the washed articles into buckets, and then taking them out into the courtyard to hang up on the washing lines.

We had a self-contained courtyard which one entered from the portaal. There was a grass patch in the centre of it, across which were strung washing lines, supported by silver-coloured metal poles. In the centre of the grass patch was a concrete drain with a black cover, and at the side a tap. Bordering the grass was a strip of flower beds with nasturtiums and everlastings in them. The everlastings looked rather gloomy. There were strong winds at this time of the year and they were continually being blown over. One of my most vivid memories of this time was during exercise time propping up these dreary everlastings by pushing mounds of gravelly sand to the bottom of each.

There was a type of nasturtium I had never seen before. We called it a 'leopard nasturtium' because we thought it had markings like a leopard. One of the base colours was a lovely wine red. There were only a few of these. As the nasturtiums as a whole were beginning to look a bit bedraggled, Wardress Taljaard, that officious, plump, growing-ever-plumper wardress, told me to pull them all out and although we tried to save the seeds of our 'leopard nasturtium' we never saw this type again.

Around this central area of the courtyard, with the grass and the border of flower beds, was a rectangle, consisting of white concrete slabs. On this we took our exercise, walking round and round. One round for me required 20 of my small walking paces.

The authorities' campaign of provocation

THERE WAS A DELIBERATE progamme of provocation on the part of the gaol authorities. No doubt instructions had come from Aucamp and one assumes that the methods to be used were decided on together with the Security Police.

One of the tactics was to prevent any routine emerging. The aim was to make us feel constantly uncertain of the framework in which we lived, to keep us permanently on the defensive and uncertain, to convince us that we had no rights and would only be granted 'privileges' if we played ball. In more general terms, their programme was directed at ensuring that we were in a constant state of psychological stress as a means of breaking us in. I cannot exclude that it was stepped up precisely after my arrival – the others had already had their share of this regime by that time. This would have been in order to ensure that I did not escape the breaking-in procedure at Barberton.

The first day I arrived and we talked at the table while we were having supper, the wardress said nothing to us about our not being allowed to talk at table, and the following morning at breakfast we talked and she did not interrupt us until we moved on to a subject she did not like. At lunchtime we started talking quietly to each other, almost whispering.

The tremendous silence of this gaol was something that had struck me when I first entered it. With well over 200 women in the building, it was an almost inexplicable silence. It seemed that the authorities managed to maintain this situation by forcing prisoners to whisper to one another. Or was it possible that they were not allowed to speak to one another?

When Dave Soggot came to visit me for the second time in connection with the appeal against my four-year sentence – this was in about January or February 1966 – he commented to Taljaard that it was a surprisingly silent gaol. She said, 'Thank you', and then, realising that perhaps he did not necessarily think it a good thing, she said, 'I do not know how you mean it but I take it as a compliment.' Laughing nervously, rolling her large hips a little and putting her hands together behind her back so that her bosom stood out even further, she'd put a self-satisfied expression on her healthy pink and white face.

As I have noted, during lunchtime on the second day after my arrival we started talking quietly to each other and the wardress interrupted – this was not Taljaard and it was clear that a general instruction had been given to all wardresses who did duty in our section – with the following: 'Julle is nie veronderstel om te praat wanneer julle eet nie.' You are not allowed to talk when you eat. So we sat there in silence, elbow to elbow.

In fact, it was to become clear that there had been a general instruction that we were not allowed to talk to each other at any time of the day. I occasionally managed to find somebody alone, that is without the wardress, and it was usually either in the bathroom section, in the tiny boiler room or out in the courtyard when I was hanging up the washing. But before we had said more than a few words, the wardress was there, telling us we were not allowed to talk. The courtyard was actually a rather uncertain place to choose to have an interchange since Matron Bester was sure to be keeping a lookout from her office window which looked out onto the courtyard.

It was a very uneasy-making space to be in because, although we could be seen through the windows looking onto the courtyard, we were unable to see whether anyone was looking at us. The result was that we felt constantly besieged by hidden eyes. And we were not far wrong for Matron Bester's eyes were often there, a fact we were to discover when we tried to say a few words to each other as we hung up the washing.

One day I attempted to say something to Jean, who was soaking some jackets with soap in a metal tub in order to remove some of the worst of the dirt before we started on them in the laundry basins. I had just begun to say something when the office window was flung open and although we could see no one, we heard that mad, unintelligible scream. Jean wandered inside with a nonchalant, innocent swing of her hips which she was characteristically to use in Barberton when confronted with what she regarded as undignified behaviour. I was left alone in the courtyard, uneasily hanging up the remaining shirts and hearing the slam of the window behind me.

In a way that courtyard summed up our situation. Looking into it on two sides were various rooms. On a third side were several windows of a storeroom, taking up nearly the whole of that side of the yard. All these windows were kept firmly closed. On the fourth side was the wall of the courtyard, which we later discovered divided us from the courtyard of the other prisoners.

It was demonstrably clear that we were not simply locked up in gaol in order to be isolated from the rest of society; we were deliberately separated from other prisoners and, indeed, as we would later learn, from the African wardresses. We were treated as though we had a dangerous infectious disease. Perhaps our message of non-racialism was regarded as such by the authorities.

The central grille and door where the wardress entered and left our section was our only means of access to the rest of the gaol, and the authorities were very careful about that door. Whenever it was opened, only a narrow aperture was allowed, enough to let the wardress squeeze her way in or out. And when somebody came to that door to give our wardress a message, she only opened it a crack and placed herself behind the door so that we could not see her.

We were not allowed to look down the passage that ran from that door, past the visiting room on the right and the office of the Matron-in-Charge on the left, down to the foyer at the entrance, let alone walk down it, except once a week when we went to the office in order to see the Officer-Commanding in the framework of the ritual designated 'Complaints and Requests'. No doubt, before this event was allowed to take place, care had been taken to remove every African prisoner and African wardress from the vicinity. Despite this, it was a real outing for us, an adventure into the 'outside world' of the rest of the gaol.

According to the prison regulations, which we were not allowed to see, an officer was supposed to see us for complaints and requests once a day but this 'privilege' was not given to us. And when we tried to speak to Matron Bester as she unlocked us in the morning, that is on an occasion when we actually had the courage to face a scream at that early hour, we often got what we had feared, some unintelligible shout. True, on occasion there was only a mutter and shake of the head that made it quite clear she had no time for us.

We were allowed some exercise in the courtyard in the morning, 20 minutes, sometimes half an hour, and, if the wardress felt like it, also a little sometimes in the afternoon, 5 or 10 minutes. We had great difficulty ensuring our afternoon exercise. According to the wardresses, the problem was that they had to be back in the gaol for night duty by 3.45 or 4pm and they wanted an hour off.

During our main exercise in the morning we marched fast around the courtyard. On the white concrete the sun was blinding, especially in the summer. Usually we marched in twos. On the first day I was there, I whispered a little to the person next to me, as did the other pairs as we walked, and evidently this was all right since the wardress made no complaint. I think it was on the second day that we did the same thing, made a few comments to each other as we walked, when our plump friend shouted, 'Julle is nie veronderstel om in die binneplaas te praat nie!' You're not allowed to talk in the courtyard. This gave rise to some argument but she insisted that we were not allowed to talk while we exercised. And so we walked round in silence.

It seemed we were not allowed to talk at all. We could not talk at the laundry basins, we could not talk at meals, we could not talk while we exercised. We were also not allowed to talk during the night.

Our exercise time was made unpleasant in another way. One day, probably a few days or maybe weeks after I arrived, I sat down in the sun on a drain in the courtyard to have a rest. I was tired. I felt I could not take the pace. Apart from anything else, I was feeling weak with hunger as breakfast was some hours behind and I had a metabolism problem, made worse by my hardly having eaten for two months in Port Elizabeth. Suddenly the office window was flung open and there was the scream again. 'Neame, wat maak jy daar? Staan op en loop!' Neame, what are

Imprisoned

you doing? Stand up and walk! There followed some comment about, 'You people ask for exercise, and then you sit.' The venetian blind fell back again, and the window slammed.

I got up and walked in the hot sun. Round and round. Round and round. It was a relief when the wardress shouted, 'Stap binne!' And we went to our food.

We dished out our meal from the large aluminium pots that were sent in. The food was cooked somewhere else in the gaol and it was good compared with the other South African gaols I had been in. It was actually edible and did not have to be forced down. The food I had at the Fort, at Pretoria Central, at the North End Prison – the very sight of it had made me want to vomit.

In the first few weeks I was in Barberton I longed for mealtimes – they broke the monotony of our lives and after Port Elizabeth I needed food desperately. But after a month or two I began to feel that the food was decidedly lacking in variety. By the time I left, I did not find it enjoyable at all. Every single day we ate pieces of fried pork, except for days here and there when we were given beef. Out of the 20 months I was at Barberton we probably had beef on 21 days, thus for nearly 600 days I ate the fried pork. We had a fair amount of vegetables although these became monotonous as well. The fatty pork was especially bad for Ann, who had developed a stomach problem and she used often to vomit after our midday meal.

We were given no fresh fruit, although two or three times, as a special treat, pawpaws or grapefruit were sent in to us from outside, usually, as I remember, connected with some Jewish religious festival. There was also an occasion when we were able to have some oranges from the huge mound outside the gaol – the (white) farmers of the area traditionally threw away large quantities of oranges in order to keep prices up, to my mind a crime in a country where there was enormous poverty.

After Matron Bester had insisted that I walk and not sit and we'd come inside from the courtyard, I was tired, hot and sticky. I had the sleeves of my blue uniform rolled up. 'Neame, roll your sleeves down, please. You are not allowed to eat with your sleeves up.' I pushed my sleeves down with great irritation and, as the edge of my cuff came in contact with the soup, I muttered, 'Shit.' The wardress said nothing.

The authorities' campaign of provocation

This was a Thursday or Friday. On the Monday I was informed that I had been charged for using indecent language to a wardress.

The provocation was continual. In some ways, it was worse than solitary to be with people with whom one was not allowed to communicate. There was continual frustration. So, for example, two of us would just manage to get away from the wardress long enough to start a conversation when she would find us and tell us we were not allowed to talk. One day I managed to corner Jean in the boiler room.

'Look, Jean,' I said, 'we've got to do something about this place. Things can't go on like this much longer. I tell you I am going to assault a w—'

'Neame, what are you and Middleton doing here? Go and do your work immediately.'

And that was the end of that.

On another occasion, I carried a bucket of washed shirts into the courtyard and rinsed them in a tub under the tap, three changes of water, and then started to hang them up on the line. I had managed about four when I began to feel I was not alone. I hung up a few more and wondered whether Matron Bester was watching me from the office window or perhaps one of the other windows. I carefully hung up another shirt, turning my body a little to the left as I did so, and then quickly darted a glance to the left. Yes, there was a presence: the wardress was standing on the concrete watching me.

I hung up some more shirts, filling up another line. And then moved on to the third line. Ah, that bucket was finished. No, one more shirt, carefully rolled up at the bottom of the bucket. I bent down, picked it up, unrolled it, turned it up to empty the water out of the top pocket, and then attached it to the line, a peg at the top of each sleeve. Well, that's done, I thought. I felt I had a virtuous expression on my face as I turned in one movement and swung my right hand down towards the bucket to pick it up.

'Neame, take all those shirts down and rinse them again.'

The anger surged in me. 'God, what I couldn't do to that woman,' I muttered.

'It is not necessary to swear, Neame,' said the wardress virtuously.

I took all the shirts off the line, flung them into the tub and turned on the tap as hard as I could so that water splashed all over me. I let the water run in until it poured over the top of the tub, on and on. The noise of the water drowned all else. I saw two thick legs with a bit of khaki skirt.

'Neame! Neame!'

'Yes?' I shouted as loud as I could above the running water.

'Neame! Neame! Turn off that water at once!'

I looked at her with hatred and a beating heart. I tried nonchalantly to turn the tap off, but I knew my anger was too obvious for me to pull off the casualness. You bitch, I thought. As the noise of the running tap stopped, I heard the yell from the office window, thereafter the venetian blind dropping with a bang and the window slamming. I bent down and pulled a shirt through the water in the tub, up and down, up and down, and then pulled it out and up, dropping more water over my already soaked white apron and uniform, and put it up on the line.

'Wring all the water out, Neame, before you hang them up,' the wardress said coolly.

I took the shirt off the line and wrung it out carefully. I was just in control. I did the same with the other shirts. The crisis was over and having done her little good deed of provocation for the moment, the wardress went inside.

'Bitch,' I muttered after her. When I had finished, I picked up the bucket and went inside and across to the laundry basins where three people were busy. 'Let me take over,' I urged. 'Somebody else can do the rinsing. I've got to get this anger out of me.'

'Neame! Neame! You are not allowed to talk. Get on with your work.'

'Okay, take over from me,' somebody murmured under their breath.

I moved over to the laundry basin with a wooden washing board, the one next to the locker on which we used to place our washed dishes while we were washing up after meals. I took a canvas jacket from the pile just behind us. No, I can't face one of these jackets just now, I thought. They were particularly tough and difficult to manage because they were so stiff, and especially hard on the hands. I wanted something I could manipulate more easily in the basin so that I could rub it furiously up and down. I had to try and get rid of this anger.

The authorities' campaign of provocation

I pulled out a pair of shorts, put the plug in the basin and turned on the tap. Ah, that smell again. Just my luck. I turned the shorts inside out and put them down on the ridged wooden surface, with the back of the shorts uppermost. I turned the tap off when the water reached a height where it would not lap over the edge of the basin. I went to the toilet and unrolled about ten squares of toilet paper and went back to my basin. Holding my breath and trying not to think about vomiting, I wiped off as much of the thick yellow ointment from the garment as I could.

The toilet paper was yellow and in shreds when I had finished, parts of it stuck in little pieces to the inside of the shorts. Taking a gasp of breath, I walked to the sluice and threw in the crumpled yellow and bloodstained wad of toilet paper, took a fresh piece, and tried to clean up the shorts a bit more. There were bloody stripes across the back with larger patches of blood. I broke off a piece of blue washing soap from a long bar on the top of the locker and started rubbing soap onto the worst parts, and thereafter rubbed these parts up and down on the washing board.

'Shame, you've got a bloody one,' somebody said next to me.

'Yes,' I said, 'I shouldn't really be using this wooden board. It doesn't clean so well. Mind if we change?'

'Neame! Neame! You are going to get yourself into trouble. You cannot work and talk.'

Matron Taljaard with the big bosom came up to the locker at the side of my basin. She stood there pompously, with a complacent smile on her face, her breasts rather more prominent than usual, if that were possible, suspended somewhere to the right of my head as I bent over the basin. We came to call her 'The Presence' because she was always there.

The other wardress, Barnard, who came on duty in our section, often on alternate weeks, we called the 'Bird of Prey' because she looked incredibly like a bird of prey and watched us constantly with beady eyes. Moreover, she had unbelievably sharp ears. She heard a whisper, a mutter, anything, and prided herself on this talent. All in all little escaped her.

As it happened, she was not only rather lacking in intelligence but a coward. Since 'the Front' – this is what we called the authorities in the prison, those to be found in the office – were after 'Neame', 'the Bird of Prey' played her 'Neame! Neame!' role with pride and determination.

Whoever was talking, say at the basins, if I were in the vicinity, it was always 'Neame! Neame!' One day she tried this trick while we were eating, and it was quite clear to the whole table that I had not said a word, and Stephanie said, 'Miss Barnard, you just pick on Neame whenever you can because Colonel Aucamp told all of you that she is a troublemaker. Is that not true?'

The Bird of Prey looked cornered, frightened. 'No, that is not true, Kemp. That is not true.'

'Oh, yes, it is true, Miss Barnard.'

Silence at the table. Then out of the blue Miss Barnard said, 'You are not allowed to talk, Nicholson.' There was real satisfaction on her face for she had now, she thought, proven her respect for justice and fair play. There were giggles at the table. 'That's marvellous,' somebody muttered, 'we've got her frightened.' However, by that afternoon the Bird of Prey was back to her 'Neame! Neame!' refrain.

The question of exercise time caused a great deal of frustration. This was inevitable since the time was not fixed (except in the prison regulations). Again in this respect uncertainty appears to have been used by the authorities as a deliberate psychological weapon. One day, rather unusually, we would get almost our full half hour in the afternoon and we would think, Ah, things are settling down at last. The authorities are finally conceding that according to the regulations we should get an hour a day. And then the next day we would have to fight to get even five minutes.

Being locked up in that little space with the constant provocations, with no emotional outlets, made exercise seem terribly important. And it was important. For in that half hour, despite the tensions that arose out of our experiences in the courtyard, we could get a small taste of freedom. We could imagine that we were walking down a long gravel road with huge bluegum trees on either side, walking, walking with the long road stretching out before us. I used to half close my eyes as I did my rounds and feel the wind blowing on my face, hear it blowing in my ears and see that road before me.

In the afternoon my dream of freedom would be rudely awakened by the shout, 'Kom binne, julle mense!' and inside we would go. During the week we used to eat supper at about 2.15 in the afternoon. By 3 or

The authorities' campaign of provocation

3.15 we were locked up in our cells for the night. At weekends we faced a similar battle.

The desire to get off early is universal amongst wardresses but it was made stronger in this situation because they hated to be effectively imprisoned together with us. They were not allowed to have a key on them and were therefore dependent on others to let them out. They felt it was an insult, an erosion of their dignity. One of them once told us that they were treated like prisoners. And so their constant battle was to get out of that place as fast as they could. They had been given instructions that they were not to speak to us, except to issue orders. They were not allowed to read on duty. And so they had very little to do except to try and make our lives unbearable and even that enjoyment palled after a bit, especially as it raised the tensions to an unbearable degree. Later some of them took to sleeping on one of our beds.

I found an interesting pattern soon after my arrival. At the beginning of the week, things in our section were not so bad. Our relationship with the wardress was just under control. But the tension gradually rose as the week progressed. By Thursday our relationship had markedly unhealthy symptoms. If it had not been for the fact that we were extremely disciplined people, with high principles of behaviour, there could have been a riot in that place.

It was extremely painful to feel this aggression building up and knowing that there was almost no outlet. However tiring the washing was, however hard on our sometimes bleeding hands, we felt it was a necessity, we felt that we must exhaust ourselves, otherwise things could get out of hand.

I used to walk around sometimes talking to myself. 'Sylvia, Sylvia, keep control of yourself. If you hit a wardress, you'll only get more years of this, and you've got to keep control for six years as it is.'

Sometimes, I felt like retaliating in some less serious way. For instance, the day the wardress told me to take all the washing down and rinse it once more, I felt like shouting at her for all I was worth. But I reminded myself that that was no answer. They would only charge me and lock me up in a small solitary cell where my aggression would only build up further. Because of my nervous stomach and metabolism problem, the prospect of being 'given meals', in other words being put on a spare diet, was a rather terrifying one.

The cold way in which the authorities dealt with prisoners who had got out of control was one of the horrifying aspects that first struck me about prison. The absolute power the authorities had over prisoners was symbolised by that key. When a prisoner showed any sign of rebelliousness, even in the smallest way – for instance, she might raise her voice to a wardress – she would just be quietly and coldly pushed into a cell. The door would bang and the key turned in the lock.

I was caught up in that restricted space at one end of the Barberton female gaol, caught, *cornered*. For the first time, I really understood the stories I had heard about prisoners overturning their sanitary buckets with all its contents onto the heads of wardresses. I really understood the animal screams that we heard sometimes coming from the other side of the gaol. They were terrifying screams, so animal it was hard to believe they issued from a human being. But I understood for they were the screams I felt inside myself.

Yet I had learned control. I had been in solitary confinement something over five months altogether in the past couple of years. There had been provocation to one degree or another in all the situations.

Finally the authorities started alternating wardresses, a week with us, the following week elsewhere in the gaol. I presumed that the wardresses had themselves insisted on such a solution.

Our weekends were even more trying than weekdays. During the weekends our lunch was sometimes brought at 9.30 in the morning. We were unlocked at 7am at the weekend, instead of 6am, so we ate our breakfast at about 7.15 and just over two hours later we had lunch; and then at 1.45 or 2pm we had supper, our last meal of the day. At first, in spite of the problems three of us had with our stomachs, we were not allowed to take bread into our cells at night, and so from about 2.15 in the afternoon until 7.15 the next morning we had nothing to eat. Some people approached the doctor about this. He said he could do nothing about it.

I am charged with using indecent language

AFTER I HAD USED A SWEAR word at the table on a day shortly before a weekend, the following Monday I was called to the Front and charged with, I think it was, 'using indecent language'. Stephanie went to the Front and asked why they had charged me when others of us used to swear occasionally and nothing was done about it and when Taljaard herself had said once to her that Aucamp talked 'stront' (shit).

Soon after being charged I had raised the issue of our having no copy of the prison regulations with General Steyn, who was Commissioner of Prisons. Without having seen the regulations, I had enquired, how was I to know that swearing was an offence? General Steyn had replied that ignorance of the law was no excuse. Swearing was an offence against God. It was a delict in the outside world, so, in the same way, it was one in prison. All South African laws operated within the gaol, and there were some extra regulations which were just relevant to gaol.

I had asked General Steyn how they could charge someone for swearing. Surely it was usual to deal with this kind of offence merely by asking the prisoner whether she admitted the offence, and then handling the matter informally? I could get a day of 'meals'. He said, no, swearing was a very serious charge and was so regarded by the Prisons Department. He told me that, in any case, he should not be discussing the matter with me as he was going to be the 'judge' in my case. Some judge!

When General Steyn came round one Sunday while we stood on parade, one of my comrades again raised the problem of our not having a copy of the regulations and the point was made that, without them, how could we know that swearing was an offence. He answered much along the same lines as he had answered my question. Some weeks later we were given a copy of a list of prison offences, removed from the brochure with the prison regulations, the latter specially drawn up for prisoners.

At some stage, soon after I had been charged, I informed General Steyn – this had been in the course of an excursion to the Front – that I wanted my own legal representative to handle my charge. Steyn asked whether I thought I could afford it. Wasn't it true that I had very little money? I responded that I had enough and was prepared to pay.

This little game had gone on for some days. The point was made that Barberton was very far from Johannesburg. It was unlikely that any lawyer would be prepared to come so far. Would I not prefer to get a local person to represent me? I replied that I did not know anyone locally and, anyway, I wanted my own legal representative. General Steyn eventually admitted that Soggot had already arranged to come to Barberton in connection with my appeal against my sentence in Humansdorp. He only admitted this after I had made it quite clear that I was going to ask my own lawyer to come in connection with the prison charge. Finally, I was allowed to write to my attorney in Johannesburg, Ruth Hayman.

One morning I was called to the office and there I was confronted by a very ugly man with a huge head and a huge nose. He looked a bit like the convict in the film version of Charles Dickens's *Great Expectations*. In khaki uniform, he was obviously a prison official. He told me he was to be the prosecutor in my prison trial. General Steyn was to be the judge. The case would be run, as closely as possible, along the lines of a proper court trial.

The 'prosecutor' was looking very uneasy and seemed to be waiting for something. I thought that perhaps he was waiting for me to say something or perhaps he, himself, wanted to say something but was not quite sure how to phrase it.

I asked, 'And when is Mr Soggot coming?'

There was a short silence.

'We are not sure ... Soon.'

'How soon? I have not yet prepared myself.'

'Are you going to call witnesses?'

'Yes, I think so, but I will have to ask people and I haven't done so yet properly.'

'Do you think anyone will be prepared to give evidence for you?'

'Yes, I think so, but I will have to ask.'

'Do you know how many witnesses you are going to call?'

'No. I will have to ask people.'

There was a long silence. This conversation had been carried on mainly in Afrikaans. In other words, the 'prosecutor' spoke in Afrikaans and I struggled away, using English whenever I got stuck. Legal language in Afrikaans was not my strength. What do they want, I wondered. Matron Bester stood silently behind the desk, a few feet from the prosecutor.

Finally, the man broke the silence: 'Now you must not upset yourself,' he said. 'This is a small thing. So don't try and make a big thing of it.'

'Yes, yes,' I responded, 'I am amazed that you can charge a prisoner for this sort of thing, especially when you people swear yourselves.'

Suddenly he pushed a brown packet across the desk towards me. 'Have a sweet,' he said.

Good God, I thought. They must be terrified. They appear to be trying to blackmail me.

'I never swear,' Matron Bester intervened. 'Have you ever heard me swear?'

'No, Matron, I have never heard you swear. But then I hardly ever see you.'

'I do not swear,' she noted. 'I know that it is very evil to swear. You ask any prisoner whether I swear.'

'Well, you know I can't do that,' I replied. 'And the swearing I heard in Port Elizabeth gaol and in all the other gaols—'

Matron Bester interrupted: 'This is not other gaols. This is Barberton Prison!'

By now it was obvious to me that they were trying to find out what sort of evidence I intended leading. So I decided to say nothing about Taljaard and 'stront'.

'Have another sweet,' the 'prosecutor' offered. 'You mustn't upset yourself.' This time it was said in a somewhat threatening, part wheedling manner. 'And the trial is going to be carried on in Afrikaans,' he insisted.

'You will have to speak in Afrikaans.'

'We will see,' I said quietly, making it clear that I would not be pushed around, that I would take this up once my lawyer was present. There was an uneasy silence.

'But can't you tell me when Mr Soggot is coming?' I urged. 'Because I want to go and prepare myself.'

'He is going to be here today.'

'When today?'

'We don't know. Probably some time this morning.'

'Well then, I must hurry up and go and speak to my witnesses,' I said. It had suddenly struck me that not only were they trying to blackmail me with sweets and trying to find out what sort of evidence I was going to lead, but they were playing for time so that I would have little opportunity to prepare myself and to arrange witnesses.

Matron Bester escorted me back down the passage to the door into our section. 'Now, don't upset yourself,' she said. She locked the grille behind me.

I quickly told the others what had happened, and was just beginning to try and arrange witnesses when the door opened. Taljaard was there, looking partly smug, partly nervous. 'Neame, your lawyer is here.' She unlocked the grille with her military twist and I went through to a room opposite the visitors' room. David Soggot was there.

Ignoring the issue of the prison charge, I started to tell him about the developments with regard to some of the things Du Preez had told me. He pressured me to get back to the subject of the charge. 'Let's get that over with first,' he suggested. 'Then we can deal with your appeal.'

I outlined what had happened. I told him about the wardresses' (including Taljaard's) constant attempt to provoke us, particularly me. He said he would go and negotiate with the prosecutor and try to get them to drop the charge. While he went to the office to see the prosecutor, I ran through a copy of the regulations which David had given me. This was the first time I had managed to get one in my hands since I had been in Barberton. I had told David that the authorities had refused to give us a copy of the prison regulations, so how did we know when we were breaking them?

I noticed, once again, that it was the policy of the Prisons Department, according to what was written on the front cover, that every prisoner should have a copy, that the brochure had been specially produced for prisoners so that they knew where they stood and what their rights were. It was also considered that this would contribute to the better running of the prison. Again, it seemed these were just words, to be shown to visitors and bodies interested in prison reform.

I ran right through the booklet, trying to memorise sections for use in the future. I noted that we were supposed to have one hour a day in the open air. So they *were* breaking a regulation! I also gathered from the section on the work prisoners were to do that the stress was on rehabilitation and that they would be given tasks suitable to their aptitudes and previous training.

In part, the regulations looked okay on paper. At least they communicated an impression that the Prisons Department was trying to be humane, but most of it was hypocrisy. Firstly, most prisoners never, in fact, saw these regulations and were discouraged from thinking they had rights rather than just privileges. But what was uncivilised and inhumane and would have been ludicrous if it were not for the fact that it affected the lives and health of prisoners, was the distinction made between white, coloured, Indian and African prisoners. Their diets were different, their clothing, their bedding, their type of work and so on.

Dave Soggot came back from the office and told me that the prosecutor was not prepared to withdraw the charge but said that I would not get a heavy sentence. I would probably get about six days of 'meals'. Six days was not a light sentence. In Barberton Female Prison swearing was usually ignored unless a prisoner actually swore at an official. Prisoners found smuggling tobacco, which was normally regarded as a much more serious offence than swearing, were not charged but were simply given one day of 'meals'. This I actually checked up on later, and it was confirmed by more than one wardress. I wondered how much they would have given me if my lawyer had not been present, probably ten days or two weeks.

At any rate, we could hardly accept the prosecution's proposal that I get six days of meals. David went to the OC and told him that he would lead evidence that I had been deliberately provoked. He also assured the Brigadier that I had not sworn at Miss Taljaard. I had sworn when my sleeve went into my soup. The Brigadier then said he had been misinformed, and would therefore withdraw the charge. I had to appear before General Steyn in the front office, and he formally withdrew the charge. He did not even reprimand me.

Some time later when the wardresses had relaxed a little with us, some of them used to swear quite openly, and Matron Taljaard even described to us how Brigadier Pretorius had said to another prison official – this was a Brigadier Viljoen – in connection with something or other, 'Hy jaag kak aan.' He chases shit. She thought this a great joke. Later I heard Matron Bester herself swear. Her favourite was 'blerrie', admittedly one of the milder swear words or phrases used by members of the Prisons Department.

We are classified as highly dangerous convicts

ONE OF THE MOST UNBEARABLE aspects of that place was the feeling that it was a no man's land, a kind of madhouse somewhere at the end of the world. The fact that we were 'D Group' prisoners, the lowest grade a prisoner could be, was used to strengthen our isolation and our sense of having been placed in quarantine. I do not think there was another white woman outside our group in Barberton Prison who was a 'D' prisoner.

Gerrie van Rensburg, who had escaped two or three times, once most dramatically over the wall of the Fort while we were there, was de-grouped to 'C' after that last escapade. She had been got for armed robbery, and had been categorised as a habitual criminal and given a sentence of 9 to 15 years. She was apparently the leader of her gang, even though there were men in it. During one of her escapes, it was known that she had an implement which she intended using should she come across the wardress on duty. She was a most enterprising escapee. Her escapes were always imaginatively and cleverly carried out. As it happens, she made a really good impression. There was something of a Robin Hood in her character.

When I passed through Kroonstad gaol on the way to Barberton, locked up in a separate section, I spoke or rather shouted across the courtyard to two of the women I'd got to know fairly well at the Fort. They were both in for fraud; one was a bookkeeper. I had also exchanged a few words with two other prisoners whom I did not know really at all but who had likewise been at the Fort. They had been locked up most of the time in single cells. One of them, Joey, had escaped over the wall of the Fort together with Gerrie. The other was believed to have been involved in the escape. According to the other prisoners, she had made a statement to the Lieutenant to this effect.

At Kroonstad, shouting likewise across the courtyard, they had told me that they were 'C' prisoners, that is a step up the ladder from the worst category, 'D', where we were. Gerrie, too, they informed me, was a 'C' prisoner. She was not in the same section with them in Kroonstad because she was pregnant. They had the free run of their section although, unlike the other prisoners, they could not go into the courtyard at night. Otherwise, they worked with the others during the day and had their sport on Saturday. We later heard at Barberton that Gerrie had escaped again while in hospital in Kroonstad where she had just been delivered of a baby.

The category of 'D' prisoner was normally reserved for 'the type of prisoner with a previous record of serious crime of a daring and aggressive nature or other aggravating circumstances, such as convictions for rape, robbery or violence in one form or another, or other gang activities, involving knife assaults or incitement thereto' (report for four years, ended 1962, by the Commission of Prisons).

Evidently the authorities did not think Gerrie fitted into this category. It was we political prisoners who did. We were not even allowed the free run of our section at night, let alone in the courtyard. Even at the time I left by which time we had been reclassified to the 'B' category and, indeed, were described to visitors to the prison as 'good prisoners' who caused no trouble, we were still locked up in our cells at night.

I assume that it was connected with the fact that we were classified as potentially violent prisoners that such care was taken with the bread knife. At meals a knife usually came in from the kitchen, which was at the other side of the gaol. With this we could cut some slices of bread. Thereafter it was immediately returned to the kitchen. We were also deprived of ordinary knives with which to eat. All we were allowed was spoons. And so we were forced to eat meat with our hands.

One day they failed to send in a knife with which to cut the bread and I had to tear off a large piece with my hands while Matron Taljaard watched. She commented, 'How can you tear bread with your hands, Neame? It seems you had no proper upbringing!' And she added with that typical proud tilt of her head: 'I myself did have a proper upbringing!' She really was rather arrogant, that nineteen-year-old, with only about a year in the service.

Our classification into the category 'D', which indicated that we had committed delicts of a violent and aggressive nature, simply did not fit the facts since the evidence against us was that we had been members of an illegal organisation, the Communist Party, and that members of our CP cell had been involved in such activities as slogan painting. That we had been committed to Barberton Prison, which was a 'maximum security' prison, pointed once again to the fact that the state had categorised us as dangerous prisoners. Moreover, printed on the gaol identity card of each of us – we had to carry it with us at all times – was 'ULTRA-MAKSIMUM' in big red letters. It is striking that the authorities never actually made reference to the security features of our imprisonment while at the same time used them as key elements in the shaping of our conditions.

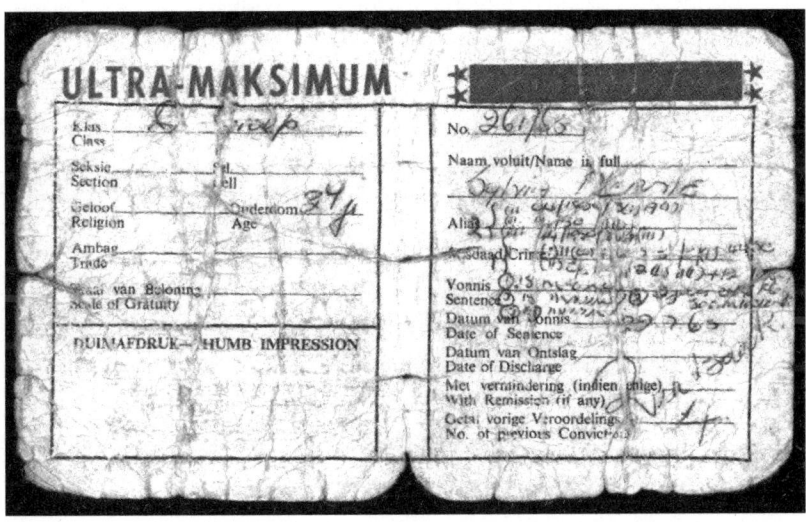

Night-time lock-up

OUR NIGHTS, TOO, WERE shaped by the general conditions of our incarceration, including our classification as highly dangerous prisoners. Three of us, Jean, Esther and I, were in single cells – orders from 'Pretoria', which meant Aucamp. According to the evidence at our Johannesburg trial, Jean and Esther had been minor officials in the Communist Party. I had just been a rank and filer, with very little evidence against me. Indeed, the informer, Gerard Ludi, had commented during our trial, making reference to the Security Branch tapes (these had, of course, been made without our knowledge), that I appeared hardly to have participated in the meetings. Was I actually there, he had asked, and he made some comment about other comrades disapproving of the fact that I did so little political work. This had not prevented the authorities stamping me as a 'troublemaker'.

In their first three and a half months at Barberton before I arrived Jean, Esther and Mollie were in the single cells, and Stephanie, Flo and Ann in the one communal cell. Then a few weeks before I arrived, the authorities had broken a door into another room along the passage and this became our second communal cell. When I arrived Stephanie was in it alone. The cell had two windows, covered with two large cages, looking out onto the front of the gaol. The golf course was to the right and the sisal lands to the left (where the black prisoners worked). I was put in the single cell Mollie had occupied and Mollie took Stephanie's place in the recently organised communal cell while Stephanie was moved to the original communal cell on the other side of the portaal, with a window overlooking the courtyard.

There was no toilet in my cell (only a sanitary bucket) and no basin.

Night-time lock-up

We were not even supplied with a metal basin and jug. Water we could only take into our cells in our metal mugs. A few days after my arrival I managed to get a table and chair so that I could study. There was limited space for me to move in that tiny cell and with the addition of table and chair it was almost impossible to avoid knocking into the furniture. My body was continually covered with bruises.

When I started doing exercises in my cell after lock-up, I had to put my chair on my bed and lie on the floor with my head under my table, the rest of my body in the space next to my bed, and with my feet reaching the grille. It was very hot in Barberton and in my cell the heat was unbearable. But it was to be far worse in the summer, especially in the very hot summer that was to come.

It was difficult not being able to speak to one another even at night. Apart from anything else, it was impossible to study with no interruption from 3 pm until lights-out at 10 o'clock at night. After working at my desk for an hour or two, I felt like getting up and stretching my legs but that was not possible. Or I felt like lying on my bed and reading a novel but there were no novels to read, as Barberton Female Prison, 'the best prison in the country', as the authorities liked to call it, had no library or library facilities of any sort. Or I would have liked to have been able to play some game but we had no games and, if we were found with a pack of cards, even if we had made them ourselves from cardboard boxes, we could be charged and put in solitary on spare diet.

Eventually, Ann suggested I cut chessmen out of the blue washing soap. This I did, and I used to try and play chess with an imaginary person. After a while Jean and I plucked up sufficient courage to call moves across the portaal to each other, and so, with a chessboard drawn on a sheet of paper and the blue soap chessmen, we used to have a game or two in the evening. But these little games were often interrupted by dreadful screams from a wardress named Bronkhorst. She had the Bester scream to a tee. She also screamed just for the sake of screaming. It was impossible to interpret what she said.

It could be argued that the maintenance of top security was especially important during the night. Perhaps this was at least a justification (amongst themselves), used by the authorities, for our extreme isolation, even from the rest of the gaol, that is apart from the danger of the spread of the infection of non-racialism. In addition to the white wardress on duty who kept an eye on us, there was an African wardress on duty on the black prisoners' side. She was not allowed to come within speaking distance of us. At the end of the passage I have described, past the visiting room and the office of the Matron, there was a locked grille, and so the African wardress could not even come into the passage that led up to our door. However, purely in terms of the risk that we would try to escape, it is to be noted that we would have had to break through seven locks.

We were not allowed to take anything into our cells at night, not a toothbrush or toothpaste, not a night cream. All we could take was our nightdress, nightgown and slippers, together with a few study books and a metal mug with water. And every hour the wardress was there, poking her head through the little window of our single cells.

Outside under a small metal shelter was a white warder with a rifle. He was relieved at midnight. We thought that maybe these guards would be friendly. On an occasion Ann put her head up at a window to have a look at the outside world through the cage, and the guard on duty that night growled, 'Ek sal jou kop skiet!' – I'll shoot you in the head! – proof enough that there was no friendliness to be expected from that quarter, indeed rather overreaction.

We were never supposed to look out of our windows, not even during the day. The windows in the *portaal* were high up and when we dusted the windowsills we climbed up either onto a chair or on top of one of the lockers. As there were no cages on these windows we could see quite clearly the trees and grass and flowers and the gravel road. We could also see the wardresses' quarters and maybe even prisoners marching in a long line to the sisal lands, with khaki hats on their heads. One day I was up there dusting the sill and I heard a scream behind me at the grille. It was Matron Bester. Evidently I was not allowed to look out of the window, never mind the fact that I was dusting!

At night we would hear the guard calling out to passers-by and he used regularly to flash his torch right along all our windows. This reminded me of our awaiting-trial period at the Fort where a wardress used to come round every hour and flash a torch onto our windows, up

Night-time lock-up

and down along the black bars to see that all were in place. After ten at night at Barberton, I would see the light flashing up and down along the cages of my cell, up and down the bars, onto the shiny concrete floor of the portaal. Flash. Flash. A pause. And flash, flash again. A light moving erratically and jerkily into our world. It was like being under siege.

Sometimes at night I heard a guard singing. A young voice, not really the voice of someone who would say he would shoot me simply because I wanted to have a quick look at the outside world of dark sky and trees and those large lights floodlighting the area around the gaol. His feet would crunch along the grey gravel as he sang one of the latest songs on the hit parade. And I would take a quick peep at his fair head as he went past and see the rifle over his shoulder.

Nevertheless, however much I tried to convince myself that his voice meant some contact with the outside world of young people and radios and records and dancing and parties and hit parades, I knew that, in the end, he was my enemy. Sometimes, especially in those early months, August, September and October 1965, there were great gales with driving rain and the guard would stand under his metal shelter in a raincoat, a small figure with a rifle. I think it was about six months later that they put African warders on guard duty at night. The white warders, we thought, must have complained about the terrible conditions of their guard duty: it was not work for white men; it was kaffir work.

And so, as the great trees swung at night in the wind and rain, there was a black guard down there with a rifle. It seemed strange that this change should have been made. Was it not a law in South Africa that a black person could not shoot a white person? And imagine the horror amongst South African whites if a black man shot white women! But, again, perhaps women who had been sentenced for membership of the Communist Party were not really white or women in the eyes of most South African whites. Very possible, I thought.

I developed an interesting symptom there in my cell, a result of the constant watch that was kept on us during the day while we worked, exercised and ate, and the regular check-ups during lock-ups. All the time I was in my cell I felt that someone was watching me through the keyhole of my grille, somebody unfriendly. It was quite irrational for it was impossible to see me through this keyhole as there was a locked door on the other side. As I sat at my desk working with my back to the door, I felt these hidden eyes boring into my back. And when I used the sanitary bucket, I was careful that I did not sit directly in view of the keyhole; I pushed my bucket into the corner between the end of my bed and the wall onto the portaal. I only lost this feeling after these long months were over, at a time when our conditions had improved somewhat.

The fact that I had six years was not, in those early months at Barberton, in the forefront of my mind. Neither I nor anyone else discussed it. In many ways, it had become a part of me, an aspect of my orientation to life, rather than playing any important role in my conscious thoughts.

It was during this period that I had a dream about the magistrate at Humansdorp. I was there under those lights in that nightmare court and he was sitting high above me, in the middle of a long brown wooden desk, looking like a judge in a high court. His face was fat, puckered and yellow under the lights, and he was talking in his lisping strong Afrikaans-accented English. Slowly. And he was sentencing me to death – with an insincere, almost tearful face.

'I hope you will use the time before your execution for meditation. You were once religious. I hope in these months you will come back to God. Let the death sentence that I am giving you be an act of grace from God.' I was conscious that I was caught in the great corrupt state machine that was sentencing me, and I shouted in a trembling, desperate voice: 'Don't try and hide your corruption behind God. It is you who are corrupt, not I.' I woke to the ringing of the 5.30 prison bell.

In that gaol one tended to take note of every sound because there were so few sounds. Needless to say this was in the main a night experience. One tried to build up an image of the outside world. The sound of wind (there were large trees in the vicinity) or a bird (what kind of bird was that?), the faint engine noise of a car or more like a lorry in the village, and trains. There seemed to be a railway line beyond the golf course. And I would see in my mind the little lights of that train moving cheerfully in the darkness along the railway line. None the less, as much as I tried in all the time I was in Barberton Prison, I could never really populate that train with people. In my mind, it travelled along completely empty, up and down that line, coming from nowhere and going nowhere.

One night soon after I arrived, as I lay on my bed exhausted after the day's washing, I felt a rush of excitement. What was that? Music? Heavens, it was music! And then there was a cheerful male voice which seemed to be coming over a loudspeaker. A fair! It must be a fair! I thought. How marvellous.

I lay on my bed in my cell and saw the merry-go-round, brightly coloured horses swinging up and down, carrying children chuckling with laughter. There were balloons and streamers. People were milling around on green grass, moving across to the skittles' booth. All sorts of exciting things merged in my mind in a crowd of people and colour and music.

Music and colour and the sound of laughter and happy people was to become a terrible hunger for me over those long months in Barberton. I remember once hearing a wardress laugh cheerfully one evening below my cell window as she went off duty and I felt a rush of relief that apparently the whole world was not the horror we were living. As for my 'fair', it was probably no such thing. Most likely it was just an ordinary party on the golf course. But I only realised this later. At this time I did not really have any picture of the outside world, even the world just a few hundred yards from my window.

Are we stoics?

WE ALWAYS HAD TO BE CAREFUL that we kept things within bounds, otherwise the authorities could have made our life there a greater hell than it already was. It was so easy to blow a fuse when you had been controlling yourself for months under constant provocation. And with no outlets. The fact that none of us had been successfully charged under a gaol regulation, that no one had been given 'meals' was a measure of our ability to keep the reins on ourselves. That the authorities had not succeeded finally in manoeuvring me into a trap so that they could have an excuse to climb in and break me, spoke, I think, quite a lot for my own discipline.

I also felt constant pressure from my fellow prisoners. They had become almost excessively afraid of taking the wrong step. On the day of my arrival when my comrades had been warned that they should not listen to me as I was a troublemaker, Mollie had spat out of the side of her mouth: 'We don't want any trouble here!'

There was something unpleasant in her response and I was quite shocked. At the same time I found it a very useful warning, which almost certainly helped me in the following months to develop a balance between the will to resist unfair and inhuman treatment with a careful weighing of the actual possibilities of the situation. I realised that I should avoid all acts of bravado while not allowing myself to be intimidated. In many ways, I think, my struggle in Barberton Prison for this kind of balance served as a training ground for the rest of my life. I developed an attitude of patience and realism, without jettisoning my principles. I believe I matured as a human being.

One of the most serious problems I was to find (and it took some months before I realised what was happening) was that the authorities had managed to produce a situation whereby there was a tendency for one prisoner to develop hostile feelings in relation to another and even to conclude that the Front could act as a kind of mediator in the face of such friction. Turning against a fellow prisoner was inevitable in that dire situation when frustrations could not be directed where they belonged, namely, against the authorities.

I came to the conclusion that an important goal for me was to build us into a unified group. Apart from anything else, I felt that, as we were, we were paralysed in face of what I perceived to be the need to struggle for an improvement in our conditions. I had to convince the others that we must act together.

I'm sure one favourable factor in my endeavours was the exposures of prison conditions that were made by Harold Strachan. They were made in an interview with journalist Benjamin Pogrund and appeared in the *Rand Daily Mail* in June–July 1965. I had heard something about this when I had been in Port Elizabeth. One result of the disclosures, it seemed, was a preparedness on the part of the authorities to make certain concessions – this is a conclusion by and large in retrospect – and to have opened some space for us in which to manoeuvre. I should emphasise that the publicity about gaol conditions, including the negative publicity for South Africa in the international arena, did not play a big role in our calculations, if at all, for we simply knew too little about what was happening outside the gaol.

BETTER JAIL CONDITIONS FOR POLITICAL PRISONERS

By BILL SMITH

JAIL conditions for South African political prisoners have improved since the Minister

I was very careful not to fall into the trap of sticking out like a sore thumb, as I referred to it at the time. That was exactly what the authorities were looking for because it would give them an argument for taking measures against me. I knew I would be used as an example to the others, discouraging them from making demands, from taking steps to improve their conditions and from trying to inform their families and friends about what our lives were like there. A key, of course, was that we should make it quite clear to the authorities that we were going to stand our ground, that we were not going to let them get away with what they were doing. We should submit our complaints to the Front and to all official visitors to the gaol.

At any rate, I took up issues like sufficient exercise and enough time out of our cells with the wardress while being careful not to go too far. I longed for the others to join me. My fellow prisoners did not know the extent to which I calculated my moves. They used to see me arguing with the wardress, sometimes quite vehemently, when she tried to cut our exercise time short or send us out early into the courtyard for exercise so that we could be locked up and she could get off or when the food was sent in with an order from Matron Bester that we should eat early.

I felt that we should ensure that we had a regular life, that a pattern should be established so that a process would be started to establish our rights. When we had 'rights', then we could afford sometimes to make concessions to the authorities, such as allowing ourselves to be locked up early one afternoon because the wardress on duty had an urgent reason to get off. We could allow a certain amount of give and take in order to improve relations.

I cannot deny that we prisoners were quite divided that first year. Different personalities react in different ways, and some were inclined rather to withdraw from the prison situation as much as possible, just by not thinking or discussing it too much. Or they simply gave in too easily to the authorities, hoping thereby to placate them. Although I had faced similar tactics in Port Elizabeth as the authorities used in Barberton, the point should be made that I had not gone through the breaking-in process the others had faced in their first months. My situation in Port Elizabeth was also rather different, above all because I was, true after a time, taken to court and thus found myself in a social context, however painful the experience was to be for me. To a degree, in Barberton I came from outside the situation and this made it easier for me to assess it. No doubt a factor in my different response was that the authorities treated me as an enemy and, on the whole, made it clear that for me there were to be no concessions.

Some of us at Barberton felt that we did not have long sentences and the attitude was: Let's just get through these few years. Prison is not the centre of the struggle, anyway. It is what goes on outside that matters. What happens to us here is not important. And: Let's show that we can take gaol as it comes and not talk about how bad we are having it. This no doubt reflected an acceptable humility in regard to our political role. However, it was not helping us to deal with the situation in which we found ourselves and I felt that that kind of approach was actually damaging us as people and as political activists.

An aspect which played a role amongst my comrades was certainly a desire to be released early if possible, with the argument that we could then continue with what was important, in other words, the political struggle outside. Indeed, this kind of approach appeared to have been suggested by Bram Fischer, who had not only been one of the accused in our Communist Party trial but was also a member of our legal team. On his last visit to us at the Fort – at that time we did not know that he had decided to estreate bail and go underground – he had suggested that we should try to mislead the authorities as to our political commitment. I do not remember exactly how he phrased the matter. All I can say is that the general idea which lay behind what he said was that we in the political movement should begin to adopt more conspiratorial methods. A new phase of struggle had opened and the liberation movement should drop its earlier tendency of political actions which often had a symbolic tendency. Forms of sharp confrontation were now on the agenda.

In a way, what he said was in line with the tactics used in the course of our trial when those who had not had a spy in their party cells, as we young people had had, geared their evidence to getting off. They denied their membership of the Communist Party and, in the case of one or two, even their communist principles. This had included members of the Central Committee. It was rather unfortunate that this tactic had tended to create tensions amongst us, between higher and lower ranking members of the party, between young and old, and, to an extent, between men and women. Initially we at Barberton had tried to follow Bram's suggestion, at least about misleading the authorities as to our political views, until the tactic had simply been dropped in the course of the struggles we waged.

Was it realistic at the time to gear our tactics to the prospect of going into the political underground? The trouble with this was that by the mid-1960s, with the breaking open of the underground movement by vicious torture and other means, the prospect of building an effective underground inside the country was fast fading. Crucial was that it was not only the political organisations that were being broken open but that the mass movement was in retreat. The apartheid regime had overcome, with the help of leading world powers and big capital, the strong crisis elements which had set in the course of the decade of the 1950s.

Moreover, in our particular case, the idea involved an overestimation of our capabilities, more especially as whites. A key weakness was that we were well known. Even if we adopted disguises, as Bram had done when he went underground, we would have found ourselves in an underground network that had all the weaknesses of a movement that had simply taken its cadres from an open movement into an underground one. Moreover, in the very widest sense, a culture of underground work had not been established.

Family circumstances to an extent played a role in our different responses at Barberton. It cannot be denied that those who had left young children at home were especially vulnerable. Be that as it may, my attitude was: Come, let's look at what this place is doing to us, firstly, in case things are happening to our attitudes that could have a negative effect on our outlook, not only politically but as people. There is nothing wrong with admitting that one is suffering. Let's be as honest with ourselves as we can. If and when we are suffering let us admit it and try to do something about it. And maybe we can even learn something from it.

In an attempt to put across my point of view without having directly to approach anybody, since at this stage I did not feel close enough to anyone to indicate how I felt about our situation, and I suspected that it would tend to put people's backs up if I discussed it in political terms – was I not a troublemaker? – I submitted a piece from a Chekhov short story to our Barberton newspaper (more about our newspaper below).

'The Stoics ... were remarkable men. But their teaching became petrified two thousand years ago, and it hasn't advanced an inch, it can't advance, because it's not practical, it doesn't answer to the

demands of life .... The majority never understood it. A doctrine that preaches indifference to riches and comforts, contempt for suffering and death, is utterly incomprehensible to the vast majority who've never known either riches or comforts. To them, despising suffering can only mean despising life itself. *Man's whole existence consists of the sensations of hunger, cold, insults, bereavements, and a Hamlet-like horror of death .... I tell you the teachings of the Stoics can never have a future, and, as you see, from the dawn of time to this day, that things that show any progress are strife, sensitivity to pain, and the ability to react to irritation."* [My emphasis]

Admittedly, what he said was geared to the conditions of people, more especially the poor, in the outside world. None the less, I thought it had something to say to us too. And it was all that I seemed to have at my disposal at that time.

---

*   Anton Chekhov, Gremov in *Ward Six*.

Washing laundry

During the day I worked long hours at the laundry basins. I gradually managed to keep my hands from getting torn on the concrete ridges though I still suffered from abrasions and wore some of my fingers smooth on the hard canvas of the jackets. I also gradually managed to work out for myself a washing routine. The shirts, the shorts and the jackets all required their own special technique. With the shirts, I first turned the pocket inside out for lots of dirt collected there, often bits of tobacco and black coal dust. Then I washed the inside of the hem of the short sleeves and then the collar, characteristically parts that become especially dirty; and then I took parts of the material of the shirt and rubbed it on other parts.

Sometimes the shirts were thick with coal dust, sometimes with red clay. Some were so dirty that the material had to be rubbed directly onto the basin's concrete ridges. The material tended to rub thin but it was the only way to get the shirts clean. I first washed the front and then the back, being careful to see that the inside of the hem at the bottom was rubbed clean. I applied a lot of blue soap, rubbed vigorously, rinsed it in the water, applied soap again in another area and repeated the process.

When the shirt was clean, I rolled it up and pushed it in between the taps and the white tiles above the basins. I turned round and bent down and took another shirt from the floor, just a few feet away under our white enamel washbasins where we washed our faces and cleaned our teeth.

When I had done three or four shirts I filled up the basin with clean water and rinsed them, changing the water about three times. Or if somebody was doing the rinsing in the courtyard in the tin tub under the tap, then I just put the washed soapy shirts into a bucket behind me.

Thereafter I might do a few jackets.

With the jackets I did the hem at the bottom of the long sleeves first, the collar, and the pocket if I could manage to turn it inside out. It was difficult to do this with the jackets because they were very stiff, especially when they were fairly new. They were also very difficult to get clean because the hard canvas seemed to hold the dirt somewhere right inside. Rubbing on the surface made no difference. Next I would pull up a sleeve and rub it up against the rest of the sleeve. First the front of the sleeve, then the back. Then on to the other sleeve. Then I would use one of the sleeves to rub up and down on half of the front of the jacket. The very dirty sections I would rub on the concrete ridges. Then I would do the other half of the front, trying not to tear off any buttons there might be. Then a shove into the water and a swing and then I worked on the back, seeing, at the end, that there was no dirt on the hem at the bottom.

Washing a jacket was often a very unrewarding task. They did not seem to look much cleaner even after one had spent 20 minutes or half an hour on just one. But the sun did marvels to the washing on the line. Often stubborn marks disappeared from articles on the washing line. The hot Barberton sun and the blue soap did their share of our work. Yet it remained an exhausting job. At the best of times, I had a painful back. The angle at the washing basin caused me agony, more particularly across the top part of my back. I used to groan with pain and was hardly able to straighten up as I came away from the basins.

Every half an hour or so, when I thought the wardress would not notice, I used to go over to my cell, close my door, and, standing at the end of my bed, I would bend backwards so that the painful part of my back was against the hard iron end of my bed, and press my spine into it. Hard, hard. And I felt the cold metal at the end of the bed pressing into my back, straightening it out with a wonderful release from pain. When I straightened up, I felt light as air, and I would open the door of my cell and slip back quietly to my basin.

'Get back to your basin, Neame!' the wardress shouted. 'There's lots of washing to do, and you'll get no exercise at all if you don't finish.' Expressionless, I would walk back to the basin, bend down and start on another shirt. And in half a minute the pain was back.

The doctor

THE DOCTOR CAME TWICE a week, Tuesdays and Fridays. His visit was a great event for us. We used to look forward to it, turning over in our minds for hours what he would say to us and we to him. He was somebody from the outside world. We did not know where he came from but there he was seated at one end of our eating table, his chair at an angle, legs crossed.

The first time I went to see him I wanted to raise the problem of both my back and my stomach. He came during lunchtime lock-up (between 12 and 1pm). We somehow expected that, because he was a doctor, he was bound to be sympathetic. He would see us as we were and not as brutal misfits. I waited to see him with a painfully beating heart. I went over what I was going to tell him, how bad the pain in my back was, my long history of back trouble. I would also tell him about my stomach, how a physician at Groote Schuur Hospital in Cape Town had put me on a strict ulcer diet (no salt, no fat) for two or three months at the end of 1961.

I was locked up in my cell behind the grey wooden door and the black grille. But I peeped cautiously through my little window on the side of the portaal, and ducked whenever Bester came into view. Then I sat myself down at my table with my back to the door as I heard Matron Bester crossing the concrete portaal and unlocking my door and then my grille with the efficient, brutal noise of her keys. There she was, not looking at me directly, seeing everything, but eyes slanted downwards and sideways, head turned to the left in the direction she was to move away. I grasped my grille, pulling it inwards. It opened into my cell and I squeezed myself between my partly opened grille and the wall. My heart was beating so much, I felt I was going to faint. Matron Bester had disappeared from sight.

The doctor

I went towards the table, looking at the doctor, waiting for him to look up and smile and greet me. His head remained down. I sat down in a chair at the table.

'Good morning,' I said hesitantly. He looked up at me with an unpleasant offhand look. 'Can you help me?' I asked. 'I have—'

'What is your complaint?' he spat out.

'Could you look at my back?' I asked. 'Because—'

'What is your complaint?' he spat out again, head down and unfriendly.

'I have bad backache.'

'What's wrong with your back?'

'Nothing much,' I said, retreating in the face of this treatment, 'just fibrositis.'

'What do you mean fibrositis? That term means nothing.'

'I have bad pain in my back when I am washing.'

'Oh, you are trying to get out of washing?'

'No, I want to wash, I just wondered if I could not have some physiotherapy. If you don't want to send me out to a physiotherapist, there is somebody here, a prisoner, who is a trained physiotherapist, and I want your permission for her to give me some massage. There will be no problem, no expense. Just a prisoner.'

'No, I cannot allow that.'

'I want you to just listen to my back,' I said, standing up and moving my arms.

Wardress Taljaard, who was standing there right up against the doctor, roared with laughter. 'Come on, Neame, back into you cell.'

'But, but ...' I said, trying to get in my bit about my stomach, 'I'm not finished ...'

Taljaard took me back to my cell and with that deft twist of the key locked the grille. The door banged in my face and locked. I went to my little window. 'But my stomach ...' I called out of the window towards the table. I was ignored. The doctor got up and swept like a prima donna out of our section. Taljaard locked the grille at the entrance and slammed the door.

I stood in my cell nonplussed and then turned and sat down at my table and tried to continue reading the British historian Christopher

Hill's *Century of Revolution*. But I could not concentrate. My mind was in a whirl, my heart beating unnaturally. I went through my talk with the doctor over and over again. Where had I gone wrong? I changed the talk this way and that. It would have been better to have started with my stomach, rather than with my back. He thought I was trying to get out of washing. Perhaps he would have been more sympathetic about my stomach. Yes, definitely. I had gone about it in the wrong way. And what did he mean, 'What is your complaint?' Did he think we came to him for 'complaints and requests'? Did he think we only went to him to make complaints about the prison authorities or the conditions of our incarceration? That was what his manner seemed to indicate. Or did he use the word 'complaint' in terms of a medical category, something like, 'What is it you are suffering from?' But he'd spat the words out in such a strange way it did not sound as if he'd meant simply that.

I usually ended up thinking that I could have handled a matter with more tact. And so did the others, despite the fact that Wardress Taljaard had told them before my arrival in Barberton that they would not get good medical attention because they were Ds and Ds did not have the privileges of other prisoners. She told them this after Jean, who had a running tummy, did not receive her medicine for some days and had made a complaint.

Nevertheless, the same excitement, the same expectancy of humane and sympathetic treatment built up before the doctor's next visit. And in spite of the fact that he was consistently awful at this time, we managed to think up all sorts of reasons to see him. And every time we did there was the same feeling of a slap in the face, of a let-down, followed by the same process of self-examination.

It should have been quite clear to us that he had either been given instructions to treat us in this manner or at least felt that that was what the authorities expected of him. We did accept this with part of our minds but the other part went on expecting and hoping. Chiefly unconsciously, we felt that it was only from the doctor that we might receive treatment which would prove to us that we were human beings with whom other human beings could sympathise. It was a hopeless battle. Our reaction to the doctor was all part of the symptoms that we were to develop over those long months.

The doctor was a short thin man, probably in his late 30s, with a rather pale, freckled face and ginger hair, the kind of man we might have called a 'weed'. And, indeed, after I first saw him, I hesitantly referred to him in an interchange with my fellow prisoners as a 'weed'. But even then I thought this bordered on sacrilege. After all, he was a man. And not only was he a man but he was somebody from the outside world. He might be employed by the Prisons Department but most of his life lay outside the gaol, somewhere else, in private practice or in a hospital. All in all, this made him not a weed but a rather exotic plant.

It worried me that he did not see me as a woman. Of course, for him I was not a human being at all, rather a potentially dangerous prisoner. A prisoner is, in any case, a distinctive category not easy to define in human terms, at least in a conservative and authoritarian society like apartheid South Africa.

I have a gaol visit

I HAD MY FIRST SIX-MONTHLY visit (30 minutes) at the beginning of September, I think it was. My friend Caroline came. And so I had a little trip down the corridor to the visitors' room. I can't say the visit was pleasant. I can remember almost nothing about what either I or Caroline said. I had the Major, a high-ranking male prison officer, on one side of me, right up against my right shoulder, and the Matron-in-Charge up against my left shoulder. To say the least, I felt most inhibited, and Caroline looked extremely cautious, even frightened. I wondered whether she had been warned by the authorities before the visit about what she could talk about. She hardly lifted her eyes. She looked hunted, cornered.

I thought I gave a rather nonchalant impression. I had got used to this sort of thing. In Port Elizabeth gaol, even when the Anglican priest came, I was put into one wire visiting cage and the priest into another, with a sort of empty cage between us. Here at Barberton Caroline was in a little cubicle, looking through a perspex window, with soundproofing around the window.

I assumed the visit was being recorded. We took this for granted, just as we took it for granted that our consultations with lawyers were always taped. I gained the impression from the visit that Caroline was being cagey, and I didn't know whether this was because she had been given a series of warnings beforehand or whether it was just the atmosphere of the place and those two ominous figures on either side of me. I guess it was both.

I told Caroline that my trial in Humansdorp had been 'terrible, a terrible nightmare'. 'Caroline, do you know that it was a complete fabrication, a string of lies from beginning to end.' She muttered something about this sort of thing happening in the eastern Cape but she was careful, I noticed, not to commit herself too adamantly.

The priest in Port Elizabeth would not commit himself either. I told him from early on in my trial that it was a complete fabrication and, when he came to visit me after I was sentenced to four years, I stressed that I was serving a sentence of four years for something I had not done. But he was uneasy, evasive. He indicated that he had been briefed by the prison authorities about what he could talk about. I understood that he wanted to communicate the message to me that he was on my side when he left a book for me, with the thoughts of the priest who was hanged by the Nazis in Germany, Dietrich Bonhoeffer. I was grateful to him for that.

To Caroline I said, 'The police are absolutely corrupt down there. People in the eastern Cape are having a terrible time.'

Caroline noted that Gillian Jewell – Gillian had come to Humansdorp to give evidence in my defence – had told her when she got back to Cape Town that I had looked terribly thin and pale in court. 'All, all your friends hope so much for the appeal.' She said that she had tried to give a picture in her letter of what our surroundings in Barberton were like and that she would be coming back to the area for her December vacation. Her friends the Cullinans had a farm about 100 miles away, and she would visit me again then. That would be for my second six-monthly visit.

Barberton was perhaps not quite no man's land anymore. At least I was beginning to feel it was not quite the unknown out there if I only had a tiny piece in the puzzle. At the same time, I did not feel that the visit had been a great success for I had learned very little about the outside world from it and, above all, there had been no real human interchange with Caroline. She was so intimidated that she was effectively not communicating with me at all.

The prison authorities later indicated to us that we were not allowed to speak about anything but family matters during visits. Our visitors could say absolutely nothing about what was happening anywhere, even if there had been a flood in Italy or an earthquake somewhere else and, of course, nothing about political happenings in Africa, Vietnam, the Middle East or China. Our world went up to the walls of our section. The authorities saw to it that it did not go further.

Our organisation, their disorganisation

ONE OF THE THINGS I first noticed in Barberton Prison was that my comrades moved around incredibly fast in the course of executing various tasks. This may seem to contradict the picture I gained on first seeing them through the central grille and I was, indeed, to have a similar picture of them in slow motion later when I had had an outing, say to the local hospital. I don't really know how to explain this apparent contradiction.

At any rate, they did move around extremely fast, and I was soon to do so too. Initially, I could not see where the organisation had its source or whether there was any pattern at all really. I simply stood dazed on the edge of a vortex, unable to fathom what it was all about. I found that people ate incredibly fast, presumably because they had got used to eating in a limited time. I had come to eat very slowly in Port Elizabeth, if I had eaten at all, because it had been such an effort to force any of the food down. In Barberton I was left at the table while the others were up and running here, running there, the dishes were washed, the floor swept of crumbs, teeth cleaned, hands washed, all in an incredibly short time.

Evidently, this was what it was all about though I was too dazed at first to focus on the meaning of what was happening around me. Over the weeks, I was drawn into the vortex, initially largely a conscious effort on my part. At any rate, as I was to discover, we lived in such a limited space, with a highly restricted range of activities allowed us, the same things repeated day after day, week after week, month after month, year after year, that each of us tended, in our physical tasks, to turn into a kind of robot.

Our organisation, their disorganisation

The whole process, the degree of our thoroughness, was powered by our sense of discipline and by our conviction that, as whites in the fight against racism, we should be prepared to do, and to do well, all kinds of tasks, even the most menial. In more general terms, we were deeply aware that we were in that situation, above all, in order to serve the country's people and it was important therefore in all situations to ensure that we maintained our dignity.

At this time we did not have all our jobs allocated, and yet things ran extremely smoothly. When I first got there, there was a roster for cleaning up the section, one 'on the floor', as we described it, and one 'on the fire'. There were three people at the laundry basins. Jean did not actually work at a basin because she had two slipped discs. When she was 'on' the laundry she helped with various things, such as rinsing in the courtyard. The 'floor' involved sweeping the two communal cells, the three single cells, the portaal, and our bathroom section, and then rubbing up with a brush, dusting as well as cleaning two toilets, the sluice and the bath. And doing various other odds and ends.

I found this quite heavy work, even though in Port Elizabeth I had swept and polished three communal cells with parquet floors, cleaned a bathroom, a lavatory, a washbasin section, the small passage that was a part of my section, beyond that a 50-yard corridor, which included removing the dust from a jutting out part of the wall that ran along the whole length of the corridor – Major Symington used to run his finger along it every day to check that I had removed the dust – and a courtyard. I had also to polish the brass and clean the windows. All this had to be completed before the Major came on his round at 10 am. It was part of a policy to break me, no doubt on orders from Aucamp.

In Barberton the person on fire duty had to clean the oven, put in fresh wood and coal – this was sent in from the other side of the gaol – light the fire, scrub the floor of the boiler room and polish the stove with blacking when required. After she was finished with this, she either helped dust or joined those busy with the laundry.

One of the things that underlined our isolation, even from the rest of the gaol, was the length of time it took for us to get the necessary cleaning materials and the wood and coal. And even clothing. We would

> Aug. 66. (1966)   Barberton prison   (159a)
>
> Fire
> Ann
> Mollie
> Esther
> Flo
> Jean
> Sylvia
> Leslie
> Vi det
>
> [Fire person lights fire as soon as possible after unlock; keeps it going; scrubs boiler-room floor; sees to tea; etc. dishes out pork at dinner; washes up after dinner & supper; washes up after breakfast the next morning, & then washes the dishcloths.]
>
> Daily Duties
> 1st Day — Fire
> 2nd " — Washes after breakfast, dishcloths
> 3rd " — Upper Dusting
> 4th " — Lower Dusting
> 5th " — Stove
> 6th " — Sweeping
> 7th " — Lavatories, basins & bath.
> 8th " — Mats, dining table.
>
> Weekly Duties.
> (1) Jean – Scrub laundry basins & basin floor., keep tablecloth & towel clean.
> (2) Esther – Scrubbing sink
> (3) Flo, Sylvia, Mollie, Ann – scrub courtyard Mondays.
> (4) Carpet person on Tuesdays – brass.
> (5) Fire person Fridays – Scrub stove floor.
> (6) Fire person Thursdays – polish stove.

sometimes wait weeks, even months, for polish for the floors or the bathbrick for cleaning bath and basins, sometimes as long as one and a half months for the disinfectant for our sanitary buckets, even though these items were often just a few yards down a corridor on the other side of our entrance grille.

We would sometimes wait a week or two for wood, and then wander round our section like caged animals trying to find something with which to get the fire started so that we could have a hot bath after a day sweating at the concrete basins. When we asked the wardress for polish, for instance, she responded that she would see to it when she went off duty or, more usually, just shrug. It was maddening, frustrating, particularly as we desperately wanted to keep our small area of living clean and orderly.

We often used to ask the wardress if we could see Matron Bester so we could make a complaint or try and settle some matter with her, for instance, with respect to obtaining some disinfectant for the sanitary buckets and toilet and anything else that might require to be disinfected. But she kept out of our way. Sometimes, though very seldom, she appeared on the other side of our entrance grille to say a few words to the wardress, and if we managed to get to her before she had closed the door, we sometimes managed to squeeze in the sentence, 'Matron, could we have some dip, please?'

'Dip? Dip? No, you can't have dip.' And she would scream out, 'Why ask *me* for dip? Ask the wardress.' Then came the shrug and the door would slam. She never came into our section, except sometimes in the morning when she unlocked our cells. Once she told us that we shouldn't expect her to come into our section because she was not allowed to do so. A very peculiar situation, the Matron-in-Charge not even allowed into a section of her own prison! Was there a suggestion here that we could not be trusted not to attack her? Or was it simply a part of the authorities' campaign of psychological warfare?

In line with the programme of discrimination against me, I was given no jersey, no bras. I think it was about a week or so after I arrived that the unseasonal heat came to an end and the temperature fell sharply. It became cold, especially in the cells at night. Gaols are always colder than other places because of all that concrete. It was so cold that most of us sat at the tables in our cells with blankets around us. And sometimes I was so cold at night that I found it difficult to sleep. So, one day, after asking Wardress Taljaard several times when I was going to get a jersey, I slipped quickly and quietly up to the entrance grille when Matron Bester appeared there.

'Matron, when am I to obtain a jersey?'

Bester's face swelled and her lips pouted. 'What do you mean?'

'I haven't a jersey, Matron, and I have asked Miss Taljaard several times if I can have one.'

Those mad eyes and lips looked at me, amazed at my audacity. 'There are no jerseys!' And the door slammed. That was that.

In a similar way, I tried to acquire underclothing but by the beginning of October, something like four months after my arrival, 'the Front' had still not given me anything. Eventually, when another prisoner joined us, and some wardresses were going off to the shops to buy her some articles of clothing, I asked timidly if, seeing they were going to the shops for the other prisoner, couldn't they buy the necessary articles for me at the same time.

A few hours later Wardress Taljaard was at our grille and she called the new prisoner over and gave her two bras. 'And here you are, Neame,' she called to me. 'Matron says you must look after these very well because you have six years.' I took them without a word. This was deliberate. She knew that I maintained that I was innocent. She had heard me say so my first day in Barberton. And I had had occasion to tell the Commanding Officer in his office in the presence of Matron Bester that I was innocent.

I could now wear a bra but I still had no jersey.

The prison experience

LIFE IN GAOL IS EXTREMELY difficult to describe. I suppose one could say that it is an eternity of sensory deprivation and about this aspect there will be more in the course of this account. At the same time, describing it in this way does not capture that special flavour which no other experience I have ever had has even a similarity. Perhaps one requires a special vocabulary for the prison experience and that is why it is so difficult to tell people who have not gone through it what it is about. The result is that most people who have been in prison do not attempt to communicate it to outsiders, in the same way, I guess, that those who have had dreadful experiences in the course of a war often do not talk about them.

Perhaps one could simply call what we went through at Barberton 'a hell'. However, it is not a place of perpetual fire, not an eternal physical torture. It is more a mental or psychological condition, an experience of *nothingness*, a universal *absence*. Above all, it seems to me, that it was not simply a suspension from life, at least not in the sense of something temporary, although there was a very strong feeling of being suspended. It was a (conscious) death in life. I suppose this has to do, in part, with the fact that prison, particularly in the form we experienced it in Barberton, is by and large a social death – this includes the emotional that is integrally interwoven with the social. And the sense is that this is not temporary but eternal. *Time stands still.* There is an everlasting cold silence buzzing in one's ears, maybe rather like being in outer space.

Perhaps, in the end, this eternal absence, this nothingness has to do with the fact that gaol involves, in many ways, the death of the individual. Without one's individuality one ceases to exist. No doubt, a (genuine) policy of rehabilitation is meant to, and to an extent actually does, serve to counter this condition. The manner in which we were being treated in Barberton was clearly meant to intensify it.

I remember standing sometimes in the centre of the concrete floored portaal and thinking, This is unbearable. Every moment is unbearable. I stand here on the concrete surrounded by prison cells for this unbearable moment. And there is another unbearable moment to face. Moment by moment right through the day. And tomorrow. And the day after. And next week. And next month. And next year. There appeared to be no way out.

I had managed to get hold of *Anna Karenina* from somebody who was studying English with the University of South Africa. And I read it alone in my cell at the time when we were not allowed to speak to each other. And my life, if I could call it life at all, stretched ahead of me. Tolstoy's character found a way out in religion. I wrote in my makeshift diary:

> 'To decide to become religious would be so easy. It would make life so easy. It would make this hell so easy. In fact, it would be a sort of justification for my suffering.'

I determined that I was not going to take that path. I wished to face this hell head on, absolutely sober and with open eyes. I needed to be honest with myself, honest about my ideas about the world, about history. At the base of my developing view of the world and my place in it – this was before I was arrested – had been a desire to investigate society, perhaps in the first place the clash of opposing historical forces, and I felt that I would learn most if I, myself, were in the midst of the battle.

In many ways what was happening to me before my imprisonment was a developing outlook according to which, by means of involving myself in significant historical processes, I would obtain knowledge in a way that would otherwise not have been possible had I merely stood on the sidelines. This experience of activism, I became convinced, I must try to carry forward in my imprisonment.

The search for knowledge had become the centre of my life. That was why always a part of my political activities had been keen observation, a search for the actual facts. I was an activist and an intellectual. This was a very difficult combination to maintain but I was not one for evading difficulty. Indeed, difficulties, contradictions were an integral part of history and by experiencing these directly, my understanding of our world and of myself, I felt, would be further sharpened. To a growing degree, in intellectual terms at least, I came to regard prison as an integral part of that journey and I became geared to deliberately increasing this ingredient.

An easing up begins

ABOUT OCTOBER OR NOVEMBER 1965 I managed to speak to Stephanie in the courtyard, out of the hearing of the wardress.

'Look, Stephanie,' I said, 'this place is unbearable. We must try to do something about it. We must try to organise classes.' I felt the eyes of the wardress boring into my back. Stephanie and I were standing on the grass under the washing lines during exercise time.

Stephanie said, 'They won't allow it.'

'I know they won't. But what about organising a prayer or Bible reading or something?'

'Neame! Neame! Will you and Kemp please stop standing there and walk.'

Well, that was that – for the moment. But some of us managed to agree to read a piece from the Bible in the mornings when we stood on parade before the porridge pot was sent in. The first morning it was Ann, who read from Ecclesiastes. We knew the Bible quite well as it was the only reading matter we had had during 90-day detention. And we all had our favourite bits. Ecclesiastes most of us liked.

I thought, as we stood on parade listening to Ann, If this is the only way we can communicate, if this is the only way we can have some sort of group life, let's have it this way. It may be a beginning. Once we have stuck this wedge into the armour that the authorities are trying to build around each one of us, keeping us separate although we live so close to each other, next time we may get away with just that little bit more. And Ann read from Ecclesiastes with the plump wardress standing watching, partly suspicious, partly with a triumphant, self-satisfied expression. Her look said, You people, you communists will come back

(34) -4-
Ann
Bible Study.

Since 67 B.C. Palestine civil war betw. 2 sons of Jewish King Jannens — Hyrcanus & Aristobulus. Pompey's legate settled in favour of Aristobulus. But in 63 B.C. decision reversed in favour Hyrcanus. (Syria won for Rome in 64-63 B.C. by Pompey) | Hyrcanus (63-37 B.C.)

In 39 B.C. Anthony's general overthrew Hyrcanus at Jerusalem. Herod, his vizier escaped to Rome & senate proclaimed him king of Judaea — installed in 37 B.C. by 2 legions. | Herod the Great (37-4 B.C.)

In 27 B.C. Augustus given Syria as province — Imperial. | Augustus (27 B.C. — A.D. 14)

In 23 B.C. & 20 B.C. Herod the Great's territory (Judaea) enlarged by inclusion of Ituraea & other districts by Augustus. [On material level did much for his country — developed economic resources, built new port (Caesarea), refortified Jerusalem & started rebuilding Temple, refounded several cities, enhanced, generally, standing of his country. But by behaving as Hellenized monarch & promoting Helleni-zation of country he won bitter hatred from more orthodox Jews. (he himself was dissenting Jew - Idumaean) He imposed his rule by force — by crushing old nobility, secret police — mercenary troops — chain of fortresses. He offended to Christianity. This gaol will make you come back. I personally will make you come back.

Before I arrived in Barberton the others had approached the authorities and asked for a priest to visit them. At one time, they had evidently spoken about it to some official – it might have been General Steyn, Commissioner of Prisons – who had visited the prison and he had smiled at them cynically and asked why communists wanted a priest. And no priest came. It was part of the strategy to keep us isolated.

One day I asked Matron Bester if we could have a Bible study class amongst ourselves on a Sunday for half an hour. My attitude was that it was a group activity where we could communicate and it might be the beginning of other classes which could make our lives more meaningful. It was also an attempt to enable us to remain outside our cells just that little bit longer. On Sundays they tried to lock us up by about 2 o'clock or 2.15. They would bring our soup and coffee sometimes immediately we were unlocked at 1 or 1.15.

Permission was given and the first class, from 2 to 2.30 in the afternoon, was quite a success. I talked about Jesus and liberation of the Jews from the oppression of the Romans. I had, in fact, read up quite a bit of historical material beforehand and found it fascinating. The wardress who was on duty that day – it wasn't Taljaard – wandered in and out of the communal cell where we were having the class. She looked suspicious and uneasy. But she could speak very little English and only seemed to understand fairly simple words. So we went on unhindered.

There were two, rather conflicting, attitudes in the Front at this time. There was the initial attitude: complete isolation for us from the outside world and from the rest of the gaol, with communication between ourselves as well as communication between us and the authorities cut to a minimum. But about September a new attitude, a contradictory one in some respects, had begun to creep in: rehabilitation. This new attitude, without doubt, had resulted from the Harold Strachan article and it manifested itself in various ways. One of these involved trying to get us to sing hymns and say prayers in the morning. The wardress told us that all prisoners were required to do this in the morning before breakfast and they tried to get us to do the same.

Another indication was something the plump wardress said one day while we were sitting in one of the cells. It was either October or November 1965. Out of the blue she announced: 'This is a rehabilitation centre.' This statement was accompanied by her characteristic self-satisfied, proud look. Around this time, too, the Brigadier started referring to the gaol as an 'institution'.

About September we had heard a rumour that prisoners, including political prisoners, were going to obtain amnesty in honour of Republic Day 1966. This information came from an unofficial source. And then the Brigadier announced one Sunday when we were standing on parade: 'I don't think any of you will serve your full sentence.' It was a response to some question put to him by one of us, probably Stephanie, since she was expecting release any minute.

Vorster had made a statement round about the time of the Armed Resistance Movement (ARM) trial, in which Stephanie had been involved, that he would consider reduction of sentence for anyone who could prove that they had been influenced by a president of the National Union of South African Students (NUSAS). The ARM had been established by liberals and a prominent member of NUSAS, a liberal-orientated student body, had been a leading light. When Aucamp made his visits to the prison, usually about once a month, he often discussed Stephanie's possible release with her. In November he told her that reduction of sentence was not only to be considered for ARM people.

Despite what might be interpreted as indications that things were getting better, our conditions remained unsatisfactory, to say the least. It took a long time for us to obtain a copy of the prison regulations. They kept making excuses such as they would first have to be translated from Afrikaans; thereafter there would be the typing. Eventually they gave us a few stencilled pages, clearly torn out of a full copy of the prison regulations, supposed to be made available to all prisoners. No doubt, not unintentionally, there was nothing about exercise.

We had managed during our Johannesburg trial to acquire a full copy from our male co-accused. The Lieutenant at the Fort had actually refused to give us the regulations and was most disconcerted when she found out that we had managed to obtain them. Subsequently, I obtained a copy from an unsuspecting wardress at Port Elizabeth's North End Prison. At the time I was trying to find out whether the authorities were breaking prison regulations by holding me in isolation while I was serving a sentence.

I think it was in the first week of November 1965 that we were upgraded to 'C' status. Colonel Aucamp arrived and all the other prisoners, except for me, were interviewed by him and told that there would be a recommendation to the Prisons Board, which dealt with such matters, that they be upgraded. It seemed that they had decided to exclude me from this privilege. However, a week later, when Colonel Aucamp came again, at a time when the Prisons Board was there, I was told that they had reconsidered my position and my upgrading to C was also to be recommended to the board.

As C prisoners we received one visit every three months and one letter (both ways); otherwise there was very little difference between C and D. While Di Schoon was with us – more about Di below in the following section – we were given our first taste of recreation. We were given a chess set, a draughts set, and dominoes. Things were definitely changing.

One day Matron Bester brought a small tortoise into the prison and put it in the courtyard. Initially I disliked the tortoise as I thought he looked so ugly. His shell was interesting but I thought he had an ugly face. And so I ignored him. None the less, a few weeks later I began to refer to him as 'Arnoldus' and would say 'Hello, Arnoldus' when I saw him in the courtyard but I did not pick him up or play with him.

Arnoldus was very unhappy at first. He used to walk very fast, round and round along the walls of the courtyard. Sometimes he would be somewhere towards the centre of the courtyard on the grass and suddenly appear to decide that freedom lay in a particular direction. He would go off at some speed and find himself up against a brick wall. At other times he would try and climb the wall, pushing himself up on his back legs, legs crinkled like a baby's, with his shell making a deep shell-noise against the wall. Thereafter he would give up that section of the wall and go off, again very fast, to another part. Round and round the courtyard. But to no avail. He discovered, as we had discovered, that there was no way out.

Some of us thought of letting Arnoldus go by asking the wardress

An easing up begins

to take him out and set him free. But we were afraid that he might be killed in the outside world because his fighting apparatus, that jutting-out section of shell under his head, was broken off. And another consideration was that we rather felt like keeping him. For, although as yet none of us had taken to him particularly, he was another potential personality in our space. And there was a great longing in some of us to have more personalities around, to try and diversify our dreary lives there a little. One of the wardresses told us later, after they began to speak to us a little, that Arnoldus had been found in the gutter of the black wardresses' quarters where a bird had dropped him. That was how he had had the piece of his shell broken off.

After some fairly cold weather in parts of August, September and October, in November the days began to warm up. And the mosquitoes started. Of course we didn't know it but we were at the beginning of a drought. In August and September there had been a lot of very gusty weather with rain, rather typical South African spring weather. In my mind, I see those driving winds in two places – in the courtyard, which looks dreary with flattened everlasting flowers, and to the front of the gaol I see in the darkness of night the black-green wind-driven trees, partly lit up by the great lights which floodlit the area. And there is the lonely guard taking shelter from the driving rain under the metal shelter.

I used, almost every day, to prop up with sand the plants with the everlasting flowers. But the next day they were drably down again, all

lying on the earth, pointing in the same direction, the direction the wind was blowing. And again I would push the sandy soil around the bottom of their hollow stems. Spring went and summer came. A long, hot, subtropical, humid summer, with no rain.

Sometime in September Ann and Mollie had been taken to Johannesburg. Ann was to stand trial for an ANC leaflet she had helped distribute during 1962. And Mollie went in connection with the suspended sentence she had as a result of the distribution of the same leaflet. She had already served six months for this in 1962. Now that she had been sentenced for membership of the Communist Party, the suspension became operative.

A prisoner breaks down

Those who had been taken to Johannesburg for further sentencing returned at the beginning of October, and they returned with a new prisoner for Barberton. This was Di Schoon, who had been sentenced in the same ANC trial as Ann to twelve months with ten months suspended. Ann had got three months. The fact that their sentences were relatively short was an indication that the authorities were not keen on keeping them in prison for a long time.

It was marvellous having Di Schoon, we thought, somebody from the outside world, somebody who had actually not long before been walking around in the streets of Johannesburg, reading newspapers, listening to the radio, going to the cinema, talking to people, eating interesting food. We could hardly believe that such excitements were possible. Di brought us news from the outside world. She seemed fairly cheerful those first few weeks, three weeks, in fact. But she, too, began to feel the walls closing in.

It was then that the trouble started.

I can't remember exactly how the drama unfolded but Di began to say that she was not feeling well and that, in particular, she was having difficulty urinating. And then one morning as the grilles of our cells were being unlocked in the early morning, Di came out of her cell crying hysterically.

At that time Di was sharing the front cell with Mollie and Esther, and they told us that Di could not urinate, however hard she tried. Later that morning she was taken off to the local hospital for an examination. She was told there was nothing physically wrong with her. And she was brought back. The next few days I did not see much of her, although occasionally I found her next to me at the basins while we were washing.

Here she sometimes asked to be relieved as she was not feeling well. She was still having difficulty urinating. Because of the instruction not to communicate with another prisoner, most of us did not really know what was going on. The only people who did were Mollie and Esther.

One morning – it must have been a few days after Di had been taken to the hospital for an examination – as I was standing at the laundry basins, I heard a high sharp scream break the silence of our section. It shook me rigid. A few seconds later I saw Stephanie and Flo carrying a limp form in from the courtyard. It was Di. They carried her into her cell and put her down on her bed.

Di was beginning to break down. People tried to help her. First Mollie and Esther. Then Stephanie. We all felt bad enough. And now we had this extra burden. But we were disciplined, determined people. And some of us made an enormous effort to help her. Yet over the next few days, she deteriorated. Several times a day I would feel the pain spark across my chest, as Di's scream pierced the silence.

She told us she had to get out of that place. She couldn't take another day. And she still could not urinate properly. One day at supper, Di was sitting opposite me at the table. And I saw her hysteria gradually building up. 'It's coming on again,' she said. I tried to help her by speaking to her. And the mounting hysteria would die down a little. But then it would mount again. Eventually, she got up from the table. She picked up something from one of the lockers – I think it was a marmalade pot. It slipped from her hand and smashed into little pieces on the concrete floor.

'Here it comes,' I muttered. Only one other person at the table saw what was happening. Di's eyes went wild. She walked rapidly round the table trying to escape from the devouring cloud of panic. And then she screamed and slumped to the floor. Everyone else was shocked rigid. And then two people got up and carried her to her cell. Various comrades over this period tried to get from Di what was worrying her. Some chatted to her for hours, trying to encourage her to pull herself together. She would be all right for a couple of hours and then it would start again.

Wardress Taljaard was terrified and admitted it. The first time Di screamed, a matron and wardress from the other side of the gaol came running to see what had happened. But they were also terrified of Di.

The only person from the side of the authorities who was not frightened was Matron Bester, and she did try to manage the situation. Di at first responded. Bester used to take her through to the office in the front and try and keep her mind off herself by talking to her. But then she would start screaming in the office too.

The Brigadier was totally unsympathetic. He told her when she went through for complaints and requests one Thursday morning that if she screamed again he would put her in a solitary cell in a straitjacket. He was going to take no nonsense from her. Di came back to the section quiet but with carefully controlled terror in her eyes. That day she did not scream. She walked up and down, sometimes round and round our eating table. She walked for hours, walking, walking from that creeping panic. Matron Bester gave her permission to go into the courtyard while we were working and she walked round and round, very fast.

At the basins we braced ourselves for the scream. Locked up in that confined no man's land we waited for the scream. At the entrance to the little boiler room there was a wire door and when it swung closed it squeaked, with exactly the same high-pitched sharp sound as Di's scream. And so several times during the day we felt our bodies jar with tension and fright as the door swung to.

'There she goes,' I would comment, trying to sound matter of fact.

'No. No. It was the door,' somebody else would say.

But that day she did not scream. She had obviously been turning over and over in her mind the Brigadier's threat. The following day, however, she went wild. She paced up and down in the portaal. And then the panic caught up with her. And she screamed and fell to the ground. Two people picked up her limp form and carried her to her bed. When she opened her eyes her pupils were large and black with panic. 'Oh God! Oh God! It's coming again.' She writhed with terror on her bed, trying to fight if off. But the panic rose and caught her in the throat and she screamed again. She got up and Flo took her and held her arm and they walked round and round the table in the portaal. Flo tried to talk to her. And the wildness in Di's eyes subsided for a few moments. But then it started again.

Some of us tried to go on washing at the basins, pretending there was nothing wrong. We made an effort to communicate to Di some sense of calm and control, that however awful this place was, we must simply go on. It was our duty as political people not to give in. 'The Brigadier is going to put me in a straitjacket,' she sobbed wildly.

'No, he won't. No, he won't put you in a straitjacket,' either Flo or Stephanie tried to calm her down. 'We will see to it that he doesn't. We won't let him.'

'But he will. I know he will. He said so,' Di sobbed.

'Listen, Di, they would never dare to put you in a straitjacket, never, not with the Harold Strachan case going on outside.' The panic went out of Di's eyes for a moment. But there was no controlling her that day. She started screaming again.

'We're going to have to do something about her,' somebody said. 'Matron Bester must come here and tell her that the Brigadier won't put her in a straitjacket.'

During this period, we had managed to get Matron Bester to enter our section at last, though it was only to be temporary. Matron Bester came that day and tried to convince Di that the Brigadier would not follow through on his threat to put her in a straitjacket. 'He won't,' she told her. 'I will see to it that he doesn't.'

Matron Bester was marvellous during this period. Her mad suspicion seemed to leave her for a bit. She felt she was needed. One or two of us were actually allowed to go through to the office to discuss Di with her. She told Flo that Di thought we were marvellous people, that it was extraordinary how we took the life there. And Flo said, 'Yes, yes, but it just makes her feel more guilty. Because she sees we are taking it. And she can't.'

So there was some communication with the Front over those couple of weeks. Once Di had gone, however, Matron Bester was worse than ever. She remained out of our section as far as possible. It seemed that the effort she had put into dealing with Di made her react even more strongly against us. We were to see this sort of pattern in Matron Bester in the future so that we began to calculate what her mood would be.

Matron Bester could not calm Di down. She went on screaming. One day I gave up my nonchalant attitude, my attempted matter of factness, and crossed the portaal to her cell to see what was going on. Di was sitting on her bed. Her long black hair was down, wild about her shoulders, and

A prisoner breaks down

her eyes like the eyes of a mad woman. God! She looks as if she is going to attack someone, I thought. And trying to control my fright and the pain of fear that crossed my chest, I walked back to the basin.

Matron Bester decided that she would have to give her a knockout dose. She gave her some strong-smelling liquid to drink. Di did not respond. Matron Bester waited a bit and gave her a second. This still did nothing. And so she gave her a third. She told us that when she gave one dose to one of the African prisoners, she was out within a few moments. After the third, Di slept. She woke up for the first time round about four or five in the afternoon, but, within a few minutes, went back to sleep again. The next day she did not seem much improved. She started pacing round and round once more with the strange look in her eyes that she had developed over the previous week. She said she had to see Matron Bester but was told that she was not on duty. That came as a shock to her.

Later she came running to the wardress.

'Matroon is in die tronk. Ek het haar behoer,' she said in her peculiar Afrikaans.

'Matron is busy, Schoon,' the wardress said nervously. She moved away from Di, looking into space, pretending she had forgotten her. But she was tensing for the scream. Di paced some more, and then she moved up to the wardress once again.

'Will you please tell Matron I must have some more of that medicine, some more of the medicine I had yesterday.'

'Matron is busy, Schoon,' the wardress said, looking nervously past Di, 'but I will tell her.'

Di was beginning to work herself up into a state. Four of us were at the basins, trying to keep our lives turning over much as usual. We talked quietly to each other. 'Something will have to be done about her. She's getting worse and worse. She'll have to see a psychiatrist.'

'Yes, I spoke to Matron about a psychiatrist but she said it is very difficult to get one here. A visiting government psychiatrist comes to this part of the world only once in six months. Di asked the Brigadier if she could see one and he responded that she did not need to see one at all, for he, the Brigadier, is the best psychiatrist she can have.'

'Yes, then he tells her if she carries on like this, he'll have her put in a straitjacket and locked up in a solitary cell. He really is a brute, so crude, and on top of it so pompous and self-satisfied.'

'I thought at first he wasn't so bad,' Ann commented, 'but now!'

We discussed whether Di was really ill or whether she was just acting. We decided that this sort of thing was usually a good mixture of both, difficult to say where one began and the other ended. And I said that I had definitely seen her trying to fight off the hysteria that suppertime when she had later stood up from the table and then, after accidentally breaking the pot into fragments on the floor, had screamed.

Ann and I decided that next time she screamed we were going to slap her. We felt that if we were tougher with her, she might pull herself together. So we went on quietly washing the smelly clothing, a smell we had more or less got used to as it was with us day and night. That musty, sweaty, damp canvas smell.

We knew the scream must come. Di knew Matron Bester was in the gaol and she would scream to attract her attention. Stephanie was talking to Di with her arms around her while Di lay on the bed. And she screamed. Ann and I ran from the basins, across the portaal and to the cell, and I slapped her across the cheek. Di caught hold of me and fought me like a little animal. Then she continued screaming, tossing around on her bed. Then she called out, 'Slap me. Slap me, please! It's coming again.'

And Ann slapped her across a cheek.

'Ah, thank you. Thank you,' Di gasped.

Matron Bester arrived on the scene. 'What's going on here?' she asked in the quiet manner she had adopted over the past week, that of a sensible person dealing with a crisis, so different from her usual hysterical shouting.

'I must have some more of that medicine, Matron,' Di insisted.

'No, I'm not giving you any more of that.'

'Oh, Matron, please knock me out. Please, Matron. I can't go on like this.'

'Come. Come with me,' Matron Bester said, and took her off to the Front. About 20 minutes later we heard a piercing scream. 'Well,' somebody said, 'even Matron Bester's influence on Di is beginning to pall.'

Matron Bester brought Di back to the section with a tennis racket and, without a word to us, took her through to our courtyard where Di hit a ball against the courtyard wall. Matron Bester was really making an effort but Di did not improve.

She still walked around with that wild look in her eyes. We decided among ourselves that one of us must assume the responsibility for Di and get her to talk about her problems. Our different approaches to her were just serving to confuse her further. Flo decided to assume the task and she took Di off alone and had long discussions with her. We also got permission from the Front for Di to move into the other big cell with Flo and Ann. So they took her over and the rest of us did not have much to do with her from then on, except at mealtimes.

The strain of having her with us did not end, however, and it must have been especially bad for Ann and Flo. We felt we had to carry her to the end of her sentence. We used to count the days and even to divide the days into fractions, right up to the day in December when she was due for release. If we hadn't been living under such terrible conditions, we would have found it easier to bear with her, but at a time when we had to preserve our own sanity, this was an extra burden. I must say my comrades stood up magnificently to the challenge.

At some stage while Di was with us the Commissioner of Prisons, General Steyn, came from Pretoria to see us. We stood on parade in the portaal, between the basins and the table, and put our complaints and requests to him. One of the main points we raised was the question of exercise. Speaking in Afrikaans, Stephanie asked him if it were not true that, according to the regulations, we were supposed to have an hour a day in the open air. His 'answer' was that South Africa was not England, that whereas in the latter country an hour might be required, this was not the case in South Africa.

We naturally asked him whether the hour was not specified in the *South African* prison regulations. He gave us the same answer, with a gentle smile on his face. We stressed that it would be a great help if we had a copy of the prison regulations, pointing out that we only had a few pages. He told us that that would be very difficult as the regulations dealt with prison officials as well as internal prison matters and, of course, we could not have those.

I explained that I was aware that there was some kind of brochure with the prison regulations stencilled, one specially prepared for prisoners, that it consisted of about 80 pages, and that we had been given only 15 or 20 pages. It was apparently specially produced for prisoners because on the front cover it was stated that it was the duty of every prisoner to make himself or herself acquainted with the contents to ensure the better running of the prison. The Commissioner looked slightly uncomfortable and, with once more the gentle smile, made some evasive reply.

Di asked him if she was going to get remission. He replied that no political prisoner was entitled to remission or parole and that she would, therefore, serve her full two months. We put various other requests to him which I do not now remember, but right through the time I was there we barraged the authorities with complaints, requests and demands. The Brigadier got a barrage once a week and every visitor to the gaol was similarly treated.

Once Flo took over, Di never again had a full-scale attack of hysteria. But she was certainly not well; she looked awful and never lost that strange look in her eyes. And she continued pacing our small area. During the day she walked up and down in the portaal and during exercise she walked very fast, with long strides, round and round our small courtyard.

At night she paced up and down in her cell between the three beds, from the window looking onto the courtyard up to the wall below the window which looked towards the wardresses' quarters. Up and down. Up and down. She often sang in a strange child-like way. Di's pacing in that small space in the cell must have been nerve-racking for Ann and Flo. She was given tranquillisers which helped to calm her. They managed to get her to the end of her sentence without a complete nervous collapse. But only just.

Behaviour of prison officials, including Matron Bester

WHEN ONE EVENING AT the end of November Stephanie was instructed to pack her things, and we realised that she was going to be moved, apparently in order to be released at last, I asked Taljaard whether she could arrange for me to have Kemp's jersey. She said she could not give it to me, that it had first to be taken to the front with all of Kemp's things, so that they could be entered into a book. She said this with the usual shrug, as if talking to a prisoner caused her to exert more energy than she had. 'Ek is besig, Neame. Jy moenie my kom pla nie.' I am busy. You mustn't come and bother me.

I spoke to Matron Bester about it, but she only got her swollen-lipped, pop-eyed look and shouted, 'Ja! Ja!' as though I were tormenting her. For the whole time I had been there in Barberton, Matron Bester had never once spoken to me. She had always only shouted and screamed. Every time I prepared to speak to her, my heart pounded and my body tensed, even when I was going to raise the simplest thing. The following day, after Stephanie had been taken away, I asked if I could now have her jersey. Taljaard told me that it had been entered in the book and sent away to the store. So that week I went to the Brigadier and told him what had happened. And he told Matron Bester that she was to give me a jersey.

Whenever I asked for things like disinfectant for our sanitary buckets or polish with which to polish the floors of our section, I got the same crazy response from Matron Bester. Sometimes I found the scream too much of a shock to my system, particularly early in the morning, and several times I collapsed into tears after Matron Bester had slammed the door in my face. Matron Bester's scream I actually found was a physical shock to my system, sparking off all sorts of feelings which otherwise would have been kept carefully under control. This woman had a power over our lives that was extremely unhealthy. If we had had other outlets, we would not have been so at her mercy.

Not only had she been given instructions to give us a bad time (this was confirmed later), but she was a sick woman, a neurotic, who found it almost impossible to control her moods. The result was that the instruction to give us a bad time enabled her to simply let go, without any idea that she should perhaps keep her moods under control.

That she was a sick woman was not only admitted later by several wardresses but by a senior officer within the Prisons Service. At the same time, it cannot be ignored that the service had found good use for her in relation to ourselves. What she was doing to us was certainly no secret. On the day of my arrival at the gaol she had started screaming at me in Aucamp's hearing; there was no question that that kind of behaviour was required of her. The admission by the senior officer was, almost certainly, an attempt to pass the buck at a time when the prisons were under pressure because of the exposures of prison conditions. A question, of course, was: had Aucamp and the Security Branch had a say in Major Bester's appointment? She would definitely have been vetted. At any rate, in relation to ourselves, it appeared that the Prisons Service, itself, was not making at least the chief decisions. Rather these were in the hands of Aucamp, together with the Security Branch. As to who, finally, had responsibility for our conditions, there appeared to be considerable uncertainty, but that there were tensions between the Prisons Service and the security establishment was certainly true.

Matron Bester was a single woman, about 35 or 36. She had been fifteen years in the Prisons Service. Here she had little need to control herself, for prisoners were not regarded as full human beings, to say the least. Although they were to be fed and kept alive, the attitude of those in the service was that even food and clothing were privileges.

The members of the Prisons Department had the word 'privilege' constantly on their lips, and it occurred frequently in the prison regulations themselves. The view was that prisoners did not have 'rights'. The fact that we identified ourselves with the aspirations of black people meant, so the view was, that we should be treated as blacks were treated. For white women to wash laundry was most unusual, to say the least, because it should be made quite clear that even in the prisons they were superior to Africans and other members of the black community. Black prisoners did the actual washing; white prisoners either supervised in the laundry, dealt with the books, or did sewing, often with machines. For white women to wash the clothes of Africans was an unheard of state of affairs in South Africa, and for them to wash the clothes of African prisoners, in particular, would have deeply shocked most whites in apartheid South Africa.

Some people, perhaps, can take this sort of attitude to fellow human beings with a laugh. But every day in South African gaols I found it a tremendous shock to my system. The initial shocks came at the Fort where I saw for the first time how prisoners were regarded by the authorities. I felt myself a part of this degradation. I remember I had the feeling continually that I was dirty.

While I was standing trial in Humansdorp I was taken from the court to a doctor's consulting rooms in order to obtain some pills, and when the doctor shook hands with me, my immediate (silent) response was, How can you shake hands with a dirty prisoner? You cannot know about me. But then he was told that I was standing trial in Humansdorp, and it did not seem to surprise him one bit. He was still charming and shook hands with me as I left. And he was an Afrikaner.

The whole attitude towards prisoners, the way the authorities spoke to us, the terrible clothes I wore in Port Elizabeth, the dreadful food, the cold, the dirt that there was so often, represented the environment that contributed to the feeling that I was 'just a dirty prisoner'. In Port Elizabeth I had no possibility to study, no good books to read that would help to maintain my normal, 'beyond prison walls' image of myself.

That fabricated trial in the Humansdorp court, those weeks of lies I had heard, added to the sense I had of a fundamental attack on my identity. One result was that I had longed to go into the witness box to give evidence in my defence and when I first entered the box, I found myself talking fast and excitedly and, I imagined, really convincingly. I could be myself at last, I could tell my own story. I did this quite spontaneously. I had made no preparations to go into the box. There was no need to do so.

The singing of freedom songs in as loud a voice as I could out of a window of my cell in Port Elizabeth across a courtyard – at least I think it was a courtyard for it was difficult to see exactly what was on the other side of my window – also helped me to establish my identity. And some political prisoners heard me and realised that I was 'one of them', as a note sent to me surreptitiously testified. It was from Zibia Mpendu, a nursing sister, who had likewise, I learned later, got caught up in the net of the eastern Cape trials.

Despite the massive working over that we got in those first months in Barberton, I was able to recover some sense of myself for here we were all politicals together. And when the authorities behaved in an uncivilised fashion, which was most of the time, somewhere hidden in each of us was a feeling that we despised them. True, there were all sorts of different and sometimes conflicting feelings within us, for most of us tried not to despise them. This was because we thought that that was a wrong attitude to adopt towards human beings, that we must understand why they were as they were, and try to change them. This was especially so with Afrikaners who, despite the criminal racist policies of the government, we were well aware had had a difficult history.

Matron Bester, many months later, when she was behaving like a reasonable human being for a few days – this was at a time when she realised that she was in for trouble – was to admit that even the Front could learn from important aspects of our behaviour. As it happened, an attitude which we maintained and actually developed towards the authorities was one of trying to encourage them to behave in a reasonable and, above all, civilised manner. Some of us, on occasion, would actually go to the Front to tell them how a responsible, humane person would behave in a particular situation and urge them to behave reasonably.

The authorities had a vague conception of what rehabilitation was, and it sometimes, especially later, enabled us to insert a wedge where there was formerly an insurmountable barrier. But this was only on occasion. For in the end their attitude was, We must be as tough as possible. These liberalistic, humane attitudes will only be our downfall.

This kind of attitude was typical of the Brigadier. He would never give an inch. One concession to humanity might send him over the precipice. He was a coward, no doubt correctly since he was also a fool, and one concession would precipitate him into a world of the unknown, which could be his doom. Flexibility would open up a world where he would have to exercise some intellectual capacity and this he did not have.

At any rate, the Brigadier was proud of his toughness, of his brutality. He seemed to find Flo attractive at one time or thought that she found him attractive (heaven forbid!) and so he adopted, especially for her, though it was an element in his relationship with all of us, a sadistic, sexy attitude. And he told Flo, with sadistic pride and a sexy look, that he was a tough man. He had a 'Bantu prisoner' in chains – his use of the term, Bantu, was clearly specially chosen since he considered that that could not be regarded as insulting to a black man, even though in chains.

He also informed Flo – and others on occasion – that no woman would ever get round him. A story he told several times was to the effect that one woman had been convinced she would get round him with tears. She had not succeeded. No woman would succeed. He seemed to long for one of us to weep in his presence so that he could show his strength. It was a sadistic longing. But I don't think he ever had the pleasure.

I move from a single to a communal cell

I MOVED INTO A COMMUNAL cell with Ann and Flo somewhere towards the middle of December when Di left. The cell was across the portaal, the one with a toilet and a tap (though no basin). It was the cell that had a window looking onto the courtyard and a window on the other side, overlooking the wardresses' quarters. Both windows were high up so that without standing on a chair we could not see out.

Esther was the first of us in the single cells to move into a communal cell. She managed to get on fairly well with the authorities, particularly Matron Bester, with whom she had a kind of joking relationship, little giggles and always smiling as though the very sight of Bester filled her with a certain amused pleasure.

Matron Bester had informed us earlier that it was on instructions from Pretoria that we three, Esther, Jean and myself, were to be kept in single cells and we were not allowed to move without the go-ahead from Pretoria. Jean was the second to move. And then I was allowed to after I had been in a single cell something like four and a half months.

Di had found her last few days in Barberton a torture. She told us, over and over again, that she didn't know how she was going to get through the last weekend. It was an agony for her. Her pacing got worse, if that were possible. 'I can't bear another day, another hour of this place,' she lamented.

She tormented herself with the idea that her mother might not be able to fetch her at nine in the morning. The Brigadier had told her that they would not be prepared to let her go, even though she was then due

I move from a single to a communal cell

for release, if her mother were not there to take her away. In this case she might have to wait until the evening, a whole eight hours longer in this hell. She even envisaged that, if her mother did not turn up, she would have to wait for a wardress to put her on the evening train. It did not seem to strike Di that other people there had years still to go. She seemed to take it for granted that we were capable of surviving.

Her mother did turn up in time, and we waved to Di surreptitiously from a window as she left. Her face in the car, driving away from the gaol, was full of smiles. She was going to have a holiday in the game reserve, not so far away. That was quite a thought for the rest of us to digest. A game reserve not so far away and one of us would be going there.

I found adjusting to a communal cell quite an effort. At first the idea of moving from a single cell made me feel distinctly uneasy. In fact, typical of our condition was that we tended to sink into a rut. We not only found it difficult but were also frightened to make a change in the particular routine we had each established for ourselves. It was one of the dangers of our situation.

In my single cell, after the grille and door locked behind me, I would rest for about five minutes and then I would walk about two paces to my chair, sit down and start reading history. I would work until about 7 o'clock, and then I would have a game of chess, using the soap chessmen and the paper board, either with myself or with Jean if the latter was possible, in other words if we thought we were safely out of hearing of the wardress on night duty. At 8 o'clock I would do some exercises, fitting myself into the very small space in my cell, until about 8.30. And then I would do some more history until about 9.30. I tried to study six or seven hours a day.

In the morning I would get up before the bell and work for half an hour to an hour. And I would do an hour at lunchtime lock-up. I would clean my teeth at a certain time, eat at a certain time a slice of bread, which we were now allowed to take into our cells at 'night' lock-up, walk the few paces that I could walk in my cell, ensuring that I did not knock myself on the bed. I had my sanitary bucket in a certain place. My eyes got used to having the walls of my cell at a certain distance from my face. I got used to hearing certain sounds from my cell, and no others. All the movements I carried out took on a regular pattern, in the framework of which I lived, as in a cocoon.

And then came the new framework of my life in that communal cell on the other side of the portaal. My space had changed. I felt I had to think first before I did anything. There was more space to move in and I had to walk around several extra pieces of furniture. Moreover, my senses were operating in a different environment. There was the sound of voices in the cell, the sound of people breathing, the movement of a chair in the same cell, the toilet flushing, the drops of water dripping from the tap into the bucket. And then there were the sounds from outside. Occasionally they came from the wardresses' quarters; sometimes I heard the distant sound of a radio or a gramophone.

I was amazed at the wider range and greater variety of sense-life the people in this cell had as compared to what I had had in a single cell a few yards across the portaal. And they had not even told me about it. But I supposed they had not realised how cut off the single cells were.

From the window on the side of the courtyard, I could see a little bit of dry, bare hill, with little strips of brown road running across it, just above and beyond our courtyard wall. And if I were careful, I could peep through the cage of the other window and have a look at the houses the wardresses lived in. Almost directly across from us were the bricks and mortar quarters of the black wardresses and above them, higher up on the rise, were the two cream-coloured plastered houses of the white wardresses and matrons.

Wonder of wonders, one could even see a wardress wandering around sometimes in mufti or a boyfriend visiting her. Or one could see them occasionally sitting at the back of a house listening to a gramophone. There was a life going on there that for four months I had known nothing about. Behind the wardresses' quarters were tall trees and behind them a piece of hill. To the front of us, a little to the right, was a huge mound of bare hill and rock. And coming over the hill the black wires for the transport of the cocopans. Sometimes in the early evening we could see little black objects moving up and down the wire, trays carrying asbestos. We found out that they were going backwards and forwards, to and fro from the Havelock mine which was just inside Swaziland. It was hard to imagine that these trays were going backwards and forwards, *in and out of South Africa.*

Despite the obvious positives in the change, I also found it somewhat disconcerting. Being pulled out of one's routine exposed one to the realities of one's incarceration just that little bit more. In my single cell the routine I had built up had served as a kind of protection from too much brooding. In the communal cell I also found that I became overstimulated. Apart from the new aspects in my physical environment, there was the conversation and comments after and between periods of study. More than anything else, I was faced with new personalities. I had not realised how much on the edge of things I had been in a single cell.

I found that I had not really got to know people as I could get to know them in a communal cell. I had seen various facets of my fellow prisoners at the table or while we were working at the basins but I had not gathered, in some cases, how deep these things went. This was especially relevant for Flo. I realised after I moved into the communal cell that her desire not to commit herself was a fundamental part of her personality. Ann I had not really got to know at all previously, and I saw and felt things in her that I did not fully understand.

No doubt, I had been on the margins not only because I had been in a single cell but because I was dazed when I arrived in Barberton, leaving aside the problem that at this time we were not allowed to talk to one another. Moreover, the very suffering I had gone through, and this went back to the time of Kathy's arrest at Rivonia and, indeed, before that, and the failure to discuss such things with comrades because, by and large, such experiences were regarded as a part of the struggle against apartheid or there were security reasons for not discussing some aspects, inevitably produced an emotional gap between me and other people.

A special problem for me was that before the Rivonia arrests I had been involved in the underground hide-out network, and, however marginal my involvement had been at that time, I could, of course, not discuss this with other people, even those who had been in my CP unit. Shortly before the Rivonia arrests there had been plans to increase my responsibilities in the underground network – this was to be in the sphere of courier duties – in the framework of which, it was envisaged, I would work together with Winnie Mandela and Adelaide Joseph.

This situation was to lead to several misunderstandings. I was, it turned out, regarded – by Jean in particular – as being unnecessarily secretive, for instance in regard to what I had been asked about in the course of interrogation. In my first detention under the 90-day law the chief question the Security Branch had been interested in was the hide-out in Mountain View and since the others knew nothing about my involvement there I could not speak about it. As for my second run under the 90-day law, I was not interrogated at all and Jean evidently found this difficult to believe.

Undoubtedly, all of us were suffering, to one degree or another, at the personal level. This is inevitable when people are wrenched out of their normal lives. There were several amongst us who had serious worries in the family sphere. At any rate, it would have appeared strange and egocentric to have started talking about one's own personal experiences, that is, apart from the 'security'/legal problems as far as I was concerned. It is always to be borne in mind that the apartheid state still existed and that for another nearly 30 years. Indeed, this is why there were matters I dared not even put down in my original manuscript.

At the same time, we failed to recognise, and this was characteristic of the political movement as a whole, that these silences could only do long-term psychological damage. Perhaps characteristic is that even I, myself, was not conscious of the bitterness that had built up in me in the context of what apartheid had done to my personal life, until later, in the framework of the poetry classes we were eventually to organise at Barberton, we discussed a love poem. I was surprised, in fact shocked, by my response.

With my move to the communal cell, I became more alive and I began to have a closer look at myself, at others, and at our surroundings. These adjustments were probably also encouraged by the fact that the year, 1965, was coming to an end. Although admittedly in a rather vague way, I felt that the new year would bring some changes. One thing that might have led me to feel this was that our conditions had been a little improved; another was that the authorities had made some reference to 'rehabilitation' which suggested that they had begun to come to the conclusion that they would have to do something about improving our conditions, if only marginally.

I expected, too, that sometime in the first months of 1966 my appeal to the Supreme Court would be handled. Soggot had told me that the appeal would come up about five months after sentencing. By the end of December five months would be up. I still did not know whether I would win it or lose it. Deep inside my gut, six years had sunk in and my appeal seemed to be some vague event which did not have all that much to do with me.

That summer I used to wake up at about 4.45 am as it was light then. Our cell got the morning sun because the window on the opposite wall from the courtyard faced east. This was the first time since I had been at Barberton that I began thinking about directions. Where was east? Where was west? But at this stage I did not think about it all that clearly for I was still cut off, to a large extent, from the life outside our windows. I had not really begun to relate myself to it, as I was later to do increasingly as my sentence started moving to an end. I was also to relate to the bird-life outside, other things too. But now I was vaguely conscious that, since our cell got the morning sun, that must be east somewhere out of that window, the window between the grille and our cell toilet.

I once watched a storm from this same window after lock-up in the evening and I was amazed and excited that I, in prison, could see the dark, ominous, purple-blue clouds in the sky above the trees, which were made bright green by that peculiar light that accompanies a coming storm. That was an extra experience, another one to add to my restricted range of impressions.

These little pictures penetrated very erratically into my mind. They were not clear or very conscious. Around those pictures there was still a lot of fluffy, disorganised material. I did not, as yet, define my lonely space, as I was to do later, into which I was to incorporate these pictures of the outside world. At this time it all flitted in an unorganised way across my mind. I was actually afraid of looking too closely at things outside the window. I would look with hooded eyes and not absorb the picture into the centre of my being. I did not want to experience my gaol situation too keenly. I did not want to feel that dreadful pain and desolation inside me, the pain of being inside, with no effective link to what was outside.

It was the ants that I found after I woke one morning in that communal cell on the surface of the water in my cup that were to become my first item of serious observation in the natural world. I had got up at 4.45 as the sun began its upward journey on the other side of our cage so that I could fit in a short period of study. But I found myself drawn to the cup of water to watch the ants. They formed bridges on the water. However, some were free-floating, that is, they did not belong to a line of ants but made up fluffy little heaps on the surface of the water. All the single ants on the water would sway their bodies so as to propel themselves across the water in order to join the heap of ants.

The heap consisted of several layers, one ant on top of another. Ants used each other, one climbing on top of another, so that they would not drown. There were special ants with strange crab-like heads. They seemed to have a special function to perform. They were always there right on top of the heap, and the others seemed to pay them special attention and help them if they were in trouble.

Little bridges would form from the edge of the cup towards the heap, with ant linked to ant. The ants closest to the surface of the water formed bridges onto which other ants climbed and the bridge moved towards the heap, the legs of the ants swaying and propelling them. Occasionally ants from the heap would move across a bridge and climb up the side of the cup.

I never worked out what they were trying to achieve on the surface of the water. I tried to find out where they came from and found that a line of ants led me to a point under my bed between the linoleum and the wall. It looked like they had a nest there, either low down in the wall or in the floor, or maybe they came from the courtyard, which was on the other side of the wall. (My bed was just under the window which looked onto the courtyard.) Before I emptied the cup of water, I carefully removed the heap of ants from the surface with a piece of paper and tried to remove all of them so none was lost. Sometimes I found that half an hour had gone by while I watched them. This, I felt, was wasting study time so I decided that I would watch them for about ten minutes every morning and would definitely cease when I heard the clock strike five.

While I was in this cell I read Karl Popper's *The Poverty of Historicism*, which was mainly an attack on Marxism and Fascism. I found it an unsatisfactory work because he tried to put together several approaches to life and history under his concept of historicism, and therefore I felt that he became inaccurate and his thinking woolly. I went on to read Theal's *Historical Sketches*, which was part of the reading for the South African history section of the UNISA History Honours course.

Aucamp had refused me permission to complete my Wits Honours course, even though I had pointed out that I would not have to use the Wits library facilities but would just write the examinations, and even though I had assured him that I would leave my small thesis on the Industrial and Commercial Workers' Union on which I had been working before my arrest – this was part of my Wits Honours course – until I got out of gaol.

I learned later that some other political prisoners in other gaols had been given permission to complete their Wits courses. The authorities seemed particularly to dislike my academic work. They had interfered with it for several years, even before I was arrested. They had removed my thesis material on three occasions, and I had spent two days on a felt mat on the concrete floor of a Bloemfontein police cell in the middle of an extremely cold winter after the Security Branch had arrested me while I was interviewing people for my thesis in a Bloemfontein township. A police officer from the local police station had actually taken me to the house of one of those I was interviewing.

I applied again to Colonel Aucamp in August or September 1965 to complete my Wits Honours course. Again my request was refused, without any reason being given. So I was forced to start another Honours course, this time with the University of South Africa, and by December 1965 I was already registered. Study was terribly important to me, to most of us. It kept me going from day to day.

Christmas 1965

CAROLINE HAD ARRANGED TO visit me sometime towards the end of December; she was to be at the Cullinans' farm from about the 10th. I looked forward to her visit. After our reclassification to 'C', which I think took place on 6 November, I had written to my brother Graham and he had not yet replied. We were told on about 22 December that all prisoners had been granted a special Christmas visit and, I think, a letter. I had organised this but no letter came, and no visitor. I started worrying. It was a feature of this time. We received so few visits and letters that we worried ourselves to distraction if they were delayed.

And Christmas was coming. We were allowed to buy small quantities of sweets, cheese and fruit and one or two other items. Early on Christmas morning we woke up to jubilant singing, with various other sounds such as drums. The black women were celebrating. It was strange, waking up to this noise in the usually silent gaol. It was summer and so there was sunlight outside. It must have been about 5 o'clock or just before. In winter at this time it would still have been dark, though the cell would have had patches of yellow artificial light here and there from the lights on the outside walls of the gaol.

That day, Christmas Day, there was warm sunlight and a blue sky. Sunlight was on the yellow-orange-brown brick of the courtyard walls, with patches of shadow under the gutter on the far wall and large patches of shadow on the wall to my right. To my left there was sunlight on the wall that divided us from the black women. We did not yet know what it looked like over that wall. We knew nothing about the other side of the gaol. From there were coming the singing voices.

I got up, put on my blue uniform and continued with my reading of Karl Popper. The only important aspect of my life at the time was study so what better to do on Christmas morning than study? This was a prison holiday, which meant that the first bell went at 6.30. There were not many prison holidays since the Department did not recognise all public holidays. I think there were about five: Dingaan's Day (16 December), Christmas Day, Boxing Day (26 December), New Year's Day, Good Friday, Easter, Republic Day (31 May) and Kruger Day (10 October). Prison holidays meant for us that we did no laundry and we were unlocked at 7 am and locked up by about 3.30 pm. That was all.

We imagined that Christmas would fit into this pattern. But the black women singing did make a difference. Unlocked at 7 am, we said 'Happy Christmas' to each other and did all the things we did on every other day – emptied our sanitary buckets, cleaned our teeth and then stood on parade, waiting for the porridge pot. Then breakfast, bread and butter and marmalade, enough for one and a half slices. Most of us had given up eating porridge. Next we washed the dishes in the laundry basin. Thereafter we rubbed up the floor, cleaned the lavatories, somebody got the fire going in the boiler room. And then we stood around since there was nothing else to do. The jubilant singing doubled in volume on the other side. The drumming sounded particularly good.

'Gosh, I wish we could join them,' somebody said.

The wardress on duty that day, Miss Wilkin, whom we sometimes called 'Pomposity', stood in the boiler room listening to the singing and watched us as we stood around with nothing to do. Suddenly something seemed to strike her. 'Dis onregverdig dat die nie-blankes kan sing en dans, and julle blankes kan niks doen nie,' she said. It is unfair that the non-whites can sing and dance, and you whites can do nothing. The fact that non-whites should have it better than whites, if only on Christmas Day, worried her pompous sense of justice! 'Ja, dis onregverdig, mense!' We listened to her, interested, and then wandered off and stood in the courtyard, listening to the singing and what sounded like happy shouting.

'Yes, yes,' we agreed.

'They allow them to let off steam once a year as a safety valve,' someone said.

We stood around silent, shifting, with the weight first on one foot and then the other, hands on hips or behind the back, leaning against the wall.

'Look,' somebody said, 'let's urge Wilkin to ask Matron Botha if we can go and watch them on the other side, as a special Christmas treat.' We had found out that Matron Bester was not on duty that day.

'They would never allow it,' I said. 'Not a chance ... But there is no harm in asking.'

And so one of us asked Wilkin who, surprisingly, said 'Ja. Ja', and then went off to ask Matron Botha.

A little later a grille was opened for us, not the grille at the entrance to our section but out in the courtyard, next to Matron Bester's office. Then followed the opening of a grey door and we were escorted into a passage to the left and finally into a room on the left of the passage. We found ourselves in what was called 'the hospital'. A wardress told us that we could go up to the large window on a side of the room. We did so. The pale green venetian blinds were down and the window was closed but we could see through into a large courtyard.

In the centre was a crowd of black women, some just sitting, some dancing. There were a few sitting with buckets between their legs drumming on the metal base. Some were blowing on combs covered with cellophane paper. Others were dressed up as men with black moustaches and little beards. Every now and again somebody from the watching crowd would come forward and do a vigorous dance which looked like a war dance. There were smiles on many faces. It was quite a scene, especially inside a gaol.

I had a look around the courtyard. On my left, it must have been just on the other side of our courtyard wall, was an area much like the centre of our courtyard with a small drain and tap in the middle. On three sides of their courtyard were rooms, most of which looked like cells, with grey concrete floors, and rolled-up mats piled up high on one side. A wardress told us that on the left was the laundry and ahead of us, just to the right, was the kitchen. She pointed out to us the woman who cooked our food. There she was standing in the courtyard with a very white apron and a red headscarf, a distant figure who was connected with the pots that came into our section every day.

Christmas 1965

One of us asked the wardress whether we couldn't put the blind up so we could see more clearly. Yes we could, she said, and she put it up. Now we just had the glass of the window between us and the courtyard filled with 230 prisoners, or so a wardress told us. The women out there now became aware that some people were watching them from the window. One of them glanced now and then in our direction. However, most of the women were too taken up with the dancing and singing to care about us. They probably assumed that we were all wardresses.

My heart was beating fast. This is marvellous, marvellous! Thank God Bester is not on duty. If she were told, there would be real trouble for these wardresses. We realised that we would get away with quite a lot if we kept up our image of white madams watching African tribal dancing. And so I tried to put that sort of white madam look on my face and say things like 'Aren't they marvellous?' We were desperate for contact with them, for them to see us and know who we were. But we had to hide this very carefully from the wardresses and appear totally taken up with the singing and dancing.

'Look, Miss ...' one of us asked a wardress, 'can't we open the window? We can't see clearly with the window closed.'

She hesitated for just a moment, and then said okay. So the window was opened. The women on the other side could see us clearly now. Some of them looked in our direction and smiled. We smiled back with fast-beating hearts. And then we saw one of the white wardresses in the courtyard hustling together about ten of those prisoners, classified under apartheid as 'coloured', and she shepherded them over to our window, where they lined up. And they sang us a few songs, songs that had been on the hit parade before my arrest.

Ann was next to me and I felt her discomfort. This was too white-madamish for her liking. She would have preferred no contact rather than contact at this level. After the coloured women had sung us two or three songs, in fact while they were singing their last song, Ann and I arranged to sing them two of our freedom songs. We decided on 'Shosholoza' for a start and so we sang, 'Shosholoza Mandela!' 'Shosholoza Sisulu!' 'Shosholoza Kathrada!' Some of the women made as if to join us but the others said, 'No. No. Don't. We want to hear the words.' Ann was shaking with excitement next to me.

As we sang, I noticed the wardress beginning to look panicky. Things were getting out of control. As we finished our second freedom song, the women standing on the other side of the window were whisked away. And all the prisoners, 230 of them, were lined up on the far side of the courtyard and made to sit down. Nobody was allowed to sing or talk.

There were some African wardresses in that courtyard, too. Barberton Prison was a training prison for African wardresses. When the wardresses felt they had things in the courtyard under control, we were told to line up and we were whisked away back to our section, with the door and grille onto our courtyard locked behind us. We tried not to look excited and pleased in front of our wardress, to look as though nothing had happened of any real importance to us. We were simply amused white madams who had just come back from a look at some local tribal dancing.

'At least they know who we are now, what we are in for.' It was crucial for our psychology to have managed to make some contact outside our little section. The white wardresses were not quite sure, I think, what had happened, and if they had grasped some of it, they chose, for their own peace of mind, at least for the moment, to pretend it hadn't happened. The African wardresses, of course, had got the message. That day and for days afterwards, as they went off duty and passed under the windows of our section, they sang 'Shosholoza' and laughed and giggled. And from then on when we saw a black prisoner, although this was very rare, we got the Congress thumbs-up sign.

We were locked up specially early that day so the wardresses could go off early to enjoy their Christmas celebrations. We must have been in our cells by 3 or 3.30. We had the long gaol Christmas lock-up ahead of us. We arranged that we would study until about 6.30 or 7 and then we would have our drink. This was to be a mouthful of tonic, a red liquid prescribed by the doctor for one of us, a liquid which went down our throats warm and tasting of alcohol. We had given a portion to each cell.

At this time the doors of our cells were left open at night, with just the grilles locked. This made a great difference to our lives. Not only because it enabled us to have contact with each other, which was important particularly for those in single cells, but also, and this was to prove more

Christmas 1965

important, because of the appalling heat that summer. All summers in Barberton are hot. But this was a particularly excruciating one for us.

It was the middle of the drought. During the day when we were out of our cells, it was bad enough. Standing at the laundry basins, we were soaked in sweat. We found that our perspiring legs stuck to our chairs when we sat at the table eating our food. It was unbearable to walk in the courtyard with the sun beating down onto the white concrete, blinding us and with the sweat running down our bodies, under our uniforms.

One of the worst occupations during this summer was making the fire. We came from the boiler room red-faced with sweat pouring off us. Barberton is in the subtropics and so it is a very humid heat, rather like Durban or Lourenço Marques. Usually in the subtropics there is rain but there was no rain here during that summer. And so, instead of the lush vegetation of the subtropics, that we have, for instance, in Durban or rather just outside Kloof – I had lived in Kloof on the way to Pietermatitzburg for a year while I taught in a school in the city – everything was dry. The hills above us were brown, bare, ominous.

It was unbelievable in the cells at night. With the doors closed, we felt we could hardly breathe. It was bad enough when they were open. As I sat in my chair studying at my table, I felt the sweat running down the side of my face, down my tummy, down my legs. There was not one single part of my body that was not wet. I actually saw the sweat making marks on the linoleum, as it dropped off me. And my feet left wet patches on the floor as I walked.

We, in the communal cell with the tap, were luckier than the others at this time for we could get up from our chairs every now and again, take off our uniforms and splash ourselves with water, and put our feet in cold water in the bucket. I used to go and lie on my bed without drying the water off so that I could feel a little cooler as it evaporated. I would then go back to my studies, and half an hour later go through the same process.

I tried taking off my uniform while I worked but then I faced another problem. That was the insects and, above all, the mosquitoes. We counted sometimes 60 at a time, like small black flies on the ceiling of our cell. Even with our uniforms on, the insects tortured us. They attacked our legs and feet, especially in the darkness under our tables. But they were so greedy that they didn't even really mind the light and used to buzz round our ears in the most maddening fashion, and nip at our faces. They would even fly under our uniforms and nip our thighs. Our whole bodies felt raw and itchy and burned.

In my bed at night, even to have one sheet over me was unbearable. It burned against my body as though it were on fire or, at least, specially heated. I slept without my nightdress, but the sheet had to be there to protect me from the mosquitoes. I turned my pillow every few minutes to try and find some coolness. Sometimes I found I could not sleep for hours. Or I woke up in the middle of the night with a mosquito shrieking in my ear. And they always found their way under the sheet and attacked my body.

About 5.30–6 in the evening we used to hear them coming. At this time it was still fairly light in our cells, especially the cells that faced north and got the light from the sun as it moved down towards the mountains in the West. I would hear a high distant whine that went on for about an hour before the first mosquito actually appeared. Evidently they were getting going in the dark places in the cells and in the portaal.

One of their favourite hide-outs during the day was in our lockers. When we opened the lockers sometimes in the morning a great cloud of mosquitoes would emerge. Another favourite place for them was in the darkness under our beds. And sometimes under our tables. About 7 o'clock, when the light had gone out of the sky, they started coming out of their dark places.

Barberton is just on the edge of the malaria belt, and I think was actually in it at one time. During this summer at Barberton we were told that one of the warders at the men's gaol was down with malaria but it was unusual in these parts at this time.

Sometimes we used to go on mosquito hunts at night. When we could bear them no longer, we used to get up and try and kill them as they settled on the walls and ceiling of the cell. We might manage to kill 20 or 30 but we knew it really did no good since there were thousands of them. At the same time, it was a way of working off aggression because they would infuriate one. I never realised before that I could so enjoy a hunt. I was literally bloodthirsty! In my experience at least there is

Christmas 1965

nothing that can be as infuriating as a mosquito, particularly when it is screaming in one's ear.

It wasn't only mosquitoes that plagued our nights in the cells. There were scores of different types of insect. Together they made up thousands. During this time of severe heat it was particularly bad. There were tiny green insects with little pointed bodies which stung us and emitted a strong unpleasant smell when disturbed. There were also brown-grey ones which looked rather similar, and little black beetles we called castor oil because when we tramped on them they let off a strong castor oil smell. These used to fly together in droves. They would arrive at about eight o'clock in the evening, and cover the floor and click against the light shades.

There were large black beetles, their bodies about four inches long, with long black antennae which they moved around ominously at the end of strangely moving heads. These very rarely actually came into our cells but they moved around on our cages, making horrible click-clack noises with their legs, and they would suddenly fly a little distance from the cage and then fly back, crashing into the cage with their bodies, which made a hard metallic sound, and whirring their wings with a terrifying noise. There were 'mis' beetles (manure beetles), fairly large but not as big as the others, with a strange shield-shaped head with a horn-like appendage in the centre and black shiny plastic-looking legs with smooth plastic-looking joints.

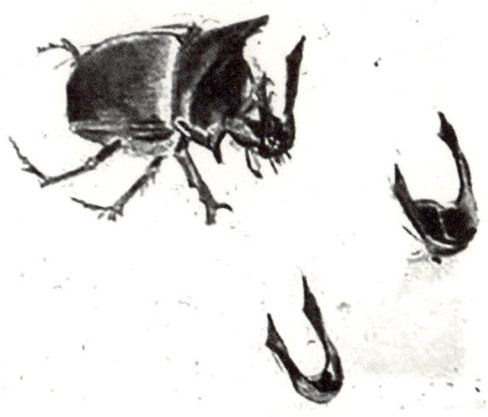

Imprisoned

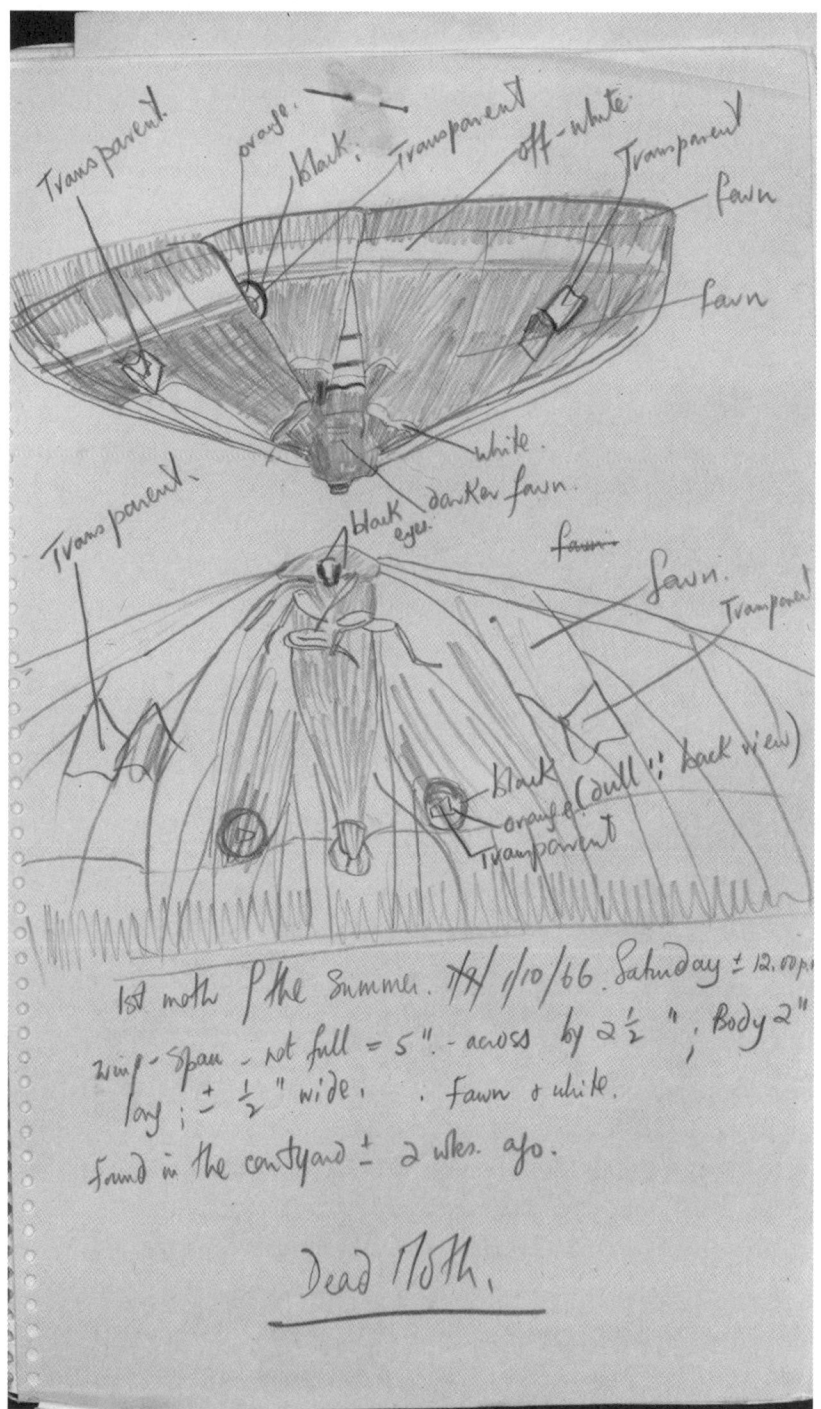

Christmas 1965

There were all kinds of praying mantises, large and small, some bright green ones, others pale green and yet others brown or grey, praying mantises with all sorts of fancy appendages, fancy wings, fancy legs so that one really had to give them a good look to identify them. Praying mantises, at the best of times, were for me rather frightening creatures, sitting on the wall, front legs up praying, and moving their small triangular-shaped heads from side to side, watching, watching with their large protuberant eyes, swaying their bodies in a peculiar uncertain rhythmic movement as though swaying on a tightrope as their legs tried to find a grip on our cages.

There were scores of varieties of minute insects and scores of varieties of moths, probably well over a hundred. There were huge moths, bigger than butterflies and as colourful. I had been terrified of moths before I came to gaol but there I had to get used to them – almost. In the past what used particularly to terrify me was not the whirring wings or the fat bodies but the thought of the grey powder on their bodies and wings. Those that confronted me in Barberton Prison also reminded me of bats. Sometimes when I saw them out of the corner of my eye, flying into the cell, I thought they were bats, and I would feel my heart contract with fear. There were frogs, too, which hopped into our cells at night, tiny sweet things, and larger ones, with salmon-brick-orange backs and pale concrete-grey legs and undersides.

Lying on my bed this first Christmas evening in Barberton, trying to get cool with the water drying on my body, I watched the scores of insects milling about on my tummy and getting stuck in the drops of water that had not evaporated. Insects on my legs, on my feet, on my face. Occasionally, I rubbed them off irritably but it was a waste of time.

In spite of suffocating heat in our cell, we closed the windows as it got dark and we put the lights on. We had decided that heat was less disturbing to our studies than the insects, though, of course, there were still the mosquitoes under our tables, nipping our legs as we studied. I put on my uniform with my body still slightly wet. The water made dark-blue patches on my uniform. We called over across the portaal to the other communal cell where the rest of us were together, as a special Christmas treat, a very crowded one.

'Come on. Time for our Christmas toast.' We each had a little in a teaspoon from our bottle of tonic. And then a second round.

'Mmmm ... lovely! Cheers, everyone! May we not have many more Christmases in gaol.'

'Freedom before the menopause!'

'To the men on Robben Island. To the men at Pretoria. To the women in Kroonstad and Port Elizabeth.'

'To all political prisoners. To all freedom fighters.'

Ann produced a Christmas card which we decided to send over to the other cell. She had drawn in pencil a Mother and Child, with the child, who had a rather dirty face, making the ANC thumbs-up sign. She wrote inside, in part imitation of a Christmas card she had received from somebody unknown in Ireland who had sent it as part of a solidarity action in the international arena, something to the effect: 'This is a drawing which these brave freedom fighters, Ann, Sylvia and Flo, drew on the wall of their cell, just before they were taken into their small courtyard and shot in December, 1988. They died bravely.' We were beginning to regard our situation with some humour by then, albeit a rather sick humour, and such attitudes were to grow in the following months.

Though we had come to laugh at ourselves and our situation, it is not to be denied that death had become very much a part of the lives of those fighting against apartheid. Death or permanent incarceration. In the first six months or so at Barberton, until probably well into 1966, several of us felt that we might never be released from gaol. The fact that the authorities had tried to get me, all in all, eleven years, made me feel this particularly strongly but the others felt it too. The hatred the Security Branch had shown us during our 90-day interrogations when they did not seem to care whether we lived or died, and during our nine-month trial in Johannesburg, and the hatred shown to us by the prison authorities at Barberton, particularly in our first months there, made us feel they might never let us go. The hatred enveloped us like an evil vapour.

Moreover, we felt that things might boil up in the country overnight, that a civil war might erupt, and we knew that in such circumstances they would never let us go. And they might even shoot us. During both my 90-day detention periods there was a real war atmosphere in South

Christmas 1965

Africa. This was the time when there were mass arrests right through the country. The 90-day law had been introduced early in 1963. Thereafter had followed the Rivonia raid on 11 July.

I was arrested for my first 90 days just before the Rivonia trial started. The Rivonia trialists faced the death sentence and I believed they would get it unless there was worldwide protest. During my first 90 days – I had been arrested on 17 October – I heard that one of my activist friends in Cape Town, Looksmart Ngudle, had in all probability been tortured to death, as it happened, in the same gaol that I was being held.

About three weeks after the Rivonia trial ended in June 1964 there were mass arrests throughout the country. It was at this time that I was again arrested under the 90-day law, together this time with several of my friends and comrades. During our detention the Park Station bomb had exploded in Johannesburg, placed by the member of the Liberal Party and of the Armed Resistance Movement, John Harris, and leading to the death of one person and the injuring of others. People in detention were met by a burst of hatred and fear from their captors. During 1964 and 1965 several sabotage trials took place all over the country and the Communist Party trial in Johannesburg.

While I was an awaiting-trial prisoner at the Fort, I heard that Babla Saloojee, who had been a friend, had died after throwing himself or being thrown from a window in the Security Branch headquarters in Johannesburg. We had heard about the torture that was being used, not simply in isolated instances, but clearly as a deliberate programme. During 1963 before my detention I had actually taken Laloo Chiba to see Helen Suzman so that he could describe to her the electric torture he had been subjected to during his detention. It was becoming widely known, even amongst liberals, that torture was the order of the day.

Electrodes were put on the head, fingers, genitals and feet of some 90-day detainees and electric currents passed through their bodies. Detainees had had plastic bags drawn over their heads and been hung upside down. Some had been hung out of windows by their ankles, from windows several floors up in buildings, and threatened that, if they did not talk, they would be dropped hundreds of feet to their deaths below. Some were brutally beaten and kicked in the genitals. Others were made to stand hours and hours, even days on end, without sleep, as had happened with some of my co-accused in the CP trial.

All the time there was the hatred and threats of brutal interrogators. John Harris, charged and convicted for the Park Station bomb, was executed just before we were sentenced. Some of us had known him though not well. All these things were not just happening to people whom we read about in newspapers. At any rate, we knew that we were involved in a struggle in which we had to accept the possibility of death. It was a feeling that sank deep, that became part of our attitude to life. The possibility of death was there all the time.

When I was in gaol in Port Elizabeth and in the court at Humansdorp this feeling, for me, was reinforced. The powerful and increasingly corrupt state machine could not only get you sentenced to a prison sentence for something you had not done, it could have you executed on a trumped-up charge.

In my Johannesburg trial Gerard Ludi, informer and state witness, had tried to suggest that I had had something to do with the murder of Justice Kuper, who had been killed by a bullet which had come whizzing through a window of his Johannesburg home. I hardly have the psychology of a terrorist, as the term is used by Marxists, in the sense of one who uses individual terror. An integral part of my political outlook was a respect for the individual, for individual human rights. I am too much of an individualist myself not to give the same right to others.

Then there was the practical side of the matter: I did not know how to use a gun. Eventually, and it took several years – was this deliberate? – the person who had shot Judge Kuper was arrested and sentenced. Kuper had in the past sentenced him on a criminal charge and the murder was evidently an act of revenge. In order to justify its brutal suppression of any political opposition, the state attempted to build up a picture of a liberation movement which was geared to violence and murder.

Death was something I thought about a great deal in prison. Part of my concern had to do with the situation whereby it increasingly appeared that the fight against apartheid was turning into a life-and-death struggle. But it also had a great deal to do with my feeling that our experience in Barberton was a living death. For me in prison, isolation and death became closely identified.

In the mind of the dying what must come especially to the fore, unless one firmly believes in an afterlife, is that death means the blotting out of consciousness, of all the senses, of any relationship with other human beings. I often wondered if the look I saw in the eyes of my comrades as I came through the grille into the section the day I arrived at Barberton was not similar for they were suffering an imposed social death, closely connected with intense sensory and emotional deprivation. I read a strange book some time in the first half of 1966 by an ex-prisoner, Starr Daily, and he noted how prisoners dreaded the idea of dying in prison. That would really be death in isolation, a kind of dual death, one death superimposed on another.

True, the idea of dying in the struggle against apartheid was something different. It could be seen as a part of a common and historical struggle against an evil system, and, thereby, was a highly social act. This was, I suppose, why the image of being shot against a wall in our courtyard did not raise that typical endless, prison feeling, that sense that the life that lay ahead was eternally meaningless.

I am not quite clear now as to why the inclination to laugh at ourselves began to emerge at this time. There had been a tendency while we were awaiting trial at the Fort, if not to laugh directly about ourselves, at least to make endless jokes about the left movement, usually in regard to some of its older leaders, the 'old guard', as we came to regard them. We tended to conceive of at least some of them as having a rather rigid outlook and, above all, as being somewhat arrogant. We were part of the 'Sharpeville generation' of young white activists who were inclined to stress the leading role of the African people and the importance of (progressive) African nationalism rather than focusing on the 'class struggle'. A reflection of our attitude towards our own political role is that, while awaiting trial in Johannesburg, we spent some months knitting baby clothes in solidarity with African mothers outside. We were never told, as far as I know, what happened to the articles we sent out.

Now at this Christmas-time in Barberton Prison we laughed at ourselves, and this was increasingly to encompass our predicament, including our conditions in the prison. No doubt our renewed capacity to laugh had something to do with the certain easing of the dreadful pressure that had been on all of us, emanating from the gaol authorities, in the previous long months.

We rolled up Ann's Christmas card and tied it up with brown knitting wool which at one stage we had been given so that we could darn the male prisoners' jerseys. We unravelled a long piece, several feet of it, attached to the card and Ann climbed up onto the lower rung of our grille and flung the ball at the end of the unravelled section across the portaal towards the other big cell. After several tries it landed within reach of someone in the other cell. We waited eagerly for their response. There was a short silence. They must have been untying the card. And then there was a roar of laugher. This must have been at the picture of the grubby-faced baby making the thumbs-up sign. They laughed and laughed. Their response was beyond our expectations.

Then there was a short silence while they opened up the card to read what we had written inside. And then they laughed again, hilariously. Again, beyond our expectations. That made us very pleased. And proud. It was so nice, too, to hear laughter amongst us on Christmas Day.

New Year

AFTER CHRISTMAS CAME Boxing Day on 26 December, a public holiday, also a prison holiday, so we had another early lock-up. There were lots of early lock-ups over this period because, of course, it was the festive season, by and large not for us but for the wardresses who went off early while we were locked up in our cells, sometimes 20 hours a day.

New Year's Eve came. As on Christmas night, we sweated in our cells. As on Christmas night, we studied at our tables and, as evening came upon us, tried to fight off the mosquitoes and other insects. We arranged to stay up until midnight so we could see the New Year in, a new year of imprisonment, it is true, but at least 1965 was behind us and, before that, the second half of 1964, with 90-day detention and awaiting trial. We had been in gaol one and a half years and that meant one and a half years less to serve. I still had more than five years.

From my cell I looked through the grille into the unlit portaal with the shiny concrete floor. The huge lights outside to the front of the prison floodlit the area so the floor was not completely dark. Our eating table in the middle of the concrete was also shiny in the strange light. The doors of the three single cells were closed because nobody was in them that night. Other than we three in the communal cell next to the courtyard, the rest were in the big cell in the front next to the locked entrance grille.

On this New Year's Eve, 1965, time was passing and not passing. In a way it stood still. No beginning and no end. I was ticking over from day to day. I had no real thought about the five years ahead of me.

Mollie – she was in the other big cell next to the entrance grille – sent each of us our 'stars', as part of our ritual of marking the coming of a new year. She told us that, if we wanted further information from 'Madame P', we could send a confidential note to her. I wrote one, asking if she could let me know something about what the stars foretold for people born under Leo – this was Kathy's star for he was born on 21 August – and to tell me what was likely to happen to people on Robben Island in 1988 as she had made special reference to 1988 in my 'stars'. I wrapped my note round a rubber, used in my study work, and flung it towards the other cell. Unfortunately, it landed between the entrance grille and their open cell door. They tried to get hold of it but couldn't.

Wardress Taljaard the next morning, opening the central grille, saw it lying there. She picked it up with a triumphant look on her face. 'Wat is dit?'

Mollie said it was hers and asked for it but Taljaard, with the smug look, unwrapped the note and took a quick look at it. 'Wie het hierdie geskryf?' Who wrote this?

'That is mine, Miss Taljaard,' Mollie said. Taljaard swung round on her heel and proceeded to walk out of our section, locking the grille behind her. 'That is mine.' Mollie was again ignored. The key turned in the grille with military precision. Nobody could turn the key in the grille quite as Taljaard did. The door slammed. We never received that note back. No doubt, it went onto my file at the Grays (Special Branch headquarters, Joburg).

New Year's Day came. We were already locked up in our cells for lunchtime lock-up when the door leading into our section was opened and we heard the Brigadier's voice. A genial, festive season, hypocritical voice, the we-are-rehabilitating-you voice. The entrance grille was unlocked. And then the same coloured prisoners who had sung to us that exciting day as we stood looking through a window into the other courtyard walked in. A wardress hustled them into a line on the other side of the grille of the communal cell next to the entrance to our portaal. We had asked to be locked up together there as it was New Year's Day. We tried to give each other knowing winks out of sight of the Brigadier and the wardress.

The Brigadier pointed out to us the woman who had led the singing in the courtyard. We learned later that she was called Spokie. She had a very powerful voice and a defiant look in her eyes. He told us that she had a stomach ulcer and had had an operation while in gaol and now she was better. He obviously prided himself on the success of this operation and that his gaol should worry about a prisoner to that extent. He asked her in his patronising, genial, boss manner whether she liked prison. And she, putting on a child-like, innocent, winning manner said, 'Ja, meneer. Ja, meneer.' And then turning towards us and out of sight of the Brigadier, she pulled a face. We smiled back at her.

They sang to us. We all felt rather uncomfortable because there was little we could do about the white madam situation we were being pushed into. But I felt it was really all right, as they, especially Spokie, apparently grasped the situation. The prisoners were reacting to us at two levels. One, which was meant for the Brigadier, envisaged coloured prisoners performing in front of white prisoners-cum-madams. At another level, they indicated that they had friendly feelings towards us and were, together with us, contemptuous of the stupidity of the Brigadier. As they marched out, they gave us friendly smiles but not for the Brigadier and wardress to see.

Captain Broodryk turns up

BY THE END OF THE FIRST week of January, I still had received no reply to the letter I had written to my brother Graham; nor had I heard anything from Caroline who was supposed to have visited me a few days before Christmas. And then Broodryk turned up. He had been the investigating officer in our trial in Johannesburg and had interrogated some of us during 90-day detention. I had had very little contact with him in the past, except to see him, day by day, sitting at the prosecution table down below the dock, into which eleven of us had been squeezed. The only two accused outside the dock were Bram Fischer and Hymie Barsel, both of whom had been granted bail. Captain Broodryk had reddish hair and moustache, brown eyes, nervously fluttering upper eyelids, and an expression of smug hatred whenever he looked in our direction. He was recognised by us as one of the cleverest interrogators and one of the most brutal. His whole being seemed to be consumed with hatred for 'die Joods en die Kommuniste'. He was a very frightening person.

Through the cage of the front communal cell, one or two of us saw a large car draw up in front of the gaol and Broodryk and a woman stepped out. Good God! Our hearts almost stopped beating. We rushed off and told the others. A look of panic and sickness came over Jean's face for he had threatened her with some very unpleasant charges while she was at the Fort, before she was removed to Barberton.

I found myself just cutting off. While tensing my body against any blows, I refused to think about Broodryk's presence there. I had six years anyway, and Aucamp had told me that the authorities were satisfied with my sentence and would not try to get a longer one. This he said after I had stressed to him that the Humansdorp trial had been a frame-up. I am not sure what his intention was. At the time I thought he was probably saying to me, Look, Sylvia, be satisfied with your sentence, even if you have got four years for something you didn't do. If you try any of your tricks we can get more for you. So you be careful.

As my appeal had not come up yet, I felt I did not have much to worry about. I did not think Broodryk would have any further charges for me at this stage. He asked to see three of us, Ann, myself and Jean.

I went through to the Front with few strong feelings that I can remember, except that I was pleased for a break in our usual routine, and particularly to see somebody from the 'outside world', however horrifying a person he was. I walked into the visitors' room. Broodryk was sitting at a table in white shirt and shorts. I sat down on a chair on the opposite side of the table. He looked up and gave me a chilling stare, filled with his own particular brand of hatred. Aucamp had a similar look of hatred but his eyes were an icy blue.

I looked at Broodryk. 'Well, Sylvia,' he said. The Branch had this habit of calling us by our first names. They took up a very possessive attitude towards us. We were *theirs*. Our whole lives, political and personal, were theirs. Their attitude was that they knew everything about us and had a right to know everything. It was a peculiar mixture of cold hatred, brutality and familiarity. 'Well, Sylvia,' he said. 'Do you know Caroline de Crespigny?'

'Yes,' I said nonchalantly, for I had nothing to fear since Caroline and I had never really been politically linked. 'We shared a flat in Cape Town for a short time.'

Broodryk looked somewhat disconcerted. I had got a name in Security Branch circles for never answering questions, even the most simple. My line during my detention had always been, 'I have nothing to say.' He asked me to make a statement to him about a news-sheet called *Focus*. He told me that Sholto Cross had made a statement. He asked whether I knew Sholto. I did not answer. He then asked me if I knew Alan Brookes. Also Fred Carneson. I did not answer.

Broodryk moved some papers lying in front of him, obviously deliberately exposing the top of one of the foolscap sheets. And I saw 'STATEMENT BY CAROLINE DE CRESPIGNY'. Oh, I thought, so she is in 180 days (90-day detention had been increased to 180 days). I looked back at Broodryk. 'Look, Sylvia,' he said, 'tell me what you know about *Focus*. We will not call you to give evidence. Nobody need know about it. We just want to know about *Focus*. It is not an illegal news-sheet.'

'Yes, you probably want to charge a banned person,' I said as he exposed Fred Carneson's name on the sheet, headed 'STATEMENT BY CAROLINE DE CRESPIGNY'. 'Look,' I said, 'you ask me to co-operate with you and to trust you but you people are absolutely corrupt. You get me on a frame-up and then you ask me to co-operate with you. You have got me four years for something I did not do.' Ever since my sentencing I tried to make my point about the case being a frame-up as many times as I could and to whomever it might be.

'That was not my case,' Broodryk said.

I countered: 'You are a member of the Security Branch and you know that I am innocent. It is your duty to do something about it. That case was lies and nonsense from beginning to end.' I emphasised, 'Absolute nonsense.'

Broodryk looked embarrassed. 'That was not my case,' he repeated. He also looked a little pleased because I had referred to the case of another Branch man as nonsense. The word indicated that Du Preez had not been very clever. In fact, it probably meant that he had been rather stupid. That made Captain Broodryk feel good for he would never have been stupid. There was a very competitive spirit within the Security Branch. They were an ambitious lot of people, determined to get places.

While I was in the eastern Cape for my fabricated trial Du Preez had spoken deprecatingly to me about the informer, Ludi, the young man who had given evidence in our trial, having been a member of our Communist Party branch that used to meet in Hillbrow. Ludi had claimed in court that he was actually a member of the Security Branch and newspapers had jubilantly referred to him as '007'. Du Preez had commented to me: 'But you know that Ludi was not a member of the Security Branch at all.' 'Yes,' I had responded, 'we suspected that.' As it happened, we had guessed he'd been caught for 'immorality' in connection with a relationship with a coloured girl and that the police had blackmailed him to become a spy.

'Ludi wasn't really anything,' Du Preez continued, with undisguised envy on his face. 'He was not like us. We do the hard day to day work. And people like Ludi get the credit.'

Ann Nicholson told us that during her interrogation a Johannesburg Security Branch man, Nic van Rensburg, also obviously jealous of the publicity Ludi had been given, noted that, 'He is certainly no 007.' Van Rensburg was one of the more sophisticated brutes in the Branch. He had a cultivated voice and movements, almost elegant. He undoubtedly projected a certain 007 image. Ann said she had found this especially frightening. He said to her once during an interrogation, she told us, that if she did not talk, he would knock her teeth into the back of her throat. And he said this with a quiet, sadistic sophistication. He appeared to be a Security Branch showpiece. Other Branch members used to tell people in interrogations that Nic had studied overseas. This, evidently, was meant to make interrogation victims feel he was the sort of person to open up to.

Van Rensburg was supposed to be my chief interrogator during my second 90-day detention. He had been in charge of the raid at 6.30 am on the house in Orange Grove which I had shared with other people in the left for over a year, different people at different times. He used to come and see me in Fordsburg police station once a week. However, he told me soon after I got to Fordsburg after the two weeks in Pretoria Central that they were not going to interrogate me since they knew I would not talk. And, in fact, I was not interrogated, though the other women who were to be charged with me were.

They were questioned for nine, ten, eleven, twelve hours, as, indeed, was Caroline de Crespigny later on. Nor did I undergo the kind of interrogation which the men in our trial endured. Some of them were interrogated for 40 hours or more while they stood on their feet. Ann had stood for eight hours. This may have been done by a frustrated interrogator against orders or it might simply have been an experiment that could be extended to other white women in future.

Having decided that there was no chance at all that I would talk, certainly not without the special techniques, they decided not to waste time. They were, in any case, very busy with the sabotage organisation, ARM, which they had uncovered. I suspect, too, that they did not want

Imprisoned

Used by SA security police in connection with their removal of my gaolen material from the house in

G.P.-S.1071307—1960-61—300,000. S.   **S.A.P. 3.**

Ondersoeker *Orange Grove,*
Investigator   **Datum vingerafdrukke geneem**
                                       Date fingerprints taken

Johannesburg, 1963   **Datum versend**
                                     Date despatched

                                     Hofsaakregisterno.
                                     Court/case Register No.

SAAKDOSSIER.—CASE DOCKET.

Stasie   **R.O.M. No.**   **R.A.A. No.**
Station   **R.C.I. No.**   **R.C.A. No.**

1. KLAER (volle naam)
    COMPLAINANT (full name)

    Adres
    Address

    Ras
    Race

2. BESKULDIGDE(S) (volle naam)
    ACCUSED (full name)

    Ras   Geslag   Ouderdom   Beroep
    Race   Sex   Age   Occupation

    (a) Persoonlik   (b) Werkkring
        Personal   Industry or profession

    Geboorteplek   Nasionaliteit   Huwelikstaat
    Birth place   Nationality   Conjugal condition

    Onderwyspeil   Godsdiens   Persoons-no.
    Education status   Religion   Identity No.

    Adres
    Adress

                 (Vervolg op folioblad binnekant indien nodig.)
                 (Continue on foolscap inside if necessary.)

3. MISDRYF(WE):—
    OFFENCE(S):—

    (a) Aard en beskrywing
        Nature and description

    (b) Aard van eiendom
        Nature of property

    (c) Waarde betrokke: R   Teruggevind: R
        Value involved   Recovered

    (d) Metode en/of instrument gebruik
        Method and/or instrument used

                 (Vervolg op folioblad binnekant indien nodig.)
                 (Continue on foolscap inside if necessary.)

4. HOF(HOWE) WAAR VERHOOR EN DATUM(S):—
    TRIAL COURT(S) AND DATE(S):—

5. UITSLAG EN DATUM VAN VERHOOR:—
    RESULT OF TRIAL AND DATE:—

                                                                       Aanklaer/Prosecutor.

6. BESKIKKING OOR DOSSIER:—
    DISPOSAL OF DOCKET:—

to use such methods on me because I had an uncle, JR (Bunny) Neame, who was a leading South African journalist. He had served, amongst other things, as assistant editor and political correspondent of the *Rand Daily Mail* under Laurence Gandar and had visited me in the course of my first 90-day detention.

During my first detention my two interrogators were Swanepoel and Van Zyl who did a great deal of questioning of people expected to be able to give information relevant to the Rivonia arrests. Captain Swanepoel was my chief interrogator. He was involved with electric torture carried out on black detainees, including Looksmart, and was one of those who had interrogated Babla Saloojee who, in September 1964, fell from a window in the Grays and died on the way to hospital.

It was hot in the visiting room of Barberton Female Prison. I took a quick look towards the windows, just to see what the world looked like out there. I could see trees and blue sky, softened by heat haze. It was pleasant to see things from a slightly different angle from my usual view. I turned towards Broodryk who was saying, 'If you don't make a statement about *Focus*, Sylvia, I am afraid I will just have to take you to court in Johannesburg and then you will get another year to serve.' I felt a look of pleasure pass uncontrollably across my face. I thought, 'How nice! Johannesburg!' An extra year in the context of my six years did not seem much. And anyway, at this stage my release from gaol at any time in the future did not seem a real prospect to me. Heavens, I thought, Broodryk must think I'm crazy.

'Well, then, you'll have to give me another year,' I said unmoved.

'You will be sorry, Sylvia,' he said. There was a silence, with the heat outside. Broodryk in white shirt and white shorts. This was certainly not the normal 90-day interrogating technique. He had probably just come to see whether five months in Barberton Prison had softened me up, especially with the prospect of six years in the gaol ahead of me. It was, I felt, a kind of fishing expedition, with no serious intention to actually interrogate me.

'Okay,' I said. 'Is that all?'

'Yes, that is all,' he said, looking somewhat deflated.

I noticed he seemed rather nervous of me, much like Aucamp looked sometimes when he was obviously saying as little as possible because he felt that I would use anything he said against him some time in the future. And Broodryk probably felt uneasy in a situation in which he did not have the support of the usual interrogating team when an atmosphere of hatred and brutality was built up as a means to intimidate the person from whom they wished to extract a statement. Broodryk was silent and uncomfortable as I walked out of the visiting room. I went down the passage and back into our section.

Ann and Jean were also asked for information. And Broodryk spoke to Ann about possible early release. He asked her not to refuse it if she were offered it. It is possible that the authorities were genuinely thinking of reducing Ann's sentence but it could also have been a manoeuvre to divide us and make us susceptible to co-operating with them in one way or another. There was no way of knowing.

Rehabilitation

ANN WAS INTERVIEWED SEVERAL times in the first few months of 1966 by a man called Brigadier Viljoen who suddenly appeared on a visit to the prison round about this time. That she was chosen for this 'privilege' seemed to be connected with the suggestion that she could possibly obtain a reduction of sentence.

Moreover, evidently Viljoen was a harbinger of the new policy of 'rehabilitation'. In our section he was introduced to us, rather pompously in full round tones, by Brigadier Pretorius as a member of the 'Institution Board'. We had heard mention of the 'Institution' around October–November the previous year, but now it appeared to have become definitely an official designation. We asked the OC what was meant by 'the Institution' and he exclaimed: 'You don't know what the Institution is!'

Brigadier Pretorius had a deep resonant voice, extremely loud. We knew whenever he was in the gaol because his voice boomed out. It was an all-on-one-level voice, very self-consciously so. This sort of voice has always worried me because I recognise in it a desire to speak with absolute authority, with utter inflexibility. It is the voice of a dictator.

Whenever Jean heard his voice, she used quietly to comment, 'The Brigadier is in the gaol. I hear his dulcet tones!' The Brigadier told one of us some time later that he had actually cultivated this tone; this was because he had to control hundreds of people. It was necessary to have that sort of voice.

After exclamations of horror at our apparently not knowing what the 'Institution' was, he made it clear that he was referring to what we had called 'The Prison'. The new designation was evidently part of the 'revolutionary changes' that were being brought about in the South African Prisons Department. We were told that because we were being 'rehabilitated', we were being held in an 'Institution' and not a prison. 'What's in a name?' was our attitude naturally. But the Brigadier thought he was very important when he boomed the words, 'Rehabilitation' and 'Institution'.

As for Viljoen, we were to come to know him, each of us personally, when we were later taken – separately – to the Front to have a talk with him or, perhaps more correctly, to be talked to. As it happened, some time passed before I was granted the pleasure of meeting him in this manner.

Apparently as part of the change to an 'Institution', the wardresses had been given instructions not to swear in front of us. It was actually rather funny. A wardress whom we knew from the past swore like a trooper, told us that ''n ordentlike mens' (a respectable person) must never swear. She never swore for it was very bad to swear. And whenever any of us used what was regarded as an indecent word, however mild, she used to put an extremely shocked expression on her face and reprimand the person concerned.

Ever since I had had anything to do with South African prisons I had heard the most incredible swearing. I had accepted it as more or less an integral part of the system. In the gaol in Port Elizabeth, the wardresses and matrons had sworn at prisoners a great deal. At all times during the day I used to hear such things as 'jou fokken poes!' 'Jou blerrie gat!' 'Jou fokken doos!' 'Jou ma se moer!' 'Gaan kak!!" (It would probably be preferable not to damage one's ears with a translation of these choice phrases, some of which are, in any case, rather difficult to translate.) I would hear wardresses screaming out such things as they chased a prisoner hitting them with a key strap. Sometimes this was done in real rage, at other times it was fairly friendly, a form of (racist-stamped) horseplay.

To hear wardresses telling us that swearing was not respectable, particularly when it came from the mouth of someone we'd heard swearing a great deal in Pretoria Central when we were there during 90-day detention, was perplexing, to say the least. When she adopted this attitude and Flo said, 'But Miss Barnard, you swear!' she pulled herself up and put a distant god-like look on her face. 'I do not swear, Duncan!'

'Come off it, Miss Barnard, you know you swear like a trooper.'

'I do not swear, Duncan.' Again the distant look.

'But, Miss Barnard, I used to hear you shouting at Pretoria Central, "Moenie kom kak skiet nie!"'

Miss Barnard's face froze. Her distant, god-like look fled terrified from her face. 'No, Duncan. No, Duncan,' she said weakly.

'We know, Miss Barnard, you can't bluff us.'

Excursion to the local hospital

Around 7 January I was taken to the hospital in Barberton. I had picked up some strange thing on my foot while I was at the Fort at a time when I was serving my two months in the hard labour section. Nobody could find out exactly what it was but it seemed to be either some sort of fungus or tiny worms which had penetrated my very soft pads. I had tried various remedies but it went on developing, so the prison doctor, Dr Scholz, said we had better try cauterising it and see if that would remove the problem. I was to have a general anaesthetic.

The Front told me to put on my prison nightdress, nightgown and slippers. I was not looking forward to the outing at all because I was anxious about having a general anaesthetic. Matron Bester was as unpleasant as usual, screaming like a madwoman at me just before I was due to go.

I was too nervous to notice much in the car on the way to the hospital, except that everything looked terribly bare and dry. I could not understand it because I thought the doctor had told me this was a subtropical climate. So why no lush vegetation? I only realised in my second summer at Barberton that this tremendous dryness and bareness was unusual and was a result of the drought. By the time my second summer in Barberton arrived the drought had been broken.

At one stage I noticed a lot of Indian shops on the right side of the road. Then we drove through a gate with a board on one side saying, 'HOSPITAL, QUIET PLEASE' and 'DO NOT HOOT', or something like that.

We drove to the front of a building. Driving the car was a man in khaki uniform, Meneer Bezuidenhout, a 'Hoofbewaarder', a Head Warder. Next to me in the back of the car was Matron Botha, the junior matron newly appointed at Barberton. I had first seen her at Pretoria Central when I was there under the 90-day law.

There was a big turnover of matrons at Barberton Prison. One who had left had known us at the Fort where we had been on quite friendly terms with the wardresses as they had not been given instructions, as they were at Barberton, to make our lives intolerable. Evidently, she had not been able to bear treating us in this way, and had eventually broken down in front of my fellow prisoners – this was before I arrived – and burst into tears. After that their relationship with her had been better. She was the blonde matron who had handled my arrival and who had been so uncertain, indeed apparently unhappy, about my situation. She had found it very difficult to get on with Matron Bester and soon handed in her resignation.

Another young matron, also one of the more pleasant people I met in the prisons' service, could also not get on with Matron Bester and found the bossiness of Miss Taljaard hard to accept, and so asked for a transfer. Matron Botha was also not to last long. She asked for a transfer and got one soon after this. So somewhere around this time, possibly January 1966, Miss Taljaard was made a Junior Matron. She obviously enjoyed the job of being unpleasant to us and generally enjoyed bossing prisoners around. She was to tell me when she escorted me on my second trip to the hospital that she had a brother in the Security Branch.

I stepped out of the car and walked across some blueish-grey flagstones, through a door and to the reception desk. The three women behind the desk and somebody sitting on a bench some feet in front of the desk stared curiously at me. Was I a prisoner, the looks seemed to say. I was in a prison nightgown made of ticking, and there were two prison officials escorting me. The woman at the desk looked a little surprised and uneasy when she was given information that definitely identified me as a prisoner. 'Who will pay?' she asked. 'The Department will pay,' Bezuidenhout said. He asked Matron Botha to phone him when I was ready to be fetched. He went off, and Matron Botha took me to the hospital matron who showed me to a private ward. She was friendly and polite.

It was strange to be treated like a human being again. I could hardly believe it. Nurses said 'Good morning' to me and smiled at me! It was unbelievable. It was strange not to be shouted at or shrugged off. There was actually a world where people were nice to each other! It may seem odd but I had almost ceased to believe it. It was not a thought out position. It was just that Barberton Prison had become my whole world.

Sometimes outsiders are surprised at how seriously prisoners – and this is especially the case with political prisoners whom people tend to assume remain, to one degree or another, geared to an outside world – take things that happen in gaol. But what they forget is that gaol is the prisoner's only world. This was especially so with us since the authorities had ensured that we had almost no contact with the outside world, not even through newspapers or the radio. We could not measure ourselves and our situation by what happened outside because we were completely cut off. And people do not usually act in terms of things they don't experience.

To some extent, prisoners with families with whom they were closely emotionally involved managed to maintain some sense of the realities in the outside world. However, even in these cases, with so little contact with the family because of very few letters and visits, this effect tended to be inconsistent. We had to be very careful to keep a watch on ourselves, otherwise we could have adopted all sorts of unhealthy attitudes. Inevitably we were affected, for only God can remain untouched by his environment.

A nurse gave me my theatre clothes and I climbed into them and lay in bed waiting for my pre-med injection. It was a pleasant hospital in nice grounds. On my right was a window, not with prison bars but with burglar bars which, for the moment, amounted to much to the same thing except that I could manage to see what was outside without having to climb up on something. Outside my window were trees and grass and right up against the window was a hibiscus bush with pink flowers. My prison escort did not leave me for a moment but she was pleasant and even offered me a sweet, which I could not take because I was not allowed to eat anything for eight hours before I went into the theatre.

I took courage and chatted to her a bit about the other gaols she had been in, and about boyfriends. She asked me how I felt about prison. She said she didn't know how I could take it. She said if ever she got a prison sentence she would commit suicide. To be locked up in that small space all the time – that was terrible! I told her reassuringly that it was not so bad if one was not ashamed of what one had done, if one was proud of what one had done. She shook her head. It was incomprehensible to her. 'I wouldn't be able to take it,' she said. 'I would commit suicide ... And the food, the same every day, and to be locked behind bars in those cells ... No ... That is terrible ... ondraaglik.'

I was really surprised by what she said. I thought prison must seem horrifying, as it seemed to her, only to people who had never been there any length of time. For prison is not quite what one expects it to be. There is perhaps a black horror of it from outside, a horror that I thought one could only experience with regard to the unexperienced, only with regard to something largely in the imagination. When one is in gaol, there is the reality to deal with and so it is different from what one expected. As I have already noted, there is a suffering that is very difficult to describe.

I remember the first time I was ever locked up in a cell. It was sometime in the first half of 1961. At that time I knew nothing about gaols or police stations. I had never really thought about them. South Africa is not a country where one tends to think about prison, if one is white. If one is black, one is either oneself likely to land up there sometime, for a pass offence, for trespassing or something like that, or relatives or friends did so. Gaol is, in this case, something tangible. The white prison population in South Africa is not large and I came from an upper middle-class white family and whites from this section do not often go to prison. In apartheid days there was a minimal interest in prison reform in South Africa amongst intellectuals or religious leaders. It was not an issue in South Africa (as it was at the same time in a country such as Britain, for instance).

Sometime during 1961, when I was 24 years old, I started taking part in 'sit-ins'. Groups of us, mainly white and coloured, and sometimes African, used to go into cafés and restaurants and cinemas. One day we went in one of these mixed groups to the restaurant of a Cape Town department store and we were arrested and taken to Caledon Square police station. There Gillian Jewell, a girl called Jill Jessop and myself were signed in. The police had determined to break the sit-ins. They had first tried to see whether they would die a natural death and, when they continued, they had decided to climb in.

I remember the cold horror that swept through me as a policeman lifted a black metal appendage on a large brown door with a spyhole, set in black metal, and banged it down several times against the door. A large woman in a white overall opened the door, saying 'Môre' to the policeman. 'Here are some prisoners for you,' he said casually. Once we had entered, the woman instructed us to divest ourselves of our watches and rings and give her all the money we had. She entered these items on a form, a copy of which she gave to each of us. At the top of the form in large letters was 'PRISONER'S RECEIPT' or something to that effect.

Excursion to the local hospital

When she had finished this removal of some of our possessions, she opened another door a few feet away from the first, also brown wood with a spyhole set in black metal. We walked into a dingy courtyard and the door slammed behind us and the key turned. That was not a nice experience. Two cells led off the courtyard with grey, dirty concrete floors. It was very dark inside. To see we had to keep the light on all day.

There were two beds in the open cell, black metal beds, with charcoal-coloured, dingy, foul-smelling blankets. No pillow, no sheets. There were white and yellow marks of food on the blankets. And from vomit. Foul-smelling vomit. Police station blankets have a sweet, musty smell. They were so thick with dirt that they did not give one much warmth. One could not get them to fold against one's body. They lay flat and heavy.

The window was high up, covered by mesh, the panes thick with dust. Almost no light could come through there. That day we tried to find some sun in the dull-red concrete-floored courtyard. It did not get much sun because there was a high building on one side above the thick netting-wire which covered the courtyard. Lying on top of the netting was a woman's bathing costume. We wondered how it had got there. It had probably fallen out of one of the windows above us in the red-brick wall. There were almost certainly CID offices up there. A little further along on the netting was one old worn shoe.

Jill Jessop got out after an hour or so. Her father was on some newspaper. I paced up and down – to the spyhole where I had a look to see what was happening every time I heard the metal knock on the outside door. Sometimes I saw the white overall of the matron swaying a little with her back to me, not far from my eye, and I would move back quickly when she turned. At other times I saw the outside door open and warm sunlight against the red-brick wall on the other side of the police station road which ran between the outside door and the police station. At lunchtime the matron brought us an indescribable plate of food on a tin plate, foul-smelling. Quite impossible to eat. And 'coffee' in two tin mugs. Cold and horrible.

I ate nothing. I found the experience of being locked up almost unbearable. I knew I would get out soon. The longest they would keep us would be until Monday morning – this was Saturday – when we would have to appear in court. None the less, I found the experience insupportable. I felt like a caged animal. I just could not bear those walls around me and that locked door. I would go up to it continually and push against it to see what would happen. But no, it would not budge. Then I would look through the spyhole again to see if anyone had come to bail us out. Back and forth across the courtyard, into the dingy, cold, depressing cell, out again and back to the door.

After some time the matron appeared in the courtyard and told me that I could go, as somebody had bailed me out, and I ran, forgetting to say goodbye to Gillian, and out through that door before anyone could close it again. I suddenly remembered Gillian and called back that I would obtain bail for her and get her out.

I never quite had that experience again. I was to be in police cells several times after that, some with worse physical conditions, such as just a mat on a concrete floor in the middle of winter, but the feeling changed from a desperation to get out to an acceptance of the inevitable and this altered, and that qualitatively, the nature of the experience.

But to get back to my hospital escort who said she would commit suicide if she ever found herself in prison. She could not have experienced that feeling. Or could a sensitive wardress perhaps obtain an inkling of what a prisoner felt? It seemed so.

I lay in the hospital bed waiting for my first injection. Every now and again I had a look at the pink hibiscus. It was in shadow because the sun was on the other side of the building. It was still early. I was beginning to get really nervous. Why were they taking so long? And then I was told that Dr Scholz had forgotten to make a theatre appointment for me. I tried to doze and forget about 'the operation' but I could not. I watched the nurses come and go in the passage outside my ward. Nurses came in and out of the ward, too, doing various jobs, putting a fresh bunch of flowers in a vase, testing the oxygen machine next to my bed.

I must have been there about three hours when they gave me my pre-med injection and I was wheeled to the theatre down several passages, through several doors. Quite a nice swinging ride! Then two doors swung open and I found myself in an operating theatre. I slid off the trolley onto the table and had a look around. It was a really pleasant theatre, with a large window in front of me, taking up the whole of one wall, and beyond it trees and flowers.

All these things were new and exciting but I saw them from captivity. The awareness of my captivity never left me for one moment. It was there, a resigned, timeless feeling. The theatre sister asked me to put out my right arm. She had a look at my vein. Dr Scholz appeared suddenly through a door. He walked fast up to the table and squeezed my arm reassuringly. Again, that was strange for was I not an animal? No doubt, it was part of the medical training. The pre-med injection had made me a bit hazy. A man with glasses and grey hair took my right arm and pushed a needle in. He asked me to clench my fist, which I did. The world began to swing and I was gone.

I woke up and tried to see whether Matron Botha was there. I opened one eye and then the other to see if I could get some sort of image. There was a vague picture of a form to the right of me. 'What's the time?' I mumbled. 'Half past twelve' came the answer. I turned onto my stomach and lay a few minutes. 'You must get up, Neame. Mr Bezuidenhout will be here very soon.'

'But I can't get up,' I said. 'I can't see yet.'

'You must get up. I've got lots of work to do at the prison.' She brought my nightdress and nightgown. 'Come on. Put these on.'

I sat up, with my eyes almost closed, peering out at the world just a little. My head was swinging. I was just awake. I had flashes of unconsciousness. I closed my eyes and dressed automatically. And then I fell back on my pillow.

'Come on, Neame. I can't leave you here and Mr Bezuidenhout is going to be very cross if we keep him waiting.'

'Okay, okay,' I mumbled, and moved my feet towards the floor. I opened my eyes as my feet touched the wooden floor and then closed them again.

'Come on, Neame.'

I opened my eyes, and moved towards the door. 'Bastards,' I mumbled. I got through the door, only just, knocking myself against the side, and walked unsteadily out into the passage. 'Which way?' I asked, peering for Matron Botha. I felt her take me by the elbow. Well, at least she offered some help. That was something. I swayed along a veranda, conscious that there were people around but too bleary-eyed and too much concentrating on keeping upright and walking straight to obtain a picture of them. I found myself inside the building somewhere right up against a wall. I felt a hand on my elbow, guiding me. 'This way, Neame.'

And there was Mr Bezuidenhout in front of the reception desk. He gave me an amused laugh when he saw me. 'Come on, help her,' Matron Botha said to him, and he took my other elbow. Together they guided me out of the door. I was conscious of stares from the reception desk. There were flashes of sunlight outside, penetrating my brain, and then a moment of unconsciousness. They helped me into the car.

Bezuidenhout was in front, Botha and I at the back. We drove out of the hospital grounds. I did not see much. I opened my eyes a little and suddenly saw a strange face in Bezuidenhout's rearview mirror. It was me. I looked like a madwoman with my pupils enormous and a pale face. 'Bastards,' I muttered.

'What was that, Neame?'

'Nothing ... nothing,' I responded. I closed my eyes.

'Sy weet nie wat gaan aan nie,' Bezuidenhout said with a laugh. She doesn't know what's going on.

The car was parked at the foot of the steep steps going up into the gaol. Botha helped me up while I held onto the sides. We waited outside the grille while somebody unlocked it. Matron Bester was somewhere around. She also had a bit of a laugh. Botha, still holding my elbow, took me down the passage to the door of our section. She opened it, and through the grille I saw the others in their blue uniforms but I could not make out who was who. Bright blue uniforms and grey shiny concrete. 'Take hold of her,' Matron Botha instructed somebody and one of my friends got me to my bed. I got under my bedcover, with my head swinging.

'God, look what she looks like,' somebody said. 'She is hardly conscious.'

I was aware that there was a bit of a gathering around my bed. Maybe they want the news, I thought. I stuck my head out from under the bedcover. 'They're bastards, aren't they?' I commented. 'I'll tell you everything later.' And I fell asleep.

A visit from Judge Boshoff

SOMETIME DURING JANUARY WE saw a large black car stop in front of the prison, together with a couple of other cars. We had sensed that something was going to happen that day for there had been an air of expectation and some nervousness from the side of the officials. We had become Geiger counters in measuring the atmosphere in the Front, noting a tone of voice in the passage outside our section, the number and pace of the footsteps there, the precise modulation of Matron Bester's voice. Often, too, when somebody was due to visit, the wardress on duty ordered us to clean the small section leading off from our courtyard, behind Matron Bester's office.

We could also tell by a certain change in the manner in which the authorities dealt with us. Suddenly everyone would be just a little more polite. Instead of shouting and shrugging at us as we approached them at the entrance grille and banging the door in our faces as we began to make a request for something, they would hesitate just for a moment and say, 'Ek sal kyk of daar is.' (I will look and see if there is any.) This was a great concession, even if there was no follow-up.

We wondered who was going to arrive. At first we thought it might be Colonel Aucamp, bringing Sheila Weinberg, whom we heard had six months for painting an ANC slogan on a wall. She had, in fact, been sentenced to eighteen months but with a year suspended which was, in any case, a vicious sentence, especially as the police spy Gerard Ludi had asked her to do it when she was a young girl of seventeen. Her father, Eli Weinberg, had been sentenced in our trial in Johannesburg to five years for membership of the Central Committee of the Communist Party and her mother, Violet Weinberg, was in 180-days detention, evidently in some way connected with Bram Fischer's underground phase. We heard that Sheila's appeal had come up round about early December or maybe late November, and we had been expecting her ever since.

However, there was an atmosphere in the gaol that wasn't quite an Aucamp atmosphere. For instance, the wardresses seemed interested in the state of our uniforms, what we looked like, and this seemed to indicate that there was a visitor who was 'really' from outside, not somebody connected with the prisons. We even thought it might be Helen Suzman on a visit to prisons. In fact, that was our strongest feeling.

The afternoon drew on and nothing happened. There had been at one stage a bit of a panic and we were told to put on clean uniforms and stand in a line. 'Staan op 'n lyn.' But this had apparently been a false alarm because we stood there 'at attention' for about half an hour. We were then told we could disperse.

We began to feel that it could hardly be Helen Suzman for surely she would not come so late? We estimated that it was about four in the afternoon. As it turned out, though she evidently went to most of the prisons where political prisoners were held, she never came to Barberton. We heard when we were released that the general view outside, even, it seemed, amongst some relatives and friends, was that our conditions were more or less satisfactory and it appeared likely that one of the relatives had spread this view, believing that it would assist in ensuring earlier release of his loved one. Helen Suzman herself was to state that she had been told we didn't need her.

We began to conclude that we must accept that the awaited 'guest' was somebody from the prisons, most likely the Commissioner. The problem was that he had visited the gaol in November, about a month and a half to two months before, and that made it unlikely that he would be back so soon. A visitor was an exciting event in our prison routine. To see and speak to somebody we did not see every day was quite something. I found myself speaking faster, walking faster, my heart beating more quickly than usual. And the uncertainty simply increased the excitement.

As time passed and no one arrived, the tension in our section died down a bit. It was now fairly late in the afternoon, too late, we felt, for anyone to turn up. We were inclined to think it must have been a false alarm.

'Parade, asseblief!' the shout came. And we went and stood in a line in the portaal. A whole lot of outsiders entered our portaal from the courtyard. They must have come either through the door of the store that ran down almost the whole of one side of our courtyard or through the grille near Matron Bester's office. First there was the Brigadier who was accompanied by a man in a smart suit, quite a sophisticated-looking chap, not the sort we usually saw in these parts. He had reddish hair and a reddish face. His well-fitting suit was a dark navy.

These first two were followed by about five other men, some quite young, some extremely ugly, and there was one woman, I think. It was strange to see such an assortment of people in our no man's land, people who seemed suddenly to appear from nowhere. It was quite impossible to work out who they might be. They walked across our portaal like a lot of sheep into one of the single cells to have a look around, it seemed. It happened to be my cell, the middle single cell which I occupied at that time. I felt a little discomfited by their behaviour since they had not asked whether they could go into the cell. They had a look at the books on my desk, the open notebook on my table. I had been taking notes from one of the history books I had just finished reading. I thought, At least, they could have asked. How could they just walk into a woman's cell like that?

At the same time I felt a strange pleasure that my life there, that our lives, were being related to an outside world, whoever these people were. It was obvious they were not prison officials. The Brigadier was nervously pompous. The visitors gathered, facing us, in a little group near the central grille, seemingly feeling a little uncomfortable. They looked at us. We looked back.

The Brigadier introduced the sophisticated-looking man as Judge Boshoff who, he pronounced, was on circuit in the district. He told us that judges on circuit visited all the prisons in the area. He asked whether we had any complaints to make to the judge. There was a silence. We had not been prepared for such a visit, and, therefore, did not know quite how to react. Judge Boshoff spoke a cultivated English, quite unlike anything we heard there normally. He indicated that he was on circuit, and said much the same sort of things the Brigadier had said.

'Well, then ...' commented the Brigadier, beginning to look relieved that apparently none of us was going to raise anything with the judge.

I gathered my courage in front of these strangers, wondering how I was going to approach Judge Boshoff. 'Yes, Brigadier,' I said, 'I would like to speak to the judge.'

The Brigadier became nervous, a smug smile on his face, with just a little look of a threat.

'All right, Neame, you can speak to the judge.'

They waited. Prisoners in blue uniforms in a straight line, standing on shiny grey concrete.

I saw a strange assortment of faces ahead of me, all staring at this female prisoner in a blue uniform and brown clodhopper shoes. For a moment I had that feeling of demoralisation I used to have at the Fort and down in Port Elizabeth: dirty prisoner, dirty criminal, convict. The judge smiled a little encouragingly.

'No, Brigadier,' I said, 'I don't wish to speak to the judge like this, in front of all these people.'

I looked at 'all these people', mostly young and unprepossessing faces, and thought, That was a bit rude, but I didn't quite know how to explain about feeling like a dirty prisoner, standing, together with my fellow prisoners, in a straight line in a uniform with brown clodhopper shoes. The looks on the faces ahead of me did not have the knowledge that we were actually political prisoners; otherwise, I thought, they would look more hostile. Instead, they just looked interested and curious, and their surprise at the books they had seen on my table convinced me that they thought I was just an ordinary prisoner. Fraud or soliciting, their looks seemed to say. I began to feel that I was, indeed, the kind of person they envisaged I was.

'All right, Neame,' the Brigadier said, as if he were granting me a great concession, and with a little threat in his voice. 'You may come through to the office and speak to the judge but I will be there. You cannot speak to the judge alone.' The threat in his voice became more emphasised. All the time he had the nervous smile on his ugly face. He stood there with his brown baton under his arm. His body fat, short and paunchy, looking rather deformed. As I stepped forward, I heard Jean saying that she also wished to speak to the judge, and I heard the Brigadier asking who else wished to see him, and saying that they would have to come through one at a time.

The line was breaking up. No longer a line of prisoners. The group of visitors was breaking up too. Judge Boshoff smiled at me in a friendly way and, talking to me, started going through to the passage and down towards the office. I almost felt human ... He asked me how long I had. 'Six years,' I said. He looked shocked for a moment.

'What are you in for?' he asked.

'Politics,' I answered.

'No, I mean what for exactly?'

'Oh,' I said. 'Communist Party.' I thought of adding 'And ANC' but thought, Then I shall have to explain that I am not really a member of the ANC but was sentenced on a frame-up. I thought that maybe I would raise that matter with him when we got to the office.

'This is a tragic country, isn't it?' Judge Boshoff commented. I just smiled as we reached the office.

The Brigadier and Matron were close behind us. Judge Boshoff went behind the desk and sat down. The Brigadier stood to his left, Matron Bester to his right. I stood on the other side of the desk, hands behind my back. The Brigadier looked very nervous.

'Well, Neame?' he asked. 'You see that I am here.'

Judge Boshoff looked irritated and, ignoring the Brigadier, asked me what I wished to speak to him about. I responded that I wished to speak to him about our bad conditions there in that gaol. I told him that there were no proper facilities for long-term prisoners, that we had no sport facilities, no library, that the space we lived in was very confined, that we were locked up in our cells for long periods, and so on. I told him about our tremendous isolation and the bad psychological effect it was having on us. The Brigadier interrupted at one point, started arguing with me on a point I had raised. The judge turned to him and said coolly and with contempt in his voice, 'I wish to hear what the prisoner has to say.'

Judge Boshoff leaned confidentially towards me over the desk and spoke to me as though he were talking behind the Brigadier's back. 'Look,' he said, 'there is not much I can do with these people' and he nodded in the direction of the Brigadier, 'and really I am only empowered to deal with complaints about assault. However, I shall raise your conditions in Pretoria unofficially. I think that is the best way to get things done. I will raise it unofficially, for I know people in Pretoria.'

'Thank you,' I said.

The Brigadier was beginning to look a bit panicky. He said in a placatory manner, 'We are going to take these washing lines down,' and pointed through the office window behind Judge Boshoff, 'so that they can have more space to exercise in.' He repeated this several times – 'We are going to take down these washing lines' – obviously trying to convince the judge of his good intentions.

'I shall take up your points about your conditions unofficially,' the judge assured me.

'And they have been allowed to study,' the Brigadier emphasised with a winning smile on his face.

Judge Boshoff ignored him. 'What did you do before you were arrested?' he asked me.

'I used to teach in a school,' I said, 'and when I was arrested I was doing a History Honours course at Wits University but I seemed to be arrested every time I was due to write my exams.'

Judge Boshoff's face froze a little at my mention of being arrested several times. I wondered why, and then thought, I should not have said that. I am giving a picture of myself as a hardened political, and then he won't help us to improve our conditions.

'Thank you, Judge,' I said, backing out of the office, with my hands still behind my back, trying to imprint on his mind the picture of a young white girl, innocent and meaning well, caught in the tentacles of the state.

'I will see what I can do,' Judge Boshoff murmured, looking friendly.

I walked down the passage back to the section. The others were sitting at the table. They had begun eating. They looked excited. 'Well? What happened?'

I was bowled over. 'He's fantastic,' I told them. 'You should have seen how he treated the Brigadier ... with such contempt ... and the

A visit from Judge Boshoff

Brigadier is looking terrified ...'

The others were drinking in my every word, except for Jean who had gone through to the Front for her turn to see the judge.

'And he was so nice ... Gosh, to be treated like a human being again.'

'What did you raise?'

'Oh, the usual things,' I answered. 'No facilities, confined space, no sport, isolation ... And Boshoff said he would take up our conditions unofficially with somebody in Pretoria. It sounded as if it might be Vorster.'

'You know that Judge Boshoff is a swine,' somebody interjected.

'Oh,' I said, flattened.

'I can't think of the trials he has been involved in, but I know he is supposed to be one of the worst judges.'

'Yes, I know he has been involved in some of the political trials and has given pretty awful judgments', somebody else commented.

'I don't see the use of raising our conditions with him,' Esther stated. 'He's just one of them.'

'No,' I responded, 'we must raise our conditions with everybody we can, every single person who comes to the gaol, whoever they are, for one never knows what might emerge out of it. And anyway, it is good for the authorities to know how we feel about this place and that we are prepared to talk about it.' I was certainly feeling somewhat deflated but still.

'I think he was involved in the MK trial,' somebody noted. 'And he gave a terrible judgment.'

'Yes,' someone else agreed.

'Still, I think we should raise our conditions with everyone possible,' I said quietly.

Jean came back from the Front. She also looked pleased and excited. 'He was very nice,' she said. 'And we may be getting a table tennis table. I suggested that it would be very easy to get a board and put it on top of our table here, and Judge Boshoff told the Brigadier that he would be very pleased if the Brigadier would give us a table tennis table.'

'Marvellous, Jean,' we said, 'but, of course, it is very unlikely. They have promised us tenniquoits since last year and nothing has happened.'

'Yes, yes, but still … one never knows. And Judge Boshoff is being very nice.'

'Yes, he is being terrific.'

'To be treated like a human being again. '

'And the Brigadier is looking so terrified.'

The excitement and enthusiasm started rising again. We talked a great deal over the table. Smiling, eager faces. I seem to remember that somebody else also went to speak to Boshoff. I think it was Ann.

'Dis laat, mense!' (It is late, people) the wardress called from the grille where she was stationed to see that nobody escaped. The grille had been left unlocked so that we could go through to see the judge. 'Julle moet die borde opwas. Ons wil nou toesluit.' You must wash the plates. We want to lock up now.

We stood up from the table, took the dishes and piled them in the laundry basin. The person 'on the dishes' that day started washing up while two people dried, and the rest of us tidied up, wiped crumbs from the table, swept the floor, and got ready for lock-up. We cleaned our teeth, washed our faces, and filled mugs with water to take to our cells. Those of us who took some bread to our cells at night put it on a plate and placed it in the cell. We talked as much as we could manage while we did these things, still very much excited.

Back in my cell, I sat down at my table in the middle single cell and tried to concentrate on my book but my mind was in a whirl, and my heart beating fast. To have somebody listening to me for a change … and treating me like a human being. Eventually, I gave up the struggle to work, flung myself onto my bed and continued reading a novel. I knew that the others in their cells were feeling just like me.

The following morning our life went on as on any other morning. We had our breakfast, and then went to the basins to do the laundry. But there was still an air of excitement. The washing smelled the same, felt the same. I had the same backache. We sweated in the heat. But we felt softer, more at peace.

I was bending over my basin, with the hard canvas sleeve of a jacket in my right hand, rubbing up and down on the front half of the jacket, rubbing, rubbing, trying to remove the brown clay marks which seemed to have sunk right into the centre of the material so that I could not get to it. The hard surface of the material seemed to be waterproof, preventing the water and soap from penetrating to the lower layers. But, of course, there was the sun baking outside which would eventually do the job. I was just going to turn the jacket over, to pick up the other sleeve in order to work away at the other front half when Mollie came up to the basins. I felt her urgency and looked up. Her face looked drawn and pale.

'Do you know what?' she muttered. 'Boshoff sentenced an African woman to death yesterday. She's in the gaol at the moment, waiting to be moved to Pretoria Central.'

That was all. Mollie walked off and we went back in silence to our washing. It was a tremendous blow. In my mind I saw Judge Boshoff sitting up high in the court, red hair, putting on the black cap, and saying, 'I sentence you to death.' A prisoner sentenced to death was one of us. Even locked up in our section, isolated in the gaol, we felt her presence. We felt one with her in her cell, grille locked with the door open all day and night, and the wardress sitting there. The gaol in Barberton was very quiet, quieter than usual, if that were possible. There was a hush.

They came to fetch food from us for the condemned prisoner. Condemned black prisoners got 'white food'. A day or two later we heard the prisoners from the other side singing the hymn 'Until We Meet Again', and we knew that the condemned woman was being taken away from Barberton to go to her death in Pretoria.

We got a table tennis table two or three months later. It stood in the centre of the portaal, and we moved aside the table where we ate to make room for it.

I receive news of Kathy

I STILL HAD HAD NO REPLY from Graham to my letter written in October or November. I had asked Matron Bester, Matron Taljaard and the Brigadier whether anything had arrived and they all said, No, nothing had arrived; if it had, they would have given it to me. I felt rather desperate. We had so little contact with the outside world, one letter in three months was terribly important.

My friend Ayesha Cajee, wife of Amien Cajee, a close comrade of Kathy who had moved into Kathy's flat, number 13 Kholvad House, Market Street, after the Rivonia arrests in order to ensure that everything was in order there, visited me about 11 January and confirmed that Caroline was in '180 days'. I had been close to both Ayesha and Amien for some time. Amien and I had, in fact, co-operated in receiving and sending news to Kathy while the latter was in 90 days immediately after the Rivonia raid. Kathy had sent out washing and I had discovered a word, written in pencil in Gujarati on a pyjama collar and asked Amien what it meant. It meant girdle, he told me, and so we examined the white cotton girdle of the pyjama trousers and found a note on tissue paper inside. We read it and on sending the clean washing back used the same method of communication.

The result was that during most of that detention we were informed what was happening to Kathy and, in turn, we gave him news from our end. In the first note Kathy had instructed me to destroy his missives immediately after reading. I did so and the result is we do not have these messages today. It was only once Bram Fischer organised the correspondence between Kathy and me after Kathy had come out of detention and been charged that I kept the communications, well hidden,

I receive news of Kathy

of course. It was during his detention that he sent me a message, telling me to leave the country immediately. I did not give it a thought.

At her visit Ayesha brought me news of Kathy, not much but that he was well and studying and very worried about me. My separation from Kathy, like my six years, had become a part of my attitude to life. It was so a part of me that I hardly thought about him with the front of my mind. He was just there, a constant presence. I rarely spoke of him and the others did not either. The news I got was usually so little and so tenuous that it had little effect on me. But I carried out the 'rites' of my relationship with him every now and again, receiving bits of news, sending bits out.

Before I came to gaol, I had thought of being separated from him five years, maybe ten at the most. In gaol I stopped bluffing myself, like I tried to stop bluffing myself about most things. Kathy had said, 'It can't be more than five years.' This 'five years' had become a kind of slogan of the Congress Movement. A lot of us had initially adopted it without much thought, even though we watched the years going by, and freedom did not come. We knew now that the movement outside had been pretty much broken up, organisations almost smashed, and that change was going to be quite a long time coming.

We knew that it would come. With 15 million Africans, about 1 and a half million Indian and coloured people and only 3 million whites, change must come. We realised now that it would be a hard battle. In the first half of the 1960s, in those years, indeed, when we were arrested and faced trial – 1963 was perhaps the turning point – international powers and capital were coming to the rescue of the apartheid regime. Change might take 15, 20, 25, 30 years. I might easily be past my childbearing age by the time it came. This possibility I faced up to in prison and I felt that Kathy on Robben Island must be facing up to it too. Indeed, he was to send me several letters from the island in which he indicated – this was in code, of course – that he deeply regretted that we had not had a child.

I remember what Govan had looked like when he gave evidence in my defence at Humansdorp after they had brought him up from Robben Island. He had received a life sentence in the Rivonia Trial. David Soggot had asked him as he stood in the box in that corrupt magistrate's court in Humansdorp – Soggot was introducing him to the court: 'You have a life sentence?' A momentary look of shock, almost disbelief, crossed Govan's face as he heard those words. A pause, and then he confirmed quietly, 'Yes, I have a life sentence.'

I felt that if Kathy had been in that box, he might have reacted in a similar way. Two levels of consciousness. There was the day to day reality of prison, dealing with each day as it came, not thinking about the life sentence until somebody confronted him with it. The Robben Islanders were, no doubt, aware that things now looked very different from the 1950s–early 60s.

We share information and letters

ON THE EVENING OF 31 January 1966 Sheila Weinberg arrived. She was to be with us until about the middle of June, I think it was. This period, for various reasons, was to be one of the most important months in our prison sentences. It was a time when we started having all sorts of reactions to our isolation, which Sheila, to some extent, highlighted. Sheila, with her gentle irony, her humour, was a valuable addition to our group. Important, too, was that it was a period in which we at last, I felt, came to terms with ourselves as a group, standing over and against the authorities.

ABOVE: Pencil portrait of Sheila by me.

In the early months of 1966 the authorities were continuing with their tactic of softening us up, one of their key aims being to divide us. This turned on the prospect of an amnesty for prisoners on 31 May, the day of the Republic. It was the fifth anniversary of the declaration of the apartheid republic.

At some stage, possibly when he delivered Sheila, Aucamp called Ann, Esther and Flo to the front. He indicated that he was going to the Minister – he meant Vorster, Minister of Justice – in connection with reduction of sentences and wished to know what their political attitudes were. Each of them told him that, for various reasons, they could not go back into active politics but that they had not changed their views.

Of course, there was great excitement at Sheila's arrival. We had expected it for so long and had prepared for her coming so often but when she came we were completely taken by surprise. We were all locked up in our cells when she was brought in and taken to a single cell. We waited for the Front to go off duty and then we asked Sheila to tell us the news. 'What is going on in the outside world?' She told us how Bram had been caught. I was shocked by what Sheila had to say. It was such a picture of bad organisation, maybe inevitable with the lack of personnel, but still. After about an hour of this information Ann developed violent pain in her stomach and had to go and vomit in the toilet.

We wanted to go on talking, we wanted to hear 'everything'. And not only political aspects. What did the streets of Johannesburg look like? Were there any new buildings? New flyovers? New one-way streets? New cinemas? New restaurants? What was the weather like when she left? Was it a hot summer there too? When had she last seen Cape Town? How was the weather there, the sea, the mountains?

But Sheila was tired and wanted to go to bed, and, anyway, she had been in prison for some weeks already at the Fort and Pretoria Central. We asked her to tell us something of what was going on in these gaols for they had become part of the 'outside world' for us. How was Matron Britz? Were the wardresses we knew still at Pretoria? How was the Lieutenant at the Fort and Mrs Lubbe and Matron Huiseman, and so on? Sheila answered some of our questions but soon asked our permission to go to bed. She disappeared from her grille and we tried to get back to our books.

About 9 February, I received a letter from my brother, Peter, as a reply to my letter to Graham. It arrived out of the three-month period but the Brigadier gave me permission to take it as my last three-month letter. The date on it was five weeks before. The Brigadier admitted that it had arrived five weeks before at Barberton Prison and he had sent it away to Colonel Aucamp because there were some things in the letter of which he did not approve.

I criticised the Brigadier for the behaviour of the authorities in this matter, asking him why he had not informed me that he had sent the letter away, especially as he knew how worried I was, and I asked whether it was necessary to lie and mislead me about the arrival of my letters. The Brigadier was furious about this criticism and shouted at me, 'Get out! Get out! Get out!', and so I left the office and went down the passage back to the section.

The Brigadier's view was that I had no 'rights', not even to letters, if he or Colonel Aucamp felt that I should not have them. He thought he had been terribly clever and subtle in the way he had misled me. He stuck his chest out and put the smug smile on his face, and, I suspected, built up an image in his mind of himself as somebody fit to be in the Security

Branch, certainly somebody fit to deal with communists. Really, he was just a stupid brute.

I never thought I would, with a clear conscience, be able to say that about any person. We tended to be careful in our criticisms for we all felt strongly that people are, to a large extent, made by their society. Because government policy was immoral and inhuman, those who administered it inevitably tended to take on these characteristics. Our view was that we should try to exercise patience as far as this was possible and try to win them over to our point of view by our example. But the reality of the Brigadier's stupidity and brutality was too much for our principles, and so we had to admit that he was a 'stupid brute'. I wrote in my 'diary' on 17 February 1966:

To understand the "other side" is sometimes difficult at moments in gaol; but we constantly make an effort of will not to lose sympathy. There is something of the young boy in their brutality.

It is interesting to see what worried the authorities about the letter from my brother Peter. The sections they did not like, and must have been considering censoring, were underlined in red pencil. They were sections about the outside world. One such section was the following: 'We read of the torrential rain in Mozambique and the E. Transvaal and the cyclones, Claude and Denise, which you no doubt heard about [which of course, we hadn't], and which you very likely felt in Barberton. The rest of the country is experiencing what is already called the great Southern African drought, most terrible this century. Even the unsuperstitious are reminded of the Old Testament ...'

I read this letter to the others because I felt it was a good one to share, a mass of detail about Christmas presents and Christmas trees and decorations and happy children. There was also something about the area surrounding our gaol. I was standing leaning on the table in the centre of the portaal, and the others were standing around, listening to every word.

ABOVE RIGHT: *A censored letter.*

We share information and letters

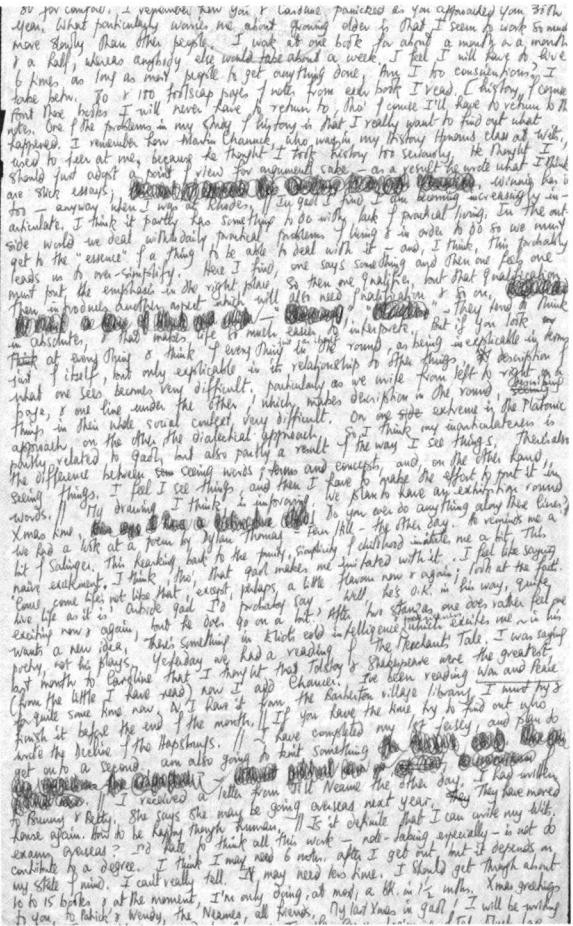

At the end of the letter I read: '... you are not very far from the Kruger National Park. Graham and I passed through Barberton on our way back from Rhodesia in the spring of 1962.* We travelled through very wild and beautiful and already at that time drought-stricken country in Sekukuniland [sic], spent a few days with Patrick and Wendy, then to Lydenburg, along the Johannesburg-Lourenço Marques road down and down through the citrus, banana, mango, avocado plantations into the subtropical warmth of the Lowveld at Nelspruit, then south

---

* Peter left South Africa in that year, when the police were after him for immorality. He was soon to marry Savathrey Naidu – outside the country, of course. Peter was a medic, became senior lecturer at Oxford University, later professor in Canada. Savi was a psychiatrist.

for a few miles to Barberton at the base of the hills into which we drove up incredibly precipitous roads to Piggs Peak in Swaziland and so back to Durban 2300 miles away. We never actually went into the Game Park, but it is just north of the LM road from Nelspruit. I seem to remember that the Lowveld area was fever-ridden in the first half of the 19th Century and that at least one party of Trekkers was all but wiped out by disease there. Then gold was discovered at Barberton itself and serious development of the area began. Now I think it's the railhead to Johannesburg for the asbestos which comes on that endless series of trays down the cableway from the Havelock mine at Piggs Peak perhaps 30 or 40 miles away. Bougainvillaea is the only other thing I can remember, bougainvillaea everywhere. Lots and lots of love from all of us. Peter.'

That was just the kind of letter we needed. We yearned to be able to place ourselves in a geographical context. We wanted to fit ourselves into the surrounding country. Thereby it would help to build up our sense of identity. The historical bits helped to relate us to the history of the area and to a wider South Africa.

I treasured these pieces of information the whole time I was at Barberton. They 'located' me, and this was terribly important in the context of our tremendous isolation and in a situation in which the authorities were on a deliberate campaign not simply to isolate us but, as an integral part of the treatment, to confuse and brainwash us. This was what the Brigadier called 'rehabilitation'. He said that before Barberton Prison was finished with us we would be good supporters of the South African government, or, failing that, we would at least not be active opponents of the government, as we had been in the past.

From this time, we all started reading our letters to each other and we began to build up a picture of the lives of people outside our little group, of the lives of Mollie's brother and mother on their farm in the Ficksburg district of the Orange Free State. I developed a sense of their personalities, of their likes and dislikes, of the sort of things that concerned them, of the farm on which they lived, of how the lucerne was growing. And we sympathised with them, identified with them during the terrible drought, and then later in 1966 when the floods came and their dam broke and flooded the lucerne fields.

Mollie Doyle.

We acquired a picture of people on the neighbouring farms, and the Andersons playing tennis on the weekends with neighbours who had diametrically opposed political views to their own but with whom they did not discuss politics. I built up a picture of the cinema in the local village, of people standing around in the streets in the hot Free State sun, of Ewald, Mollie's brother, big and strong and sunburnt, removing the stumps of willow trees after the trees had been burnt. Then there was the pergola, draped with wisteria on the veranda, the long walks across the lands with the two dogs, and so on.

Then there was Esther's family, her husband, Hymie, with a chronic disorder, who had stood trial with us in Johannesburg but had been discharged at the end of the trial, and her three daughters, one ten, one sixteen, and one eighteen. We came to know them as people we knew personally. We saw what they did in the evenings. We saw them going to the cinema with a boyfriend. There they were in the sun on Clifton beach in Cape Town. We understood the little one of ten, terrified of being left alone for one minute because her mother had suddenly disappeared out of her life to go far away to prison.

Earlier some of us had gone away alone into the cells to read our letters, to enjoy them all to ourselves. But, as we came more and more to consider the emotional needs of one another, we came to share our friends and relatives almost as though they were the friends and relatives of all of us. My friends, my brother are just as much yours as mine. In this way, not only did we share with each other and so give a little of ourselves in this unloving situation, but we enlarged our social circle, and our mental and emotional range. That little section at one end of the Barberton Female Prison began to house more than just the seven of us. We brought into our lives our own friends and relations and those of the others.

Flashbacks

ROUND ABOUT THIS TIME, in early 1966, I began particularly to notice symptoms in myself and in the others which were obviously developing as a result of our situation there. Fairly early on I began to have flashbacks. These are not just ordinary memories but they are a flash of some experience one has had in the past. The visual aspect is important, seems to be central, for the flash is rather like a quick look at a snapshot through a viewer, a click and the picture is gone. Very often I could not even remember a moment thereafter what the picture had been or even from what part of my life it came.

Often with this momentary visual experience, there were other sensations, also intensely experienced just for a moment. There was, for instance, an odour which came from the past or a sense of chill. Interesting is that the senses seemed to play an extremely important role. The pictures were often extremely detailed, details which in normal memory I could not possibly remember, if I could 'remember' the situation at all. Often I used to have one flash after the other, in a succession of five or ten. What was particularly interesting was that their succession was quite unrelated to any chronology. One flash would come from an experience of mine from way back in 1952, the next would be from 1965, the next from 1955, and yet another from 1948, and so on, one flash after the other, seemingly unrelated.

I started writing them down as they occurred so that I would have a record. Sometimes they followed each other fairly slowly, say five minutes between; on other occasions they followed each other so fast that I could not possibly have got them down. They were actual flashes, like flashes of light going through my head, disintegrating my mind, blocking out all impressions around me.

Sometimes I not only failed to discover any link between the flashbacks but also whether the first in a series was linked to something in my present experience. At other times I did find a link. In my diary for 28 February 1966 I have the following entry:

> *There is a nip in the air – Monday evening – a flashback of a short holiday at the Katberg Inn, then a flash of Cape Town, then ... I've forgotten ... with other thoughts between. Just flashes of places with a nip in the air. It is a very still evening. A slice of moon with a small fluffy grey cloud on the right. A dove now and again and another bird, heard often in Barberton, don't know what it is, and crickets. Quiet footsteps of the guard with the rifle. I've got to close the window before the big beetles come when all the light has gone out of the sky. A rectangle of sky with a cage. An occasional sound of a chair being shifted in another cell. Clank of a lid going down onto a sanitary bucket. Voices from a cell. The rumble of the lavatory in the big cell ... This is a very unusual mood. I am usually too tight, too bottled, too afraid to think about anything outside this window and sometimes even outside my cell.*

Some flashbacks kept coming back, again and again. One I kept on having and couldn't think what it related to. It was a flash of the inside of a large pigeon cage – it was so large that one could remain upright in it – belonging to some friends of ours who lived in Port Elizabeth in the same suburb of Mill Park. I was seven or eight years old. I only realised the significance of this once I was out of prison: there in my cell I was inside the cage.

I began to become much more self-conscious round about this time – I mean this in the psychological sense – and increasingly aware of my environment. I began to 'place' or 'locate' myself in the world more clearly and meaningfully, in terms of what I could see and hear from my cell or information contained in letters but also philosophically and historically and in terms of my place in the family unit. It is noteworthy that it was only in February 1966 that I started to keep some sort of diary. I was discovering my indentity again and taking steps to strengthen the process.

No doubt, too, it was a form of communication of what I was experiencing.

In about January we had started regular poetry classes on a Monday morning. The washing usually only turned up about 10 or 10.30 and, if we could, that is if Matron Bester did not come storming in to drive us to the basins, we did not start washing until the afternoon, and continued with the poetry discussion until exercise time. After a while we managed to pluck up sufficient courage to take a table and chairs into a corner of the courtyard and there we sat for one and half or two hours discussing usually a poem from the University of South Africa's English I syllabus. In this way we could assist those who were doing the course and at the same time have some kind of group activity in the framework of which we could exchange ideas. It was Ann who suggested having this class, and it was one that was still going at the time of my release over a year later.

There were some people who were keen on classes and some who were not. Prison produces a feeling of apathy in some, for, unless one struggles against it, it can be a pretty useless sort of life, and lack of love does tend to produce apathy. But some of us fought against this feeling, and, in doing so, went perhaps to the other extreme. We were determined to make our sentences a really worthwhile experience. We kept ourselves constantly busy and were determined that classes should be kept going.

Also round about this time we started an art class, with Ann as teacher, and Ann and I ensured that it should continue despite a certain lack of interest on the part of the others. When Leslie Schermbrucker came in August that year, she became one of the people who was particularly keen on the idea of classes.

The poems we studied knit themselves into the very texture of my life there. In general, I wished to widen not only my knowledge of history but my familiarity with literature of various kinds, not only poetry but also novels. A crucial aspect was that I was searching for a language which would express my ideas and view of things clearly and accurately. This was a really important concern of mine during my sentence. I grew interested in Chekhov, whom I thought had managed to say what he wanted to say in clear, simple language.

A key question was that of emphasis. I felt that the language and method of writing at our disposal, one word after the other, one sentence after the other, made it very difficult to put across a universal outlook, one which was organised around some central ideas, which was consistent within itself and where every aspect was related to every other, but where every aspect was not of equal weight. To make the whole problem more difficult where the main weight was located was always changing. Nothing was ever completely static. As it happens, though I seemed to be particularly concerned with accuracy of language, it appears to have been a part of our reaction to our situation, affecting the others, to one degree or another, too.

It was from about the time Sheila arrived that we, I think with one, possibly two exceptions, started having a look at what the situation was doing to us. At least this seemed to be reflected in that we started laughing at ourselves, sometimes parodying ourselves. One day Ann, Sheila and I were walking together around the courtyard trying to discuss the whole problem of accepting reduction of sentence. Unfortunately for us, Barnard was on duty and she, as I have noted, had extremely sharp ears. She stood there against the wall, looking as usual like the Bird of Prey. We discussed our problem as we walked but as soon as we came near to Barnard we would break into a mad conversation. This reflected in part what that place was doing to us, and ties up with the point I have made above about our almost obsessive concern with accuracy of expression but also our increasing capacity to laugh at ourselves.

As we got near to where Barnard was standing the 'innocent' conversation would start.

'How about Chekhov and the past tense?' I said in a clear voice. 'He always wants to use the past tense. He said "The cow *had* four legs"! Why is he so taken with the past tense? He should have said, "The cow 'had', 'has' and 'will have' four legs" ...'

As we got out of the hearing of the Bird of Prey we went back to the problem of reduction of sentence. And then round again until we came up to where Barnard was standing, and Sheila said, 'The problem is the verbs ...'

'Yes, but he could leave finite verbs out,' Ann interrupted. 'He could use the infinitive. The cow "to have" four legs ...'

concerned with the 1917 Revolution & 6 years thereafter.

(2) Some thoughts about Zhivago.   March 66
         → (from our newspaper) (by myself)
          The novel (is it really a novel?) consists of a
     series of situations which Pasternak creates to put
     across Zhivago's (i.e. Pasternak's) views. This
     method accounts, to a large extent, for the rather
     static, artificial & erratic nature of the plot & the
     static, artificial nature of the "characters." Pasternak
     remains the poet and the book's failures failings.
     Successes partly stem from this fact.
          Most of his characters are symbols, symbols
     portray Zhivago's views — note, the girl Sima,
     for instance. She is merely introduced to put across
     Zhivago's views on religion. She does not — even
     superficially — interact with Zhivago. One afternoon
     he is lying on a couch trying to sleep & Sima
     comes to visit Lara (Zhivago's mistress) & what
     Sima says is recorded as Zhivago lies & listens
     to what she has to say. Sima does not even
     interact with Lara. Lara just asks her to talk.
     Thus the scene is really just a monologue.
     Pasternak uses the monologue (or sometimes a dialogue)
     on several occasions;
     he surrounds the ideas with a few concrete
     images to make it all look real, but we are
     conscious that he is perpetrating a fraud on us.
     At one point he uses the diary method —
     perhaps the whole novel would be better as a diary.
     He also has a small section of notes on art which
     were, he says, found among Zhivago's papers.
what → Zhivago wrote has to say cast an interesting light
Pasternak's "The seemingly incongruous and arbitrary jumble
novel: of things & ideas in the work of the Symbolists (Blok
     Verhaeren, Whitman) is not a stylistic fancy. This

ABOVE: Article from our Barberton newspaper.

And so on, round and round the courtyard, two conversations going, one concerning a political problem and the other as a decoy but also a method of laughing at ourselves and at our predicament.

During this time, I became particularly interested in 'escape poetry' and escape techniques in literature in general. In our discussion I approached Andrew Marvel's 'The Garden' in this manner. I wrote an article on Zhivago along these lines, and I did an analysis of Wordworth's 'Tintern Abbey'.

It was in the earlier months when we were discussing poetry that I was so irrationally angered by what I regarded as escape poetry. It must have been related to the fact that I felt I had made a choice and that Kathy had made a choice in favour of dedicating ourselves to political change in South Africa, that we had rejected a nice cosy garden of love and accepted the arid suffering of prison. This sense had undoubtedly been much strengthened by my fabricated trial. I felt under attack as an individual, an attack which had to do with apartheid's denial of human rights, of my rights as a human being. I felt the unjustness of it all intensely.

I would become so upset while we were discussing poetry that I would almost choke. This must have been unpleasant for the others who could not have missed the tension. Moreover, Jean in particular completely rejected my concern with the question of how the particular pieces of poetry we were discussing reflected societal influences. She had studied under Geoff Durrant at the University of Natal, Pietermaritzburg, and he followed the Leavis school of literary criticism whose adherents considered that poetry should be considered for itself, separate from societal or historical factors.

Anyway, I was one pole and Jean the other and for quite a while at Barberton we had considerable differences on this. I presume that not only was Jean's position too rigid but mine also. I was trying to run away from my own suffering, exactly what I had been urging we should not do. Somewhere towards the middle of 1966, I think it was, I had overcome my vehemence when discussing love poems.

Three chameleons join the tortoise in captivity

ARNOLDUS, THE TORTOISE, HAD gradually become a part of our scene, and I had formed quite an important relationship with him. During our poetry discussions he used to come over to our table and wander in and out amongst our feet and the legs of the chairs and the table. He had ceased to pace the walls. It seems he had come to the conclusion that there was no way out … He was right.

I used to pick him up quite a lot and carry him around like a sandwich, as Ann described it. And I would put water in the little hollow in the centre of the drain in the courtyard so that he could drink. He began to get used to me and sometimes, when I was sitting on the grass, he would come haring over to me; now and then he would creep into the darkness and warmth under my uniform. I'd hold him up in the air, with four fingers of my right hand on the top of his shell, and my thumb underneath his body, and sometimes his legs would hang there relaxed, just slowly moving, and he began to stick his head out and look at me with his blue-black little jewel eyes.

At other times his back legs would kick and, with his front legs, he would try to prise open my hands so that he could free himself. This was what I called his ugly mood. It was only slowly that he got used to me and the rest of us and stopped pulling his head back nervously into his shell whenever one of us came near him or whenever he saw a movement close by. For food, he ate flowers and grass and the leaves of some plants.

Somewhere towards the beginning of that year, Matron Taljaard brought us three chameleons. She carried them in. One, I remember, was sitting on her arm, twig-feet clinging onto the top of her forearm, eyes swivelling suspiciously, or so it seemed to me. We had a large plant in a container on top of a locker, and Taljaard placed the chameleons there and they sat, merging with the greenery, two large ones, with mottled bloated cushion bodies, twig-feet clinging onto the stems, eyes swivelling, and one little one who was not as brightly coloured as the other two. The two big ones were deep green with orange and yellow and charcoal patches. The little one was more uniform in colour, grey-brown, with a firmer body, and not such swivelling suspicious eyes.

We prisoners neared the locker to have a look. I went up but not too close because they looked rather terrifying. If one of us came up too close or put a hand out the chameleon's head would turn slowly and its mouth would open wide, in a hideous manner, and make a frightening hissing noise, rather like a snake spitting, only there was no 'spit'. They were on an island there for there was no plant life around them, just this one plant on top of a locker, and down below grey shiny slippery cold concrete.

Gradually we became a little more used to these creatures. I had never seen such huge chameleons in my life or such highly coloured exotic ones. I had not known they existed. When Taljaard first brought them in, I had asked with horror, 'What on earth are these?' I thought they must be some strange tropical animal. They looked as though they came from a prehistoric past. The little one was more like the kind of chameleon I had been used to, little grey-brown things running over rocks in our garden when I was a child, looking rather like lizards but with the peculiar swivelling eyes.

I would never pick up these new inhabitants in our space, although I did run the tips of my fingers along their cushiony rough-textured bellies just to see what they felt like. Then the mouth would open with the hissing noise and with the eyes swivelling and I would back away.

Jean was one of the first of us to pick up one of the large ones. She was always good with animals there. She was also one of the first to pick up the frogs. But once the chameleon was on her arm and clinging there, a twig-toe of one foot lying on the top of her forearm, the other twig-toe of the same foot clinging to the side of her forearm, and the other legs in various positions, she tried to gently pull the creature off her arm just to test that she could get it off. No, it clung tenaciously to her arm, eyes swivelling and mouth beginning to open to hiss.

I saw the panic rising in Jean's eyes. She tried to suppress her rising fear and pulled at the chameleon's body more firmly, her fingers making indentations in the cushion-sides of its belly. Then she pulled more insistently and managed to disengage its front legs, and then prised away with her fingers at the back legs, and then it was free. Then with shaking control she placed the chameleon back on the plant.

The two large ones had such fat bellies we wondered whether they were pregnant. Taljaard said maybe they were. We christened them Schleswig and Holstein but often referred to Schleswig as Paranoia because of its swivelling suspicious eyes and its nervousness of us. Paranoia used to hiss a lot.

The day after Taljaard brought them in we decided to move them from their plant on top of the locker and put them in the courtyard. We felt sorry for them because their space was so confined on that plant, and there was no bridge of greenery to take them across the concrete to the courtyard. As it turned out, that was no answer for they were very unhappy in our courtyard. Once there they stretched their fat bellies into something rather long and elegant, stretched their legs, using their twig-toes very elegantly to grip onto the white concrete, and paced the courtyard walls. Paced and paced. Round and round, swivelling their eyes and looking ever more despairing.

We came to the conclusion that they were desperate to get onto something that had some height for weren't they climbing creatures? Their twig-like feet looked as though they were meant for climbing. We placed our broom in the corner of the courtyard near to the boiler room and one of them – was it Holstein or Paranoia? – used to climb up the handle. It climbed and climbed and then put a leg out, with the twig-toe beginning to curve to grasp onto something ... and there was nothing. That was as high as the broom handle went. So then there was the problem of twisting round, carefully adjusting the feet, so that it could come down the handle again. Once down, it would get back onto the rough concrete, baking white in the sun, stretch its body gracefully and start pacing the walls once more.

This pacing underlined our own captivity as prisoners. At the same time, it was good to have new life around us, new personalities. Moreover, observation in gaol of animal life is a great relief for a prisoner. I found I could lose myself completely in the act of observation. I forgot the burden of those walls pressing in on me and lying heavy on my back when I crouched down in the courtyard and watched every single movement of an animal. But the animals were unhappy and we felt that it was bad enough being prisoners without imprisoning other creatures.

As it happened, the chameleons' pacing reminded me of my first detention under the 90-day law. At that time I had found my captivity for 23 hours a day in a cell 6 feet by 9 feet particularly painful in the face of the panic building up in me as I sought to deal with the Security Branch's threat that they were going to hang Kathy. One day when the Matron-in-Charge, Matron Britz, brought me back to my cell, a small black cat with a white patch on its neck and little white paws slipped into my cell. As Matron Britz turned to close the door and the key began to turn in the lock, the cat pushed against the door and, finding it could not get out, began to meow loudly and persistently, throwing itself against the door.

I began to feel the hysteria breaking from my control and I cried out, 'Matron Britz! Matron Britz! The cat's in here. Please take it out!'

Matron Britz opened the door of my cell and, with a smug and frighteningly sadistic look, understanding perfectly how I felt, said in her whining voice, 'Wat makeer, Neame, wil jy nie met die kat speel nie?' What's wrong, Neame? Don't you want to play with the cat? And I said, 'No. It doesn't like it in here. It will just scream. You had better take it out.' 'Ag nee, Neame,' whined Britz in her high hypocritical lilting voice. 'Ek het gedink jy wil met die kat speel.' I thought you wanted to play with the cat.

With that she opened the door and the cat vanished like lightning, thinning itself out like a sausage to get through the small crack as quickly as possible. As Britz closed the door and I heard the key turn in the lock, I worried that she had seen my weakness and would tell my interrogators.

The chameleons showed us that they were unhappy not only by pacing the walls of our courtyard but by the change in their physical appearance. After a few days their fat-bellied look completely disappeared. Their bodies thinned out and lost their cushiony appearance, their skin hanging loosely. And they began to walk very slowly. Their eyes developed a strange dead hopeless look. Instead of swivelling suspiciously they became droopy and almost immobile. We tried to help them by carrying them around and letting them climb up our arms or by putting them in the canna which was the highest plant in the courtyard.

A few months before I had asked Taljaard if we could have an azalea bush and a frangipani to plant in the flower bed. She had said No, we would use them to climb out of the courtyard and escape! I don't know whether she was joking. She looked quite serious. An azalea bush or a frangipani could never grow to a height where they could assist us in an escape. At least I did not think so.

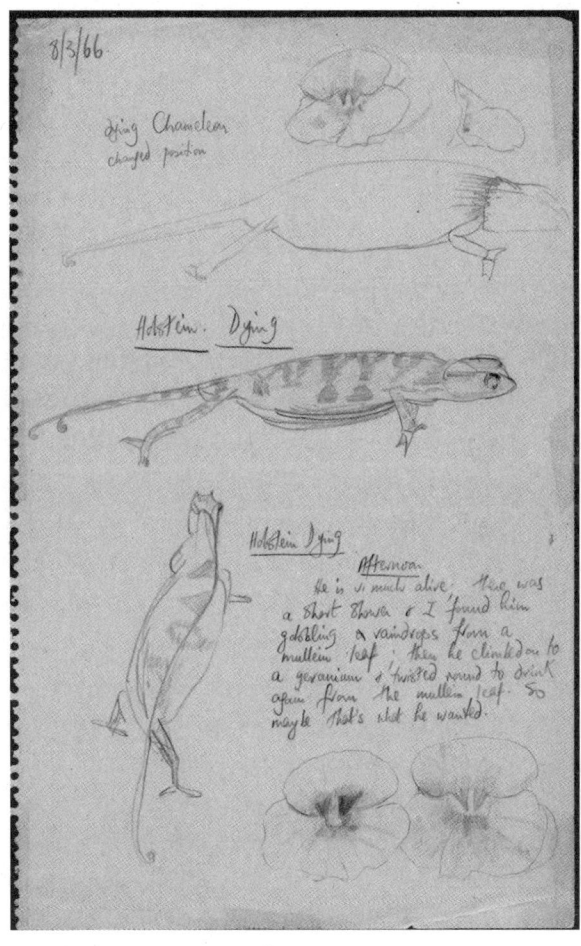

There was really very little plant life in the courtyard. There was an unhappy-looking elephant-ear, two cannas, some geraniums, a mullein and very little else, and they did not seem to have much life. We tried to make the two large chameleons enjoy what there was but they were having none of it. Paranoia began to look so ill we were frightened it would die in our courtyard. That we did not want. We asked a wardress to take it out and put it in the outside world where, we thought, it would probably perk up, once there were trees and all sorts of exciting plants.

A few days later the other large chameleon – Holstein – began to look really ill and eventually lay down on the concrete on the side of the courtyard near the store. When I went to feel its body, it did not even bother to move or hiss. It had just given up and lost all fight. And it had probably decided, I thought, that it could not get away from these large blue-uniformed creatures anyway because there were no trees and so little space. There were just four walls and two unsatisfactory cannas.

As a last resort and feeling that I had to try everything for Holstein was now, I concluded, too sick to be put out, I put it in the canna and poured water onto the plant. At first the water dropped down onto its limp body without causing any response. Later I went to have a look at it and it was drinking the little droplets that had got caught in the plant's leaves; and later I observed that its body was firm again and its eyes were no longer completely hopeless. However, the whole process started again a day or two later. And it died. We found Holstein lying limp on the concrete. We put it in the ash bucket the following morning and the dead body was taken out of our section.

I used to try and shape the courtyard in my mind as something romantic, a place strange and exciting, and I was surprised when Ann once described it in this way in a rather humorous and slightly cynical moment: 'Grass, geranium trees, animals, like Arnoldus, stalking in the courtyard.' Much later I did a large picture of the courtyard for an art exhibition we organised. My picture reflected a fairyland attitude to it, plants against a red background. The background had to be red, a bright red.

I did this picture at a time when the drought had broken and the courtyard was looking a little less arid, but in fact it never developed into anything remotely lush. We did try, Mollie especially, to make something out of 'the garden'. It was a strip of about a foot and a half across, on all four sides of the central grass patch where the washing lines were. On the other side of the beds, on all four sides, were the concrete slabs on which we walked, up to the walls of the courtyard. All in all, the courtyard was about 20 of my walking paces one way, 21 the other.

One chameleon did survive, the small one, which Jean had named Hegel. Hegel was her particular chum. In fact, it flourished. It was a very friendly creature. We used to carry it around a lot, especially Jean. It would sit on her hand, clinging to her thumb. It seemed to like the warmth. And we used often, too, to put it in the courtyard, where it would sit on the geranium and blend with the plant so effectively that we could not easily find it. Sometimes it would sit in the grass, which was rather risky because we could easily have tramped on it. Ann wrote a little poem about Hegel on a card, marking Pesach, the Jewish Passover festival, which Esther sent to her youngest. On the front of the card was a little drawing of Hegel. The verses went like this:

> 'Our friend Hegel's hard to beat,
> Although he has such funny feet
> And with his twirly eyes
> He sneaks and peeps and spies
> at us; always on his guard.
>
> 'And though his body's cold and hard
> And sometimes flecked and sometimes plain,
> Sometimes striped with coloured rain
> As if it's left a streaky stain,
>
> 'And though he puffs his pleated jaw
> When he gets cross and digs his claw
> Like any old chameleon –
> Oh yes, I know he's not so hot –
> But, my dear, he's all I've got.

'And till I'm back again with you
I've got nothing else to do
But lavish all my love on him,
That silly old chameleon!'
26/3/66

Other than Arnoldus, Hegel was the only animal at this time that appeared capable of surviving the prison experience. Another animal we had with us at one time was a rabbit. It had been brought in by Matron Bester and had been absolutely desperate, throwing itself a great deal of the time against the various walls. That had not prevented Matron Bester bringing us a second, bigger rabbit. A similar situation developed, with the animal throwing itself against the walls. Sometimes at night it would come into my tiny cell and proceed to throw itself against the walls there. I wanted to have it put out as I not only considered it unfair to keep it captive but it was also likely to die there – in our space. Ann, with what I thought a child-like response, objected.

As for the chameleon, Hegel, it disappeared one day, much to our disappointment. Was it on the orders of Matron Bester who, I asked myself, might take a sadistic pleasure in noting our suffering when our various animal friends died rather than wanting to give us a companion, as some of us believed? Or was it instructions from above where there was apparently an increasing interest in our psychological condition? More likely was that it was on the instructions of the Brigadier who had undoubtedly noted the pain, communicated in some of our letters, at the death of one of our friends. At any rate, it was clear that Hegel was not playing a role in the framework of the psychological warfare of the authorities.

My appeal: the authorities play cat-and-mouse with me

It was sometime in February 1966, I think, that I had moved from the big courtyard cell to the middle single cell. We all, at one time or another, had to take our turn in there. This was the worst cell of all because it had no side window and the other windows, other than the frosted part, were covered with white paint. In other words, it had no clear pane at the top as did the other two single cells. The authorities must have decided before our arrival that this was to be our punishment cell. It was rather dark during the day and altogether more claustrophobic than the other cells. Sheila moved over to the front big cell, sharing it with Jean.

Round about this time, I was expecting my appeal to come up. By the end of February, over seven months had already passed by since the date I was sentenced in my Humansdorp trial. Although, as I have mentioned, in the first months of 1966 I was beginning apparently to recover a stronger sense of identity, it was, at the same time, a peculiarly unhappy time for me. Indeed, did my beginning a prison diary at this time not reflect an intense sense of loneliness?

My state of mind had partly, I think, to do with the fact that I had had seven months of Barberton Maximum Security Prison and was beginning to be very much affected by it. There was also the authorities' continued determination to break me and to use me as an example in order to intimidate my fellow prisoners. One of the problems that seriously complicated my life was the question of possible reduction of sentence for some prisoners and how this prospect was affecting the responses of some of my comrades.

However much on the surface of things my appeal did not make much difference to me since I thought that, even if I did win it, the authorities would find some other means to keep me beyond my two years, it was definitely there, hanging over me. It was, above all, my sense of the unjustness of the four extra years that so upset me.

ABOVE: Prison diary written on tissue paper.

My appeal: the authorities play cat-and-mouse with me

On Friday, 1 April, I went through to the Brigadier for Complaints and Requests and asked him whether anything had been heard of my appeal. I had determined not to ask him because of his unpleasantness in the past when I had told him I was innocent, and he had answered, with a sneer, 'That's *your* story, of course.' But I wanted to know very much. He drew himself up importantly, smiling smugly at me. 'Yes, Neame, I did hear something about it, I think.'

'What did you hear, Brigadier?' I asked.

'I don't think I can tell you that, Neame.'

'Why can't you tell me, Brigadier?'

'Well,' he said, smiling benignly at me. He was really enjoying himself, cat playing with mouse. 'I'm not sure what I heard.'

'Heard, Brigadier?'

'Well, yesterday, Neame, I think I heard something on the radio.'

'What did you hear, Brigadier?'

'Well, you know, Neame, it was my lunchtime, and my wife was waiting for me – you know what it is, and my son wanted to listen to another programme ...'

'Yes, Brigadier ...?'

'Well, Neame, I am not absolutely sure what I heard.' He was delighted. Everything was going very well. He was on top. He was the boss. At the same time, he felt, his manner was kind and that was, indeed, satisfactory. All in all wasn't he proving himself to be rather clever?

'Surely you have some idea, Brigadier. Did I win my appeal or not?'

'I can't tell you that, Neame. You know what it is. My wife was waiting for me at the table, and my son wanted to listen to another programme.'

'But can't you find out, Brigadier?' I insisted, my tone becoming just a little bit desperate although I still managed to maintain the atmosphere of smiling friendliness.

'I did hear something, Neame, but I may have been wrong. I have my opinion of what the outcome of your appeal was but I cannot tell you because I may have made a mistake.' His tone was deliberately becoming more businesslike.

Then he added, winningly, leaning forward across his desk towards me, 'And you wouldn't like to be told the wrong thing, would you?'

I did not answer.

'What do *you* think the outcome is?' he continued.

'I think I must have won my appeal because I am innocent,' I responded. 'Can't you find out from Pretoria?'

The Brigadier just sat there smiling and smug, watching his mouse. Then his voice became deep, resonant, matter of fact: 'Yes, Neame, Head Office in Pretoria will let me know in due course, and then I will certainly let you know the outcome.' His intonation was self-conscious, and he lifted himself, twisting his fat body slightly to the side, and then leant over his desk confidentially. 'When Head Office lets me know, I shall tell you immediately. Immediately, Neame.' And he leant back in his chair, looking at me with a kindly expression. 'I do not want to make a mistake,' he added. 'When I am informed officially by Head Office, then I shall let you know immediately.'

'When do you think they will let you know, Brigadier?' I asked.

'That I can't tell you, Neame. But Head Office will let me know in due course.'

'Thank you, Brigadier,' I said quietly, and I turned and walked out of the office and down the passage. Matron Bester locked me up in my cell. The others were already locked up as I had been the last to go for Complaints and Requests. Matron Bester went out, locking the central grille behind her and closing the door into our section.

'Any news of your appeal?' somebody asked.

'Yes, it's out,' I said, 'but he won't tell me.' I was struggling against my tears.

'What do you mean, he won't tell you?'

'He said he heard it over the news yesterday at lunchtime, but he won't tell me.'

'The swine!'

'He says he might make a mistake. He must wait for official notice from Head Office.'

'But that is nonsense,' Mollie whispered across the portaal. 'We were always told immediately it came over the news. When I was in gaol at Pietersburg, and our appeal came over the news, they let us know immediately. In fact, most prisoners can hear it over the radio themselves, if it comes over on the news.'

'Well, he won't tell me.'

'He's just trying to be nasty,' somebody commented.

'Yes. Yes,' I agreed.

'But what sort of impression did he give? Do you think you may have won it?' somebody asked.

'I don't know. I'm not sure. Yes, from his attitude I think I've won it … because he didn't tell me that that was "my story" when I told him I thought I must have won my appeal since I am innocent. But still, maybe I've just had the sentence reduced. And, anyway, maybe I've lost it.'

Nobody said anything more. The faces I could see behind the bars of the grilles just looked sympathetically miserable.

During the afternoon I tried to find out from the wardress on duty. In addition I enquired from any wardress who appeared at our central grille whether she had heard anything about my appeal. They all said they knew nothing about it. In fact, most of them did not seem to know I had an appeal.

I found it very difficult to work that night. I decided to try and forget about my appeal. After all, I had already waited over eight months, what did a few days more matter? But I was really desperate to hear, not so much because of the four years but because I was determined that these people should be exposed. I hoped beyond hope that, if I had won my appeal, that the judges had commented on the sinister aspects of the state case. They could not avoid doing so, for the defence had on many occasions drawn the attention of the court to these aspects. And even if they didn't let me off, they couldn't avoid making some comment in this connection.

As it happened, I had received a letter from Graham on 26 March: 'Dear Sylvia, I'm sorry this may be a little later than you had hoped. I thought the judgment might be handed down within a day or two. But it now appears that it will definitely not be given before Friday 1st and possibly later. I expect this makes sense given the length of the record – 14 volumes of it, I think, which I now have. The proceedings on Monday were fairly short. It was over by lunchtime, largely because the Attorney-General did not have very much to say. I thought Counsel* 'brilliant',

---

* Counsel to whom Graham refers was Advocate Harold Hanson QC.

and I was on the verge of tears most of the morning, as you can imagine I emerged from it all very hopeful, but don't let's count any chickens etc., etc. Just sit tight and wait. I expect you ought to get word well before I see you (my visit is arranged and confirmed for April 12th – the Tuesday after Easter), in fact perhaps before this reaches you, as letters seem to take a fair time to get in …'

The day after I had spoken to the Brigadier, however much I tried to leave the matter aside, my mind turned over and over on the question of my appeal. There was news of it in newspapers and on the radio but we had no access to information in the media. We did not know what was happening in Vietnam, what was happening with the Labour government in Britain, what was happening in China, Africa and in our very own South Africa. We knew nothing about what was going on in the art world, in literature, in music, in the field of fashion. And now I did not even know what had happened with respect to my own life here and now, behind these bars.

A new phase in our washing duties

THE MORNING AFTER I HAD spoken to the Brigadier proceeded very much as usual. It was a Saturday morning. We had finished with the prisoners' clothing by the end of Friday afternoon. At the beginning in Barberton, we used to wash on Saturday morning as well, and on Saturday afternoon we would do our own washing, our bedclothing, uniforms, underclothing and we ironed them on Sunday – a Day of Rest usually in gaols, but not for us. But gradually they allowed us to get away with not doing any of the outside washing on Saturday. We finished up with this on Friday afternoon, and then did our own washing on Saturday morning.

As it happened, we never established this as a 'right' with the Front. We managed, in this respect as in some others, to improve our conditions somewhat by simply changing our routine gradually, cutting down on the amount of washing we did, diminishing our working hours just a little bit one day and a little more the next. We even organised a conspiratorial go-slow early on. And it worked. But the problem with doing things this way and not establishing our 'rights' was that when the authorities felt like being nasty, when they felt, for one reason or another, that they wanted to put the screws on, we would just suddenly get more washing, and there was not much we could say.

Initially we would usually do the extra work, without a word. But we were a stubborn set of people and we had learned the hard way. They had taught us how to deal with them. And so as time went on, without a word, we would go-slow or try some other technique. The Front would realise that something was happening but found it difficult to put a finger on it and, before they knew where they were, we prisoners had gained what we had set out to achieve. Then for some months the drift would proceed, with our doing less and less washing, until the authorities decided to put the squeeze on because we had annoyed them for some reason, perhaps complained to a judge or to the Prison Board. The same process would start once more.

Yet, as regards the washing, the authorities did not have much of a leg to stand on for certainly, according to their own regulations, we should not have been washing. It was about this time that the Front started sending us in the white warders' sheets, pillowslips and bedcovers to wash. We still did a bit of the black prisoners' washing but just a token amount. I'm sure the Front felt that this was a great concession for us, in other words, to do the washing of whites rather than of blacks. The prisoners' clothing was certainly tough to wash but, at least, however unpleasant it was to live and eat with the stench of sweat and blood and sulphur ointment, it was better than living and eating with the stale smell of extremely dirty bedclothes.

Most of this new round of washing was from the white warders who worked in the farm gaol, down in the valley, a couple of miles from us. From the state of these warders' bedclothes, it appeared that they lived and ate in their beds, and defecated there too. Their sheets were stained with urine, faeces, night emissions, snot – it seemed they used their sheets to blow their noses on – blood and pus, and a great variety of foods. And their pillowslips were literally black with the dirt and grease of their hair. Moreover, it was quite clear from the clay marks at one end of the sheets that many warders got into bed with their boots on.

After a few days, we decided to complain to the authorities. Matron Bester said she would tell the Brigadier about it. We asked her to come and have an inspection 'in loco' but she chose, wisely, I think, to refrain. Another disgusting aspect of the whole business was that we had to wash the dishes we ate from in the same basin. After our complaint, there was no improvement. So we complained again, this time to the Brigadier, and he said he would speak to the warders concerned about the issue. But again there was no improvement so, when a sheet was sent in that was particularly disgusting, we refused to wash it and sent it out of our section.

A new phase in our washing duties

With sheets, bedcovers and pillowslips, we had to learn a new technique of washing. It was extremely difficult to wash such large articles in such a confined space. It was difficult enough, standing elbow to elbow, to wash at all but with sheets and bedcovers, it was well-nigh impossible. All of us developed our own particular techniques. I folded my sheet into four and placed it in the basin, making sure that the water was low in the basin, otherwise it would splash all over the floor, over me, and over the person on the basin next to me. I would then soap one side of this exposed quarter of the sheet, then turn it over and do the other, then unfold it once, exposing the two other quarters, and then rub away at them.

The result was that I washed only one side of the sheet or bedcover. However, I used a great deal of soap – my basin was always filled with white soapy suds, the envy of my friends on the other basins – and, once the sheet was hung up on a washing line in the courtyard, it whitened marvellously in the sun.

It was hard work, particularly as it was so hot. Round about March–April the sun was in a particularly bad position for us. It used to beat down on our necks and backs through the high windows a few feet behind us. It would burn into us. This made the Barberton subtropical heat even more difficult to bear. And during lock-ups at this time of the year, particularly lunchtime lock-up in the north-facing cells, in fact all the cells, except for one, the sun would beat down on our backs as we tried to study at our tables, and fall onto the pages of our books, almost blinding us.

I win my appeal

MY APPEAL WAS CONSTANTLY on my mind. During lunch the Saturday morning after my exchange with the Brigadier a wardress came to our central grille and handed me a telegram. It was from my uncle and aunt in Johannesburg, Bunny (JR) and Betty Neame, and ran like this: 'Wonderful news, Many congratulations.' It was almost certainly because Bunny was a journalist, and that on the *Rand Daily Mail*, which had shown an interest in prison conditions and had run the Harold Strachan exposures, that I was allowed to have the telegram. I doubt very much that the Front would have given it to me otherwise.

I read it to the others. 'I wonder what this means?' I asked. 'Does it mean that I have won my appeal or does it just mean my sentence has been reduced?' The others would not commit themselves because they felt they did not want to raise false hopes. I sobbed, 'I'll never forgive them for all they have made me go through.' Esther cried, too, because of my frustration at not knowing the outcome of my appeal.

Luckily I had arranged that my lawyer in Johannesburg should let me know as soon as possible about the outcome of my appeal because I had feared that the authorities would try something like this. That Saturday afternoon I received a communication from Ruth Hayman, stating that my sentence had been set aside and my appeal upheld. The authorities could hardly refuse to give me information of this sort from my lawyer.

I think it was about six weeks later that I was called through to the Front. The Brigadier, with great pomposity and self-righteousness, told me that Head Office had informed him that I had won my appeal against my four-year sentence, and he congratulated me.

I win my appeal

On the Sunday, following the communication from Ruth Hayman, I wrote in my diary:

> *'I suppose it is a relief though I still have the feeling that my sentence is endless, i.e. that I won't get out anyway when my two years is up. The Brigadier is looking somewhat down in the mouth. I think he must find it a bit confusing after Aucamp's portrait of me as a troublemaker. I'm looking forward to hearing the judgement. Graham comes on the 12th and will, no doubt, have news for me.*

Graham did come on the 12th and he told me that it was a 'muted judgment'. It said nothing about the sinister aspects of the state case and there was no criticism of the police. I was very disappointed. He told me that the appeal had got a great deal of publicity, the whole of the front page of the *Evening Post* and front page headlines in other papers; and later I heard in a letter that the *Rand Daily Mail* had written a leading article on it, pointing out that, without the defence provided by the Defence and Aid Fund, which had just been banned, I would most likely not have got off.* I heard also that the magistrate in Humansdorp had made a vicious attack on Defence and Aid, just before its banning. A fine upstanding magistrate!

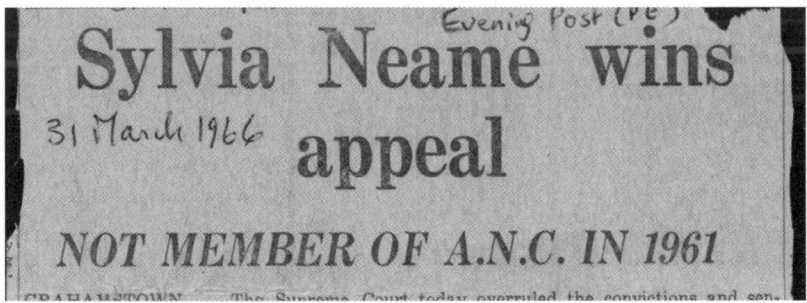

After my release I spoke to David Soggot concerning my disappointment about the fact that counsel had not underlined the

---

* As it happened, the Defence and Aid Fund had not paid for my case. My brother, Peter, did so. The full amount was later – after my release – paid back to him by International Defence & Aid, based in London.

fact that the state case was shot through with indications that it was a fabricated case and he then admitted that he had possibly made a mistake. His caution, together apparently with a similar caution amongst other members of the legal fraternity, was probably a reflection of the extent to which the viciousness of the apartheid regime at this time had tended to put the opposition on the defensive. I had hoped, indeed expected, that my case would point to what was happening in the eastern Cape.

One morning we found the rabbit dead in the boiler room, with a puddle of urine next to him. We sent him out in the ash bucket. My comment in my diary was: *'What else can we expect in this place?'*

SOUTH AFRICAN TRIALS from MARY BENSON

Mystery of the State witnesses

[1965]

PORT ELIZABETH, July 24

MISS SYLVIA NEAME, a 27-year-old teacher, has been sentenced to four years' imprisonment after being convicted of belonging to the African National Congress and of having attended meetings where plans of violence are alleged to have been discussed.

Miss Neame is the only white person who has figured in the trials of about 900 people which are proceeding in a number of towns and villages in the Eastern Cape Province.

She was a student and a member of the Liberal Party when the shootings occurred at Sharpeville in 1961. The impact of this event led to her participating in "sit-ins" against colour-bar restaurants.

Miss Neame's case is significant not because she is white, but because of the methods which the police have used to secure her conviction. Her counsel, Mr David Soggot, referred to "some of the most extraordinary evidence ever placed before a court."

'Nothing to explain it'

His complaint relates to the manner in which the police are building up evidence to secure the conviction of hundreds of people in obscure courts in dozens of little villages, like Humansdorp, where Sylvia Neame stood trial for weeks before she was finally convicted. She had been awaiting trial for several months.

The police seem to be relying on witnesses who appear regularly in one case after another. One of the witnesses in the Neame trial has already testified against 60 people.

The case against Miss Neame rested on the evidence of four State wit-

Letting off steam

ABOUT THIS TIME I HAD a bad time dealing with feelings of aggression. It had been a problem all the time really while I had been at Barberton, particularly when the wardresses were on a deliberate campaign of provocation. This is a problem I have already dealt with. But during the period while I was waiting for the outcome of my appeal, my aggression got really bad.

I had had to deal with it at various times before I came to Barberton. It had plagued me during my first 90-day detention in Pretoria Central. There I was locked up in my cell 23 hours a day, a cell in which there was very little space to move, and with very little to do, except read the Bible and play patience with a pack of cards I had made out of cardboard from various boxes. I had had to be very careful to keep these well hidden from the authorities.

And I was fighting with the possibility of Kathy's hanging. I had not been feeling particularly well before my arrest on 17 October 1963, as the Branch well knew. There had been a series of events from the second half of 1962 which had affected my health.

And then out of the blue, one day, on 11 July 1963, I was walking along Kotze Street in Hillbrow, Johannesburg, after having bought some meat and vegetables to deliver to Kathy at his hide-out in Mountain View, just off Louis Botha Avenue. At about 11 o'clock on a lovely blue-skied morning, I looked down at a pile of newspapers lying on the pavement at the corner of a street, next to a newspaper vendor. On a front page I saw Walter Sisulu's photograph. I grabbed a paper and found that it was a special issue, giving the news of the arrest of several men at a place in Rivonia. I glanced quickly through the names of those arrested and read, quite far down, 'Among those arrested was a Johannesburg Indian, Ahmed Kathrada.'

The blue-skied morning fell like a dark cloud on my head. The people in the street turned suddenly into static forms, only I was moving, rushing forward, away, trying to prevent the people around me seeing my tears. I thought, If they see me crying, they may connect me with these people. As it happened, I had the previous evening taken Kathy from his Mountain View hide-out to the Liliesleaf Farm in Rivonia. I did not go into any of the buildings. I had merely parked my car near a kind of outhouse, close to the entrance I used, as I had done on several occasions in the past. Now I drove down to Market Street in the centre of town to flat 13 Kholvad House, Kathy's flat. There I found some of my Indian friends. Without a word, I handed over the meat and vegetables to Tommy Vassen and sat down and wept. They already had news of the arrests.

During my first detention when I was in that cell in Pretoria Central I was taken for one hour a day, usually from about 12 to 1 pm, from my cell up in that hall, past the condemned cell, down the concrete steps with the black metal handrail, through a door and along a bit of slate paving, through a corrugated-iron gate into the courtyard of the white prisoners. A courtyard for the black prisoners was on the other side of a high red-painted corrugated-iron fence, which ran along one side of the exercise yard I was in.

While I exercised the wardress who escorted me never left me for one moment alone and she watched my every movement. I remember so clearly what she looked like. She was new, still in mufti for she had not yet been given a uniform. She had red hair and a milky white complexion. Young, very young, and I guess she meant me no harm. But the way she watched me constantly and her presence on the bench in the yard, there behind my back, drove me into a frenzy.

I used to talk to myself, to her, in fact, but not allowing her to hear what I said. 'I will hit you if you don't stop watching me there behind me. Don't you know that I only have an hour out of my cell, and I want this hour, I need it to try and relax, to try and forget for a moment where I am, to try and forget that rope which is going to hang Kathy.' And I started picking up little bits of gravel, and trying to find small stones, so that I could fling them against the metal bins that stood on one side of the exercise yard next to the steps that led up to the closed door of the laundry. I loved to hear the tremendous clang as the stones hit the bin. I tried to find bigger pieces to make an even louder noise. And as I flung the stone I muttered to myself: 'If you know how I hate you there behind me watching ... Can't you leave me alone?' And back in my cell, I used to think of all the terrible things I would like to do to the police ...

Down in Port Elizabeth in the North End Prison after some weeks of isolation, I would note that my aggression was mounting. The Major (Symington) attempted to find as many charges as he could against me as well as working me physically to the bone with cleaning not only my own relatively large cell but two other cells, a bathroom unit, the large passage outside as well as the courtyard, all this before he came mid-morning on his round. And when he was there he would run his finger along the narrow ledge somewhere in the middle of the wall down the long passage to check whether I had removed the dust.

With the aim of countering my aggression I would walk up and down in my little red linoleum-floored inside passage, tramping up and down, singing freedom songs as loud as I could. And I would go into the bathroom and shout long speeches out of the window towards where I imagined the administrative block was, towards the Major over there, whom I hated. I told him what a ghastly man he was, how cruel, what a brute. And I could see the hatred in his eyes when he looked at me, and yet, I said, in real platform tones, imagining myself shouting across a huge square, 'You are not in gaol. You are not locked up alone in a small section 23 hours a day, and one hour alone in a courtyard. And yet you hate. You are not facing a trial every day which has been fabricated against you. You don't have to listen to a string of lies every day in court, day after day, week after week, and you can say nothing. And yet you hate. Everything that is happening to me, leads me to hate and yet I try not to. I try to understand what makes you people what you are. I have a right to hate. But it is you who do the worst of the hating …' And so on. I used to try and let off steam that way.

This business of being watched all the time, it does terrible things to one's system. We were watched continually the first few months at Barberton, my comrades for 7 or 8 months non-stop, me for 4 or 5 months. To have eyes watching your every movement, listening to every single thing you say is a peculiar experience. It means you can never, for one moment, let go. This is partly because when anyone is being watched intently and by someone who is not a friend, and is, in fact, hostile, it is simply not possible to forget that one is being watched. Moreover, we had to be terribly careful not to make any security slip, not only as regarded politics in the wider world but also about the way we organised our lives there in our section. This response to being watched has, no doubt, something to do, too, with our animal past, like our response to captivity. The stare from another animal is usually a prelude to an attack.

During March–April 1966 when I had to face the extra burden of waiting for my appeal and after two years of tremendous strain when I had had to exercise enormous control over myself, the anger in me built up to an almost intolerable degree. One of the unbearable things was that the outlets I had, either emotional or recreational, were so limited. And I was getting a constant hammering from the authorities.

It was a very painful business dealing with that aggression. I tried to get it under control by washing in a frenzied manner and walking round the courtyard as fast as I could. Generally, too, I sought to find outlets, some kind of creative activity, such as our poetry discussions, drawing, animal observation. I tried to channel it as much as I could. I started suffering from a kind of hyperactivity. My heart started beating at a tremendous pace so that, amongst other things, I found great difficulty sleeping. I take it that my thyroid was playing up as a result of the strain I had been under as well as months at a time of hardly eating.

We meet the Rev. Canon Langley

GAOL IS MADE ARID BY ALL kinds of deprivation: deprivation of love, of colour, of exciting food flavours, of sounds, such as music, and, more fundamentally, of space. And I suppose also a sense of time.

Barberton Prison was peculiarly devoid of atmosphere. It was hygienic, with shining grey concrete floors, clean walls, no graffiti. All the cells, except for the front big cell next to our entrance grille, had walls that were part light green, part cream. The portaal was in the same colour. The front big cell was partly painted in rather a cold blue and part cream. The bars of our grilles were painted grey, the bars of our windows cream.

As a child I had imagined gaols to be like the dark medieval dungeons I had read about and seen in pictures: nothing in the cell, except a slab of stone on which the prisoner slept, no table, no bed with sheets and a bedcover, as we had at Barberton. Perhaps one small window, high up in the concrete, unpainted wall, giving very little light. And a dark grey concrete floor. True, the police cells I had been in were something like this.

I remember how surprised I was when I first saw the white female cells at the Fort, beds with pink bedcovers and shiny polished concrete floors and large sash windows at eye level; and grass and flowers in a small area between two cell sections. In fact I was amazed. I had never thought that gaol looked like this. The Fort as a whole, however, did look like a gaol. There was a high red-brick wall right round the buildings inside, and there was definitely a gaol atmosphere because of the attitudes of the Lieutenant and the wardresses. There was, of course, also a large number of black prisoners, who existed in rather different conditions, certainly no beds with or without pink bedcovers.

Barberton was even less like the kind of gaol I had had in my mind. In a way, it was much better but in a way it was worse. A dark dungeon definitely has an atmosphere, something tangible. There is a suffering there that one cannot miss, one can grasp it visually. In Barberton the suffering was not so obvious. I remember trying to look at our section objectively, as an outsider, as somebody who had never been in a police cell or prison before. For a gaol, it did not look unpleasant. The suffering it evoked was insidious.

It was with this kind of consideration in mind that I was particularly interested in the reactions of the Rev. Canon Langley, the Anglican priest. We had had quite a struggle getting a priest to visit us. When my comrades had first made such a request (this had happened before I arrived), as I have noted earlier, General Steyn had laughed and asked what communists wanted with a priest. We had gone on trying and were met with varying cynical responses. The authorities were obviously not keen on having a priest there because they wanted to keep us as isolated as possible.

It took about six months of asking but finally a priest did turn up – the Rev. Canon Langley from the All Saint's Church in Barberton. This was no doubt as a result of the *Rand Daily Mail* exposés but we knew almost nothing about these at the time. While he was with us we had a wardress present all the time, within hearing distance. We once heard the Matron-in-Charge giving Langley a lecture in the office about how to conduct a service for us.

It was somewhere towards the end of 1965 that we were to meet him for the first time. This was not in our section but in the visitors' room. He asked each of us when we were going out and when I told him I was due to go out in 1971, his eyes popped out of his head. I could see the word 'murder' going through his mind or at least 'grievous bodily harm'. Then he started talking about how we felt as prisoners, how we felt about our rejection by society, and suggesting we should come to terms with it and make decisions about our futures, never to do what we had done again. We must not be ashamed and beaten down by our rejection by society; we must become strong and, with God's help, make resolutions for the future.

Mollie, at this point, thoroughly discomfited by his approach, insisted that she was not at all ashamed of what she had done. On the contrary, she was proud. He responded, a little bitingly, 'Well, happy are you!' We concluded that he almost certainly did not know that we were political prisoners. However, we were not absolutely sure. Maybe, we thought, he did feel that we should be ashamed of having opposed apartheid in the way we had. Mollie continued undaunted, 'I am proud of having opposed apartheid.'

Light began to dawn on Langley's face, although he tried to keep the expressions that were hurrying to the surface of his face under control.

'You are a political prisoner then?' he asked.

'Yes, yes,' Mollie said eagerly.

'Well, then,' he said, 'I understand. Are any of the rest of you political prisoners?'

'Yes. We all are. There are no non-political prisoners here with us.'

That was settled. All the same we never built up a completely happy relationship with Canon Langley while I was there. I think he found the situation very difficult. The Matron-in-Charge was consistently unpleasant to him, and the wardresses would giggle behind his back. The Junior Matron, Taljaard, used to imitate his hot potato-English voice to us after he had left. He could not have missed the disrespect with which he was treated. So he looked generally rather unhappy in the gaol.

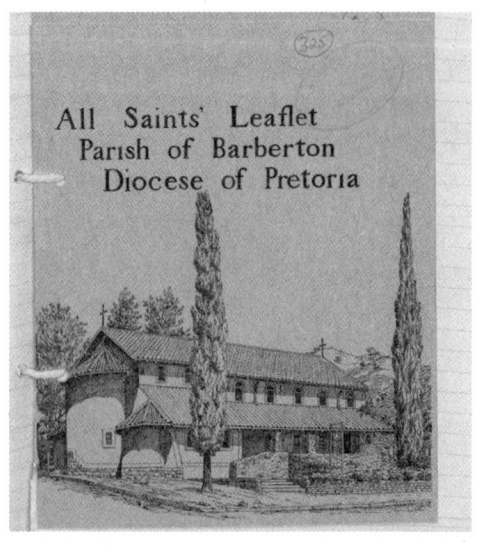

But he looked absolutely miserable after it was arranged that, instead of meeting us in the visitors' room, he should come into our section and be locked in there with us. The claustrophobia of the place, the isolation, the silence, the sense of a no man's land, the kind of social unreality of the place clearly weighed on his soul.

One assumes that security reasons played a role in the change of venue. However, almost certainly a reason had been that Matron Bester did not like having us so close to her office for fear that we might see and hear what was going on in the Front. I think that made her feel more paranoid than usual. It was interesting to note how terrified the authorities were of our seeing what they did and said in the normal run of a prison day. One of the reasons why we were so isolated was definitely because they feared that we would see how they treated other prisoners and how they ran the prison.

Their anxiety in this respect gave us rather an interesting insight into their attitudes, though, of course, we had come up against these in the outside world. We had often observed the police trying to hide their brutality, and they were careful to deny to the public all allegations of torture. We were used to all the window dressing, hypocrisy and lies that the South African government went in for. So what we saw of this attitude in gaol was not new to us.

The authorities were, in general, brutal, and yet they felt continually uneasy and guilty and uncivilised. English-speaking South Africans and the British had always tended to make them feel like 'boers', uncultured people fresh from the veld. Once the Afrikaners had taken over the reins of power, as they struggled to maintain their role as rulers in what was a parasitic and predatory system in the face of rising opposition from the black majority and growing criticism in the international arena, they began to build a police state. They were now at the helm, yet they never really lost their sense of an inherent inferiority. The Brigadier was a typical product of these contradictions and conflicts, perhaps an extreme product but typical none the less. He was also a measure of the type of society they were trying to maintain.

We were, of course, keenly aware of the psychological conflicts that were so typical of South Africa's rulers and which were reflected so graphically amongst prison officials. Here we had to take into consideration not only the inclination to brutality and even sadism but their deep feelings of inferiority. A psychologist would point out that the two aspects often go together. Striking was that we tried our utmost to ease their feeling of inferiority, amongst other things by mostly conversing with the wardresses and more senior officials in Afrikaans. Day-to-day Afrikaans we could all speak. It was only aspects like legal terms that we found difficult.

In retrospect, I think we did an excellent job. A big problem in this context was Matron Bester, who often felt we were laughing behind her back, and she would react aggressively when she thought this was the case. In fact we rarely laughed behind her back. We considered this inhuman and uncivilised behaviour. I must admit, though, that we did laugh at the Brigadier. His stupid pomposity was too much of a bait to ignore.

When Canon Langley visited us we would sit with him at our eating table – to call it a dining table would be inappropriate – in the portaal. Seeing his unhappiness at where he found himself, we tried desperately to make him feel 'at home' by laughing and chatting and trying generally to lighten the atmosphere, but there was no pulling him out of the gloom into which he sank.

I wondered how he saw our section. I tried to see it through his eyes. Yes, it was rather bare. Yes, he was locked in, but then he was locked in the gaol when he was in the visitors' room too. In our section I supposed he was *more* locked in, and there was an atmosphere here that there was not at the Front. Indeed, an atmosphere seemed to have built up in our section, one which seemed to have a kind of independent existence. It had grown there, had become something almost tangible, existing in its own right, quite apart from its inhabitants, although it had originally grown from our reactions to the place. Possibly the deaths of the animals that had occurred there had become a part of that atmosphere too.

The spirit that pervaded our space seemed to be something almost primeval, the response to captivity of the human being who had in him the whole of his prehistoric past and the original animal in him. It was a response to this kind of atmosphere that I think I saw in Langley's eyes, on his mouth, in the sag of his body. His eyes were shifty and uneasy and our endeavours to be hospitable seemed merely to embarrass him. He simply could not respond in any genuine manner.

The prison look

We prisoners sometimes saw our section with the eyes of an outsider. This was particularly so when we came back to the section after a trip outside, say to the dentist. I would come down the passage, past the office of the Matron-in-Charge on the right and then past the visitors' room on my left, and another room on my right, past a room on my left, where there was a bed and a hotplate with a kettle and a black prisoner who made tea for the wardresses; thereafter on the right the closed door of a small store where they kept various things, together with our luggage which we would take with us when we were released, if we were released. Then the wardress acting as escort would open the grey-painted door that opened into our section.

I would be feeling excited and exhilarated because of my brief encounter with the world outside. I would be thinking of all the things I could tell the others, about the trees and the kind of flowers I had seen, what was on at the local cinema and so on, and the trays carrying asbestos going up the hill in the direction of Swaziland, high up over the road.

I would be brought up with a shock by what I saw of our section through the central grille which had not yet been unlocked for me to go in. There was a tremendous silence and stillness there, as if the world had suddenly frozen stiff. There would be one or two people at the laundry basins, perhaps one person ironing a uniform. But they were strange figures suspended immobile in space. And, as the sound of our door opening and then the grating sound of the key in the grille reached them, they all looked up and round at me, as if in slow motion, and in their eyes was a most peculiar stare, as if they weren't living or seeing or experiencing that moment but were looking back far into the past.

The prison look

And as their eyes met mine, there was no look of recognition, no friendliness, no response at all. That was the terrifying thing – no response. I thought, My God, something terrible has happened, while I was away, somebody has died or collapsed or something. They just looked silently at me, with that dead look. We came to call this look 'fish eyes'. I did not know whether this was an accurate description. I thought it was a look I had seen in the eyes of schizophrenics. It was so close to that look that I would say that that place, our section in Barberton Prison, had given us some of the symptoms of schizophrenics.

It was rather a terrifying thought and I pushed it from my mind. We just had to grasp that we were developing to an extent pathological reactions to our isolation and our deprivation, and try to find other outlets. That was all.

I heard the grille locking behind me and I took a few steps forward across the portaal towards the others. They seemed to realise something, and the slow turn of the head and the look in the eyes, looking suspiciously sideways, receded and they came towards me, asking me for 'the news'. Yet they came up to me slowly and hesitantly and formed a rather questioning circle round me, like wild animals circling something they were not quite sure of. And I talked gaily and excitedly about what I had seen and heard, forgetting my initial shock at what they'd looked like. And they told me I was looking marvellous, that I had an 'outside world' expression on my face.

We used to notice that people's faces had changed when they came back from the visitors' room, from a visit from relations and friends, or from a trip to the dentist or hospital. They looked alive, their eyes were shining, the skin of their faces smoothed out, colour came into their cheeks. Those dark rings under the eyes, so typical of prisoners, had receded. Even the colour of their hair changed and began to glisten. It was an incredible transformation. It sometimes lasted the whole day and sometimes even the day after.

I remember the first time I was ever in a prison. This had happened in the course of the sit-in campaign in Cape Town. On this occasion, rather than releasing us at the Caledon Square police station after payment of bail, they decided to send us on to the Roeland Street Prison. This was

Gillian Jewell, a girl called Ann and myself. It was obvious that they were going to hold us for 48 hours up to Monday morning. The police had evidently decided that a police station had not broken us, had not frightened us off the sit-in campaign, and so this time they were going to try prison. Maybe that would do the trick.

There was a feeling of horror in me as we were told to strip in a bathroom at Roeland Street Prison and our clothes were searched by a woman in khaki uniform, who looked challengingly at us and spoke to us in a rough manner as though we were dogs that had misbehaved. Evidently, this was not a special manner for us because we were involved in politics. It was just the normal way of handling prisoners. I found it terrifying.

Eventually, we were taken through the gaol, through an open courtyard with washing lines. Sun on white concrete, red corrugated-iron roofs and old red-brick walls is the picture I have. We were taken through a red metal door into a small courtyard and, at the sound of our coming, several prisoners came through a door from the other side of the small courtyard and stared at us. Pale faces, dark rings under the eyes, and a peculiar suspicious wild animal look.

I think we must have pulled up short and the shock showed on our

ABOVE: Photos supplied by Val Bijl (née Hutchinson), who was a participant in the sit-ins in Cape Town.

faces, for the wardress with us suddenly let out a tremendous, amused and sadistic laugh. The prisoners were in dark navy uniforms with white collars. That was my first taste of the 'prison look'.

Although visits and 'trips' made us look better, more alive, it was not always a pleasant sensation, for we often became overstimulated and in our section there was no outlet, and so our discomfort was, to some extent, increased. As a reflection of the effect of visits, it is noteworthy that we came to ask each other, 'Have you got over your visit yet?', as though it were some illness. Visits were often a tremendous shock to our system, so that all sorts of feelings that we had been keeping carefully under control and of which we were even, to some extent, unaware, came boiling up to the surface. And so sometimes just before people went through for a visit, they burst into tears.

My second hospital outing

About this time I had a second trip to the Barberton hospital for another attempt to deal with the problem on my foot by cauterisation. This time I was not so afraid and was able to look at my surroundings on the way to the hospital. It was Meneer Bezuidenhout driving again. I walked down the steep steps of the Barberton female prison, leading down from the front door to the grey gravel driveway below. Through the iron-grey cages that covered the windows of our cells, we used sometimes to see African prisoners, in red headscarf and brown overalls and often barefoot, sweeping the gravel of the drive smooth so that it looked nice and did not form bumps and ridges on the edges of the driveway. Barnard was escorting me this time. Meneer Bezuidenhout asked her to sit in the front but she said, No, she could not, her orders were to sit in the back. 'Ag nee,' he said and laughed.

The car, a Consul, swung round the central piece in the driveway, stones cemented together and a pond in the middle. There were some reeds growing out of gaps in the stones. The car travelled on past flower beds on the right, great trees on the left, then on the other side of a low wall, out of the driveway and onto a brown gravel road that ran between the golf course on one side and some grass lawns and the quarters of the wardresses on the left. Behind us the road ran along the sisal lands, for about a mile down to the farm gaol. We travelled between 50 and 100 yards along the gravel road and out through an open gate with a board saying something like 'Department of Prisons. No Trespassing.' And we were out of prison property.

We travelled between houses, mostly of a cottagey kind. I was amazed, again, that there was no lushness. I knew already that the hills were bare and dry because we could see them from our section but I thought maybe that was just the hills and that down below in the little subtropical village of Barberton there would be flowers, azaleas, frangipani, moonflowers, bouganvillea, honeysuckle, and greenery, and general lushness, but, no, everything looked arid, bare. I was disappointed. This was probably because I longed to build up a tangible atmosphere around Barberton Prison, to take away from the tremendous aridity of the gaol experience. A wild tropical lushness seemed to be the answer.

Barberton was just an ordinary dorp, nothing special. We drove, or rather Bezuidenhout drove, towards what appeared to be the centre of the village. I saw the large glass windows of shops and big painted signs and advertisements, and a bank. And then we came to a stop street and turned left down a carriageway, the longest road I had seen in Barberton, and I saw poinsettias. I ventured to ask, 'Where's Johannesburg from here?' And Bezuidenhout said the road to Johannesburg was down this road and straight on.

On my left there were some prisoners working on a sports field. They were in shorts and red and white striped jerseys, and I remembered how I had felt about 'convicts' when I was a child. They were black men whom I had seen marching sometimes in a long line on the road, with picks and shovels and buckets, or I had seen them working on a road, and once I had seen them in the quarter acre garden of my home in Port Elizabeth, clearing away a rockery, moving huge boulders and doing something to a hedge. I had been taught to be terrified of these men. They were dangerous criminals who would kill me and rape me at the slightest opportunity, and that was why a white man with a gun stood over them all the time. And I read about 'dangerous escaped convicts' in newspapers when I was a little older.

But now I was a prisoner, one of them. I, too, was sometimes referred to as a 'convict'. One day Matron Taljaard gave me a form to sign agreeing to have a general anaesthetic at the hospital. At the top of the form I was shocked to see, 'Convict Sylvia Neame'. Now, too, I washed the prison clothes of convicts, and we waved and smiled at them and gave them the thumbs-up sign from our courtyard when they came to work on the roof above us. And when a group of them came to work on our tenniquoit court in our courtyard we looked into their eyes and smiled and waved. As I have noted, the kindest smile I got at Barberton was from one of these men, our fellow prisoners, our brother convicts.

Bezuidenhout turned off left, past the Indian quarter, with Indian shops on the right, and up the road to the hospital gate, and in, up the narrow tarred road. The car swung round in front of the building, and I was escorted to the reception desk as on the previous occasion.

Again there were the curious stares and the politeness from the hospital staff and I was taken to the same private ward, looking into a garden of grass and flowers and hibiscus bushes, between hospital buildings. They gave me my pre-med injection early. Evidently the prison doctor had remembered to make an appointment this time for the operating theatre, and I was put on the trolley, and again I went swinging down long passages, many passages, swinging this way, swinging that, and then doors swung open and I was in the same little bright theatre with the trees and flowers and grass on the other side of the large window. And then the Pentothal injection.

I woke up with my face almost buried in a pillow, and I heard Barnard saying, 'But, Neame, Matron Bester does not hate you.' I gathered that I must have been having a conversation with her. She was somewhere behind my back next to my bed. I decided I had better continue the conversation. 'How can I go on living in a gaol when the Matron hates me,' I said, and I heard myself saying this in a rather weeping voice, and I felt the tears wet on my face. I turned over onto my back and opened my eyes. Barnard was next to me, on the left side of my bed, and there were five or six nurses staring at me. One of the nurses said, 'Look at how red your eyes are. You have been crying so much.'

'Have I been crying?' I asked.

'Yes,' she said, 'and talking.'

'Talking? What about?' I asked.

'Oh, you have been talking a lot.' And Barnard added: 'About Matron Bester, how she ill-treats you, and about a boyfriend, whom you say you love so much and long for.'

'Oh,' I said.

'You must get up now, Neame,' Barnard changed the subject. 'Mr

Bezuidenhout is waiting.' Nurses were still staring at me.

'I can't get up now,' I said, 'I can hardly see. And because I am a prisoner it is not necessary to treat me like a dog.'

The nurse who had said I had been crying such a lot said, shocked, to Barnard, 'She is not a prisoner, is she?' She turned to me. 'You are not a prisoner?'

'Of course she is a prisoner,' Barnard responded. 'What else do you think she is? Do you think she is a wardress?' She said this with some distaste.

The nurse was staring at me, horrified. 'You are really a prisoner! How terrible. You are so young!'

Barnard was beginning to look a bit embarrassed. 'Come on, Neame, you must get up now. I have work to do at the prison. I can't stay here all day.'

'I'm not going now,' I said, beginning to feel rebellious, and feeling I could get away with more than usual as I was obviously not yet fully round from the anaesthetic. 'I am "doing time", as prisoners say. I am in no hurry.'

'Come on, Neame,' Barnard said, 'get up, at once.' I did not move. 'Come, here are your clothes.' And she passed me my ticking prison nightgown and my nightdress. I struggled into them, blacking out for moments as I tried to struggle up. The nurses were still there, watching me. Whatever I had said while I was unconscious had obviously interested them. I struggled out of bed, almost falling over.

'Where are my slippers?' I asked. 'I can't see.' I peered around, trying to find them.

'Come, Neame, sit on the bed,' Barnard said, and she put my slippers on my feet. 'All right, come now. Mr Bezuidenhout is waiting.' I struggled up, took a few steps and nearly fell over.

One of the nurses said to Barnard, 'You'll have to take her in a wheelchair.' And they brought one, and pushed me into it. We went down the hospital passages. I closed my eyes. I opened them as we got to the reception desk. Bezuidenhout was there. I was aware that the women at the desk were staring at me in my prison nightgown and my heavy half-conscious face. I was wheeled to the car, and they opened a back door.

I waited for somebody to help me but nobody did. I looked at the seat, and tried to get up but couldn't move. The space I had to manoeuvre myself through in order to reach the seat was not very clear because my eyes were not focusing properly. With a tremendous effort, I pulled myself up and threw myself onto the seat in one movement. I was quite surprised when I landed firmly on the seat. As I had done before, I saw myself in Bezuidenhout's rearview mirror as we drove along, the pale swollen face and the eyes with huge pupils.

When I walked down the passage past Matron Bester's office towards the door leading into our section, nobody attempted to help me, and I found myself against the wall of the passage, and heard Bester's roar of laughter behind me. 'A great joke!' I muttered to myself.

Some time later I went back to the hospital, this time for a stomach X-ray. Taljaard told me to put on my prison nightgown and nightdress. I told her I wanted my private clothes. I told her I was not prepared to go out in my prison nightclothes. She was furious, and shrugged, turning to slam the door.

'You can tell Matron Bester,' I said, 'that if I have to wear my prison nightdress, I am not going.'

Later Matron Bester came to the section and told me to accompany her to fetch my private clothes.

There is a prison regulation which says that no prisoner should be exposed to public curiosity and interest. The effect of it is that no prisoner should be embarrassed by being recognised to be a prisoner by a member of the public. But, as with so many South African prison regulations, the authorities did not pay much heed to it. They evidently bore it in mind in regard to ordinary white prisoners but not at all with black prisoners.

Whenever we political prisoners at Barberton were taken to the dentist or the hospital we were accompanied by a female escort in the khaki prison uniform and the man who drove the car was almost without exception also in uniform. This situation exposed us without doubt to public curiosity. Then, when we went to the hospital we were dressed in prison nightclothes. Admittedly, members of the public might not identify these as prison clothing but none the less the particular nature of this clothing would tend to arouse curiosity.

Some months later several of us were to raise this issue during Complaints and Requests with the Brigadier, pointing out that we should not be taken out by escorts in uniform and quoting the relevant prison regulation to him. His response was, 'Oh, you are trying to pretend you are not prisoners when you go out of here. But I want to tell you you *are* a prisoner, whether you are in the gaol or whether you are at the hospital or the dentist. I don't care what other prisons do. This is Barberton Prison.'

I also complained about the way in which they had removed me, not fully conscious, on two occasions from the hospital, thus drawing attention to me, quite apart from the dangers for my health and physical well-being. Much later I would also raise the matter with the Prison Board.

Black prisoners were transferred from one gaol to another in their uniforms. To any member of the public, they could be nothing else but prisoners. I had travelled down to Port Elizabeth in a large prison van with five African women in the back with red headscarfs and brown overalls. They were serving sentences for membership of the African National Congress.

From the front big cell at Barberton I saw on one occasion a whole lot of African women prisoners arriving on an open lorry in their prison uniforms. The wardress on duty told me they had come all the way from Lydenburg.

Condition of our prison clothing and other matters

ONE OF THE PROBLEMS about prison clothing is that it is often most unfortunately stamped. For instance, a nightdress I had to wear to the hospital had a large black stamp on it, B↑P (Barberton Prison), quite obvious on the back of the nightdress. It was also not very pleasant wearing clothing even in the gaol with large stamps on them, particularly for visits. I remember that Jean once had a uniform with a large red stamp across the back of the skirt. It really looked most unfortunate. I was on one occasion given two pairs of panties with large red gaol stamps on them, making them look quite revolting.

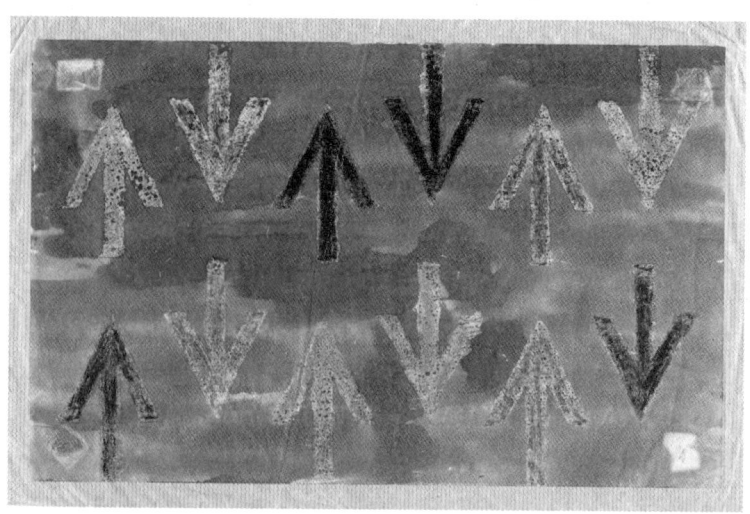

ABOVE: *A picture with prison arrows on wrapping paper.*

I told the Brigadier about them during Complaints and Requests, and said that I refused to wear them. In the course of a long cat-and-mouse conversation, during which there were touches of sadism and much lechery, he asked me why I should object to such panties since nobody saw them. I said that, quite apart from whether anyone saw them or not, it was demoralising for me to have to wear them. I saw them, I told him. After about ten minutes of this playing with me, he ordered me to go and put on one of the stamped panties and to return to the office. I noted that Matron Bester was beginning to look panicky. The Brigadier was getting out of hand.

I went back to our section and put the panties on. The whole business was revolting. Matron Bester came after me down the corridor and told me, nervously, not to show them to the Brigadier. When I got back to the office, the Brigadier had pulled himself together, and he did not even refer to the panties again. Matron Bester told me I could tear them and hand them in for 'condemning'.

Talking about 'condemning', we were each issued with two new blue uniforms, my fellow prisoners in about June and me in August 1965. Sometime in the first half of 1966 my uniforms started looking really terrible. They had torn under the arms and I had sewn them. They tore again, and I sewed them again and again until there was not enough material to bring the two ends together, and so I had to leave them open. My underclothing, in particular my bra, showed quite clearly through the gap, and the gap started moving right towards the centre of my body. The material of my uniform became thinner and thinner. The cuffs of my sleeves frayed and I put a thread through them so that they might look a bit better. And then the material began wearing through at the back, on the seat.

The same kind of thing was affecting other people's uniforms. Over and over again I went through to the Front and asked Matron Bester if we could have new uniforms, and she said she had none. She used often to shout at me, telling me that she could not help it, that this prison did not have a store for white women. Then she said she would try to get some from another gaol. Weeks, months went by, with our uniforms getting worse and worse.

I went to Matron Bester again, and this time she asked me how I could possibly expect a new uniform if I had not 'condemned' my uniform. She told me that the Department would not send her new uniforms unless she sent the old uniforms to them first. Only then would they replace them. This, we learned, through long and bitter experience, was a process which could evidently not be reversed. I asked her what I was going to wear in the meantime. She said she did not know. All she knew was that she had to follow the accepted procedure.

In the face of the complete lack of interest she showed in the demoralising state of my clothing, I therefore raised the question of uniforms with the Brigadier during Complaints and Requests. He said he would see what he could do. Weeks and months went by. Every time we raised it with him, he told us he could not help it, for he had written to the department but had heard nothing. We must remember, he insisted, that our gaol was not a 'factory prison' like Kroonstad where they made uniforms. We must be patient.

Nothing happened. No uniforms arrived. So we went to the Brigadier again and, with great pomposity, he told us that he had just received a note from the Department saying that an order had been put in for the required uniforms, and they were on their way.

Weeks passed by. We went to the Brigadier once more. He told me with his deep resonant boss voice that he had just received a note indicating that the uniforms were already on the train. They would be arriving any day. Weeks passed. Nothing arrived. I don't know what happened to that train! But we were used to the lies, hypocrisies and incompetence of the prison authorities. Thus, tenacious as we were, we just went on battling. We had been battling for uniforms for about six months. Mine were almost falling off my back. The Prison Board arrived some time in October that year and its members were horrified to see the state of our uniforms. They said they would see to it that we got our uniforms within a few days. We did.

We had a constant struggle over clothes. I have already described how I had to fight to get a jersey and some underclothing in the first few months I was there. Most of us had, at one time or another, to fight for underclothing. The trouble was that we had to follow the 'condemning' procedure, handing the article in before we could receive a replacement.

Usually we had to hand in the article on the Thursday before the third Monday of the month. The result was that for at least four or five days we would be without the particular article and in fact we were very, very lucky if we had only four or five days to wait. Jean walked around without panties for about one and a half months. Polishing and scrubbing floors without panties isn't particularly pleasant. When we asked Matron Taljaard or Matron Bester for the required article, they would look at us as though we were asking them for an unusual 'privilege'. They would shout and shrug and slam the door. They were 'te besig!' Too busy.

Being so dependent on the authorities was a real problem and, because they isolated us completely in our section, we, even more than the ordinary prisoner, became even more dependent on them. We could not go to the store like ordinary prisoners could and organise cleaning materials for ourselves or fetch wood and coal for the fire or get clothing. Not only did they lock us up in our small section so that we could not organise anything outside it but they would not allow us to do anything, even within our section, towards the running of the gaol. We were aliens in the framework of their prison.

The South African Prisons Department, whatever it might try to pretend to the outside public, had no real feeling about rehabilitation of prisoners. It was only when they were criticised by outsiders that they would grant prisoners certain privileges. Blue uniforms – for white female prisoners – were the great banner of a new programme of the Prisons Department. Flo wrote an amusing story for our *Barberton Bladsy* about a man who came from overseas to have a look at Barberton Prison to see if all the stories about bad treatment of political prisoners were true, and it gave a good picture of the authorities' attitude.

The Brigadier used so often to stress to us and to visitors that we were allowed to study. 'Allowed' is the operative word. They thought this was a great privilege instead of regarding it as an inherent part of a prison system that focuses on rehabilitation. We were never really encouraged, though. Matron Bester did not support in any way the organisation of classes amongst ourselves. We did it despite the authorities and often behind their backs. They sometimes let us get away with it by turning a blind eye but occasionally Matron Bester would storm in while we were in the portaal and lock up all our cells in order to prevent us going into our cells to study or hold a class. She would tell us that during the day we were supposed to work for the prisons, never mind that they would not give us proper work to do.

Then suddenly we were not allowed to do Honours courses on the grounds that it was a postgraduate course and no prisoner was allowed, they held, to do a postgraduate course. For an Honours course with the University of South Africa, a distance learning institution, exactly the same procedure was followed as for a BA degree (undergraduate), that is, one read the lecture notes, wrote regular assignments which were sent to the university and wrote examinations. Yet a prisoner was not allowed to do an Honours course because it was a postgraduate course.

The attitude of the authorities to the running of their prisons was just a part of the attitude to their society. There was a certain distrust of learning in general; they thought it encouraged 'liberalism' and 'communism'. They would not allow books in to us from the UNISA library if they gave any facts that might serve to make anyone believe that the system of apartheid was ludicrous or which expressed any type of anti-apartheid opinion, even if the book was in the syllabus. The Brigadier obviously felt that the whole equilibrium of the prison would be disturbed if we read such literature. This sort of attitude was a measure of their feelings of insecurity and, of course, of the authoritarian nature of the regime.

I have a depression

I FOUND, AS MOST OF US DID, that we began to become very inward and cut off after we had been in a single cell for a month or a month and a half. It was something that happened almost without our noticing, behind our backs, as it were. However, the depression I developed had to do with more than the effects of a single cell. In addition to the tension surrounding my appeal, it was clearly a kind of psychological reaction to the series of traumatic experiences I had gone through over the previous years.

A more immediate factor was what I heard from Jean. I still do not know why she decided to offer this piece of information when she knew what I was going through at the time my appeal was due to come up. At any rate, apparently out of the blue she told me that I had been 'under a cloud' for a while after Babla Saloojee had seen me climbing out of a Special Branch car in Market Street, Johannesburg. This had been around mid-September or early October of 1963, not long before I was arrested for my first 90-day detention.

POLICE SEIZE MATERIAL FOR GIRL'S THESIS [Oct. 1964]

STAFF REPORTER

What had happened was that I had had to go to the Grays in connection with the removal of two trunks of research material from the cottage I was staying in in Orange Grove. Five Security Branch men had raided the cottage while I was not present and had taken two trunks of research material, leaving politely(?) a receipt for me. Kathy had already been arrested. I do not remember the exact details but I was without my car at the Grays. In my presence the Security Police had gone through the material, a long procedure. It was on this occasion that a leading member of the Security Branch, coming into the room as the sorting was going on, had said to me, 'All we want to know is about Kathrada.' And then he had gone on to comment, making a gesture at his throat, 'You know that we are going to hang him!'

When they were apparently finished with packing my material back into the trunks, they had asked whether they could drop me somewhere and I had said, 'Yes, in Market Street.' This was in the centre of the business district and I wanted to be dropped somewhere near Kholvad House where Kathy had lived before his arrest and which his friends were looking after for him. Babla Saloojee had seen me climbing out of the Special Branch car and he reported this, of course, not realising how innocent the situation was.

Amongst others, it was reported to Jean and Bram Fischer, both of whom were in the CP cell into which I had been incorporated after arriving in Johannesburg. Bram was on the Central Committee but there was evidently a decision that members of the committee should be delegated to branches. I am not sure why but it was likely to have been, at least in part, a measure to prevent the bureaucratisation of the party, a tendency that arises more particularly in underground conditions. Jean was our contact to the area committee, I think it was called.

At any rate, an unfortunate result of Babla's report was that a point which I had made to Jean on my release from my first detention at the end of November 1963 that I had come to the conclusion in the course of my interrogation by Swanepoel that Gerard Ludi was a spy was not taken seriously. Indeed, Jean did not even pass on my suspicion about Ludi to a CP structure. This was because she was so taken up with 'the cloud' I was under. The worst aspect of all this was that a new member was thereafter taken into our unit (Costa Gazidis) and, having become known to Ludi, he spent a year in gaol for membership of the Communist Party.

What Jean told me at Barberton was to spark off in me a deep depression. I wrote in my makeshift diary at the time:

> '*I was sitting at the lunch table, 11.30-12, and suddenly I felt as though I were sitting on the bottom floor of myself and of the portaal ... I felt I would never be able to move from that position again – this was a physical reaction*'. Later I '*developed strong heart palpitations which almost knocked me over.*'

I took steps to move into a communal cell. I arranged that I would go in with Jean and Sheila into the front big cell. The usual procedure by this time was for us to ask permission from Matron Bester to move and there was never any problem. However, when I asked her, she told me I could not move into that cell and, when I questioned her decision, she said she would have to speak to the Brigadier. I had become used to this sort of discrimination. For instance, whenever I wanted to write my three-monthly letter, Matron Bester told me I would have to ask the Brigadier for permission whereas all the others obtained permission straight from Matron Bester.

At the time I asked Matron Bester about my wish to move into the big cell at the front, the Brigadier was not coming for some days – he was, in fact, in control of two gaols, the one at Barberton, the other at Nelspruit, so he was not present every day and all day in our gaol. I was beginning to feel desperate. I felt it was essential that I get out of a single cell immediately and so I went through to Matron Bester and told her I was not feeling well and that I must go to a communal cell. She then gave me her permission.

The front big cell measured, approximately, 11½ feet by 11½ feet. I could walk just over five paces one way and five paces the other. There were three beds in there, and three tables, and three people, and a locker. Quite a squash!

As for my state of mind, I realised that the others needed me. At that time I was still in the midst of my battle to unite us and to ensure that we struggled together for improved conditions. As it happened, just at this time I heard things that made me conclude that the situation was reaching a crisis. With a supreme effort, I managed to pull myself together. I actually had a picture of my physically pulling myself up out of the depths.

What strikes me as strange in retrospect is that I never discussed what had sparked off my depression with my fellow prisoners, either then or later. As for Jean, she could not have missed the link with what she had told me. I wrote in my diary:

20 April 66, Friday
... I realised I was needed. Since then I have lain on my bed in the evenings, staring at the globe, and let my mind wander where it will. Have played games three days running. Played monopoly which has just arrived from Mollie's people, then scrabble two days running with Jean and Sheila, and also some chess. Slept at lunchtime and often went to bed at eight. Have done very little work and felt no obligation to do so (or very little). Have only just started reading a little of Bonhoeffer, 'Letters and Papers from Prison'.

Bonhoeffer, a priest, was picked up as a suspect in Germany in Hitler times. While he was being held it was discovered that he had been involved in the attempt on Hitler's life in July. After expecting to be released any moment – he had been held for two years – he was fetched and realised that he was going to be shot. His ideas about a religionless Christianity are interesting. I mean to take down a few extracts when finished. Canon Langley lent it to us. I actually read about three-quarters of it in Port Elizabeth Gaol after the Anglican priest who came to visit me not long after I had arrived at the gaol had given it to me. His name was Father Louw.

I have been thinking a great deal about the sociology of knowledge. I don't think I agree with E.H. Carr's view that history is 'shot through with relativity' etc .... I have ordered from UNISA library, Karl Mannheim, Sociology of Knowledge, also Maurice Conforth's In Defence of Philosophy, which I read in 1963 at Wits, but would like to read again, and a Treitschke biography. Have just received Ranke's History of England, vol. I; will look at a few chapters. Also Tawney on Business and Politics in the Reign of James I has arrived ...

... Today one of the laundry basin taps made a sort of trumpet noise when it was turned on. I found the noise a great relief.... Sounds here are the trilling of bells – front door of the gaol and cells, keys in locks, voices, steps in the corridor just outside our section, and we have a window in this big front cell, looking onto the corridor – the glass is painted over. Other sounds are the lids of sanitary buckets clanging as they are placed back on the bucket, taps dripping, toilets flushing, the clash of tin plates. I don't think I shall ever forget that typical sound in gaols of a tin plate clanging onto concrete as somebody drops it in another part of a gaol – if this is the clanging noise I hear, I am possibly quite wrong. Sometimes beetles and other insects outside make various noises, scratching their legs together, on occasion but seldom, lorries, vans, cars. Wind in the trees is a relief too, and, very seldom, Jean's 'self-expression' – Jean on the comb with cellophane paper.

We are developing 'home industries' which is helping the taste deprivation. We make various things on the stove in the boiler room, keeping it out of sight of the authorities – sweets etc. The 'Coffee Bar' is going ahead. We now save coffee or tea from mealtimes and heat it on our stove round about 9 in the morning after we have cleaned our section. As well as being a nice break in the gaol routine, it brings us together as a group. The Coffee Bar started a month or two back.

We marked Pesach, the Jewish Passover (spring festival). The concern with Jewish culture emanates chiefly from Esther who is strongly oriented to Jewish customary observances. We also marked Easter, not that there was any outward change at the time, just a series of early lock-ups. Playing table tennis is quite nice. The grass for our tenniquoits' patch is growing very slowly in spite of constant watering. If it had not been for Judge Boshoff, we would still have no sport. Arnoldus, our tortoise, is becoming very tame. Every evening 'Our Friend' (the frog) comes under the metal door of our cell to eat insects. He is fairly tame but if we go too close, he lets out little squeaks of fright or is it his feet squeaking on the linoleum? A pale pink tongue, catching insects with a soft tongue-noise.

Arnoldus appears!
(from our Prison newspaper, Barberton)

28 April 66

It is very quiet in the cell. Sheila and Jean are lying in bed reading. The sound of a beetle outside and the occasional click of one small insect on the bare light bulb of our cell. 'Our Friend', the frog, was in here again tonight though I can't see him at the moment. Saw him eat a fairly large (for the size of the frog) winged insect a night or two ago. What a procedure! It was so large that it distended his body in various parts as it moved down and he would suddenly make a jerking movement as he pushed it lower. A little later he chased another largish winged insect but the insect fought him off and escaped under the metal door of our cell. The frog grapples with these insects, in the initial stages, rather like a lion and its prey. He paws the air.

Yesterday we heard that 'C's' now have two visits in three months and two letters. 'D's' now have the same as C's had – 1 letter and 1 visit in three months. To bed. To Orwell. Last night started reading Animal Farm. Should be amusing. The 9 o'clock hooter went about half an hour ago. A very still night. Has been raining slightly but has now stopped. Not a sound in the gaol.

I write as a form of therapy

AROUND THIS TIME AFTER lock-up – it must have been shortly before I was allowed to move to the communal cell – I started writing the following and was busy with it into the late hours of the night. I wrote it as a form of therapy, a means of dealing with my existing state of mind. I had gone through a series of traumatic experiences in the last years and I concluded that it might be a good idea to have a look at one of them more closely:

Sometime in the last months of 1962 I went into a house somewhere in a Johannesburg suburb and spoke to an ugly woman. I said, 'I want an abortion.'

She answered after a searching pause: 'How long are you pregnant?'
'About two and a half months.'
'Well, we don't usually do abortions as late as that,' she said.
There was a long pause.
'Come back tomorrow at nine o'clock,' she said.
'Oh, can't you do it now?' I asked. 'I would like to get it over with. Won't it just take a few minutes?'
'No. We can't do it now. The doctor isn't here. And it won't take a few minutes. You will have to come back tomorrow.' There was another long pause. She seemed to be feeling me out. 'Have you ever had an abortion before?'
'No. This is the first time.'
Another pause. Then, 'Who gave you the doctor's name?'
I made up some name. 'Mrs Thomas,' I said.
'I don't remember her … Did she come to us?'

'Yes. I think she came about a year ago.'

Pause. We were standing in a rather ordinary sitting room, ordinary on the side of drabness. A round table with those ugly paws on the end of the legs, lace curtains at the windows, and rather tasteless floral curtains. Couch and chairs covered with a different but similar material. Floral carpet. Old photographs on a cabinet. All very, very ordinary. Difficult to imagine that any drama took place in this house. Very quiet. And this rather distastefully ugly woman in an ugly floral dress and slippers on her feet. It was evening. The sound of traffic came from a main highway about a hundred yards away but the street outside was quiet.

She broke the pause. She was obviously feeling her way, trying to assess me, trying to gauge whether I was a police trap. 'Why have you decided to have an abortion? ... You look a very nice girl ... You come from a good family.'

I hadn't been expecting these questions so wasn't prepared. I thought I had better not say 'Because the baby wouldn't be white.' She didn't look the sort of woman who would approve at all. And she might, in some way, expose me to the police, especially if she were in trouble herself at any time.

'I just can't get married at this stage,' I answered. 'Only later.'

Another one of these slightly suspicious pauses.

She asked, 'What do you do?'

'How do you mean, "What do I do?"' I wondered how to answer that one, so played for time.

'What is your job?'

'I am a university student – history,' I said.

'Yes, yes. You speak as though you come from a good family.'

Another pause.

'How long will it take?' I asked.

She seemed to come to a decision. 'Come back at nine tomorrow morning.'

'All right, I'll come then,' I said, trying not to think of the whole night I would have to face. If only they could have done it now, right away, I thought.

'And you must bring some things with you. Will you remember, or must I write it down?'

'I'll remember,' I answered.

'You must bring half a pound of cotton wool, and pyjamas and a dressing gown. That is all. Just go to a chemist first thing tomorrow morning before you come here, and ask for half a pound of cotton wool.'

'Right,' I said, trying to sound firm.

'We will give you ether,' she said.

'Ether!' I exclaimed. 'Isn't ether awful? Can't you give me Pentothal, or something like that?'

'No. The doctor likes to give ether. But you won't be under for long. Of course, you will be a bit sick afterwards.'

'Oh, does it make one vomit?' I asked. 'Like chloroform?'

'Yes, it makes you feel very sick afterwards.'

'How long?'

'You'll feel better in a few hours.'

'A few hours! Good Lord, I didn't think it would take as long as that!'

'Yes, you can just lie here until you feel better. Everything will be all right,' she said in a way that didn't reassure me at all. There was something squalid about her.

Another pause.

'How much do you charge?' I asked. I became even more conscious of the rather unwholesome atmosphere. I felt there was going to be a bit of bargaining.

'Do your parents know about this?' she asked, obviously trying to judge how much she could ask me for.

'No,' I responded.

'And the man? Can he pay?'

'Yes, but he hasn't much money.'

'We can't do it for less than fifteen pounds.'

'All right, all right.' I was placatory, fearing that she might finally reject me. 'Okay,' I said as firmly as I could. 'I shall come back at nine tomorrow.'

'And remember the cotton wool and the pyjamas and the dressing gown,' she said.

I went out through the kitchen with the green linoleum floor and there was an African woman there in white cap and apron. She turned and looked at me in a searching, interested way, but as though she had looked at many others in the same way.

I spent that night alone, somewhere in Bellevue in a rented room in an annex to a hotel. I couldn't sleep the whole night.

The next morning I went to the chemist and bought the cotton wool. I had my nightdress and dressing gown with me. Somebody dropped me on the Main Road and I walked the hundred yards to the house. I went to the kitchen door and knocked. The African woman in the white cap and apron let me in without a word. The same interested look, first at my face, and then at the little parcel wrapped in brown paper which I carried under my left arm. She sat me down in the same sitting room with the floral curtains, the floral chair covers, and the floral carpet. I was there a few minutes alone, and then the rather sordid woman entered.

'Oh, you have come,' she said as if slightly surprised. 'And on time.' She looked at the brown parcel. 'And you have remembered the things … Come with me and we'll get you ready. The doctor isn't here yet.' She tried to speak a little kindly and reassuringly but even her kindness had a sordid touch.

We went through another room which was not unpleasant but cluttered with objets d'arts, and then to a bedroom. In the room was a large old cupboard and a bed, and in the middle a table covered with newspaper. Sitting on the table was a large black cat, with leaking infected eyes. It was the most horrible, dirty-looking cat. The woman told me to change into my nightdress. She looked at me, as I changed, 'Yes, you come from a good family,' she commented. 'It is a pity this should happen to you. You're young and pretty.'

I said nothing. I wondered how she could bear to have that cat around, and, even more, why she didn't appear the slightest bit embarrassed by my seeing the wretched animal.

The woman told me to get into bed and relax for a while. I lay there with body taut. On my right were windows, looking onto a back garden. The cat jumped from the table and came onto my bed. I tried to encourage it to jump off by kicking a little with my feet. At last, it decided things were a little uncomfortable and jumped back onto the table.

I wondered where they would do the job. The room must be somewhere in this house, I thought.

The woman came back.

'Where is the doctor going to do it?' I asked her nervously. 'Will it be somewhere in this house?'

'Oh, yes,' she said, 'he'll do it in this room.'

'He'll do it here?' I exclaimed, surprised.

She rearranged the newspaper a little on the table. I wondered why on earth they had newspaper on the table. Couldn't they afford a cloth? They didn't seem poor, to tell from the rest of the house.

And who was the doctor she referred to – her husband? Probably not, I thought, she didn't look like a doctor's wife. She looked like a housekeeper or even like an abortionist herself, or how one imagined women who made a living by abortions looked, the sort of women who lived in back streets, and had a rather sordid view of life.

In my fear, I had a strong desire to communicate with some human being, and, as she happened to be the only one available, I ventured to tell her some of my feelings.

'I couldn't sleep all night,' I said.

She didn't look a bit surprised. 'Shame,' she commented. 'There was a girl here the other day. Her young man brought her. She was pregnant, but he didn't want to marry her, poor girl. Men are rats, aren't they?'

She obviously felt that in my position I must agree with her view of the male, and she seemed to be waiting for my story. I made no comment. I didn't know quite what to say. I did not feel like that, and, at the same time, I was so busy thinking how sordid she was, and what a squalid view of life she had, that I couldn't think what to reply.

The woman went on, 'And when the doctor put the mask over this girl's face, and began to give her the ether, she started screaming and screaming, and struggling. It was terrible, what with the neighbours. So the doctor refused to carry on. And even though the young man spoke to the girl, she refused to have it done.'

She paused, and gave me a slightly leering but penetrating look. 'You aren't going to scream, are you? Otherwise the doctor won't do it. He can't, not with the neighbours.'

'No, I won't scream,' I said, feeling sick in the stomach. 'I may struggle, but I won't scream. I don't like the thought of the ether.'

'Have you ever had it before?' she asked.

'No, no, but I've had chloroform. That was when I was a little kid and had my tonsils out ... Is it at all like chloroform? ... It's cold, isn't it?'

'The doctor just puts this mask over your face, and I will tell him to drop the ether slowly so you won't get so frightened. I'll tell him that you are afraid of ether.'

'I don't like the idea of the mask either,' I said.

'It's just one of these gauze masks that he will put over your face, and drop the ether through.'

There was a pause. That ghastly cat was still sitting on the newspaper on the table.

'Have you the money with you?' she asked. 'The doctor won't do it unless he has the money first.'

'Yes. Yes, I have it here,' I said, leaning from my bed to pick up my bag on the floor. I counted out the pound notes and handed them over to her.

She counted them carefully, and left the room for a few moments. I wondered where she put them. Probably hidden away carefully in a mattress or something or maybe she went running down the road to hand it over to somebody to keep. I thought the latter a bit unlikely. Dear God, I thought, I wish the doctor would come, and it could be all over. It had to be done. I had resigned myself to it, so the quicker the better.

The leaking-eyed cat jumped from the table covered with newspaper onto the floor. I looked at my watch. The doctor was late. It was already 9.45, and she had told me to be ready at nine.

The woman came back without the pound notes. 'The doctor's a bit late, but he will be here soon.'

'I can't stand this waiting,' I said.

'It will be all over very soon,' she said comfortingly but always with that slight leer, as though she knew and I knew the ways of the world. We were both common sluts, and all men were rats, nasty lecherous creatures, wanting a woman for only one thing. Well, she's wrong as far as I'm concerned, I thought, and about my man.

'I don't suppose the man is helping you at all with the money'.

Remembering that I had indicated to her that I couldn't pay much, I responded, 'No, he is helping, but he hasn't got much money.'

I lay back. It shouldn't be so bad, I thought, except for the ether. I imagined a very doctor-looking doctor, with very white coat and stethoscope round his neck, coming into the room, and moving across to me with a competent manner as I lay in the bed. I thought, It will be all over very soon, as soon as he comes. Abortions, as far as I knew, weren't supposed to be particularly terrible events but I was worried about the woman looking at me in that leering sorry-for-me way, and also by the fact that they had to give me ether.

The woman went out of the room and came back a few minutes later, this time somewhat more briskly. 'The doctor is ready. Come here and get up on the table.' And she indicated the table with the newspaper, on which the awful-eyed cat had been sitting.

Good God, I thought, are they going to do it on there? Not only had the ghastly cat been sitting on the newspaper but the table was so small, too small for me to fit on surely?

I climbed out of bed and walked the few steps to the table.

'Which way?' I asked, trying to sound as firm as possible, not for her benefit but for my own. 'On which side must I put my head?'

'Here,' she said, and indicated the side of the table nearest to the door and furthest from the window.

I climbed up on the table.

'The doctor will be here in a few minutes.'

'I wish he would hurry up and come,' I said. 'I can't stand this waiting.'

'Here is the doctor.'

A male form walked past my head and stood at the end of the table, with his back to the window and facing me.

My God, I thought, he doesn't look like a doctor. He looks like the convict from the film *Great Expectations*, based on the book by Charles Dickens.

The doctor certainly wasn't a very prepossessing sight. He did not have on a white coat, as I had expected, and no stethoscope. To make matters worse, he had a rather ugly, in fact, distinctly frightening, face. Nothing of the slick doctor I had imagined. I wondered whether he was a doctor at all.

'This is the girl, doctor,' the woman said irrelevantly.

'Have you had an abortion before?' he asked.

'No.'

The woman said, 'Doctor, I have told her you will give her the ether very slowly so that she will not be frightened.'

'You look as though you come from a good family,' the 'doctor' said.

I said nothing.

'She says she won't scream, doctor,' the woman said, 'but she might struggle.'

'We'll hold you down,' he said, 'but you mustn't scream, otherwise I won't do it for you.'

'I definitely won't scream,' I said firmly.

He moved away out of my sight and came back with a gauze mask and a bottle. I wondered where the instruments were, or an instrument anyway.

'I will do it slowly,' he said, 'so don't worry. I will put this mask over your face, and then I will drop the ether slowly. When I tell you to start counting, you must count out aloud, "one, two, three", and so on. As long as you can.'

He put the mask over my face. I wondered whether I was going to struggle but the fact that it was gauze made me feel better. At least there were some air holes. I felt I wouldn't be smothered. I usually hated things being put over my face. The fact that I was resigned helped, too, resigned because we had decided to have it done. It must be done.

The man's voice said, 'Start counting ... One, two ...'

I counted, 'One, two, three, four, five ...' I wondered what he was doing, dropping drops of ether, I supposed. And then I felt myself beginning to sink gradually, as I got to the twenties. I felt as though I was dropping through down layers of my past. There were pictures from my childhood flashing by. There was my sister, and my mother, and then my father. My head was beginning to whirl, and there was a drumming in my ears. Well, at least I'm going, I thought. Getting me under an anaesthetic usually took quite a time. When I was a kid and they gave me chloroform, I remember the nurses were surprised it took so long, and I remember wondering whether they would ever get me 'under', and whether they might not make a mistake, and do the operation while I was still awake.

'Twenty-two, twenty-three, twenty-four, twenty-five, twenty-six …' There was a tremendous buzzing in my ears, but I felt somebody shaking me roughly by the shoulders, and a voice saying, 'Why didn't you tell us you bleed so much? … Why didn't you tell us you bleed so much?'

I felt myself lying in a bed, with my back to the woman's voice and the hands that were shaking my shoulders.

I remembered where I was. I thought, Oh, I must be dying. They didn't know I was going to bleed so much. I felt resigned. Strange, I didn't seem to mind the thought of dying.

The shaking continued. I thought, Well, why the hell don't they get an ambulance and take me to hospital, otherwise I'm going to bleed to death. I felt as though I was bleeding a great deal. Then I thought, Maybe they can't call an ambulance. They're too frightened to. And I'll have to lie here and bleed to death. For a moment I indulged in wishful thinking: I imagined the ambulance coming and me inside, comfortable and being looked after properly.

But the shaking at my shoulders was continuing. There was still a buzzing in my ears. 'Wake up, wake up,' the woman's voice said.

I turned over onto my back, and then realised I was going to be sick. Through a haze, I saw a hand holding an enamel basin. I vomited, and fell back. I could see a little more clearly now. The woman said, 'You should have told the doctor you bleed so much. You bled so much he could hardly see what he was doing. This whole floor was a flood.'

I looked down towards the wooden floorboards. I was feeling very sick again. The African woman with the white cap and apron was down on her knees on the floor. There was nothing to see. She had obviously finished the mopping up. She looked up at me again in that interested, impersonal way, as though she had seen this sort of thing many times before.

I found myself crying and saying, 'He loves me and I love him but we can't have the baby.'

The woman on her knees on the floor was still looking up at me, as though waiting for more. I stopped talking.

I write as a form of therapy

The sordid woman came into sight. 'You bled so much the doctor could hardly see what he was doing but he did do it ... He definitely did do it.'

I realised that she was worried that I might think I had paid for something he hadn't done.

It's strange how clearly one thinks in these kinds of situations, as though one is looking from the outside in at the world and other people's worries. I decided that I was probably not dying ... I felt very sick. 'The basin,' I said. I vomited again.

I turned over onto my side, with my back to the room.

The woman's voice said, 'You mustn't go to sleep ... You ...' She was shaking me by the shoulders again. 'Mustn't go to sleep.'

Oh, yes, I thought, they're afraid that somebody might come and find me asleep, the police or somebody else. I was amazed at how naive I had been. I hadn't thought before of all the intricacies of the situation. I had merely told him what had happened and he had indicated that he had important political tasks, including in relation to Nelson Mandela who had recently been arrested. He simply could not leave the country. I accepted that it just had to be done and, after obtaining the necessary information, I came to this house and asked them to do it, closing my mind as far as possible to the whole situation. Now for the first time I faced the facts more squarely, in particular in relation to the legal dangers for them and for us.

I turned over onto my back and looked at the woman. 'You're a very brave girl,' she said, with real admiration and relief in her voice. 'You gave the doctor no trouble at all.'

'Is everything okay?' I asked.

'Yes, yes,' she said. 'He definitely did do it.' She looked nervous and somewat shifty as though I wouldn't believe her.

'Can I go now?' I asked.

'Oh, no, no,' she said, 'you must lie there a few hours and rest. You just lie there quietly.'

'But somebody is going to fetch me at twelve o'clock,' I said. I looked at my watch. It was only 10.30. I couldn't have been under very long, I thought. I was surprised. When I woke up, it felt as though I had been unconscious for hours.

'I think he should come and fetch you a bit later,' she said.

I noticed she assumed he was a man.

'No, I think it'll be all right,' I said. 'I think I'll be all right by twelve.'

'Well, just you rest,' she said. 'But I think you should get out of that nightdress and into your clothes.'

Fear of the police again, I thought.

I got out of the bed unsteadily, and she helped me dress. I got back onto the bed, and she put a blanket over me.

Oh, well, I definitely am not dying, I thought.

'I've got things to do,' she said, 'so you just lie there and rest.'

I wondered how I would be feeling by twelve o'clock. I was still feeling sick and rather weak.

The next time I looked at my watch it was nearly 12.30. Heavens, I thought, he must have been waiting for half an hour already. I felt I couldn't move. Another half hour passed.

The house was very quiet except for the phone ringing now and again. And occasionally quiet steps in the passage.

The phone rang once more, and the woman came through. 'There is a man for you on the phone. He wants to know when you will be ready to be fetched.' She looked at me knowingly. To her, this was obviously the responsible man.

I tried to say coolly, 'Oh yes, I left my car at the garage to be serviced and told the garage man to bring me my car about twelve. Not to this house,' I added reassuringly. 'I asked him to come to the road down there.' I named the main road a hundred yards away. 'Tell him to be there in half an hour.'

I decided to start moving around a bit, just to see how steady I was. It wouldn't do to collapse in the road outside.

'Are you sure you are going to be all right?' the woman asked. 'You lost a lot of blood, you know ... I think you should leave it a bit longer.' She was obviously afraid that I would collapse in the road.

'No, no, I'll be all right,' I said.

She gave me some antibiotics – just in case, she said, a slight infection developed.

'Don't you think I should go to a hospital?' I asked naively. 'Just to see everything is okay?'

Her manner since I had come round from the ether suggested that all was not right. I wasn't sure whether I was imagining it.

'No,' she responded, almost rudely, 'there is no need to go to a hospital.'

It only struck me then that that would be the last thing she would want me to do.

I got up and wandered around the room a bit, feeling very weak, and into the next room with the telephone and all the objets d'arts. There was no sign of the 'doctor'. He had just quietly disappeared while I was still unconscious.

When about twenty minutes had passed, I told the woman I was ready to leave.

'Are you sure you are all right?' she repeated.

'Yes, I am all right.' I went through the kitchen with the brown parcel with my nightdress under my arm. The woman with the cap and apron gave me that same impersonal searching look. I walked out into the sunlight through a weather-washed green gate and onto the tarred road. I crossed the road and walked on some grass down to the main road. I tried to walk as steadily as possible. The message about fear of the police had penetrated at last. I turned and saw the woman watching me from the gate. If I collapsed, she was going to see that she got hold of me. Well, that's sensible, I thought.

I walked onto the main road, crowded with lunchtime traffic. It was summer. A hot day with a blue sky.

I saw the car fifty yards down from the corner, walked towards it and climbed into the back.

That night alone in my rented room I aborted. I knew then why the woman had looked so worried. They obviously had not been able to do the job properly.

After writing this I slept a few hours and woke at 5.30 with the first bell ringing. I dressed slowly, putting on my blue uniform and my army shoes. And then waited to stand to attention.

Something of the life of black prisoners at Barberton

THE FRONT BIG CELL WAS A NICE cell, as cells go. At this stage I did not yet internalise that it was north-facing and that we could look to the west. All I knew was that we could see the sun setting over the mountains there across the valley. At this time, April–May 1966, I still could not look with open eyes at the landscape outside because I feared the pain that it would give me in my chest and the gaol feeling. I dared look just a little, not allowing my eyes to relax and drink in the picture of the trees across the gravel near the golf course, the sisal lands down there to the left of the golf course, the farm gaol, a mile or so away in the valley, down in the west, and the mountains over which the sun set.

I tensed my body and kept the shutters just a little over my eyes. I did not yet see the detail, the lines of sisal plants, the colour of the leaves of the trees, all the different colours in the valley and of the mountains when the sun set. I was only conscious of the orange sun setting, making the cages on our windows orange and creating a square of orange on the wall above Sheila's bed. I was here inside with the orange reflection. The sun made itself a part of us by coming inside through the cages and bars. But the rest of the outside world was beyond. Out of reach.

True, I would observe ordinary gaol things through the window, in other words aspects that belonged to the life of the gaol. I used to watch the African prisoners in the morning, sweeping the gravel smooth below our windows, and I used to observe their babies, often on their backs, but sometimes put down on the gravel on a grey blanket while their mothers worked. Other women filled buckets of water at the pond, treading carefully on the stones on the edge, and bending over, stretching their arms forward as they pushed the mouth of the bucket into the water, and allowing it to fill, and then drawing their arms back and lifting them as they placed the buckets on their heads. Then they moved slowly up the stone edge of the pond and to the flower beds, where they emptied the bucket in big splashes. All in slow motion. Life had lost its real purpose, and the same job had to be done, apparently meaninglessly, every day.

We politicals were the only prisoners I have ever seen who went about bustling, walking fast. We became almost compulsive in our hurry to do useful things, to keep ourselves busy all the time. One of the wardresses once said to us, 'I have never in my life seen people like you inside or outside gaol. You are moving and busy all the time.'

I used to watch the long line of African women every morning going down to the sisal lands but I had to be careful that no wardress saw me looking out of the window. It was easier for us now because the wardress on duty with us was not there all the time. She would sometimes go and sit on a chair in the boiler room or sit at one of our tables in a cell, and dream the day away, utterly bored, and with nothing to do, for we ran our own lives without any supervision now. We did not have to be told to work. Everyone diligently performed their tasks and we did not fight amongst ourselves like other prisoners did. The wardresses were not allowed to read or smoke on duty. It was not pleasant for them.

I watched the long line of women, in red headscarves and brown overalls, walking in twos across the grey gravel with the little stones crunching. Crunch. Crunch. Crunch, crunch, crunch. There were probably 150 to 200 women. Most of the black women prisoners worked in the sisal lands. Only a few worked in the laundry in their section, did odd jobs in the gaol or worked below our windows on the gravel and flower beds.

Those who worked with the sisal went down to the lands about 7.30 in the morning. Each of them carried a folded kitchen towel over one arm, and some carried large tin containers which must have had their food. At intervals amongst them there were African wardresses, dressed differently from the white wardresses. Each was dressed in light khaki shirt, khaki skirt and jacket and with a topee on the head to protect her from the sun.

Also with the women going to the lands were African warders, in khaki too, with rifles. At various points in the lands there were platforms from which look-out points wardresses kept an eye on the prisoners so that none escaped. An African warder with a gun was on one of the platforms. And about 50 yards from the first row of sisal, close to the prison building, was another platform with a white warder with a rifle. He was on duty there all day. He kept a keen eye on the lands down below him. We could see him from the window of the front big cell. The prisoners only came back at half past three in the afternoon.

Our wardresses told us proudly that the policy of Barberton Prison – the 'best prison in the country' – was to break prisoners. They told us that the most difficult, the most dangerous prisoners were sent to Barberton. If a prisoner caused trouble in another gaol, somewhere else in South Africa, or tried to escape, they were sent to Barberton as 'C' and 'D' prisoners. Here after one day in the appalling heat of the subtropical summer, with the sisal blistering their hands, they were broken in. They never gave trouble again. The wardresses insisted that they, themselves, would not go into the sisal lands even for a few minutes on a summer's day because it was unbearable.

At some stage, we politicals tried to get the authorities to allow us out of the prison for short periods, just to get the feel of the outside world. The white women in Worcester prison in the Western Cape, we had been informed by prisoners who had been there, including Stephanie Kemp, were not confined all the time to their section (Worcester Prison was built according to the same plan as Barberton Prison). They were allowed outside in their grounds for sports' activities, and they used to go for tea to the quarters of the Matron-in-Charge, and were even allowed to go to milk bars in Worcester.

When I asked the Brigadier during Complaints and Requests whether he would not allow us to go into the prison grounds occasionally, particularly as there was no public to see us – the grounds were self-contained – Matron Bester threatened that she would send us into the sisal fields. She obviously felt this was a dire threat. The Brigadier confirmed that the policy of Barberton Prison was to break prisoners. He knew that one could not reform a convict unless they were broken down first. Only then was it possible to reclaim a prisoner. We knew that it was not an unusual occurrence for the black women prisoners to be severely beaten by the wardresses. One day, sometime in the first half of 1966, we heard terrible screams coming from the other side of the gaol. It was nothing new. We had heard wild screams quite often before. When we first heard them we were shocked rigid, but one gets used to anything, on the surface anyway, and so when we heard screams, one of us would simply look up from our work and say, 'The wardresses are at it again. Listen to those screams.' And go back to our work.

But every time it happened, I felt something snap inside me. Every time I heard one of these piercing cries my determination to fight the South African authorities was strengthened and I waited for the day when I would be out of there, and could tell the world about them. I think these kinds of thoughts entered the minds of all of us. We could do nothing about it then because our wings were clipped, but one day ...

On the day I am describing, the wardress who came from the front to lock us up for lunchtime lock-up (the Bird of Prey, Barnard), had a bandage around her hand and wrist. As she crossed the portaal in the direction of the courtyard big cell, with her keys jangling, she held up her arm importantly before her. At lock-up we all had to stand just inside our cells, behind the grilles, with our hands behind our backs, at attention, and so she knew we were all watching her. She looked so smug. Somehow it was all so naive. In a way I felt sorry for her, except that I knew that she had just beaten up a woman. 'O, ja,' Barnard spoke partly to herself, partly to the other wardress with her but she was performing above all for us. 'O, ja, ek het haar gedonner!' Oh yes, I beat her up.

Most of the wardresses we knew at Barberton were proud of being able to fight. It is something that was apparently a part of the culture of young Afrikaner girls of their particular social group. If you couldn't beat somebody in a fight, you weren't worth your salt. When they began talking more freely to us, they used to tell us stories, not only about beating up prisoners but even beating up other wardresses, or at least threatening them, and beating up men, too. One of them, who had once been a nurse, described to us how she had beaten up the boyfriend of a member of the prison staff. And she was proud of it.

The prisons service

THE WARDRESSES DID NOT come from a very different social background from many of the white prisoners. Even before they came into the service, they had often known of people who had gone to gaol. It might have been a chap across the road or the brother of a friend. And being able to use your fists and be tough was something desirable.

Many of the wardresses with whom we came into contact had joined the service when they were seventeen or eighteen. Most of them had not gone beyond Standard 6. They came into the prisons service often because they could not get a job elsewhere. They weren't trained for anything. Or they had to choose between going into an office to do odd jobs, dull work at a very low salary, or working in a prison. Some of them had friends whose brothers or boyfriends were in the service. Another reason for taking such a job could be in order to find a boyfriend amongst the warders and then get married.

Several of the wardresses told us that the issue of the uniform had been an important one in their choice of a job. The alternative was in some cases between nursing and the prisons, and some of them chose the prisons because they thought the uniform was smarter; or they chose the prisons because nursing was more difficult and you had to pass exams. When I went to the hospital one of the first topics of conversation between my escort and the nurses was their respective uniforms. 'My, daardie is 'n mooi uniform, ne!' Gosh, that is a lovely uniform. And my escort would swagger a little.

After some months the sense of pride which came with the wearing of a uniform and the novelty of working in a prison would wear off, and the long face and complaints would start. Some of the most dissatisfied people I have ever met were wardresses. They usually hated their job. At least this was the case in Barberton.

The whole atmosphere of the gaol was not conducive to a feeling of well-being. The prisoners longed to get out of there, and so did the wardresses. They were always trying to ensure that we ate early so that we could be locked up. They longed for their 'four hours', the one afternoon a week they had free. And they longed for their alternative weekend off. This attitude of the wardresses made the atmosphere of our section just that little bit more unbearable. The wardresses hated being locked up with us. They felt they were being treated like prisoners. As noted, they were not even allowed to have the key of our central grille on them so they couldn't get out even if they wanted to. They were locked in with us by another wardress.

Matron Bester often treated them like dirt. As her attitude to black prisoners rubbed off on her treatment of white prisoners, so her whole attitude to prisoners rubbed off on her relationship to wardresses. She used to scream at me consistently but she screamed at wardresses as well. Once you do not respect one lot of human beings, you tend to lose your respect for all. It is something one sees so clearly in the prisons. Some wardresses found the way they were handled by Matron Bester almost unbearable, and many of them reached a point where they felt they could not take one more day in that gaol. A lot of them left. Our problem was that we could not leave.

The disappointing thing about most of the wardresses was that they might complain about their treatment by Matron Bester and even make such general statements as 'It is terrible to treat human beings in such a manner.' But very few of them carried such thinking to its logical conclusion. I saw them treat prisoners like dogs, and I saw them treat each other on occasion in a similar way.

Although my comments about wardresses held for most of them, there were some quite nice people amongst them, particularly one who was a civilised human being. She was not a wardress who built up any sort of relationship with us which could in any way worry the authorities. She was absolutely correct. But she was a human being, somebody we felt we could respond to, not somebody absolutely alien. I have mentioned, too, the young matron who broke down because she could not bear treating us in the way demanded by the authorities and was soon to leave Barberton.

One of the basic problems in our relationship with the authorities was that we were completely alien to each other. We had a completely different code of behaviour, completely different principles on which we based our lives, and our interests were completely different. The wardresses thought our concern with study something very strange and wonderful. They could not understand how we could get excited about a problem of the French Revolution or a TS Eliot poem or a Picasso picture.

They were catty, swore at each other, gossiped. One of them asked me one day in absolute amazement after being with us a few months, 'Don't you people ever fight?' Of course, we prisoners had disagreements and, of course, we got almost unbearably irritated with each other in that situation where we lived on top of each other, where we could never get away for one minute. But we believed that civilised people should control themselves and deal with disagreements and irritations in a civilised and reasonable manner.

We had one altercation where two prisoners had shouted at a third. The altercation had arisen from a misunderstanding. Immediately after that we started having regular get-togethers where we talked out our problems. Every so often things would boil up to a certain point, and then we would have a full-scale discussion. This was an absolute necessity. The wardresses found our approach in such situations strange too.

We used sometimes to tell Matron Bester and the Brigadier how we felt they should have tackled a particular problem, indicating, for instance, that they could have settled it with far less trouble if they had dealt with it in a reasonable manner. Needless to say they found this very odd behaviour from prisoners, for the Brigadier intolerable.

It was something, in the end, we just had to accept: we could not get through to one another. If Matron Bester had not been so suspicious and lacking in self-control, it might have been possible in her case. As I have already noted, the Brigadier was a brute, stupid and a coward. Basically, Matron Bester was none of these. She was uncontrolled, verging most of the time on the hysterical, and, after fifteen years in the South African Prisons Service, quite unused to treating prisoners as human beings.

Prison symptoms

DURING THIS PERIOD THE symptoms of our condition, however the latter was to be described in psychological or medical terms, intensified, reaching, it appeared, a kind of climax towards the middle of 1966. Instead of keeping it all to ourselves, however, we would try to speak it out and, especially, joke and laugh about it.

One afternoon we were standing in the portaal near the laundry basins and Sheila said in the sort of strange Afrikaans working-class accent she had cultivated while there: 'My ma says I can maar go to Cape Town when I get out.'

Ann responded with disgust. 'Go to Cape Town! No, not to Cape Town. I'm going zoom, zoom' – she made movements with her arm like a plane diving – 'I'm going zoom, zoom to London.'

Sylvia (with a similar arm movement): Yes, zoom, zoom to Paris.

Ann: Zoom, zoom to Rome.

Sylvia: Zoom, zoom to Prague. Zoom, zoom to Budapest.

Ann: Zoom, zoom to Peking.

Flo (this was her pet joke): You're very limited – only socialist countries. Dogmatists! Communists!

Ann: But I said London!

Sylvia: I said Paris!

Ann: Rome!

Sylvia: Berlin, too! Yes, Berlin, both sides.

Esther (in her mock Yiddish accent): Come, Flo, how's it for a date in Haifa?

Flo: No, I don't want to make any dates, no dates. Maybe I'll just bump into you in a street in Haifa and I'll think I can't say hello to Esther because she's a named communist and I'm banned. So if I talk to her I'll probably get a three-year sentence. And I'll just walk past you with my nose in the air.

Esther: Nonsense! You walk past me! That'll be the day!

Sylvia (singing): That'll be the day when you say goodbye ...

Flo (joining in, singing): Oh, that'll be the day when you make me cry ... (talking) You know when that was on the hit parade? In 1950.

Sylvia: No, it wasn't. It was on the hit parade when I went for a holiday to Cape Town with my brother and we stayed in that ghastly house in Pinelands. That was in ... (thinking) ... that was in .... end of 1958.

Flo: No ...

Sylvia: Definitely. Because I remember we had the record and my brother adored it.

Flo: Oh, was it? (singing) That'll be the day when I die.

Sylvia (singing, ending off the song): ... when I die, when I die.

Ann: Oh God, I had a terrible nightmare last night about dying.

Flo: I wondered what was wrong with you. You were bouncing around from side to side. Bang! Bang!

Ann: What about you? You were tossing and turning and I was getting more and more furious and I was just going to say to you, 'Flo, why are you making such waking noises?' And then I thought, Oh hell, what does it matter! It won't make sense because she'll just say, 'Well, I am awake.' So, I thought the bitch is always keeping me awake and then I fell asleep and woke up this morning having this terrible nightmare about dying. I was just lying on my bed dead and I couldn't move. I just couldn't move and I heard my mother saying that breakfast was on the table, and I wondered when she would find out I was dead. I just couldn't move. I thought of calling her and telling her, but I found I couldn't open my mouth ... I just couldn't move ... Then I woke up.

Flo: I had a terrible nightmare, too. I dreamt I couldn't open my eyes because everything went into strange shapes. I remember trying to look out of the courtyard window of the cell at the hill, and it was terrible. I had to close my eyes. And there was my grandmother – the grandmother who's dead – and she was going into strange shapes ...

Sheila particularly used to get great enjoyment out of parodying our state of mind. My diary has the following entry for 6/6/66:

Conversation between Ann and Sheila at the laundry basins:
    Sheila: Ja, my pa sold your pa a shithouse.
    Ann: Yes, he did.
    Sheila: How was it?
    Ann: Okay, except that the wind blew rather cold in there.
    Sheila: Was there a peach tree nearby?
    Ann: Yes, but what has that to do with it?
    Sheila: Well, you see if there was a peach tree nearby that would account for the cold wind.
    Ann: No, it would affect the wind but I said a cold wind.
    Sheila: No, but the point is, when did this peach tree blossom?
    Ann: Like normal peach trees.
    Sheila: How do normal peach trees blossom?
    Ann: Once a year, I think.
    Sheila: What time of the year?
    Ann: I don't know what time of the year.
    Sheila: But it is terribly important to my thesis when the peach tree blossomed, because, if it blossomed in a particular season, it might account for the cold wind in the shithouse that my pa sold your pa ... etc., etc., etc.

This kind of conversation used to amuse the listeners, we prisoners, but usually it would become too much. I would suddenly feel myself spinning off into space in tiny fragments. I remember Ann and Sheila once had a similar sort of exchange, in which they tried to establish a 'thesis' about the relationship of parrots to chocolates. We laughed at them and then it became too much, and somebody said, 'Please stop. Please stop. I can't bear another minute of it.'

My 'flashback attacks' got much worse during this period. It was a peculiar state of mind. It was as though I were moving quite freely in the 'layers' of my mind where every single impression and experience I had ever had in the past had been recorded. In ordinary memory past experiences are recreated and one sees them from one's present position. It is a looking back. One feels that one, that is, oneself, one's personality as it exists at the relevant moment, is in control. It is the centre from which one looks back, and, because one is looking into the past from one's present position, what one remembers is often not very clear. One does not see, smell, feel, experience everything that one experienced at that moment in the past.

And memory is not a thing just of the senses. One's mind is operating in relation to these experiences. Thinking becomes an inherent part of the remembering process. Then, too, memories are not just quick flashes in one's mind. One may remember for minutes, moving one's mind slowly over one's past. A flashback, on the other hand, is a momentary flash, mainly, it seems, of the senses, though it is difficult to make this kind of distinction. It is far too quick for any thought to be formed at any conscious level. And it seems that the whole previous experience occurs, every detail of it. It is not as though one is looking from the present into the past but as though one is directly experiencing the past, as though one's present self has ceased to operate for the moment, and one is moving up and down in one's mind amongst all the recordings of one's previous life.

I don't know whether I should use such spatial terms as 'up and down'. We tend, especially since Freud, to talk about 'deeper' layers of one's mind, of the 'subconscious', but whether this is a valid description I do not know, or even whether it is useful. Maybe there is a more meaningful term we could use.

Sometimes there were five minutes or so, sometimes more, between separate flashbacks, but occasionally they followed one another directly. I experienced the latter particularly when I first started playing table tennis, watching that little white ball going away from me as I hit it, over the net to the other side of the table, and then moving towards me, after the person I was playing with had hit it, seeing it going in all sorts of angles across the table. All this seemed to encourage the very shaky balance I had established to disintegrate to some extent and I would go hurtling around amongst the recordings in my past, one flashback immediately after the other. Mainly they were visual, but with other things involved, particularly sometimes very intense odours.

I did not exist at all, except for those recordings. It was as though a series of lights were flashing through my head, and I could not even see the present. I could not see my present surroundings at all, not the table tennis table, not the brown lockers in the portaal, not the grey shiny concrete floor, not the cells looking onto the portaal, not the prisoners walking around in bright blue uniforms. They were for a few moments completely blocked out by the pictures flashing in front of my eyes.

The flashbacks which followed each other directly were difficult to get down because once they had passed through my mind they were gone and although I could remember I had had one, I could not remember what it was, so the flashbacks I wrote down were usually ones that followed each other at five- or ten-minute intervals.

More diary entries

MY ATTENTION TO FLASHBACKS, to our dreams, to our jokes, my decision to jot down aspects of our experience, was all a part, it should be clear, of my concern with the prison experience. Much of what I set down was written in a minute hand on tissue paper, which I kept well hidden; or there were 'diary entries' buried in the midst of my study notes. The activity was a reflection of the fact that I was determined to make my prison years useful, a genuine experience, and a part of it, naturally, was turning over in my mind intellectual problems which arose in my studies, the efforts I made to develop or polish up a world view. Even with regard to the suffering, in the end result I accepted it as a part of life, to be dealt with and understood.

> *Feb 66:*
> *To whom can I speak today?*
>   *Hearts are grasping*
>   *None has a heart on which to rely.*
> *To whom can I speak today? (Egyptian, Middle Kingdom) It seems I am not the only one amongst us who responds to this piece for somebody put this in our Barberton newspaper – without further comment.*

> *Thursday 17/2/66:*
> *The Afrikaner increasingly, as things tighten up for him, believes that to have understanding is a sign of weakness. The Nazis felt the same. Van Jaarsveld is an example of an Afrikaner who refuses to move in this direction.*
>   *... Gaol and death. The experience of death is very much with*

me here ...

To understand 'the other side' is sometimes difficult at moments in gaol but we constantly make an effort of will not to lose sympathy. There is something of the young boy in their brutality.

20/2/66:
I dreamed last night that I couldn't take a boat to leave South Africa until I had given 1,000 pints of blood. This links up with a conversation I had with Jean about donating blood as a symbol of socialisation.

7/3/66:
Aggression. Must be careful not to let it out on each other, rather than authorities. I am very hyperactive, find I am not listening to people when they talk to me, and am writing peculiarly, like 'succcess' for 'success' and 'sidid' for 'sordid'. Reading ahead and writing ahead.

End of March 66:
Scream like an animal from the other side of the gaol, about ten minutes.

The sound of doves stops in the evening – sunset? Sound of tin plates, tramp of the guard on the gravel. A squeaky bird? Insects squeaking, scratching their legs.

I dreamed about Arnoldus. I found he had dug a hole in the red sand of the courtyard and laid an egg. I realised he was a female. I felt disappointed.

Jean made a spider from paper clips, and wound navy blue wool from the male prisoners' jerseys around the clips. He has become one of our friends. We call him Hieronymus.

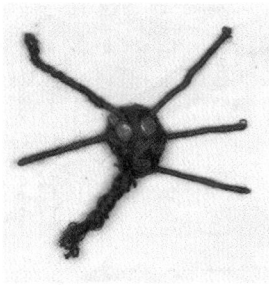

Imprisoned

20/4/66:

... On Monday we discussed a Shakespeare sonnet. I don't know what I think of it – rather flat rhythm. So much poetry is anti-action, e.g. Marvell's Garden, Donne's Canonization and the Good Morrow, Yeats's Prayer for my Daughter and Ann Gregory. Yeats's poetry – is it flat or is it just a sophisticated simplicity? Romantic poetry also the escape.

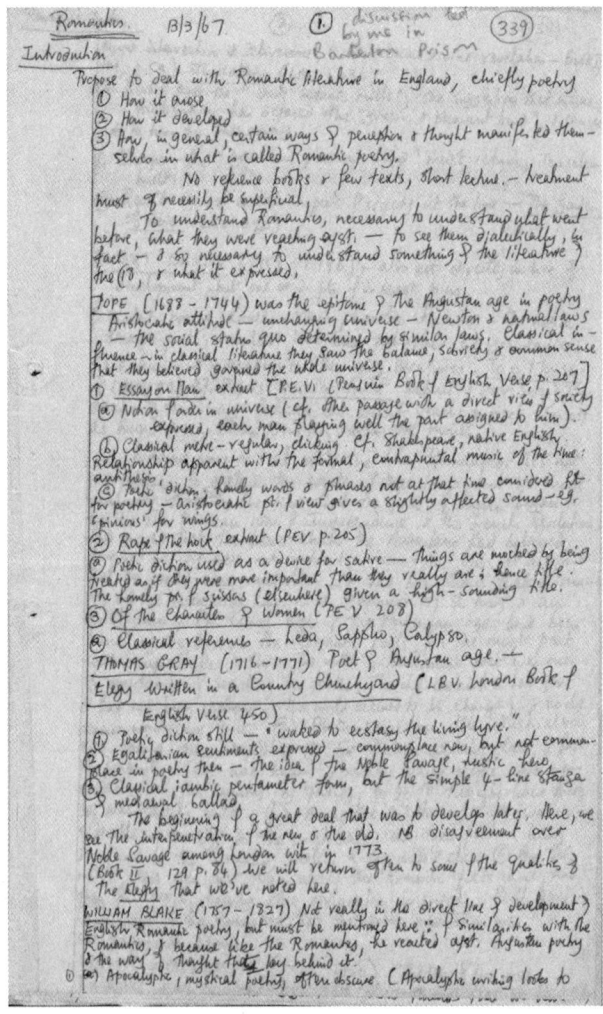

ABOVE: *Notes for a talk on the British Romantics.*

More diary entries

Sheila is working on Bible Study – the entry of Jesus into Jerusalem, arrest, crucifixion and resurrection. Last time Jean did teachings of the Early Church (as shown in the gospels) and its relation to Judaism and the thought in the Old Testament. It is interesting how the Old Testament appeals to those who are politically involved – 17th century Puritans in England, the Afrikaners, Bonhoeffer, my own instinctive liking of the Old Testament, how depressed I was in 90 days when I read the New Testament ... The Old Testament is fighting, healthy, this-wordly, socialised. The New Testament is passive, inward, somewhere a feeling of hopelessness (about this world).

Ann's drawing of Christ on the Cross etc, for her tapestry does not appeal to me. Somehow too critical, too ideological. I am too conscious of the terrible suffering, not only physical but psychological – God, why have you forsaken me? – to portray the crucifixion like that. Also a wincing that men could crucify other men. It seems he was caught in a misconception of his own (political) role in relation to Roman domination. Or not? At the same time, I suppose the crucifixion had long-term historical value. Of course, Christianity had its ups and downs, including periods of dreadful dogmatism and inhumanity.

There are, it appears, growing difficulties in our modern world with Christianity. See Bonhoeffer's difficulties, also somebody like Herbert Butterfield and especially the development in the 19th century – here the UNISA course useful. Improving all men's conditions, their material needs, their intellectual needs, the need for love, security etc, peace and humanity – what else is there to fight for? The way people treat each other here in South Africa too terrible, so against the grain, and one becomes even more conscious of this aspect in gaol. Science and social justice and peace ... I read up to about a week ago about 100 pages of a book, edited by Hans Kohn, a German who is professor of history in New York ...' [I go on to make a comment about the 'idealism and romanticism in German thought, particularly 19th century German thought, about its inability to make a realistic analysis of its history and politics'.] A problem of excessive nationalism.

30/5/66:

Jean's fantasy: Say they gave us something in our coffee so that we went through two days instead of one without knowing.

9 o'clock at night – Sheila's voice from a single cell to Flo who is also locked up in a single cell. Sheila: Flo, turn my light off. I don't want to have to get out of bed. Flo: Okay, just wait a minute while I undo the bolts on my grille.

Clash of tin plates and metal cups. My hearing seems to be so sharp here.

Dream of Ann's: I put red strawberry jam with a knife onto my shoe, and threw it away. And I told the people standing around that I was throwing away the sins of white people perpetrated on blacks. I was chased by the white people.

Dream of Flo's: I dreamed I saw everything, the outside world, through a glass window. I was on one side behind this glass window, and everything else was on the other side.

We hear a siren from the village regularly at 6 am, 9 am, 1 pm, 2 pm, 9 pm. Our only way of telling the time. The prisons, of course, take away our watches on arrival, part of our time deprivation. Timelessness of the gaol experience. We can hear the clock strike if the wind is not blowing the 'wrong way'. Also in some of the cells we can't hear the siren. And on a stormy night none of us can hear it. Church bells on Sunday 6.30, 7.00, 7.30.

1/6/66:

Arnoldus has begun to walk so slowly. He looks so hopeless. It frightens me. I hope he is not going to die, like the rest.

7/6/66:

I am alive at a time when it is possible to look at and consider the whole world. In the Middle Ages one's knowledge was limited. Life was very confined. Now what happens all over the world affects us. Thus we should have a broader view of our planet and of life. This should prevent us from being too dogmatic.

19th century European thinking began to take an historical view of

More diary entries

the world. And in the course of the 20th century Marxism, at least in Europe, is becoming more historicist and less positivist, and thus more humane and less dogmatic. But China, with her back to the wall, feeling very insecure in the world situation, not able to compete economically on an equal basis, stresses the positivist aspects of Marxism. Historicist thinking, ie the belief that social and cultural phenomena arise out of a particular historical/social situation, has vitally affected the thinking of 'the West'. It is something which cannot be ignored ...

Ann and I ordered atlases a couple of months ago, and we spend quite a bit of time looking at maps. There is the whole world in the atlas. And we have also found out exactly where Barberton Gaol is in relation to the rest of South Africa, Swaziland, Zululand, Lourenço Marques. I get a feeling of relief when I look at a map. These four walls seem to stop bearing down on me for a time.

Dream of Ann's: I drove and drove and drove from Barberton to Lands End where I knew I was to be shot. And I fell in love with somebody there. I was only there a day.

Footsteps. Noise of grilles closing.

Chekov's Ward 6. Society treats those who don't fall in with them, as mad. We here in Barberton have been isolated from society as though we have been declared insane.

Today I saw the reflection of the bars of a window in the portaal in the mirror which stands on the top of a locker. The bars were apparently lurching sideways. This picture reminded me of the shadow of bars lurching in a small rectangle of light in the police cell in Fordsburg where I spent most of my second detention under 90 days.

10/6/66:
It horrifies me to think we are 'pushing time' when life is so short.
There is a knot in my stomach when I ask Matron Bester for anything, anticipating the screams.
Our friends: Arnoldus, Hegel, Aristophanes the frog. And our artificial friends – two spiders, made of paper clips and wool,

Hieronymus Major and Hieronymus Minor. And there is Cuthbert, who is a piece of wood which came in a bucket of wood for the fire. He looks just like a seal, and I have become quite fond of him.

18/6/66:
Children's cries on the golf course. Taps making a noise when they are turned on. Pipes in the boiler room make a noise as the water heats. And the geyser in the boiler room, too.

20/6/66:
Flashbacks while reading Weber, Methodology of the Social Sciences.
 It is a great comfort here for me to feel that my ideas are in harmony with the future, the needs of humanity, human dignity. It helps me to feel more integrated in a rather disintegrating situation.
 A cow mooing. Very unusual.
 Jean's dream: 'I was looking at myself in the mirror and instead I saw a girl I taught at school, a very pretty girl. I knew I was so ugly, but I asked myself whether I preferred to be her rather than myself. My own face appeared in the mirror and I decided I preferred to be myself.' Some prisoners, particularly very isolated prisoners, often begin to feel they are ugly. Must tie up with lack of love here and the limited potential for self-realisation.
 For me, Arnoldus is at present a constant, friendly presence.
 Dogs bark occasionally. Birds twitter.
 When I play doubles in table tennis when partners have to take every alternate ball, I get the whirling feeling, the world breaking up and fragmenting, something like the feeling when I have a lot of flashbacks. I seem to be whirling around in all the material my mind has collected since my birth. Possibly in the pre-natal period, too? Jean refuses to play doubles. Says it makes her feel too ghastly.

28/6/66:
The effect of a conflictual transition period on an activist can be painful. See Zhivago's feelings for instance. In a way one becomes so focused on outside things, one sees things too clearly so that one

loses a softness, a gentleness, a certain passivity which, amongst others, the Christian religion tries to encourage. Activists deal with a conflict of social forces. The Christian tends to withdraw from the battle. Of course, I cannot deny that there are Christian activists but they are exceptions except perhaps in places like Latin America and some other places also, of course, such as amongst African leaders in South Africa.

I see the inclination to withdraw into a comfortable cocoon in Rev Langley's approach to life. In a way, I envy this kind of attitude. But, at the same time, I don't like the dishonesty, the shying away from reality, looking at the world all the time not as a real, living, changing world, but just extracting symbols and inserting them to back up one's own philosophy of life, taking them, thus, out of their real context, and changing their meaning to suit oneself. So often, we say to Langley, 'But what you say is not historically correct.' This has usually to do with the Christian story, and his answer is, 'That does not really matter. I am merely using it as a symbol or set of symbols.' And we can see how our historical approach to religion worries him and how he pushes our questions, with controlled irritation, out of sight.

Also as an activist, you can see yourself operating. You are not afraid to face yourself in a concrete situation, at a time when you are being pushed about by circumstances, by other people etc. Not the cloud cuckoo land of mysticism where you withdraw from the arena, introspect and arrange your feelings and thoughts according to your own wishes, mental balance or whatever.

Flo's dream: 'I went out of gaol and met a policeman who asked for an identity card. I said I didn't have one as I had just come out of gaol but I had a gaol card in my bag. Then I found I didn't have the bag.'

Esther's dream: 'There was a change around of the beds and tables in the cell. I am in the front big cell. I walked into this cell where there were lots of beds, mattresses and blankets. I couldn't find my own. I felt lost and angry with Ann who had played a trick on me. I then went to wash a set of bedclothing, nightie, thinking they wouldn't be dry by the night.

Ann writes poetry

Here is some of what she wrote:

Close prison days
have broken back
to warm ones bright with berries picked for jam
to fresh ones sweet with juices crushed upon the tongue:
to days of ease
and leafy finger-fumbled mysteries.
(or days with easy deedless fingers fumbling new mysteries of leaf
and thorn)

Warm days. A friend
and flat stones skipping lightly on the Dee
her great back swelling darkly by,
with ruffled edges laced upon the rocks:
and grand tales told
of men who died within her folds.

Pungent days of pine
exploring grey slate pockets in the hills;
Rob Roy and Cousin John Ray- Park-
heroes both with jaunty swinging kilts:
And love perceived
with unfamiliar vague unease
(A vague uneasy meeting with unfamiliar love.)

Safe ways the crunching gravel paths of home

Imprisoned

Safe the hatstand in the hall,
A Great-Aunt's hair and glittering hands,
The curly footstool brought in awe:
The sheets turned down
and milk and biscuits by the bed.

And long the fast-returning road:
The flashing days of long ago,
A hundred thoughts, a hundred more,
The untold moments leading back ….

To four safe walls;
To countless safe and shapeless days.

The one above is dated 14/1/66. Earlier, July 1965, she had written the following:

I had forgotten
These many years
The liquid of your eyes,
their tender fears,
Our pain,
And my guilt.

But here,
Imprisoned with my past
these bleak days
have plumbed unguessed-at depths
And memories of you
have suffered darkly in my dreams
through wells of hidden tears.

And I, waking,
chained again,
must live each futile day

Ann writes poetry

a penance,
in memory of you.

Here is another poem, this one written in October:

Can I in confusion speak of it?
This and that
awhirl
The why, the what:
a trenchant strand
traced with lightning memories
from darkness
back to darkness.

Worse:
glimpsed for a moment on the way
a myriad more
close-knotted in confusion
grown rank in tears and laughter –
a mother's warning glance,
a father's ease
and bed-time tales of dogs
with blue-bell legs,
And I the Goldilocks.

And back,
struggling through the tangled black
fingering familiar, well-forgotten fears,
the what done
and the what not
and the perhaps
and the only God knows what.

Can I clearly in confusion speak of it?

Venetian blinds

ONE OF THE PROBLEMS WE had in our section round about March–April–May 1966, as I have indicated earlier, was that the sun shone through the windows behind us while we worked at the laundry basins, beating down on our heads, necks and backs, and thus making it more unpleasant than usual while we did the washing. And in the middle of the day, during lunchtime lock-up, the sun poured through the windows of the front cells and because there was so little space in our cells, it was difficult to find a shady spot where we could sit.

The people in the single cells had their difficulties in this respect, and so did Jean, Sheila and I in the front communal cell. We managed to have one of our tables out of the sun but it was impossible with the other two, and so we worked with the sun beating down on us and its white light fell onto the pages of our books, almost blinding us. We asked the Front if we could put up curtains on the windows near the laundry basins, and curtains or venetian blinds on the windows of the front big cell. We also told the Front that another reason why we would like curtains in the front big cell was that the guard outside or anyone else who happened to be around could see us at night when our light was on. They could, for instance, see us getting undressed.

I raised the matter first with Matron Bester. For once, she was quite reasonable, and said that there had earlier been venetian blinds on the two windows of the front big cell; they were stored away and thus still available; she would get them out and see that they were put up. Nothing happened. Of course, we were very used to having to ask over and over again for things, and so we went on asking. Jean took up the matter and was told that something would be done about it. Eventually, when neither curtains nor blinds had been forthcoming, I raised the question during Complaints and Requests. I did so very carefully, not even telling the Brigadier that we had been waiting for them for weeks already.

'Brigadier, would it be possible for us to have some venetian blinds up in our cell or curtains because the sun comes onto our tables in the middle of the day so that we find it difficult to study. And it would also be a good idea because people can see us at night from outside ... And Matron Bester has said there are venetian blinds available.'

Matron Bester was standing next to the Brigadier's desk. The Brigadier was pompously holding his pen over the large 'Complaints and Requests Book' which lay on the desk in front of him. I could hear the others exercising in the yard. Tramp, tramp, tramp. Such fast steps, and so insistent. Like soldiers marching. The venetian blinds in the office were down.

I saw Matron Bester's face beginning to swell. Her mouth began to pout, partly like a spoilt child, partly like somebody insane. And her eyes began to pop out of her head.

'How can I give them venetian blinds when they are interfering with the wall next to the window!' she burst out.

'I beg your pardon, Matron,' I said. 'What do you mean "interfering" with the wall? Who is interfering with the wall?'

Matron Bester turned to the Brigadier. 'Yes, Brigadier, you go and look at that wall. The brick is all broken away. How can I then put venetian blinds up there?'

'What is this, Matron?' I said, feeling I had a right to be angry. 'Are you accusing me of breaking down the wall?'

She turned to me. 'Why are you asking me that question?' She walked towards me round the side of the desk, pushed her face at mine and leered. 'Are you guilty?' she sneered.

I addressed the Brigadier. 'How dare Matron accuse me of breaking down the wall! I object most strongly to this. Indeed, according to the regulations, people have no right to throw accusations at other people without a firm basis.'

The Brigadier pulled himself up. 'Yes, well, Matron has made a complaint to me and she has every right to do so. And I must investigate her complaint.' His voice was resonant.

'She has no right to make such accusations, Brigadier,' I insisted.

The Brigadier's eyes turned black and his face pale. 'Get out of here!' he spat, leaning across his desk. 'Get out. Get out, at once! At once!'

I backed out of the office and walked down the passage back to the section. I told the others what had happened. 'She's accusing us of breaking down the wall in the front big cell,' I said.

'Good Lord!' somebody exclaimed. 'Why on earth should we do that?'

'I don't know,' I responded. 'She's just a crazy woman. I don't even know whether she believes it herself.'

'But does she genuinely believe that we would try and escape out of a front window of the gaol? Can you imagine! We would first have to remove a few bars, then we would have to undo the bolts to remove the cage, and then what?'

We went into the cell to have a look. The brick was breaking away at a point between the window and the cage. 'So what are we going to do when we've got the cage off?' somebody asked.

I pressed my head against the bars of the window, looked through the bottom of the cage to the concrete path 20 or 30 feet below. 'Then we're going to throw the cage down onto the path below with a loud metal clang,' I answered. 'And, with the guard watching us quietly, make a jump for it, probably breaking a leg or two, and maybe an arm, and then make a dash for it, crunch, crunch, crunch across the gravel, past the gun of the guard who continues to watch us in silence and down the gravel road into Barberton where we'll wait patiently on the road and try and hitch a lift to Swaziland.'

'God, she really must be crazy if she believes we are trying to escape from here.'

'You can see why the wall has broken away at that point,' I noted. 'There was obviously a bolt in there … Look at that line into the brick … And look just in front of it there is a hole for the bolt in the cage and that bolt has been taken out, obviously because they didn't want it there. Instead they put it here on the side.

A little later the Brigadier came importantly to our cell, together with

Venetian blinds

Matron Bester. He had a look and, without a word, left.

I decided to drop the matter there since, it seemed to me, the Brigadier must have been convinced that Matron Bester's allegation was nonsense. And I thought Matron Bester had probably not been serious as she had not raised the matter before. If she had really believed it, it was a serious matter. I presumed that she had probably raised it because she felt guilty about having done nothing about the venetian blinds and just wanted to put the blame elsewhere.

This was a favourite tactic of the authorities. Whenever we made a complaint which they felt was, to one degree or another, justified, they would accuse us of something else so that we felt guilty and, in trying to defend ourselves, would forget about the complaint we had been making. The Brigadier used this method a lot, as did Aucamp.

The Brigadier's favourite tactic was to establish in some way that we prisoners had discussed the complaint beforehand, and then throw this in the face of the prisoner who was making the complaint. 'Oh, so you people have been discussing this, have you?' he would say, threatening and leering. And the prisoner would immediately go on the defensive, trying to prove to him that we had not discussed it. The Brigadier knew this was a good point for there was a prison regulation that stated that it was illegal for any prisoners to conspire together, and this was so wide it seemed it could cover anything – any common action, any common decision even to raise a problem with the Front.

When on occasion the Brigadier discovered we had obviously not discussed the complaint, and that one prisoner was just raising it on her own, he would comment, 'But you are the only person making this complaint. Nobody else has made this complaint to me.' What he was saying, amongst other things, was, You are just a troublemaker. You just want to make complaints for the sake of making complaints. So I'm not interested.

If you countered with, 'But, Brigadier, the others do feel the same about it,' he would say, 'Oh, the others do feel the same, do they? So you have all discussed the matter amongst yourselves, and you have been made the spokesman.' Then he would add, threateningly: 'Is that the case?'

I decided not to refer again to Matron Bester's allegations concerning the wall, but just to go ahead and continue asking for venetian blinds. However, it was Matron Bester who made the next move. A day or two after the brush in the office, as she was unlocking our cell in the morning, she muttered, not looking at us, 'Middleton and Neame, you are to move out of this cell and go to the other big cell.' And, without waiting for an answer, she swept out of our section, banging the grille behind her.

In the days that followed I tried to obtain some explanation from Matron Bester. She said it was the Brigadier's orders. 'I don't know,' she said rudely when I asked her whether she knew why I had to move. 'It's the Brigadier's orders.'

'But surely, Matron, you know why the Brigadier gave such orders. Didn't he discuss the matter with you?'

'I know nothing,' she said sullenly.

I could see she was lying. Jean and I discussed the whole matter. This sort of action was quite unprecedented. We had only been a few weeks in that cell and none of us had asked to move. In fact, the move was inconveniencing some of the others, who had made plans about cell arrangements which were now impossible. If the Brigadier's order had something to do with the broken brick near the window, why was Sheila not involved? She was also in the cell. Why only Jean and I? Did they seriously believe that Jean and I were involved in a plan to escape? And, if they did, why were they not interrogating any of us, particularly Sheila?

Perhaps Matron Bester just wanted to show who was boss, that she could make any allegations she pleased against prisoners. That was likely to have been the Brigadier's view, which would also have been that it should be made clear in every instance that a prisoner and not a prison official was in the wrong. And then I remembered that Matron Bester had initially refused permission for me to move into that cell when I had asked a few weeks before, and had said I would have to ask the Brigadier. Thereafter she had changed her mind and herself given me permission. Had he asked, I wondered, why she had taken this decision alone?

A factor may have been that in the big front cell we could now hear something of what was happening in the Front. Some panes of glass had been taken out of the top of the window that looked down onto the passage, leading up to Matron Bester's office. This would have been done in order to give the people in the big cell some cross-ventilation as it had been absolutely unbearable in there, especially in the summer.

So now we could hear some of what was going on in the Front through the wire mesh which replaced the glass panes. That was why I had been able to hear Taljaard shouting and threatening a woman who had broken her cup, and, as far as I could remember, I had told my fellow prisoners in front of the wardress on duty with us about this incident. Had the wardress reported this to the Front? Matron Bester was absolutely neurotic about being 'caught out', and it was Jean and I who were regarded as being particularly keen to take up any misdemeanours on the part of the authorities.

At Complaints and Requests I asked the Brigadier why he had given orders that I leave the front cell and he told me he did not have to tell me why he did things – orders were orders – and I was to move over to another cell immediately.

Following instructions was another prison regulation, one which obviously could very easily be abused. A prisoner had to obey the instructions of a prison official; in fact, I think, they had to obey the instructions of any member of the Prisons Service. This regulation in the Prisoners' Handbook says nothing about instructions which may be contrary to other regulations or instructions which may be immoral or actually illegal, etc. Nothing.

This was a problem for us even when we were trying to maintain our modicum of 'rights' under the prison regulations. For instance, what does a prisoner do if an official orders them to come in from the exercise yard when they have only had ten minutes' exercise whereas the regulations specify an hour exercise? Or what does a prisoner do if a member of the prison staff orders him to have sexual intercourse with another prisoner, as evidently happens on occasion in men's gaols.

At any rate, I asked the Brigadier whether he really thought that I had been responsible for the brick breaking away next to the window. He responded in his pompous manner that he had made a full investigation. It was quite clear to him that the brick had broken away when one of the men had tried to drive a bolt into the wall.

After this whole typical Barberton Prison palaver/diversion, I at last managed to come back to my original request, which was for venetian blinds. I told the Brigadier about the sun pouring in onto our tables and the fact that people could see us from outside when our light was on. With his lascivious inclination, he naturally ignored the first point, latching onto the second.

'But who comes around at night?' he asked.

'There's the guard,' I answered 'And various other men come on rounds.'

'And who else?' he inquired significantly.

'I don't know,' I said. 'Just people on rounds ... and sometimes wardresses.'

'Who else?' he insisted, pulling himself up behind the desk. 'Do you not know that I come regularly on rounds.' He leaned over the desk with his sadistic-lecherous-macho look. 'I,' he stressed again, 'come round regularly at night.'

'Oh,' I responded. He seemed to think this piece of information would excite me.

'And,' he continued, 'I have had a look up at your windows at night, and people can't see anything from outside.'

'They can if the prisoner is a certain distance from the window.'

'Well,' he said, 'just see to it that you are not at that distance from the window.'

'It is difficult to avoid. We in the cell can't always be calculating whether we can be seen from the outside.' Attempting to come back to my original request after this characteristic seemingly endless diversion on the part of the Brigadier, I then pointed out that Matron Bester had said there were venetian blinds available. Was it not possible for us to have them?

Throughout this conversation Matron Bester was sighing with impatience and pulling faces. The Brigadier's meandering style often irritated her. She thought he was an idiot, which he was, of course. And she was irritated and angered by me.

'Anyway,' she spat at me with a swollen face, 'you are not in that cell any longer. And the others haven't asked for venetian blinds.'

The people who moved into the front big cell decided they couldn't face any more of the cat-and-mouse tactics of the Front and did not ask for venetian blinds. About eight months later the whole campaign started all over again and, after weeks of raising the issue at Complaints and Requests, we were given a curtain and a venetian blind.

Judge Ludorf visits

I THINK IT WAS IN THE COURSE of May or June 1966 that Judge Ludorf visited the gaol. We noted that there was a similar black car at the front as there had been the afternoon Judge Boshoff had come. And a similar number of mainly goofy-looking men. They all trooped into our portaal with the Brigadier in front, accompanied by a short, rather ungainly man in a grey suit. He had iron-grey hair and the purple face of a heavy drinker. He did not look spruce as Boshoff had looked. However, I noticed that his trousers were fairly narrow, not the huge flapping trousers the Brigadier wore. He was obviously a city man.

The Brigadier, with a smug smile on his face, introduced him as 'Judge Ludorf' and asked if any of us wished to speak to the judge. We were, as was usual in such circumstances, standing on parade, with our hands behind our backs, in a line just outside the laundry basin area. I said I would like to speak to him. And one or two others expressed a similar wish. Sheila said she wanted to speak to him about her mother who had been arrested.

The Brigadier made a gesture to Ludorf, inviting him to have a look at the cells. The judge, looking very unwilling and, I thought, rather unsteady on his feet, walked towards the back big cell, the one overlooking the courtyard, and had a quick look in, quite obviously completely disinterested. It was just a gesture. And, as he crossed the portaal, he had a quick look at the single cells and out he went up the passage, with a peculiar unsteady, rather rolling gait.

'Come on, Neame.' Matron Bester was looking relaxed. So, come to think of it, was the Brigadier. I went up the passage and, as I did so, noted a strong smell of liquor. I followed the smell to the office. As

I entered, the Brigadier and Matron Bester proceeded to leave, and the Brigadier said, with a very smug, relaxed smile on his face, 'Well, Neame, you see that we are leaving you alone with the judge. I am not going to be present.'

I stood in front of the desk. Judge Ludorf was sitting behind it, together with a youngish man with black or dark brown curly hair, not an unpleasant face. I looked at Ludorf enquiringly. His was not a very nice face. Apart from anything else, he had rather bleary, bloodshot, unfriendly eyes.

He said, 'I have come to hear your complaints. I have come direct from the Minister of Justice and I will go straight back to him. The Brigadier or the Matron will know nothing of what you have said. Only the Minister will know what your complaints are. Moreover, what you tell me will be completely confidential. No names will be mentioned.' He turned to the younger man. 'This is my secretary and he will just take a note of any complaints you have. I have been visiting other political prisoners, too. I have already seen the men in Pretoria.'

I wasn't particularly interested in his undertaking to keep what I said confidential. This was, firstly, because it would have no influence on the kind of complaints I intended making, and, secondly, because I had learned to take nobody at face value, to trust nobody, particularly somebody so obviously connected with the authorities. And I had noted that the Brigadier was quite happy with the Ludorf visit.

I looked carefully again at the expression in the judge's eyes. I decided that they were definitely not sympathetic. And I tried to work out why. Was he unsympathetic to my political views, indeed not only unsympathetic but even hostile? Or was it just boredom? He certainly did not look interested in the job he had to do. Maybe he was just longing to get away so that he could have a drink.

I did not feel encouraged but I went ahead anyway, following my usual routine of raising our dissatisfactions. I spoke about our tremendous isolation, our wish to be reclassified to B Group, the group where most ordinary criminal prisoners start and which we had been fighting for for quite a few weeks already. I also took up the issue of the very confined area in which we lived our whole lives, the fact that we were not integrated into the life of the prison and the bad psychological effects this situation was having on us. I had often spoken to the Brigadier about our confined space. It had become my favourite topic.

'Oh,' the Brigadier had said with a sneer when I first raised it with him, 'you are beginning to find the space confined, are you? Well, let me tell you that we are pleased when those four walls begin to close in on you –' he brought his palms together carefully and sadistically, two hands, podgy white, with black hairs '– for then we know that your prison sentence has really begun.'

I spoke to Ludorf about the very different conditions of ordinary women criminal prisoners in a gaol such as Kroonstad, where they did not work, eat, exercise, sleep, live their whole lives in just one small section. They had a cell section where they slept and took a bath. They had a workroom where they were busy during the day, a separate dining hall where they ate their meals, a library, a hospital, a common room, a chapel where they attended services on Sunday.

I told him that we washed the dishes from which we ate our food in the same basin as we washed filthy washing. I said that the women at Kroonstad saw films regularly, and had a gramophone. I asked that we should be left free in our section and courtyard at lunchtime lock-up and at night, as were the ordinary prisoners at Kroonstad. I asked that political prisoners should get remission and parole like ordinary criminal prisoners. Etcetera, etcetera.

While I was speaking Ludorf's secretary did a bit of writing but I imagined that everything I said was being recorded on tape anyway. The secretary seemed fairly interested, not so much in what I said, perhaps, but the sort of person I was. Ludorf's dull eyes didn't really seem to be taking anything in. It was certainly a most discouraging atmosphere. None the less, I felt it had to be done since I was of the opinion that we must use any opportunity that offered itself. I told him that was all I had to say and excused myself.

By the end of the interview I felt my jaw quivering. To speak to someone new, to speak to anyone for any length of time, was a great strain. Any new situation taxed my strength to the maximum. Every nerve, every muscle in my body tensed and my heart beat fast. It was like struggling against the child in me, as though a part of me had retrogressed into my past when I had only faced limited situations and found new ones difficult to handle.

If I remember correctly, the other people who went to see Ludorf were Jean, Sheila and Ann.

Jean was always very good and conscientious about raising points and about how she approached the matter. She would plan, often for days, sometimes weeks, the way in which she was going to tackle a problem or approach a particular person. However rude the person was to whom she spoke, she never lost her ladylike manner.

Ann complains about Matron Bester

ANN, MUCH TO MY SURPRISE, was to raise with the judge the issue of the behaviour of Matron Bester. She told Ludorf she didn't know whether Matron Bester had been given instructions to conduct herself in the way she was doing but that it was having a most terrible effect on us. She did not know whether Matron Bester was on a deliberate campaign to confuse us and make our lives unbearable. If that was not her deliberate intention, then she was an extremely neurotic woman and should have nothing to do with prisoners.

The point she stressed was Matron Bester's inconsistency. Indeed, it was true that despite her ingrained moodiness, which tended to make her at most times unbearable, Bester was now and again fairly pleasant. To me, of course, she was inclined to be consistently awful. To the others, out of the blue one day she would be nice. And their morale as human beings would strengthen. Then, without warning, without any apparent reason, she would smash them down again.

Mollie, for instance, might ask Matron Bester at Complaints and Requests whether we could have a large jug for the milk that was sent in to us. And Matron Bester would smile and say that was a good idea and she would see that a jug from the 'back' would be sent into our section immediately. And Mollie, with a polite 'Thank you, Matron', would return to the section.

She would give Matron Bester a couple of days and then at morning unlock she would politely ask whether Matron had managed to organise a jug for us. Matron Bester's face would swell, her lower lip would swell into an enormous pout and, with wild eyes, she would scream at Mollie, 'Do you think I've got all day to think about you people? You sit in this section all day while I've got to run a prison. Don't you know you are not the only prisoners here? I have hundreds of other prisoners ...' She would be shouting this as she hurried from cell to cell, crashing the keys into the locks as she opened them and ignoring everyone's polite 'Good morning, Matron'. 'And anyway,' she would say as she backed out through the central grille, 'I've got no jugs. You will have to do without.'

I would look at Mollie's face as she came out of her cell with her toothbrush, tight and pale with a clenched mouth, very close to tears. This sort of shouting, particularly at six in the morning, was a great shock to anyone's system. It was a tremendous shock to Mollie. She was consistently polite to the authorities, and, as she once told me, she had never in her life come across this type of behaviour.

Mollie came from a very affectionate, almost protective family. She was the niece of Bram Fischer, who was strikingly soft spoken. Mollie was devoted to her father, who had died some years before, and her mother and brother were very loving and conscientious about seeing to her requirements while she was in gaol. She had served a six-month sentence in 1962 for distribution of a leaflet of the banned African National Congress and so the family had a good idea about what to do in order to keep up her morale.

Anyway, here was Mollie who, because of her family background, had only experienced politeness and affection and gentleness from other human beings, precipitated into the world of Barberton Prison. It horrified her. I saw the horror sink deep into her being. After one of these shouting incidents she would wander around in the section for days, tense and tight and as if thunderstruck. Her natural inclination was to trust people. When they told her something she believed them. This was something natural to her personality.

It was during the first half of 1966 that Mollie's attitudes and beliefs went through a furnace. And she realised, not only rationally but with her whole being, that the authorities were liars, hypocrites and brutes. For somebody as gentle as she was, it was a terrible lesson to learn. Later she would speak once again to Matron Bester in the front office about a jug for the milk. Matron Bester, apparently forgetting what she had said about there being no jugs, agreed to see to the matter immediately and sent somebody off to the back of the gaol to fetch a jug.

As for Ann, I think her desire to have good relations with the authorities, in the first place with Brigadier Pretorius and Matron Bester, lasted about a year. She was immediately popular with the wardresses, with Matron Bester and, indeed, with the authorities in general. She was, in fact, the type of person who desperately needed to be liked and she would make great efforts to ensure that she was. Moreover, I assume that Bram's advice to us to try to mislead the authorities as to our political intentions had influenced her in regard to the way in which she initially shaped her relations with the authorities.

In this context, the fact that she took up the behaviour of Matron Bester with Judge Ludorf was an indication that she was rethinking her approach. It was at this point that she was to grasp the nettle. She did not discuss it beforehand with me or, as far as I know, with anyone else. She told Judge Ludorf, and Ann could be very eloquent and because she was a 'favourite' she was in a good position to make criticisms, that prisoners inevitably became very dependent on the authorities, particularly on the Matron-in-Charge, because they are a vital part of their world, and so Matron Bester's inconsistent behaviour was having a terrible effect on us.

She insisted that if things went on as they were, we would all go out of that prison insane. She told Ludorf it was unacceptable that a Matron-in-Charge should be allowed to scream at prisoners like a mad woman. And what was worse, one moment she would be screaming at us from the central grille and a few minutes later she might be back there smiling at us. Ann asked whether there was a deliberate campaign on the part of the authorities to drive us into mental illness. She said it was a matter of great urgency for our psychological balance was already very shaky.

It was shortly after Ludorf had been there that the Brigadier asked me whether I had criticised any of the staff to the judge, and, if not, why not. He knew perfectly well that I hadn't; he just wanted to find out if I had used Ann as a kind of proxy. It was apparent from the Brigadier's questions and attitude that he knew what complaints each of us had made. I was not surprised.

Colonel Aucamp came soon after Ludorf had visited us. I think the two people he specially spoke to were Mollie and Ann. Aucamp said we were wasting our time going to judges. We had wasted our time going to Ludorf for as soon as the latter had got back to Pretoria, he had come straight to his (Aucamp's) office and told him all the complaints we had made, and the complaints made were listed against the names of the people who had made them. Aucamp told us that the only reason why Ludorf had come was so the authorities could find out who the troublemakers were. They were not interested in our complaints.

Well, that was that. I don't think any of us were particularly surprised. We had come to know the authorities. And we knew that Ludorf was a red-hot Nationalist, anyway.

Judge Hiemstra on a visit

THE ONLY OTHER JUDGE WHO visited us while I was there was Hiemstra, who came, I think, in about July or August 1966. He was on circuit in the area and so I suppose he came to the local prisons. We were out in the exercise yard when he arrived and we were lined up 'on parade' in the courtyard. He looked spruce to us. I don't know whether he would have looked spruce in the outside world but against the male prison officials we saw, he did. He was short, wore a grey suit, grey hair combed back. He stood, too, with some presence and self-confidence, unlike the Brigadier with baggy pants, fat backside and large paunch, with a goofy smile on his face.

The Brigadier introduced the judge, who did not even say 'Good afternoon' or 'How do you do'. He merely said, 'I don't want to hear any complaints because I can't judge.' And the Brigadier took him off before we could open our mouths. We turned and looked at each other.

'Well, I like that,' somebody commented. 'He can't judge, so why does he come? Why is he a judge if he can't judge?'

'He's supposed to hear complaints of assault, isn't he?' somebody asked. 'And he doesn't even ask what complaints we have.'

'And he was so rude. He didn't even greet us.'

'Well, anyway, it will make a nice story for my next visit,' Jean said. Soon her face lit up. She looked perfectly delighted. 'Think what an extensive acquaintance we will have amongst judges and magistrates!' she said. We caught her mood.

'Yes,' I said, 'we'll hardly be able to go into the Supreme Court without greeting somebody.'

'Indeed,' said Ann. 'You mean as you go in your chains into the dock.'

'Yes,' Sheila joined in, not wanting to miss out on this, 'you'll have your chains in your hands and you'll be bowing from side to side, saying, "Hello Ludorf, Hello Boshoff, Hello Hiemstra." And Judge Boshoff will say, "Can my secretary carry your chains for you, Miss Middleton?"'

'No, that's really sick,' Flo intervened. 'Come on – let's walk.' The group broke up and we marched, two by two, around the courtyard.

Brigadier Viljoen

Ludorf's visit occurred not so long before May 31st, Republic Day, the day on which the government had planned, we had heard, to grant amnesty to prisoners. They were using this rumour as a bait to discourage us from fighting for better conditions. Apart from anything else, if you think that you are going to get out soon, you don't bother too much about your conditions. Moreover, the authorities clearly worked on the assumption that if a prisoner wants release as soon as possible and feels that 'good behaviour' is the only way to get it, they will stop fighting for better conditions. At any rate, they had made it clear to us that 'complaints and requests' were regarded as an indication of what the authorities regarded as unsatisfactory behaviour on the part of a prisoner.

Brigadier Pretorius had on an occasion, in support of his argument that I was a troublemaker, pointed to the 'Complaints and Requests' book. 'You are not a good prisoner,' he told me. 'Here is the proof.' And in a rather theatrical manner he turned over pages of the large book. 'Here, in this very book, there is proof. Look at all the entries next to your name. I don't think there is a single day when you have not made some complaint or request.' He used a similar argument with Mollie later.

The continual allusions to and rumours about reduction of sentences made life there even more uncomfortable for us. The authorities seemed deliberately to be trying to induce an atmosphere of confusion and uncertainty. One of the people they used for this purpose was Brigadier Viljoen, the man whom the OC had told us was on the '*Institution* Board' and who was apparently a harbinger of the policy of 'rehabilitation'.

This man, in the course of the first half of 1966, saw Ann several times, the rest of us at least once. His aim, he told us, was to bring us back to God. And he gave us various pieces of literature to help us on our way – so Starr Daily books as well as Norman Vincent Peale's *The Power of Positive Thinking*. We were horrified particularly by the latter. It is a typical product of business America. Norman Vincent Peale had taken it upon himself to use God to become influential, to make friends and influence people. And make money. He told his readers that, with God's help and the confidence that a firm belief in God gave people, a man could become an extremely successful businessman.

I think it was at the beginning of 1966 that Brigadier Pretorius had first introduced us to Brigadier Viljoen. This was as a group in the portaal. And Viljoen was very pleasant, particularly in comparison with the rude manners of the OC and Matron Bester. He told us he would be seeing us soon but, except for Ann, quite a long time passed before he came to see the rest of us. He told one of us that he had had a great struggle with himself for he had found the thought of visiting communists unbearable. He had had to pray to God, night after night, for months before he could overcome this feeling. With God's help, he had managed, and so there he was.

As always, any change in the routine evoked great excitement and I rather looked forward to going to have a chat with Viljoen, particularly as he seemed quite a pleasant chap. Matron Bester came to the section to call me and escorted me to the visitors' room. Viljoen was sitting on the other side of the table. 'Hello, Sylvia,' he said in a loud hearty voice and with a big smile. 'If I may call you Sylvia?'

'Yes, yes,' I responded. That was certainly different from the 'Neame, Neame'.

He smiled at me. A clear pink and white complexion. A bit podgy. Black, curly hair, close cut. Saliva at the corners of his mouth. He had a strange accent – in English – and a loud, rather high voice. He smoked a pipe. Later, we always knew when he was in the gaol because we came to recognise the smell of his tobacco. It had a very nice perfume.

'Well, Sylvia, and how are you?' he asked in a cheery manner, as though he had just met a pal at a cattle sale. I found myself responding.

'Well, I can't say I feel so hot,' I said.

'Why is that, Sylvia? Why is that?'

Imprisoned

I took up my usual subject. 'Well, Brigadier, we are very isolated here, and very confined.'

'Yes, I know that, Sylvia. We know that. I, and the Department of Prisons, don't like locking people up like this, especially young girls like you. It must be terrible. In fact, I know it is terrible.'

'Yes, Brigadier, but can't you do something—' I tried to hold a dialogue with him but he was obviously used to monologues because he ignored what I said, and went on talking.

'And Mr Vorster is a close friend of mine. And he has spoken to me about all of you, Sylvia. He is very worried about you. As he lies in bed at night, he thinks about you. He thinks about you and prays for you …'

'Really, Brigadier!' I said with an edge in my voice.

'Yes, Sylvia. You must believe me. Mr Vorster is most concerned about you. I know because he is a friend of mine. And you know that he knows one of the prisoners in Pretoria Prison and he actually went to visit him and offered him cigarettes.'

'Oh, really, Brigadier!'

'And Mrs Vorster too. You know that she specially chose the colour of your uniforms.'

Heavens! I thought. This guy can talk. But it was pleasant in the visitors' room. It was not so often that we had a chance of getting out of our section for a little chat in the Front. It was a bright sunny room. Two windows to the left of me with the bars painted in a cream colour. And what was especially nice, there were no cages so that I could see the outside world clearly. Tall trees on the other side of the little stone wall at the edge of the grey gravel driveway. Quite a hot sun outside but cool here, with one of the venetian blinds down. Brigadier Viljoen's high loud voice went droning on.

'I know what it is like to be in gaol … Maybe I don't know all that prisoners know but I have been in the prison service for many, many years.'

'Is that so, Brigadier,' I commented.

'Yes, yes, Sylvia.' He was pleased with this encouragement. 'I was in Pretoria, too, so I know what it is like. And I sympathise very much with you. For I know that prison is a terrible thing for anyone. I also know about Bantu prisoners. They know me and trust me. I am very kind to the Bantu. One of the Bantu prisoners who had finished his sentence, I took to work for me, and I help him whenever I can. I am very good to him, and he knows it ... I give him food and clothing, and he is fond of me.'

'You sound very patronising, Brigadier. You talk about him as though he were a child.'

Viljoen paused, and I saw the struggle going on under the surface of his eyes. A strange sort of convulsive movement, as though an amoeba were trying to absorb a foreign body which it did not like very much and was not quite sure whether it was actually edible.

That was the thing about Viljoen. He had built up his own private view of life, struggling with himself, but not really looking at the facts or thinking about anyone else's point of view. He was not a listener to anyone, it seemed. I found out later that Matron Bester and Taljaard despised him. They laughed at him behind his back, even in front of prisoners. Taljaard used to speak to us about him, laughing and pulling a face. They said he talked too much and wouldn't let them get on with their work.

Viljoen's approach to life meant that he was unable to deal with my comment about his being patronising and so, ignoring it, he continued: 'Yes, the Bantu know that they can trust me, that I will be good to them. The Bantu is a human being too,' he confirmed. He was clearly especially proud of the latter statement. He seemed to feel that he had just discovered some very important fact. 'And they know that we know what is good for them.'

Then, getting back to me, he said, 'I want you to trust me, Sylvia. I want you to come to me with any problems you may have.'

'Yes, Brigadier, do you think you could do anything about improving' – I tried to slip something into the pause in the flow of words and the apparent invitation. Viljoen was not to be interrupted, however. There was not even a glimmer of an expression on his face to indicate that he had even heard me say anything.

'Yes, yes, Sylvia,' his loud voice continued, 'whenever you are worried about anything tell me about it. You can even at any time ask Matron

Bester to phone me if you want to discuss anything with me. I am always ready to help you, Sylvia.'

'Yes, Brigadier,' I tried to interrupt. 'Isn't there something you can do about –'

The endless verbal stream went on. A little piece of white saliva dropped from the left corner of his mouth onto the end of his chin. 'Yes, Sylvia, do you know that I have a degree in psychology?'

His eyes cleared a little. He looked at me expectantly, searching for my reaction. He could not take the naive look of pride off his face. I was watching the saliva at the end of his chin. 'Oh, really, Brigadier?' I pretended to be impressed. But this time he was watching me and he saw my eyes on his chin. He glanced down and managed somehow to catch sight of the white speck. The look of pride went suddenly from his face. He looked embarrassed. He looked into my eyes and his eyes were filled with a sense of his own foolishness. For a moment he looked cornered. Then he hurriedly pulled himself together, brushed his hand across his chin and, leaning again over the table towards me, he said softly, with his chubby red lips, 'God is with you, Sylvia, even though you are a prisoner. In fact, he is especially with you because you are a prisoner. He is waiting for you, Sylvia, waiting and waiting for you to come back to him. How long are you going to keep him waiting?'

Viljoen paused with a dramatic gesture. He seemed to expect an answer. I wasn't quite sure what to say now that he was actually giving me an opportunity to say something.

It was warm and quiet in the gaol. No screaming for the moment. Bester was probably somewhere at the back. It's rather nice sitting here, I thought. Nice to be spoken to so kindly. But he was waiting for me to answer his question as to how long I intended keeping God waiting.

'I don't know, Brigadier,' I said, pulling myself back in my chair, embarrassed by his wheedling expression across the narrow space of table.

'Look, Sylvia, I know that you do things here that you shouldn't do.'

I latched onto that immediately. 'What do you mean, Brigadier?'

'You know what I mean, Sylvia,' he said quietly and significantly.

'I don't know what you mean, Brigadier.'

He ignored me. His eyes were cut off again, turned inwards, looking at his own benevolence. He was pleased with himself. He had forgotten about the saliva. He felt he was making a good impression. He was impressed himself. He was again absolutely sure of his benevolence. His chubby round soft face portrayed a self-satisfied expression.

'But I believe in you, Sylvia ... I believe in you ... I believe in every prisoner ... I have worked with prisoners a long time, Sylvia, a long time, and they know that they can trust me ... And I know what it is like to be a prisoner. It is a terrible thing ... truly terrible. I know, Sylvia ... I know.' He paused. 'But you must have patience with them, Sylvia.'

'With whom, Brigadier?' I asked quietly, lulled by the heat around the trees outside and the blue, blue sky, the pale green venetian blinds and the sunlight on the floor.

'They have a terrible life, you know, Sylvia. Matron and her wardresses have to get up early in the morning, before six o'clock, to come to the gaol, and they have long hours. Very long hours. What other people have to get up so early in the morning? So you must have patience with them.'

'They chose their job, Brigadier.'

'They have a very hard life, Sylvia. And Matron Bester gets very tired sometimes. I know that.'

I suddenly felt the exhaustion and tautness of my body. My spine was stiff with tension. My lips taut and beginning to tremble. I couldn't listen to another word. I can't take any more of this, I thought. It was nice to get out of the section, to talk to somebody new, to somebody who spoke gently, but I was very tired now. The Brigadier's voice droned on. I let him go on for a bit and then, half getting up when he paused a little, I said, 'Well, thank you very much, Brigadier.' He looked startled for a moment and then he looked as though I had slapped him in the face.

'Thank you very much, Brigadier,' I said again, politely and with a smile, as I backed towards the doorway, feeling the tension in the upper half of my back, at the top of my arms, and in my neck. And a dry, taut feeling in my mouth.

'That's all right, Sylvia,' he said, standing up politely. 'Best of luck. And remember what I said to you about being patient. I have confidence in you.'

'Right, Brigadier,' I mumbled as I turned down the passage towards the door of our section.

Back in the section, everyone wanted to know exactly what he'd said. I told them, word for word. They looked excited. 'At least he speaks to one decently,' I said, trying to hang onto something positive.

'Do you think it is worth seeing him?' somebody asked.

'Yes, I think so. He's nicer than the others, anyway. At least he doesn't scream and shout ... And his pipe smells nice.'

'Yes, his pipe does smell nice, doesn't it?'

And the inevitable question: 'Did he say anything about reduction?'

'No, not to me. He just said how much Vorster and Mrs Vorster think about us.'

Cynical laughs all round.

As it happened, Viljoen did drop very broad hints about possible release, particularly to Ann.

We win a battle

VILJOEN'S TREATMENT OF US was just a short break from the general nastiness of the authorities. We still had to fight every inch of the way for everything.

One afternoon 'Pomposity' was on duty in our section – Miss Wilkin with her large breasts carried like a shelf before her, and her pimply face from which she continually squeezed blackheads, using Jean's eyebrow tweezers, without Jean's permission and much to Jean's disgust. Miss Wilkin used to disappear into our small storeroom many an afternoon with one of our little mirrors from the top of a locker in the portaal and the tweezers.

This particular afternoon her blackhead squeezing was interrupted. It must have been about 2.30. A wardress from the Front brought in the large aluminium pot with soup. Flo and I happened to be in the vicinity of the grille at the time and we asked Miss Wilkin if she wouldn't keep the pot on the stove for us as it wasn't yet time to eat and we didn't want cold soup. And could we do the same with the coffee in the kettle? She said she would go and ask Matron.

Flo and I then joined the others who were exercising out in the courtyard. We were there about two minutes when Miss Wilkin's ample bosom and narrow legs appeared in the doorless doorway opening out into the courtyard. 'Matrone sê julle mense moet nou binnekom. Julle kan nie nou oefen nie. Sy wil vroeg toesluit.' (Matron says you people must come in. You cannot exercise now. She wants to lock up early.)

'But, Miss Wilkin, we haven't had our exercise, and it is too early to eat. We are supposed to eat at 3.30.'

'Ek kan niks sê nie, mense. Matrone sê julle moet onmiddelik binnekom.' (I cannot say anything, people. Matron says you must come in immediately.)

'Come on,' somebody said, 'we had better go in.'

We gathered near our table in the portaal and started arguing with Miss Wilkin.

'Miss Wilkin,' said Jean, pulling herself up and with her most ladylike look, 'will you please tell Matron that we would like to see her so that we can discuss this matter with her.'

'Ag nee, mense, ek kan niks doen nie. Matrone het gesê sy will vroeg toesluit. Ek weet nie waarom nie.' She couldn't do anything about it. She didn't know why Matron had to lock up early.

'Miss Wilkin, we have not had our exercise.'

Miss Wilkin was beginning to look extremely nervous. She adopted a placatory, apologetic manner. 'Ja, ek weet, mense. Ek weet. Maar ek moet doen wat Matrone vir my sê. Ek is jammer, mense.'

'Look, Miss Wilkin,' said Flo, 'we have not had our exercise and, according to the regulations, we are entitled to an hour's exercise a day. Will you please tell Matron Bester that we would like to speak to her.'

'Look, don't let's eat,' said somebody.

'Yes,' I said. 'We just won't eat until 3.30.'

Miss Wilkin's face relaxed a little. 'Ja, dis beter, mense. Solank julle nie oefen nie, want Matrone het gesê julle moenie nou oefen nie.' As long as we didn't exercise, because Matron had said we mustn't.

'No, Miss Wilkin, but we are entitled to an hour's exercise and we would like to discuss this with Matron ... Miss Wilkin, please go and tell Matron we wish to speak to her.'

'Okay, mense. Ek sal haar gaan vra, maar ek weet, sy sal nie kom nie.'

'Yes, Miss Wilkin, nevertheless go and ask her.'

She went out into the courtyard to Matron Bester's little window. Within a few minutes she was back.

'Nee, Matrone sê sy kan nie kom nie. Sy is baie besig.' Matron says she cannot come; she is very busy.

'Yes, this is what she always does, as you know, Miss Wilkin. Whenever we want to see her about anything she won't come. And we haven't had our exercise, and she expects us to eat one meal on top of the other.

We've got to eat at half past two and then we don't eat until quarter past six tomorrow morning. Do you think that is good for our stomachs?'

'Ag nee, mense, daar is niks wat ek kan doen nie. Dis nie my skuld nie.' She was placating again, nervous, telling us it wasn't her fault. Matron Bester must have threatened her with some sort of disciplinary action if we went out into the courtyard.

Ann said, 'Well, let's just go out into the courtyard. We're entitled to our exercise. Let her try and stop us.'

'Yes, yes,' said some of the others, 'let's just go out and exercise.' And they began moving away from the table towards the courtyard. Miss Wilkin was watching us nervously.

'No,' I urged. 'We mustn't go out as Matron Bester has said we must not. We just won't eat until half past three.'

'Okay,' said some of the others. 'We just won't eat until 3.30. That is the time we are supposed to eat.'

Miss Wilkin was in agreement. We could eat at half past three but we must not go outside.

'If we do this, then we aren't breaking a regulation,' I explained, 'because she hasn't told us to eat.'

Some sat round the table waiting; others went to their cells to work. It was about 3.05. A few minutes before half past, I went out of my cell to the table. The rest appeared and we started eating at 3.30. When the wardress came to lock up at 4.15 we had finished eating, washed up our dishes in the central laundry basin as usual, and were waiting on parade. We had not put a foot wrong.

This kind of victory made one feel good. We had learned to undertake such actions in a disciplined way. We had learned that we were tough and organised enough to make Matron Bester and the wardresses bend to our will. We had learned that if we were persistent they could not keep up the pace, so that, although sometimes they seemed to be defeating us, if we just carried on they eventually gave in. When the wardress came to lock us up, we were careful to keep the smugness off our faces. And we went quietly to our cells. They had not managed to get off early.

Early release – Amnesty 31 May?

In the days following this incident, I had a feeling that the Front was gunning for me again. I can't remember exactly how I picked this up, perhaps from the attitude of Matron Bester or the wardresses. But nothing was said at this stage directly to me.

One morning, not long afterwards, we were all gathered in the boiler room having our mid-morning coffee. This we did behind the backs of the authorities. We saved coffee (tea during tea weeks) from lunchtime and suppertime, and then we heated it on the coal stove in the boiler room. The person whose 'fire day' it was was also responsible for the beverage. Obviously, the wardresses on duty with us must have observed what we were doing but we guessed they were turning a blind eye and that they were careful to keep it from Matron Bester. Whenever anyone came to the grille, we kept out of sight. We later found out that Matron Bester did know but, for some reason, she decided to do nothing about it (a 'privilege' as long as we 'behaved'?).

During this particular coffee-break we had started talking about the importance of telling one another what the authorities discussed with each of us when we went to the Front, for example when we went to see the Brigadier once a week. I said I felt that if the authorities made some comment about somebody else in the group, that person should be told.

I had sensed that the Front at times made comments about me and that I was not always told about it. Ann apparently usually did so. She informed me after Broodryk's visit in January that he had said I was a troublemaker, that the authorities did not like my behaviour or something to that effect, and she did likewise when Brigadier Pretorius accused her of coming under my influence (about which more below), indeed all the references to me that were made by Viljoen, Aucamp and Pretorius. But it seemed to me that others of my comrades might not be doing so.

Crucial also, I noted, was the issue of reduction of sentence. When they were told about reduction or broad hints were dropped we should all be told so that we knew as far as possible the kind of situation in which we were operating.

The first rumour of early release had been about September 1965 when we heard that there was to be an amnesty for all prisoners, including political prisoners, to be granted in honour of Republic Day the following year. I do not think any of us took this particularly seriously at the time. A few months later Brigadier Pretorius told us – this was in the portaal and he was addressing us as a group – that he did not think any of us would serve our full sentences. On an occasion Aucamp called Ann, Esther and Flo to the Front and told them he was going to the Minister about them and he would like to know what their political attitudes were now.

Matron Bester also participated in the rumour-mongering, indicating at one time that we would all be released in April 1967. When asked about it, she would tell us such things as, 'Yes, I have seen mention of it in the newspaper. Remission and parole for political prisoners is coming up in parliament soon.'

Stephanie informed us before she left that Aucamp had told her that it was not only the ARM people who were going to get reduction. Early in 1966, Broodryk spoke to Ann about reduction of sentence and asked her not to refuse it if it were offered to her. Thereafter Brigadier Viljoen spoke to her on several occasions. And then one day while Taljaard was on duty in our section she told Ann – this was apparently in confidence – that she thought Ann was going to be released in the near future.

Ann did not tell us about what Taljaard had said and I suspect that it was soon thereafter that, evidently sensing that matters were coming to a head, she decided (on her own, it seemed, without discussion with anyone else, certainly not with me) that she must finally take a stand on the issue. She informed the authorities that, in response to the several indications, and this from different people, that she was going to be offered early release, she wished to make it clear that she wanted no favours. She insisted that she was only prepared to take remission or parole if it were offered to all political prisoners.

In South Africa political prisoners did not get remission and parole, like ordinary prisoners. Those people imprisoned for activities in connection with the ARM, to which Stephanie had belonged, were evidently getting something called 'reduction', something completely new. There was at least no mention of it in the prison regulations.

Ann did not tell us that Brigadier Pretorius had accused her, after she had made it clear what her position was on the issue of early release, of coming under the influence of some person whom he did not name. Later it became quite clear that the person to whom he had referred was myself. Moreover, during a visit, Hymie, Esther's husband, told her that he had had information from the Prisons Department (this had come to him indirectly) that the only reason why the women at Barberton had not been released was because of Sylvia Neame.

Initially, rumours about early release created some tensions amongst us, not only because some of us were obviously more favoured by the authorities than others but also because we had different opinions on the issue. I assume that Bram Fischer's suggestion that we should try to mislead the authorities as to our political views influenced people although this is only a view in retrospect. Following Bram's proposal, all of us for quite a while used to say things in front of the wardresses that suggested we had changed our political views, though I do not remember that this had any connection with the prospect of actual reduction of sentence. Indeed, at this early stage it was by and large a non-issue since the authorities had evidently not considered the matter in relation to the fifth anniversary of Republic Day in 1966. As we saw it, it was only ARM people, like Stephanie, who were candidates for early release. We regarded the question of 'reduction' as having nothing to do with us.

There came a time, I cannot remember exactly when this was, when I came to the conclusion that attempting to give the impression that we held political positions that were not our own was serving actually to demoralise us. As I remember, no definite decision was taken on the matter. Rather, as we stepped up our struggle for improved conditions and became more united as a group, such tactics simply faded away.

However, in the context of the rumours that began to be spread by the authorities the matter clearly became of some concern. The tension in our section intensified as Republic Day 1966 neared. We would blow up the slightest thing into something terribly significant. For example, we asked ourselves whether the fact that we had not yet been given new uniforms was not perhaps an indication that we would get early release. On the other hand, when at last they got working on our tenniquoit court we took this as an indication that we were *not* going to get early release.

The Front planted disinformation. One day we were led to believe that all of us were going to be released, on another only one of us and on yet another occasion three of us. I found the continual uncertainty painful. And the fact that I felt we weren't all being as open with each other as we should have been made it doubly so. I knew the authorities were always trying to play me off against the others and to use me as a scapegoat and as a focus for dissatisfaction.

Of interest perhaps is that one of us expressed the opinion that she actually found the uncertainty helpful. It was assisting her in getting through her sentence. She said she found she could break up her sentence by saying to herself, 'Okay, I haven't all those long years ahead of me. I've only got another six months to go till May 31st.' Then when May 31st had gone and there she still was with the prison bars staring her in the face, she could say, 'Well, I haven't got nearly two years still to go, I've only got till April '67.' Perhaps she was not being all that serious or only in part.

In general, there is no doubt about it that the rumours and our expectations had a very disintegrating effect on the psychology of each of us and on the cohesion of our group. The authorities knew, as a later conversation I had with Brigadier Viljoen confirmed, how susceptible we were to suggestions of any type. Prisoners, even those being held under reasonable prison conditions, are vulnerable. We were especially so, living, as we did, in that peculiar situation of isolation within the gaol, cut off from outside news, with no newspapers, no radio, no magazines, with our visitors only able to talk to us about family matters, together with all the other techniques the authorities used against us.

We used to jump to conclusions not only with respect to the possibility of early release but about all sorts of things. For instance, we would decide that on a particular day Aucamp was definitely coming because we had been asked to clean the courtyard or because out of the blue Matron Bester smiled at us as she unlocked our grilles in the morning or we had just been given polish to polish the floor of the portaal, something we had been fighting for for weeks.

Somehow we never seemed to learn from our mistakes. We behaved like caged animals, picking up the faintest scent on an evening breeze, analysing it and preparing ourselves to deal with what information the breeze had provided us with. This was something we never lost. It wasn't so bad at the beginning of our time at Barberton. It started becoming really bad round about April–May–June 1966 and it was still there when I left in April 1967.

As 31 May neared Matron Bester told us we would have to bring our cards to the office on that day. She said the whole prison would have to do that, the black prisoners as well, so that our date of release could be checked. Each prisoner had noted on their card a specific gaol number, the date of committal and date of release. The information given by Matron Bester was an obvious attempt to make us feel that indeed we were to obtain an amnesty.

I longed for 31 May to come and go. From about April, I was saying, 'Yes, things are bad for us but after May, when we realise we are not getting amnesty, things will be better.'

On Republic Day we were unlocked at 7 o'clock. The morning passed by. From what we could gather, the black women prisoners were lining up in long lines in the passage and going with their cards into Matron Bester's office. Morning exercise time came and went. Then lunch at 10.15. As usual several of us helped with the dishing up of the food, one person to each aluminium pot. It was the usual fried pork with vegetables.

We all settled down round our table, rather cramped, seven of us, one at each end, three on one side, and two on the other. We referred to the central seat on the side with three seats as the 'claustrophobic seat'. The three people at that side ate knocking elbows. It wasn't a good seat to be in if you were feeling irritable, although Sheila said she liked it because it made her feel secure – one of her ironic jokes, no doubt.

That lunchtime we had one of our mad fantasy conversations. It was about the big Afrikaner celebration at the Voortrekker Monument in Pretoria to mark the fifth anniversary of the Republic, with BJ Vorster and our Officer-Commanding discussing us. Around this time we used to have a great many of these exchanges. Very often the theme was reduction of sentence and how well we got on with the authorities, how they liked us and wanted to help us. For instance, we would take up Viljoen's story about how Vorster lay in bed at night and thought about us and worried about us. Though the sort of fantasy world we created was primarily a means of ridiculing the authorities, it also deliberately exposed in comic fashion what was happening to us psychologically.

In December the previous year, 1965, we had started our monthly 'newspaper', the *Barberton Bladsy*. It was Mollie's idea and we took it in turns to produce it. Each of us made contributions every month but most of the work was done by the editor of a particular edition who was responsible for the layout, etc. Contributions were anonymous and half the fun of reading the *Bladsy* was to try and guess who had written what. Sometimes one edition ran to 120 foolscap pages. I remember how marvellous it was when the first one came out, about 4–5 months after I had got to Barberton.

We had to produce the newspaper behind the backs of the authorities because Matron Bester had forbidden the activity. There was an elaborate system of hiding it and passing it after lock-up from cell to cell on a conveyor belt consisting of a long thread of yarn. It took each person about two or three hours to read. What was so exciting was that it gave us a sense of group identity and of achievement. We felt we had really produced something. I remember absolutely splitting my sides over it. There were what I thought screamingly funny descriptions of the authorities. They were ridiculed, their hypocrisy, crudity and brutality were shown up so clearly. That was a defiant document!

In our newspaper we also laughed at ourselves, laughed at our aggressions, at the way we washed shirts, scrubbed the floor, about the lack of adequate utensils and cleaning products. We also ran advertisements, promoting the kind of utensils and cleaning products we were given by the authorities, like a broom without a handle – evidently the authorities feared our using it to beat a wardress. We picked out idiosyncrasies and chuckled over them. We described our peculiar states of mind and laughed and laughed.

On this Republic Day Ann was sitting at one end of our eating table, hunched up as was her wont and fingering little grains of sugar on the white tablecloth with the index finger of her left hand. Hunched up, head very close to the table, she said contemplatively, taking a sip of 'coffee' from her white cup. 'Just think of all the volk celebrating at the Voortrekker Monument, hundreds, thousands of them,' she said.

'Yes,' I responded. 'Think of them all dancing volkspeletjies there.'

And Mollie joined in: And the Briggie must be there.

Esther: And Balthazar.

Sylvia: Yes, BJ Vorster.

Flo: And BJ and the 'Brigadier' (using Matron Bester's pronunciation) will be dancing and, as they link arms, BJ will say to the Brigadier: 'Kyk hier, Sarel, hoe gaan dit met daardie lieflike meisies in Barberton?' (Look here, Sarel, how is it going with those lovely girls in Barberton?)

Mollie: Sarel? Who's Sarel? Is the Briggie's name Sarel?

Flo (ignoring Mollie): And the Brigadier will say, 'Dit gaan goed, baie, baie goed. Hulle is lieflike meisies, behalwe daardie Neame. She's just a troublemaker. Maar daardie Flo Duncan, o, sy is lieflik. Ek wens dat sy my dogtertjie was. En sy is so aantreklik, ne? Ken jy haar?' (But that Flo Duncan, oh, she is lovely. I wish she were my little daughter. And she is so attractive, not so? Do you know her?) And Balthazar will say, 'Look here, Sarel …'

Mollie (interrupting again): Is the Briggie's name really Sarel?'

Ann: We don't know what his name is but he looks like a Sarel.'

Flo: Stop interrupting, Mollie. If we say his name's Sarel, it's Sarel, and anyway the Minister is calling him Sarel … And so the Minister will say, 'Sarel, give these lieflike meisies by best wishes, my love in fact. Tell them how they are constantly in my thoughts.'

Sylvia: Yes, and he says, 'Give them remission maar, man, Sarel – eight months off for the two-year girls, nine months for the three-year girls. And remember to give them my best wishes, Sarel.'

Flo: Don't be silly. BJ will say to Sarel as they are resting on the hill next to the Voortrekker Monument, as he mops the sweat from his brow: 'Come on, let's get on the road, op die pad Barberton toe. Ek will met daardie Barberton meisies praat, veral daardie lieflike Flo Duncan. Kom ons gaan hulle self sien en ons sal vir hulle sê dat hulle kan dadelik huistoe gaan. Ek wil self hulle mooi gesiggies sien wanneer ons dit vir hulle sê.' (I wish to talk to those Barberton girls, especially that lovely Flo Duncan. Come, let's go see them. We'll tell them they can go home immediately. I want to see their pretty faces myself when we tell them.)

Ann: Don't be mad. BJ Vorster will stand there on the steps of the Voortrekker Monument with the crowd at his feet – hundreds of them, thousands of them – and he will be standing there high above them on the steps, and he'll call for silence, and he'll say, 'What can we do for these girls in Barberton? Will you give me your permission to give them remission? Just say Yay or nay.' And the crowd will shout in indignation, 'Hang them ... Hang them!' And by mistake somebody will say 'Crucify them ...' (muttering) That idea must come from our Bible class ... And Vorster will then turn to the Brigadier, who is standing there on his right hand, high over the volk, and he'll say, 'You hear what they say, Sarel. Do it. I wash my hands of it.'

Jean: No, Ann, that's a bit sick.

Ann: But I feel sick, Jean, I am sick.

Flo: You look it too.

Republic Day afternoon went by. Suppertime. And then lock-up. We were not summoned to bring our cards to the office.

We heard later that about 100 of the black women had been released. Their number dropped from about 230 to 130. And more went out later. Many of them got many years off their sentences. No political prisoners received amnesty. We also learned later that our relatives had been reading in the newspapers for many months that political prisoners, people sentenced under the Immorality Act, and those for dagga or illegal gold-buying offences were not to get amnesty; that category of prisoner, in other words, who in normal circumstances do not get remission.

Republic Day might have passed but this did not bring an end to the game the authorities were playing with us. Just a few weeks before I left Barberton in April 1967, Brigadier Pretorius told Esther, who had still a year to serve, that he 'could give her a date'. She responded that she did not want to hear about dates. The Brigadier was not to be discouraged. 'But I will give you a date: April 1967.' Esther served her whole three-year sentence. She was released in April 1968.

Aucamp comes with a high prison official

IN THE COURSE OF THE discussion we had had in the boiler room about telling each other things that the officials had said to them, Mollie commented that the Brigadier had held that one of our number had encouraged us some days before to march out into the courtyard in open defiance of Matron Bester who said we were not to exercise. Later Mollie spoke to me separately, telling me that the Brigadier had said that 'Neame' had told them to go out into the courtyard and they had all followed her. Mollie said that the Brigadier had demanded information from her about 'Neame'. He would not regard her as co-operating unless she gave him such information. Naturally, Mollie refused to do any such thing, advising that if he wanted any information he must ask me for it.

I was furious with Wilkin for having told such lies, if she had, indeed, done so. It may have been that the Brigadier had just been baiting Mollie with what he knew to be wrong information in order to get her to talk. Anyway, I had got used to this sort of thing and I did nothing about it, not wanting to get Mollie into trouble for having passed the information on to me.

It must have been a few days or a week or two later that Colonel Aucamp turned up. As usual we had been expecting him for a long time. He had come to pick up Sheila, who was almost at the end of her sentence. It must have been between 10 and 16 June. I think I went through to Matron Bester's office somewhere towards the middle of the queue, although I usually seemed to end up last in these queues to the Front. When Aucamp came we were eating; then we'd gone back into the courtyard, and we went one by one to the Front. This was an extra excitement: not only did we have a visitor to see and from whom to try and gather information but we could walk in the courtyard while darkness fell. We could go and turn on the courtyard lights at the switch on the wall next to the window of Matron Bester's office. Only two or three times over two years did I have the sky above my head while darkness fell. And the stars! Stars above my head! And no bars or cages in front of my eyes! Just a stretch of sky! And the mysterious look of the courtyard at night. Little insects squeaking in the grass. We tried not to tramp on the frogs as they hopped around on the cement.

We marched round and round, out of habit. Exercise was so important. In any case, we were too tense to stand aside for a moment, to lean against a brick wall of the courtyard. No: we marched, tramp, tramp. There was the dark purplish sky and the stars swinging above my head. Over our courtyard wall in the distance were the hills in the direction of Swaziland. In the courtyard the electric light fell on the cannas, on the elephant-ears, on the mullein, lighting them up in little patches, with different intensities of darkness splattered all over the leaves and, towards the centre of the plants, darkness.

In fact we were not yet certain that it *was* Aucamp who was there. The wardresses had not informed us who the visitor was. The Front was trying to prevent us from preparing complaints for whoever it was. As we swung past the office window, we tried to take a look in. Could we not catch a word here and there? Was it Aucamp? I could see a woman with blonde hair sitting at one side of the desk. Present, too, was Matron Bester, with her pouting lips, standing with her chin tucked into her neck, her eyes peering from under her eyebrows.

On another round, as I passed the window, I heard a man's voice. Whose voice was that? Was it the Brigadier's? Was it Aucamp's? I asked the others what they thought. They speculated. It could be the Brigadier. On the other hand, it might be Aucamp. In any case, I felt that the person we were destined to see was the blonde woman. Who was she? But then again she might be an escort. But why then was she sitting behind the desk? That looked official. She must be somebody of some importance ... Round and round the courtyard I went, with the stars above my head and the sounds of a subtropical night, always thinking, speculating.

Somebody came back into our section but she was not allowed to communicate with the rest of us so, as I walked fast down the corridor, with the wardress at our open grille watching me, I did not yet know exactly whom I was about to see. I tried to think of the sort of complaints and requests I would put, at the same time keeping an open mind in case I found somebody quite unexpected there. It was difficult to keep one's mental flexibility in gaol, especially at the end of the day when one was tired.

I entered the office and confronted Aucamp's cold blue eyes. Oh, so he *is* here! I realised from my sense of shock that I had not really been expecting him. I took a quick look at the others. There was Brigadier Pretorius. And the blonde woman. I greeted Aucamp: 'Good evening, Colonel.'

I discovered the woman was Lieutenant Muil, a high official in the Prisons Department. I had heard of her before. At the Fort prisoners had spoken of her. And she had been expected to come on a tour of inspection while I was in Port Elizabeth. There they had tried to improve the look of my clothes for her visit and fussed about everything looking clean and shiny – the brass and the parquet floors of the cells, the linoleum on the floor of the basin and toilet section and the little passage in my cell section as well as the long passage outside. I had had to clean the windows, to be careful that there was no dust on any of the windowsills, and clean the walls in the long passage outside, including the long narrow ledge jutting out of the wall that so interested Major Symington. And I also had to remove the dust from the white grooves between the little red bricks. Then I had to clean my exercise yard.

There had been a great bustle in the part of the female gaol in Port Elizabeth that I could see at the other end of the long passage, the opposite end to my courtyard. There were black women working on the other side of a green grille.

After all that activity in the end Lieutenant Muil had not turned up. But I was to meet her after all for here she was behind the desk in Matron Bester's office in Barberton Prison. The light was on in the office. A really snooty-looking woman. Nice hair. Her face might have seemed quite good-looking from a distance, but close up it was ungenerous, prim. She had pursed-up lips and a disapproving expression. She looked as if she had a very bad smell under her nose. Perhaps she did not like political prisoners; or perhaps this was simply her response to prisoners in general.

I turned to Aucamp. 'Well, how are you, Colonel?' I tried to say in as friendly a manner as possible.

'Not too bad,' he said. 'And how are you, Sylvia?'

'I'm all right, Colonel.'

'Well?' He looked at me questioningly.

I started with my complaints and requests: when were we to be reclassified to B Group? We had already been C prisoners for going on eight months. We heard that the men in Pretoria Central who had been sentenced in the same trial in Johannesburg were already Bs, so why weren't we?

I referred to my little green notebook where I kept a list of complaints and requests, ready for any visitor. Most of us kept a note of the complaints and requests we wished to make. I asked that we should be moved to Kroonstad Prison. I said that I had often complained that we lived in a very confined area. I was making that complaint again. We worked, ate, slept in one small area. This was obviously not a suitable prison for us. There was space and facilities at Kroonstad for long-term women. Aucamp responded that such a move was out of the question.

I asked for tennis dresses and tennis shoes. They had them at Kroonstad. Aucamp referred me to the prim lieutenant, who pulled up her nose a little further as though the smell was quite unbearable, and said, without looking at me and in such an abrupt manner that it seemed I had in some way mortally offended her, that she did not think it would be possible.

I made the usual request for remission and parole. I asked when the prison was going to be supplied with proper library facilities. And so on.

The Brigadier suddenly interrupted my address to Aucamp, saying out of the blue: 'Do you know what Neame did the other day, and yet she asks to be made a B prisoner? She went and walked out in the courtyard on her own and exercised against Matron Bester's express orders. On her own she went out and walked in the courtyard while the others sat down and ate their afternoon meal.'

'I did what, Brigadier? What absolute nonsense!' I said, then added:

'And may I ask, Brigadier, where did you get that inaccurate piece of information? I certainly did not go out and walk in the courtyard.'

The Brigadier was looking smug and triumphant. He always tried to show off in front of Colonel Aucamp. He was eager to impress him with his finesse in dealing with these 'kommuniste'. 'Yes, yes,' he said, turning to Colonel Aucamp. 'Do you know that Neame is the leader here? She is the leader of these prisoners.' Then he leaned back importantly in his chair, satisfied that he was making an outstanding impression, and had produced some extremely significant information.

His face was red and bloated, black dots on his cheeks and on his red nose, either blackheads or the black roots of hair. By the look of it, he probably had to shave quite a way up his cheeks, above the level of his black moustache. He really was a very unattractive man and yet he constantly preened himself. He actually looked much worse standing up because then you could see his ungainly body, his hanging paunch and large backside. Sitting behind the desk gave him a certain advantage.

'Brigadier,' I asked, 'from where did you get this strange piece of information?'

He stuck his chest out. 'I have my sources.'

I looked at him silently, wondering how to respond to such an idiot, and, anyway, what could one do against the allegations of one's Officer-Commanding. Then I said: 'I object, Brigadier, to your making reports to Colonel Aucamp, an official from Head Office, when you have not even checked up on the facts and when you have not even asked the prisoner concerned whether what you have been told is true.'

I turned to Colonel Aucamp and described the whole incident. I told him that the funny thing about the whole story was that it was diametrically opposed to what had actually happened. Other people had suggested going out to exercise in the courtyard, and I was the one who had said we should not do that.

I then went into the whole story of the discrimination that I had been subjected to ever since I had been in Barberton. I told him how Matron Bester had deliberately refused to give me certain articles of underclothing and a jersey, how she had constantly screamed and shouted at me from the day I arrived, that she had made quite unfounded allegations against me, such as that I had broken down the brick next to the window of the front big cell. Now there was this new unfounded allegation.

I must have been talking for about 20 minutes when I suddenly caught sight of Matron Bester's face. I stopped in my tracks. She was looking absolutely distraught, wild. I felt suddenly sorry for her. I turned to Aucamp and said, 'Anyway if it wasn't for the fact that one gets caught up in this whole prison situation, this would all seem very childish, and I'm sick of having to worry myself about such trifles. And I don't know why Matron has been doing this to me. I don't know whether she is doing it on your instructions.'

Colonel Aucamp carefully controlled the muscles of his eyes so as to prevent his surfacing feelings from being mirrored there. '*My* instructions?'

'Yes, Colonel. You know very well that the day I arrived in this prison you told the other prisoners here that they were to be careful of me, that they were not to listen to me. And you spoke to me along similar lines here in this office in front of Matron Bester, the Brigadier and your wife.'

Colonel Aucamp's eyes were cold. Icy blue. Matron Bester looked as though she were on the edge of a nervous collapse. Aucamp made an effort to appear friendlier. Trying to put a little of a confiding tone in his voice and opening his eyes wider to make room for an expression of innocence, he said, 'Yes, Sylvia, but you know I did not do this behind your back. I did it in front of you.'

'That is not my point, Colonel. My point is that you did it.'

He changed his tactic. 'Isn't it funny, Sylvia? Nobody likes you. In Port Elizabeth they did not like you, and here they don't like you.'

I was used to that kind of tactic. They had used it on me during my first 90-day detention. I ignored what he said and went on to say that the trouble was that Matron Bester was inconsistent. For instance, some of the trouble the other day over exercise was caused by the fact that Matron Bester had given us a timetable. She set down times for our exercise, for our meals and for our lock-ups, and that timetable was up on the wall in our section. But, I said, Matron Bester chose to ignore aspects of that timetable when it suited her. One day we had our full exercise at the correct time. The next day we would get a message that we were to exercise and eat early because she wanted to lock up early; or she would just send in our food and try to prevent us from exercising.

Colonel Aucamp interrupted, 'Yes, but Matron Bester only does that when it is absolutely necessary, when she has to get off early.'

'Oh, no, Colonel, the other day the wardress on duty informed us that Matron Bester had told her to ask us to eat early because she wanted to do this wardress a favour, and let her off early. And—'

I was interrupted by a peculiar noise from Matron Bester, half growl, half sob. She jumped out of her chair and disappeared from the office. I heard later from the others that she had come rushing through into the portaal – they were already locked up – beside herself with rage and had torn the timetable off the wall. She did not return to the office while I was there.

I carried on speaking to Aucamp. 'Look, Colonel, we are quite prepared to exercise and eat early sometimes if Matron Bester or one of the wardresses wishes to go off early, and we have done this in the past without any complaint when Matron Bester has asked us decently to do it as a special favour.'

Colonel Aucamp broke in again: 'Oh, but you know that the Matron-in-Charge can give you any instructions she wishes and you must carry it out. That is a regulation.'

'I know that, Colonel. That is why I did not go out into the courtyard to exercise when she instructed us not to the other day. However, we want to live a regular life here, Colonel. And we are entitled to an hour's exercise a day according to the regulations. And why does Matron Bester not come and discuss things with us when a situation arises as it arose the other day? This is one of the big problems here, that Matron Bester tries to avoid us at all times. She will never discuss any matter with us in a reasonable way. And another thing, it is extremely bad for us to have one meal on top of the other. As you know and as Matron Bester knows, several of us here have trouble with our stomachs, and yet Matron Bester wants to lock us up at 2.30 or 3 in the afternoon of a weekday, and then we don't eat again until the next morning.'

All this time Lieutenant Muir was sitting there silently behind the desk next to the Brigadier with the bad-smell-under-her-nose look. The

Brigadier turned smugly to Aucamp. 'You know that Neame comes into this office almost every week complaining that they don't get sufficient marmalade, that they don't get what they are entitled to?'

Aucamp took up the point. 'I must tell you a story, Sylvia. There was a prisoner at Pretoria when I was there, and one day he came to me and said he wasn't getting enough to eat. So we took his food to the kitchen and we carefully measured it all out on the scale and we found that he was getting more than the regulations specified, and so from then on we cut his food down to the regulation requirements.'

'Yes, Colonel, but I know we are not getting the regulation amount. We should get two teaspoonfuls for the day, but often we only get one. And, anyway, the Brigadier had it measured out the other day, and it was too little, and he gave instructions for it to be increased. That did not happen.'

The Brigadier wasn't to be put off, 'And you know what a fuss she made about that letter that she received from her brother. She accused me of all sorts of things.'

'Yes, Colonel, you know about that letter that came five weeks late.'

'But I am entitled to withhold any letter from you, Sylvia,' Aucamp responded. 'That is up to me. If the Brigadier thinks there is anything in a letter which you should not see, then he must send it straight on to me.'

'Yes, Colonel, you may have every right to do that but then I mustn't be lied to and told it hasn't come.'

'You see,' the Brigadier turned triumphantly to Aucamp, 'you see what she accuses me of.' He turned to me. 'You cannot make allegations like that, Neame.' His voice was stupidly triumphant as though he had proved something very important to Colonel Aucamp. It was not quite clear to me and possibly also not to Aucamp what he had actually proved.

Aucamp looked irritated by his stupidity. 'We may do anything we like, Sylvia. Letters are a privilege, remember.'

I was beginning to feel exhausted. I excused myself and went back to the section. A wardress locked me up. The others told me I had been away an hour. The rest of us went through, one by one, to the Front.

I did not have time to tell the others that night what had happened as Sheila was due to be taken away early the next morning, and so we spent the evening chatting through our grilles to her, across the portaal.

Aucamp comes with a high prison official

The next morning Matron Bester unlocked Sheila before six o'clock and, without looking at her, growled, 'Kom.' Sheila asked her if she could not say goodbye to us. We heard Matron Bester's screams, 'Nee! Nee! Kom dadelik.' (No! No! Come immediately.)

The screws are on and Matron Bester breaks down

AFTER SHEILA LEFT, THE Front gave us a really bad time. As we put it, 'The screws are on.' The atmosphere in our section could be cut with a knife. The wardresses had obviously been given instructions to treat us badly. In all sorts of ways the screws were tightened. While mostly this applied to small things, to a prisoner caught up in a situation where these 'small things' are her whole life, this can be unbearable. Similar methods to those that had been used in our first months in Barberton were applied, except that we got our regular exercise. All the little 'favours' Bester had granted us, such as extra sugar, were withdrawn. Additional washing was sent in.

Whenever she came to our grille, she screamed hideously at us. We found it impossible to have any classes or to have our coffee break in the morning. If we spoke to one another in the courtyard while exercising, up would come the venetian blind in the office and Bester's wild swollen face would scream at us across the courtyard. Sometimes she would suddenly sweep into our section and have a quick look in our cells, with the most frightening expression on her face. She was clearly trying to find something to use against us.

The wardress on duty with us ceased to speak to us at all, except to give us orders in a most unpleasant way. She would not leave us alone for one moment. Even during mealtimes she stood deliberately watching our every movement and listening to our every word in spite of the fact that Matron Bester had a few weeks earlier agreed that the wardress should not stand and stare at us while we were eating, and in fact need not even be in the portaal at the time. Our central grille was, at all times, kept firmly shut. Nobody was allowed to come near it.

All this had a tremendous effect on us. Things had eased up over the past few months in small ways. The wardresses had been friendlier. They left us on our own very often, so they would go and sit in a cell while we were eating, even in our work time. Matron Bester used actually to be fairly nice, off and on, to some of us. They were not so strict about people coming to the central grille so we sometimes saw faces there. All these apparently small things had made our lives more bearable, and the Front, as had become quite clear to us, was very conscious of this.

They knew precisely how to put the screws on. For prisoners, it was really painful to have things taken away, things you had gained, fought for. It could be morale breaking. One tended to think, Oh, we had better let them get away with giving us only half an hour's exercise sometimes, just so we can have a more pleasant atmosphere. The authorities, particularly Matron Bester, used such techniques right through our sentence. She would give us what she called 'favours' and then if, in any way, we annoyed her, and she was, of course, easily annoyed, she would remove these 'favours'. She would give us no explanation. She did not need to. Prisoners get the message.

By this time, however, we had learned our lesson. We had learned how to deal with the authorities. We dug in our heels, ignored the fact that the 'favours' had been withdrawn, started a go-slow on the washing, went on demanding improvements in our conditions.

Meanwhile Matron Bester was in a terrible state. My criticism of her had come five to seven days after Judge Ludorf's visit when Ann had made a very moving exposure of Matron Bester. Bester obviously felt she was in for trouble from senior officials and must have realised that the complaints about her could have reached Vorster, either directly through Ludorf or via Aucamp. Bester said nothing to me but she spoke to some of my comrades in the office, telling them what I had done, and saying that I had said I was their spokesperson and that they all agreed with what I had said.

This, of course, was nonsense. What she was trying to indicate was that I was not the only one who had put her in this state but that Ann was responsible too and that Ann had done this under my influence. Because of Judge Ludorf's promise that our complaints to him would be kept confidential, she could not refer directly to the complaint Ann had made to the judge. She told my fellow prisoners that she was on the edge of a nervous breakdown and that Neame was responsible. She said that I had deliberately, against her instructions, walked in the courtyard.

None of us, of course, responded to her manoeuvring. We felt that this was an important battle, that this was to be one of our main battles. In fact, our slogan became 'an NB for HB' which stood for 'a nervous breakdown for Hester Bester'. Actually, we did not know what Matron Bester's first name was but we knew her initial was 'H', and so one of us decided it must be 'Hester' because that might account for her being so extraordinarily neurotic since it rhymed with Bester. Obviously, our slogan was not meant all that seriously, but it was not completely off the mark either. We really felt that maybe things had come to such a pass that we must break her or she would break us.

We came to the conclusion that if we made things unbearable for her, she might leave or might be forced to leave. I think she realised, too, that this was her last chance to try and break us. She certainly had a good go. She made us feel, again, like trapped animals. But we stood firm. We had in the past months knit together as a group. By this time we had had some planned 'campaigns', more and more as time went on, and we would decide on what role each of us was to play.

A key problem with Bester was that she could not bear to be criticised. She saw criticism everywhere. She felt we were attacking her, even when we were just making a request for something, more particularly if what we asked for was an item that was not available in the gaol. It had become clear that Barberton Prison was simply not geared to having white political prisoners (in particular in terms of the regulations – and attitudes – of the apartheid state) and female ones at that. And she was particularly touchy about us. I think this was because in a strange way she respected us and she seemed constantly to feel guilty.

Any criticism seemed to spark off something inside her, something totally uncontrollable. She would hit back savagely and irrationally at the most suitable object. It must have seemed to her, from what Aucamp had said, that I was the most suitable object.

She had a very expressive face, expressive eyes. She was not very used to having to control her expressions, to try and hide her inward thoughts and feelings. She had lived her whole working life with people whom she considered little better than animals so why should she try and exert any control over herself? And so her violent aggressions would transform her face, her mouth, her eyes. If any outsider had seen her in this condition, I'm sure they could not but have thought her insane.

I used to observe sometimes as she was locking us up or unlocking us, after somebody had made some criticism or some suggestion or request, that she was looking around with a vacant, searching look in her eyes for an object on which to pin her aggression. Her face at first would look fairly normal, except for the distraught, searching look in her eyes, and then, if she caught sight of me, her lips would suddenly pout, her whole face swell, her eyes pop out of her head and flash and, of course, a scream would follow. What exactly she was saying was usually not to be made out and, in any case, was often quite unrelated to the request that had been made. She might shout at me to stand up properly, to stand to attention, or ask me why my uniform was torn (after I had been asking her for months for a new one).

Sometimes, realising that she was looking for an object, I would quietly move out of her sight. She would then look around for something else on which to pin her aggression. Later, as we forced her to learn more control, she might think it wise to find no special object and she would go from cell to cell, mumbling and muttering to herself with her pouted lips and bang our central grille – GUNG! – still muttering and then slam the door.

She was a sick woman, as a high official later admitted to us. At the same time, the prisons service had evidently thought her suitable for the post of Matron-in-Charge at Barberton and, moreover, had kept her there as, it appeared, a fitting person to deal with politicals. Her behaviour could hardly have escaped Aucamp. She was not one for hiding her tantrums.

Perhaps the conclusion can be allowed that the authorities actually needed a sick person to do the kind of job they wanted done. Anyone with a sense of morality and humanity could not have done the job, as had been the case with the young matron who had left towards the beginning of our stay. Something similar can be said about the members of the Security Branch who engaged in torture and framed-up charges. One needed sick people for the job, like one needed them in Hitler Germany, or at least people whose ambition was such that they were prepared to perform even tasks they would normally have refused to carry out.

True, when things were going well in her personal life, which was very rare as it often is with highly neurotic people, Bester was fairly reasonable. When she felt needed, as she did when Di Schoon was with us, she could be an acceptable person. Round about the end of 1965 and the beginning of 1966 she actually had ordinary chats with us. She spoke to us, for once, as though we were normal human beings. We discovered that some man had come into her life. She was very excited and began to look rather blooming. But, unfortunately for her prisoners, this did not last long.

Wardresses had told us that Matron Bester had been left at the altar by the man she had planned to marry, and this had made her terribly bitter. Whether this story is true or not, it is significant that it existed.

What must have contributed to her unpleasantness was that she disliked Barberton. She had been at Roeland Street Prison in Cape Town and her family were down in the Cape, in Worcester. Her mother was there, and evidently she was very close to her, indeed, according to all reports, neurotically close to her. Apparently she had not wanted to be transferred from the Cape but Prisons Service people had to go, according to South African prison policy, where they were sent, although sometimes, by threatening to leave the service, some of them managed to be placed where they wished to be.

A Prisons official told us that Bester had entered the service as a young girl. When I arrived in Barberton she must have been about 35 years old. She had evidently been encouraged to come to Barberton because she was offered her own prison. But she hated it, or so she commented to one or two of us, and was living for the day when she could leave. The fact that she disliked Barberton so much certainly did not make the lives of her prisoners more bearable. She told one of us that she had a contract until April 1967 and this makes one wonder whether her suggestion to us, or more specifically to Esther, that we all would be freed by April

1967 was not somehow connected with this.

Suddenly Matron Bester disappeared from the prison. She had gone away for a holiday 'because she was on the edge of a nervous breakdown'. It was wonderful to be without her. I felt an enormous sense of release, almost free for a few weeks. While she was away the wardresses were much nicer to me. When she came back she made a big effort with us. She had either had a talking to from senior officials or she realised herself that things were getting out of hand. On her first day back she came into our section, smiling nervously, and asking how we all were. This was an unheard-of thing for her to do. And what was fantastic for me was that I realised, this was after a few weeks, that the pressure was off me. I was no longer to be used as the scapegoat.

Further extracts from my diary

HERE ARE SOME JOTTINGS from 29 July 1966:

I have seen more clearly the possibility of getting out of this place and the thought of going out does not fill me with such fear as before. I see that things can't be as bad as when I went out at the end of November 1963 from Pretoria Central. At that time the threat of the hanging of the Rivonia trialists was still a possibility and I was in quite a bad psychological state. Moreover, I feel I have more of a future now, especially in connection with the idea of going overseas, and I feel I have achieved some things since July 64 when I was arrested and then faced trial.

I am in a way more myself and think this is not only a temporary feeling, connected with the fact that Bester has been away two weeks so far. At any rate, I now feel rested as I did by the end of February this year when Bester was away for a month. I have been enjoying yoga exercises and been walking around the courtyard with a book on my head for improved posture. We are inclined to look on the ground when walking here because there is nowhere to look really and one tends to be deep in thought.

Still waiting for reclassification to a higher group. There is, true, the continuing cat-and-mouse game with us but we have learned patience. That is something I don't think we shall ever lose. We have waited for everything from cleaning materials to release.

I have read about two-thirds of the Keith Feiling [history] and am over halfway through Gogol which is brilliant. I remember reading this in my first year at Rhodes when I found it boring. I think I am less introverted now and have more of a sense of humour. The story told by the postmaster about Captain Kopeikin is fantastic ...

Arnoldus has been hibernating under the mullein for weeks and weeks now. There have been within the last few months three changes of season, summer to autumn, autumn to winter, winter to spring. The tree behind the gaol, that is behind the back wall – I can see it from the boiler room – has sprouted some green leaves on one side, the morning sun side, first a few leaves on the outer edge and now moving towards the centre. Nearly half the tree has now green leaves.

I thought a great deal about Mom on the 24th, the anniversary of her birthday. Anna's birthday, my maternal grandmother, her name is actually Maude, is on 5 August. I received a wonderful letter from her. Very heartening. I think about her a lot, too, and my other relatives. I like placing myself historically, as it were, in the family. I thought of my sister, Jennifer, today as I talked to Mollie while we were walking around the courtyard. Half past nine has struck. I am going to get into bed with the Gogol and read for about half an hour. Late unlock tomorrow, thank goodness. First bell goes at 6.30 instead of 5.30.

7 August 66:
It is evening. The tree behind our wall has been completely green for quite a few days now. One of the Kaffirboom trees near the staff quarters sprouted an orange-red flower a few weeks ago and now the three or four trees there have quite a lot of red flowers. Yesterday came the first spring rain, the first rains of summer. It is getting light earlier so that, instead of it being black as pitch when we are opened up at 6, there is now a lighter sky in the east and more faded stars than about a month ago.

I had a look at some prints of the Impressionists in a book by John Rewald which came from the University of South Africa for Ann who is doing art history as a course. What a wonderful feeling of sunlight and air! And then I played table tennis with Mollie. I was on the far side from this cell with the lav that I am in now, that is, the back cell next to the courtyard.

So, as I played I could look through the window towards the staff quarters and see the trees and hibiscus hedge and the hills behind. I saw it all as an impressionist picture, light, air, joyousness, spring, the outside world – one day! I feel it's round the corner, even if I have quite a long while to go.

I have read very little of Gogol. I want to climb into bed early tonight and try to do a good bit of reading. I must go through the poem for tomorrow again once or twice – Robert Browning's Grammarian's Funeral. I went through it about three times at lunchtime lock-up.

Church bells have been going – six, half past six, again seven and half past seven. When I first came the church bells were for me a harbinger of the outside world, like Langley. Now both have become painfully associated with gaol. However, this evening for the first time for some months, the bells give promise of the outside world.

Last evening the frog came out, plopping in the puddles on the concrete pathway underneath the east-facing window of this cell. It was the same colour as all those we see here, a rust-pink back with the rest light grey. It must have come out from hibernating for the first time. Still no sign of Aristophanes, and Arnoldus has not yet appeared from hibernating under the mullein. Life goes on with new promise.

Up to a few days ago I had been pushing time rather dreadfully. Pushing time is one of the most painful psychological experiences I know. Not only had I begun to push months – that I started doing, to a degree, after passing halfway and after I had learned that I had won my appeal – but weeks, and, far worse, days.

This is what Jean has been doing all the time, marking off every day that passes on her calendar – her pattern, as she calls it, for she uses some method of blocking in squares so that she gradually produces a rather nice decorative design. I have refused to mark off days on a calendar, as so many prisoners do, since I see this as a completely negative attitude to the gaol experience and I avoid as far as possible seeing any of my experiences as completely negative.

Brigadier Viljoen was here last Monday, and now I am not pushing time so dreadfully. Trouble about being halfway, around halfway, is that you start pushing time and yet there is still half your sentence to go. Evidently, prisoners often have a bad reaction at halfway. They are right there in the middle, being pushed in from behind and from the front, and though this has to do with time it recreates in a way perceptions connected with the confined space. More and more my gaol experience is convincing me of an integral linkage between time and space in human (only human?) perception. Perhaps the close connection, interpenetration, exists in the objective world, too?

Tonight I also want to draw and colour-in with pencils. We are planning an art exhibition for Christmas. We are no longer doing life or figure drawing. Instead we are having a history of art get-together every Friday morning, with Ann teaching. The result is I must work on my own. I also intend copying from prints.

I want to get a half day job when I get out so I can work on my Wits course. I hope to be able to write exams within a few weeks of getting out and then go overseas.

We wait for everything. I think I have learned a great deal of patience, not that I ever was a particularly impatient person, don't think so. Life moves on even here. Over the past month I have at last I think begun to be merged into the rest of the group, no longer the scapegoat, I hope.

My first German exercise and 3rd lesson haven't yet been sent to me. My German seems doomed to slowness.

I went to hospital for an X-ray on Wednesday 3rd for my stomach. Get spasms in the pylorus, duodenum, have tender duodenal cap, no ulcer. A very pleasant trip. Barberton was looking lovely. I think I have been out about five times before, no six. Twice to hospital for the operation on my foot and now a third time for the X-ray, three times to the dentist. I think mostly in the summer months, maybe one at the end of last spring.

Usually Barberton looks rather dry, sometimes almost barren, a barrenness accentuated by the bare hills which hover over the village. But on Wednesday everything looked quite lush. Beautiful bougainvillaea, especially on the fence of the Brigadier's house which Taljaard pointed out to me. The hospital garden looked beautiful. After my X-ray Taljaard and I waited on the road in the garden of the hospital and I looked particularly at the three colours of Barberton daisies. I almost felt as though I was in Cape Town – the flowers, with the hills showing through the trees. I had that quiet, suspended, outing-from-gaol feeling, passive, silent, except for quiet conversation now and again. I thought 'one day I could be standing in a place like this – free!'

The car drove up and I went back to gaol.

The gaol feeling is a very specific feeling, quite different to any other, and it is extremely difficult to describe, especially to people who have never been in gaol. It is an utterly hopeless, heavy, emotionless feeling, one of being trapped in nothingness, a cessation of existence while still alive, the loss of an individual, and, therefore, human identity and that for eternity. Time has stopped.

In the framework of a normal human life choice plays a crucial role. In gaol there are extremely limited possibilities for personal choice. In the first place, you would not choose to be in gaol. In little things, too, the choices are often made by the gaol authorities. The gaol feeling is necessarily an utterly passive feeling. This may sound like a depression but it is not. The prisoner has no inclination to be passive. On the contrary, but you have no other choice for your life, more or less your every movement, is in the hands of others.

On Friday afternoon Langley brought a second tape of a service in the local Anglican church. I didn't have such a strong reaction as the previous time when I was quite tearful. Suppose I am slowly coming out of the depths. Langley prayed for all prisoners serving sentences at this service. Unfortunately, the tape was not clear enough to hear the prayer. I think he may be feeling easier with us. I hope so.

Our alcohol industry

EVER SINCE ABOUT APRIL 1966 we had been forging ahead with our 'campaign' to be reclassified to B group. This is where all ordinary criminal prisoners start, those with no record of violence before arrest nor especially bad behaviour in the gaols. Not one of us had been officially charged with any misbehaviour for which we had 'done meals' (solitary with spare diet). This was actually a remarkable record for it is very easy to obtain 'meals'. There are so many gaol regulations a prisoner can break and most prisoners go in for 'trading'. You acquire tobacco for anything you can offer, and in any gaol, however strict the security, tobacco always manages to find its way in, like other items. When there are awaiting-trial prisoners, trade tends to be brisker and more variegated.

One of the tough things about our life at Barberton was that we could not enter into what I might describe as some of the lighter aspects of gaol life, aspects which at least promote contact with other human beings and may contribute largely to relieving the monotony and the culture of simply pushing time. Instead, especially in our first months, all our time and energy were spent trying to say something to each other before the wardress noticed. In any case, we were so isolated from the rest of the gaol that it was impossible to trade. It was a harsh, cold, arid, characterless life.

Gradually, as things eased up a little, and at times we could escape from the staring eyes and out of the hearing of the wardress, we started trying to get a life going for ourselves. I have already referred to our morning 'coffee' gatherings. Some of us started making toffee and fudge on the stove in the boiler room. Then we hit on the idea of alcohol. The idea came to us when one of us found that some marmalade, which had been left for some time in a small face-cream pot, had begun fermenting. We put the marmalade, about an inch or two or three, at the bottom of a milk bottle and added water. We placed this out of the way behind the bathroom door and left it for a week. It certainly produced something slightly alcoholic though it did not have a particularly nice taste. And so we made up the following rhyme:

'Oh, the baby's vomit and the baby's pee,
What will the bootleg liquor be?'

I think Flo was responsible for those two lines.

We found, too, that the stalks of the strange tea that was sent in twice a day every alternate week had some properties we could use. We put the stalks with some water and sugar into a large bottle, and left it for a week or two. This produced a rather delicious cool drink, one which bubbled but was not really alcoholic.

Somewhere towards the end of 1965 – I think it was just before Di Schoon left a few weeks before Christmas – Matron Bester sent in some grapefruit. This was the first taste of fruit we had had for seven or eight months. We put it to good use. Not only did we eat the fruit, some of us made glacé grapefruit by putting some of the fruit with sugar in one of our tin plates on the stove in the boiler room, and we packed the peel with sugar and this was also delicious. And we added some of the peel to the bottle with the tea stalks, and also put some in separate bottles with sugar and water.

Sometime during the first half of 1966 we started receiving about sixteen prunes each a week for medicinal purposes. Each of us used to donate two of these to the alcohol pool. Nobody really got drunk on these drinks, at least if we stuck to one kind at a time, though they were definitely alcoholic. However, at some stage, probably about May, we mixed them all together in a carefully cleaned sanitary bucket, and let the brew 'cook' for a few weeks behind the bathroom door.

And then on one of our celebration days on the 12th of the month (our release date was 12 April, some in 1967, others in 1968) we had a drink together in the bathroom. This was carefully behind the back of the wardress though the smell was so powerful that it could not but have reached her. This punch was really potent. Esther was so drunk that she had to sit for about half an hour on the edge of the bath before she could make her appearance in the portaal, and when she did she was definitely weaving.

Matron Bester, unfortunately at this point, appeared at the grille, asking for 'Barsel', and Esther, somewhat unsteady on her feet, went to the grille, trying to open her eyes wide to make room for a look of innocence and matter-of-factness. She managed to get through the ordeal though she did not really seem to know what Matron Bester was asking for. She wanted some dish or mug or jug or something. Esther managed to carry it off by pretending that her vagueness was caused by the fact that she didn't know where the required object was. And the more sober of us moved quickly to the grille to join Esther so that Matron Bester's attention could be diverted.

I drank very little in prison. I used to have a few sips or nothing at all. I seemed to fear what it would do to me though I never quite formulated my reasons, even to myself. I think it was because I was living so under control and I felt that control was so necessary for my survival that I feared what drink would do to me. I also found most of the stuff too raw for my sensitive stomach. It made my stomach hurt without making me nicely high.

But I was the chief drink-maker. I can't remember quite how that happened but I think it was because I first got on to the possibilities of the marmalade. Later Ann joined me. She became responsible for the tea cooldrink. This alcohol production served a useful purpose, in the same way as did the cooking. It introduced into our lives a little bit of variety and independent activity, that is, independent of the prison authorities. Independent activity and creativity seem to be essential for the human being's sense of well-being. And, of course, it had a definitely social ingredient.

I was convinced that such undertakings were vital for us. I was constantly thinking of ways and means to help us to reduce the starkness of our lives and to relate our lives, as far as we could, to the outside world. Even drink seemed to be another strand linking us to the outside world. And concern with its 'manufacture' made us forget a little our enclosed condition. There was also the humour and laughter with which we carried out such activities, above all the laughing at ourselves.

I used to sit in the bathroom on my haunches taking the pips out of the prunes – we referred to these prunes as the 'spares' – forcing them through the mouth of the bottle, and then adding a few spoons of sugar from the 'spare' sugar. If we added just a little water at a time, instead of filling up the whole bottle, we discovered the drink wasn't so raw. So I used to add just a little water, leave it for about five days, until it bubbled a bit, and then add a bit more. This was a definite improvement.

I also made an experiment with the mealie-meal porridge we got in the morning and which very few of us ate. I put some spoonfuls into a bottle, again with water and sugar. A few weeks later I had a 'taste'. It was definitely alcoholic and had a peculiar chemical flavour, a bit like methylated spirits. I was rather afraid of it and didn't like the taste so thought we could use this as a last resort, in case any of our other supplies dried up for some reason or other.

At some stage, I think it was at the beginning of 1967 (our alcohol 'industry' had then been going a year), our supplies did dry up. However, we decided not to use the porridge idea. Some of the others had a taste and decided it wasn't worth it. In any case, we still had the cooldrink, made from the tea stalks, for our 'celebrations'.

This was how our other supplies 'dried up':

We had complained to Matron Bester that the drain in our bathroom was blocked. Of course, as usual, we repeated the request, week after week, but suddenly one day a white Chief Warder appeared, with two black prisoners. At this point, there were eight bottles behind the bathroom door. Some of them were those large bottles one sees in chemists and which contain all sorts of strange-looking liquids. Several of these had come into our section filled either with cough mixture or with a liquid, used for constipation. We carefully cleaned them and filled them with our products.

Unfortunately, when the men came to open the bathroom drain we had forgotten all about the bottles behind the door. Sadly, as it happened, we had a really good product going. At Christmas-time we had been allowed to order 1lb of dried fruit each as a special treat, and some of us had ordered mixed dried fruit. In each of these packets were several peaches, and Leslie – more below about the arrival of Leslie Schermbrucker, together with Violet Weinberg – who had taken over the organisation of the alcohol from me, had made the most delicious peach 'brandy'. It was the only alcohol there that I could drink without discomfort, and actually gave me a nice warm feeling inside. It really had body. Although Leslie was, on principal, opposed to drink and did not drink herself, she really had had great success with this effort. We had decided to save it for our celebrations.

Evidently, while the black prisoners were opening up the drain, the warder had moved the bathroom door, thus exposing the eight bottles. He drew back startled and muttered, 'God! Hulle maak hier bier!' And the eight bottles were hurriedly removed to the front, to Matron Bester's office. Naturally, this caused some panic amongst us. And we quickly had a look at our copy of the prison regulations to see what penalties we could suffer. We found that it was a serious offence to introduce liquor into a gaol. However, we felt the authorities could not get us on that one as we had not introduced it. We had *produced* it.

At the same time, there was another regulation which really made our position look rather serious. This declared that it was an offence for any member of the prison staff or any prisoner to 'trade' in liquor. For this offence, the prisoner could be taken to a magistrate's court and, if found guilty, was liable to a fine and even a prison sentence of some years. This gave us all a bit of a shock but we concluded that it would be difficult for the authorities to prove that we had been 'trading' in it. We decided that nobody must admit to making the stuff.

The authorities kept ominously silent about the whole affair. This silence usually indicated that they were considering framing a charge.

When we went through for 'Complaints and Requests' at the end of the week, we found, to our great embarrassment, the bottles standing side by side under the office desk. The fact that neither the Brigadier nor Matron Bester made any reference to their presence under the desk or even to the incident itself made the situation even more embarrassing.

As it turned out, they followed their usual technique of dropping questions out of the blue to one or two of us. Nothing was said to me. One of us who was asked about it said that we had 'all' made it. Somebody else told them that it was just cooldrink. The rest of us said nothing.

The days passed by ominously. We wondered whether they were keen for any of us to add another two or three years to our sentences. Needless to say, our prunes 'for medicinal purposes' stopped coming. No explanation was given, and Leslie immediately went on a 'campaign' to get them back – with utter innocence.

We did not see prunes again. Nor did we ever hear of a charge. They probably realised they could not get us under the regulations. I wonder whether they sent it to a laboratory to test the alcohol content? It would be quite interesting to know how successful we had been.

The authorities evidently decided that some 'favour' or other should be removed in order to make it quite clear that they did not approve of what we had been doing. Matron Bester was the instrument of such an approach. She muttered that we thought we could do what we liked and one morning she came crashing into our section as we were working. She locked the grilles of our cells so that we could do no studying during working hours, although, by this time, we had so little work to do that, without access to our cells, all we could do was to sit around or stand around, waiting for the long hours to pass by.

The Front would have known that the cutting down of our space to just the portaal and the bathroom area would be specially hard on us. Matron Bester knew what it was like to take away from prisoners something they already had and she knew – we had told her and the other prison officials often enough, after all – how our confined space caused us considerable suffering. I could see the pain in the eyes of the others and could feel it in my own as the grilles, one by one, banged to and the keys clattered in the locks while we stood in the portaal. Our study space, that part of our life which was really our own, was, at least during the day, only accessible at the behest of the authorities.

Matron Bester was very good at using her keys as a symbol of our 'degradation' as human beings. The sound of keys has great meaning for a prisoner because the key and the lock are the mechanical objects which keep you in your situation. The keys were in the hands of other human beings, those who controlled your life, by and large every minute of it.

I had the 'master' once in my hands, that is, the key that could open any door in the prison. I took it from Matron Taljaard on one occasion and, although we had all been standing around her having a friendly chat and I would have to get through at least two grilles, if not three, to get out of the gaol, leaving aside the doors, a look of panic crossed her face. Trying to maintain a friendly expression, she said, 'Give the key back to me, Neame.' I gave it back to her. It was a thick heavy key.

She had just been telling us how the black prisoners felt about that key. She said that if ever they touched the master by mistake (they never touched it on purpose), they went through a magical ceremony to take a sort of curse off themselves. We felt certain that the authorities had over several decades told prisoners that they would have a curse on them if they touched the key until this myth became a part of prison culture.

Yet we were sure that some of them, such as Spokie, who had escaped once before and who seemed to have a cynical attitude towards the authorities, wouldn't have fallen for this story. Apparently, Spokie had 'a nine to fifteen years', and, with 'good behaviour', would probably have got out after nine. However, after trying to escape, she would have to 'do' the full fifteen years, six years more. Clearly the master, together with the other keys, was crucial to a prisoner's life.

Reclassification from 'C' to 'B' group

I THINK IT WAS ALREADY at the time of Judge Boshoff's visit in January 1966 that the Brigadier started telling visitors to the prison that we were 'good prisoners'. We had done a year and we were still C group prisoners, and we felt we really had a good case when we insisted that we should be reclassified to B. It was from about April that we went on a campaign for reclassification. As was usual with the authorities, there was always a different explanation as to why we had not yet been reclassified. I cannot remember all the intricacies of the explanations given in the months from April until 9 August 1966 when we were eventually reclassified but the general approach was again to confuse us and keep us on tenterhooks. Each week at 'Complaints and Requests' the same person would be told a different story; different people could be told different stories on the same day.

The trouble was that in our situation of enormous isolation we tended to take seriously the explanations we were offered, even though with one part of ourselves we didn't believe them. People are inclined to believe the information that is available and so, also because there was often no other information to measure it against, we tended to accept, to one degree or another, what we were told.

This is how it usually went: one week we would discuss backwards and forwards the reasons given that particular week, and find all the arguments we might use in a 'campaign' to show that these reasons were invalid. And we would look forward to the following week's 'Complaints and Requests' so that we could show the Brigadier how wrong he was.

The Brigadier would then coolly come out with another explanation, sometimes one in complete contradiction to the one he had given the previous week. We would be so busy working out all the arguments to use against the previous explanation we would hardly notice that he was busy shifting his ground. And the fact that he had given a quite different explanation to somebody else on the same day didn't make you feel, as in normal circumstances it would, that the Brigadier was just shooting his mouth off or just trying to keep us from finding the answer, namely that they wanted to keep our conditions as bad as they could until pressure from outside forced their hand.

The men in Pretoria Central who had been in our trial and had two-, three- or five-year sentences (and a couple of them had been on the Central Committee) had been reclassified in April or May, I think it was; this was obviously because Pretoria had hit the public eye in connection with the Harold Strachan case and because Helen Suzman, the lone Progressive Party MP, had visited the prison to check up on what conditions were like there.

I have already pointed to the false information outside concerning our conditions. It was only after some of us started coming out of Barberton Prison that people began to obtain some picture of what it was really like there, and even then there were difficulties. For instance, Di Schoon was a banned person and therefore had to be terribly careful whom she saw and she was not likely to risk another sentence. In any case, it is unlikely that her view would have been taken all that seriously.

Sheila Weinberg had also to be careful. She had been in 90-day detention before serving her six months, and her father, Eli Weinberg, had been convicted in our trial for being a member of the Central Committee of the Communist Party and was still in Pretoria Central. Her mother, Violet Weinberg, had been held in 180-day detention for interrogation purposes and had been connected with Bram Fischer's underground activities. And so on.

At the same time, the point should be made that we women were possibly not regarded as especially worthy of public attention, not only because there were no top leaders amongst us but because we were women and mostly young. And there had also been the smear campaign indulged in by the police spy, Gerard Ludi, about 'naked orgies' which made it appear, apart from anything else, that our political stand against apartheid and racism was perhaps not to be taken all that seriously. It is undoubted that at this time the security police were especially keen to suggest that white women who identified themselves with the anti-apartheid struggle were in general morally degenerate.

The extent to which the white liberal press fell for such tactics was, in my view, an indication of the state of (white) liberalism in the country. Ludi, in replying to a question from the defence as to whether any of the accused had been involved in these alleged orgies, had answered in the negative. This was simply not reported, despite the fact that the newspapers had used the theme of naked orgies in bold letters in headlines.

At the time we were fighting to be reclassified to B, we also went on a campaign to be moved to Kroonstad. Even if they did eventually reclassify us, many of the facilities that were available to Bs according to the prison regulations would not be available to us, simply because Barberton did not have them. For instance, in Kroonstad prisoners saw a film once or twice a week. For us, that would have been an important link with the outside world. White women prisoners worked on sewing machines in Kroonstad, making prison uniforms, sports' dresses and nightdresses. We were still washing laundry and it appeared would continue to do so as there were no facilities for anything else. Even our washing facilities were extremely restricted. Above all, the women at Kroonstad had space to live and work in, and they could move around the prison. When I had spent a night in the Kroonstad prison on my way from Port Elizabeth to Barberton, I had noted various boards, indicating a LIBRARY, a HOSPITAL, a DINING HALL and the prisoners there with whom I spoke told me that there was a workroom where they worked during the day, a chapel where they went to church on a Sunday, and a common room. Relative freedom of movement was not confined to ordinary white prisoners at Kroonstad Prison but also encompassed ordinary black prisoners.

Viljoen and a conflict: Prisons/Security branch

It was sometime in July that Brigadier Viljoen visited us again. As usual, we were in quite a state of excitement. I was taken through to the visitors' room. There he was sitting behind the table, black haired with a white hair here and there, ruddy cheeked, plump, happy with himself.

On his last visit he had told Ann that, amongst us prisoners, the person who really interested him was Sylvia Neame. She had had a bad time, he'd said. I imagined that he was either baiting Ann to talk about me or was trying to win me with kindness. It was probably a bit of both.

Viljoen leaned over the table with a friendly smile as I entered and said heartily, 'Hello, Sylvia. And how are you?'

'I'm all right, thank you, Brigadier.' And I sat down in the chair opposite him.

'Well, well, Sylvia. And how have you been getting on?'

'Brigadier, when are we going to be reclassified to B?'

'I cannot tell you that, Sylvia …' He put a hypocritical look of humility and detachment on his face. 'That I cannot tell you. That lies in the hands, as you know, of the Prison Board.'

'But why haven't we seen the Prison Board, Brigadier? It hasn't been here for over a year, and we should see it once a year.'

In fact I had never seen the Prison Board and at this time I had been serving over a year. I had seen a man once, soon after I arrived at Barberton, whom, I was told, was on the board but I did not ever see him again. And all that happened was that he'd looked at me and I'd looked at him, and he'd asked whether I had anything to say, and I, completely nonplussed, not knowing what the Prison Board was anyway as we had no copy of the regulations in which were stated its duties said, 'No.' And he'd said, 'That is all.' And I walked out of the office.

We were told on several occasions in the early stages of our sentences that, in fact, the board had no jurisdiction over us since we were 'Security Prisoners'. We discovered when we did eventually get a copy of the regulations that there was no such category. Later, the authorities sometimes said we fell under the jurisdiction of the board and at other times that we did not, according to which was the most suitable argument for them at the time.

One of the many reasons the OC had given us for the fact that we had not been reclassified was that the Prison Board had not yet seen us and that they were responsible for our reclassification, as we could see from the regulations. They were the main body responsible for the conditions under which we lived, he told us. They were responsible for the type of work we did, for the timing of our release, etc. He could do nothing without the board. Of course we followed up this piece of 'information' by going on a campaign to see the Prison Board. We even threatened to take legal action.

The Brigadier then about-faced. He told one of us who raised the matter at 'Complaints and Requests' that the Prison Board had, in fact, no jurisdiction over us as we were 'security prisoners'. When we raised the matter with Colonel Aucamp, he did the same sort of thing. And yet we went on, fighting each week on the basis of the most recent information given us by the authorities.

Brigadier Viljoen leaned confidentially over the table towards me and said, 'Sylvia, the board is very, very busy. We have been expecting for months that they would come here. They tell us they will do so in a few days or a week, and then they send a telegram with the information that they have been held up at another prison. You must remember, Sylvia, that this is not the only prison they have to visit, you are not their only prisoner. There are many, many prisoners whom they have to interview and think about. There are only five of you.'

'Yes, but, Brigadier, according to the regulations, we should see them within twelve months and that period is up long ago.'

'Sylvia, you must be patient. They have a great deal of work to do ... We, too, are worried about the fact that they have not yet come to Barberton.'

'Anyway, Brigadier, isn't it irrelevant whether the board comes or not? Colonel Aucamp has told us, and Brigadier Pretorius has told us, too, on occasion, that the board has no jurisdiction over us because we are political prisoners or whatever special category you wish to place us in.'

Brigadier Viljoen drew himself up importantly and began to look very patient. I knew what was coming. We had had this little sidetrack so often from all of them, from Colonel Aucamp, from Pretorius, from the Commissioner of Prisons, from Matron Bester. 'Sylvia, there is no such category as "political prisoners". The Minister himself said so in the House the other day. You prisoners are subversive prisoners, *staatsmisdadigers* (state offenders). That is a very serious offence.' Clearly the word 'state' was the operative word; and it was true that we wished to *subvert* the apartheid system and what, indeed, had become the apartheid state.

'What term you use, Brigadier, is quite irrelevant. My point is—'

But Viljoen thought this an extremely significant point. 'You are all state offenders, Sylvia. The Minister, himself, said so.'

'Brigadier, the point is, is the board responsible for our reclassification or is it not? If it is not, who or what institution is?'

'Of course the Prison Board is responsible for your reclassification, as it is responsible for your training [!] and conditions of imprisonment.'

'Then why did Colonel Aucamp tell us that the board had nothing to do with us, that he, himself, was responsible for our reclassification, he, in consultation with the Minister of Justice?'

A look passed across Viljoen's face. 'Don't talk to me about Colonel Aucamp. He is not one of us. *He* is not in the Prisons Department. He is Security.'

This was to become a favourite sidetracking technique of the prison authorities, playing themselves off against Colonel Aucamp. Brigadier Pretorius began to use it too. No doubt there were differences on this question in the government camp and, no doubt, most immediately between the Prisons and the Police or, more directly, the latter's Security Branch. However, as far as we were concerned, there was an important element of bureaucratic manoeuvring, amongst others, in order to evade our demand for reclassification.

In the past we had been encouraged to believe that Colonel Aucamp was mainly responsible for us. In fact Aucamp had told us this himself. This was reinforced by what the OC told us as well as Matron Bester. And the certain trepidation and excitement that accompanied Aucamp's visits made it pretty clear where the power lay. Behind Aucamp were the Security Police and the Minister of Justice, to whom Aucamp passed on information and from whom he received instructions of one kind or another. Prison officials admitted this when they found it useful to do so, in particular when they tried to deny their own responsibility for our conditions.

They developed a technique of passing the buck to somebody who was not present, someone who, most probably, we might not see for many months or even a year, such as the Prison Board or the Commissioner of Prisons; or someone we would never see, such as the Minister of Justice. And they were always giving us different explanations.

'I tell you,' Viljoen continued, and I saw the blue sky on the other side of the bars and the sun falling in large yellow patches on the floor of the visitors' room, 'don't talk to me about Colonel Aucamp.' A sneer and slight look of disgust crossed his face. I tried to assess whether it was genuine or not but could not make up my mind. Strangely, it looked genuine. There was much rivalry between the strictly prisons' officials and Colonel Aucamp as well as the Security Branch.

The Officer-Commanding, Brigadier Pretorius, was, in fact, by rank senior to Colonel Aucamp, and yet it was clear that he had to take instructions from the colonel. It was a peculiar situation. I remember Brigadier Pretorius saying to me that if Captain Broodryk had said I could write a letter, then, of course, I could. But this, I think, was a slip. For definitely, by that time – it was a couple of months before I was due for release in 1967 – the authorities, prisons, police and government, were trying to build up a picture according to which we were ordinary criminal prisoners.

It was in the latter framework that they held that we fell under the jurisdiction of the Prison Board. In the second half of 1966 whenever we asked Colonel Aucamp something, such as when were we to be reclassified, he would say, 'Don't ask me that. Ask the Brigadier.' But this was after we had started the campaign to find out where we stood and after we had stressed that we knew we were being discriminated against as political prisoners and that, according to the regulations, this should not be so except in the case of remission and parole (of course we fought against that piece of discrimination too).

I was still trying to get some clarity from Brigadier Viljoen in the visitors' room of the Barberton prison. 'But, Brigadier,' I said patiently, really expecting no outcome but determined to go on pushing at the authorities, 'if we fall under the Prison Board and our reclassification depends on them, don't you think it is important that they should come here soon, especially as they are long overdue?'

'Yes, yes, Sylvia, we here are very worried about their not coming to Barberton. We are expecting them any moment, any moment. In fact, we received a telegram from them saying they will be here within the week.'

We had heard that story about the telegram for a long time from the OC as well, and were to hear it many times in the months to come. It was like the OC's story about his having received information that our uniforms had already been put on the train and were on their way. The uniforms did not turn up for months and months, not until we had spoken to the Prison Board and they had seen the rags on our backs – the blue rags, the remains of the peacock blue uniforms, specially chosen for prisoners by Mrs Vorster, wife of the Minister of Justice and strongman of South Africa's racist state.

'I am told,' Viljoen changed the subject, 'that you people have been causing some trouble.'

'Trouble, Brigadier? What trouble?'

'You are not the prisoners you used to be, I have been told.'

'I don't know what you are referring to, Brigadier.'

'Just that some of you are not the prisoners you used to be.'

One of these contorted conversations was apparently starting in the framework of which the authorities would not commit themselves, and, therefore, we prisoners weren't absolutely sure what they were getting at, leading to endless discussion amongst us about what they were actually after.

'I really thought, Sylvia, that some of you would have been released by this time.' He suddenly looked uncomfortable. By saying 'some of you', which would almost certainly have excluded myself, he realised that he had made a slip. 'Really, Sylvia, I would like to have seen you people released by this time.'

It seemed to me that he was trying to indicate that I was responsible for people not being released, in particular for the apparent change of attitude amongst us on the issue. Or perhaps he was trying to get me to commit myself on the point, to say, for instance, that I was against people accepting remission and parole unless it was given to all political prisoners. 'Sylvia, you prisoners are behaving differently from how you used to.'

I wondered whether he was referring to the fact that we had knit together as a group over the past month and that our 'campaigning' had stepped up its pace.

'I do not know what you mean, Brigadier. Can't you put it more clearly so that I can understand you?'

'It is just that you people have changed.'

'Well, Brigadier, I am not sure what you mean but there is no doubt that this situation is having an effect on us.' I pointed a finger towards our section. 'Locked up in that confined space down there.'

Viljoen caught onto this eagerly. 'Yes, that is what I thought ... as prisoners, you begin to change. That is inevitable. It is not the fault of the Prisons Department. It is that imprisonment is having an affect on you people.'

I couldn't work out what he was referring to – perhaps to our complaints about Matron Bester and all the other 'complaints and requests' we had been making. Here, of course, Ann was important. The authorities must be worried then, I thought.

I was beginning to feel extremely tired. My mouth was dry, my body stretched and tense, my eyes felt increasingly immobile. I leaned forward across the table and said, with a dry mouth, 'Yes, Brigadier, that situation down there is definitely having an effect on us. And you people are always telling us different stories so that we get confused ... more and more confused.'

'Who tells you different stories? That is impossible.'

'All of you, particularly Brigadier Pretorius. He has one story for one week, another story for the next.'

Viljoen got a hypocritical look of indignation on his face. 'That cannot be, Sylvia. The Brigadier is a very, very kind man ...' He paused. 'You people may not realise it but he gives you all a lot of thought. He thinks about you, worries about you. He is always trying to think of ways of helping you people.'

'That is nonsense, Brigadier,' I said tiredly.

Viljoen did not seem particularly worried about my comment. I don't think he especially liked Pretorius and, anyway, he had been present on several occasions when Pretorius had claimed that he was a hard man and, if that was the image Pretorius wanted to project, Viljoen must have thought, why worry to change it.

'You say we have changed,' I said, 'but you must remember it was you people who were always trying to indicate to us that we were going to be released early, constantly trying to confuse us.'

'Who told you you would be released early?'

'Brigadier Pretorius himself,' I said. 'He told us all one day as we stood on parade that he didn't think one of us would serve our full sentences. And all of you were always dropping hints and even saying things directly.'

'No, no, Sylvia, that is the trouble with prisoners. All prisoners are like this. They misinterpret what people say. They take a small statement and build it into something big. Prisoners are always discussing and talking and blowing up small things into big things, and then they begin to feel confused. I know this, Sylvia, for I have worked in the prisons for many, many years.'

'Look, Brigadier, I can definitely tell you that Brigadier Pretorius told us this, and Colonel Aucamp also said something to some of us when he came here once.'

'No, no, Sylvia. You must remember that the judgement of prisoners becomes confused.'

So he knew all this, I thought. That was interesting. He wasn't such an old fool as I thought he was. But where was he going? What was he trying to get out of me or tell me? I felt so exhausted by the whole conversation that I felt I couldn't say another word. 'Yes, Brigadier, we have changed. We feel very confused. This is what that place is doing to us. We are very isolated, very confined and you try to confuse us.'

It was July in Barberton, a cold month for some parts of South Africa but warm here, warm in the visitors' room. I had that suspended feeling. I was out of our section, the section in which I was living my life, if one could call it living. And here in the visitors' room I was thinking about our situation there down the passage. Our section was like a square box in my head with us in it. With the part of my mind, that part in the visitors' room, I was looking limply at us there, my mind turning over just a little. My body, my mind, was continually, eternally and inevitably, in a straitjacket. Inside me was a large, tired feeling of resignation.

Viljoen seemed to come back to his original point, whatever that was. 'You people are not what you were. You have changed.'

'I don't really know what you mean, Brigadier.'

'Sylvia, I can say sincerely that I really hoped that you people would be released by now.'

There was a long pause. Brigadier Viljoen's face was ruddy, soft and chubby across the table. My eyeballs felt as though they were set in concrete in my head, sunk right back into my head. I turned and looked outside towards the trees, large Australian gums, were they? I did not really know. The green venetian blind was down on one window, up on the other, so I could see the blue of the sky and the green of the trees through my taut eyeballs.

Brigadier Viljoen leaned confidentially towards me. 'Sylvia, I want to tell you something, don't tell the others ... I warn you, don't tell the others. It will only cause trouble.' The Brigadier paused. He was searching for the kind of manner with which he could communicate something to me. It should be subtle but dramatic. Chubby red lips with a bit of saliva in one corner. Blue eyes fixed on me. 'After you people are reclassified to B group, you are going to get something which no other prisoners have ever been given. You are going to get something which is going to make you people so happy, so happy. But, Sylvia, don't tell the others, I warn you, for it will only cause trouble.'

I felt too tired to ask him what we were going to get. I knew he wouldn't tell me anyway. I wondered whether he was telling the truth or whether he was trying to further confuse us. I had never seen him quite as subtle or, perhaps better, so focused on achieving a distinct goal. He was usually such an old introverted fool. Was he trying to convince himself and perhaps others what a really good psychologist he was and how he might be used much more extensively as an instrument to manipulate prisoners? Of course, he had told me that he had a psychology degree and he might have developed the ambition to be engaged in a more professional capacity in the prison service and perhaps even serve as a link to the Security Branch (instead of Aucamp?). Did Viljoen have ambitions, I wondered, which he felt might be satisfied if he could win the approval of the Security Branch.

From what I had gathered from several interchanges I had had in the past couple of years, there was a growing feeling, especially in the public service, that it could be very useful to gain the approval of the security police in order to satisfy personal ambitions. I had not quite expected this from Viljoen but I had possibly underestimated his desire to get on in the world at whatever cost to principles.

Yet I suspect that another conclusion emerges from his visit and that was that the prisons service was trying to convince the security establishment and further the government that it was able itself to perform the job of psychological manipulation – in our case, they liked to identify this with 'rehabilitation' – that the security arm had been directing.

I left the visitors' room, tired and limp. I told the others what Viljoen had said, including his promise that after reclassification we would obtain something very special.

On 9 August 1966 we were reclassified to B group. We did not see the Prison Board first. Nothing happened thereafter, despite Viljoen's promise.

But we were much tougher than we had been before July. Their techniques could either break us or make us stronger. They had made us stronger.

We had fought for reclassification but we did not expect much of a change in our lives as a result of it because the facilities simply did not exist in Barberton. Nevertheless our reclassification did improve our lives quite a bit. A visit a month and two letters a month was a big improvement. Perhaps even more exciting was that we got some news via fashion and film magazines (although we were allowed no newspapers). This made me really feel that I had some contact with the outside world. At first, though, I found it a bit painful to see luscious women in gorgeous clothes or even spindly-legged Twiggy in her minis. We all longed to get out of gaol so that we could put on a mini-skirt!

Leslie Schermbrucker and Violet Weinberg join us

SOON AFTER OUR RECLASSIFICATION Aucamp brought Leslie and Violet to join us. Leslie had been in gaol for about nine or ten months by then. She had been under 180-day detention for interrogation and had had quite a rough time. She had been kept awake for days to try and force her to make a statement. She had then been taken to court to give evidence against Bram Fischer but had refused to do so and was given about 300 days' imprisonment for refusing to give evidence. She had then been tried herself, together with Violet Weinberg, for furthering the aims of the illegal Communist Party, and they had each been sentenced to two years. We had been expecting them for months and had almost given up all hope that they would join us when one afternoon there they were. Of course, there was great excitement.

I noted in my diary on Thursday, 18/8/66:

Today I moved into the single cell, with the side window looking towards the mountains. Violet and Leslie arrived so I have done very little work today …

When people arrive (I think I have had this impression before, when Di and Sheila arrived but not so strongly) I feel how well organised we are, how well organised I am. Every action of mine, every word, feeling, thought, seems to me to be well ordered, directed, my mind clear and unencumbered. I suppose that here the world is so restricted that we perfect each action. Even our thought and emotional life appears to become efficient, so with our manners which I thought must be appalling, both table and social. On the contrary, I find when I compare us with new arrivals that, in a way, our manners are so perfect. We are careful about every word we use, every tone of voice, every gesture, every movement with the knife and fork at meals. It must be because we are so likely to get on one another's nerves here that we are especially careful.

I was conscious, after Leslie and Violet arrived, as I walked around in our little space, how straight and firm I walked, how sure I feel within myself, how clear my views about everything have become. I know what my intellectual position on most things is without any effort. I find I analyse problems so crisply and clearly if not so clearly in words, at least in my own mind.

Yet I felt, as I listened to Violet talking with a roughness and inaccuracy, a kind of muddling through, that perhaps I had lost something, nevertheless also gained. I felt my principles were so straight and firm. Maybe this sort of feeling is merely a feeling of here. Perhaps in the outside world, that fast-moving world, this crystal clear consciousness will begin to become somewhat ragged at the edges.

I find that I am beginning to be able to construct more complex sentences. I seem to have more flow. I noticed this in my last two letters – to Caroline and to my grandmother. I have always found in the past that I had to use short simple sentences, otherwise things went more wrong than usual with my intention of putting down on paper what I had in my mind. It is something I have thought about a great deal since I have been here, i.e. how to express myself more clearly. I started thinking about it when I read Anna K. soon after I arrived; then much later, particularly when I read Chekhov, and now, above all, Gogol. The latter has such flow, such unselfconsciousness of style – helped by humour? Gogol is a strange man – this unselfconsciousness, this humour, combined with his messianic attitude towards his writing.

Anyway, to get back to my point: What I found particularly difficult was to put down on paper the complicated picture I have of life somewhere in my mind. The consecutiveness of sentence construction, the fact that one sentence follows the other on the page and thus in time as you write or read it I found a real problem for the picture in my mind never fitted in with this. I felt, too, that the dialectical way of seeing *things – with the interest in the horizontal view, with the interest in questions of emphasis, 'quality' as against quantity, in primary factors as against secondary factors, more fundamental factors and superstructure, interconnectedness, overlapping, etc. – this complex view was very difficult to express. I felt that we had not yet found the language to convey this kind of view of life and of history sufficiently accurately.*

I think that my difficulties were, in part, a genuine reflection of the difficulties of language but I guess that my inarticulateness was also a psychological thing, caused partly by introversion – too much of it – and, no doubt, because I was still struggling to find a solid position. A great deal, too, had to do with impatience, not wanting to take the trouble and concentration to put the 'picture' down as accurately as possible. In addition to impatience, I used also to feel that I would lose the whole picture if I concentrated on its details, i.e. on seeing that I had the details accurate.

I don't feel this so much anymore. I have become more interested in accuracy of detail. In this connection, think of the limited nature of the world here and thus our concentration on details. Connected with this seems to be the clear details of memory. My memories outside were always so vague. I had a very poor memory and rarely remembered many details, just the flavour usually. Now I am surprised to see the details of my 'memories' ... I am still having flashbacks.

Well I have done very little work tonight. The hooter has gone. I must finish Gogol. I have about twenty pages or so. Then I can start Moll Flanders which I want to read for the 17th century ...

Though there was a bit of coldness and calculation in our relations with each other, it was, by no means, only that. Without doubt, we learned to give to each other and to respect each other. We learned to share what little we had. I wrote in a letter to my sister, 3 January, 1967:

'... I liked your story about Twiggy. Your cutting introduced her to me for the first time. However, just recently I have read an article on her and Jean Shrimpton, the other English model, in one of our magazines. Now she has become one of our friends. We are so limited in our social *contacts here that we go out of our way to make new friends. We all get to know each other's friends and relations. So you, Anna, Graham, Peter, Mizan, Dion and Caroline are well-known personalities in Barberton Gaol. And I know what Ann's uncle, aunt and two cousins look like, what they do, etc etc. This sort of thing is a great enrichment of our lives here. We share, we have learned to share a great deal with each other – and that helps us to make life more tolerable.'*

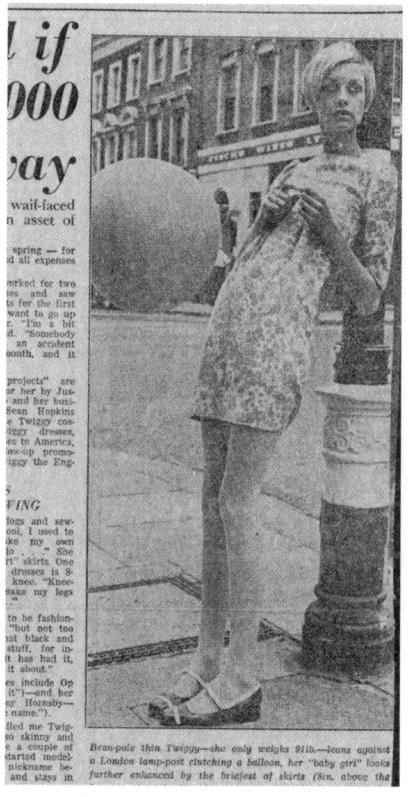

It was in August–September 1966 that my life, and I think this was true of the others who had been in Barberton with me all this time, changed its quality and became more bearable. There were several reasons for this. First and foremost for me was that we had knit together as a group.

I had felt tremendously isolated in my first six or nine months at Barberton. There had been my Port Elizabeth experience, and then, above all, the fact that I was used as a scapegoat. At the same time, I was very keen to ensure that we were cemented as a group and this necessarily meant that I stood outside to a considerable extent. The certain outsider location I, in fact, never quite lost while I was there.

Leslie was an important addition to our community. She had a family outside, an eighteen-year-old daughter, Jill, and a sixteen-year-old son, Peter. Her husband, Ivan, was in Pretoria serving five years. I am not sure why she lived her whole life with us. It may partly have been because Ivan was in gaol and would be for several years. Her children were also somewhat older than, for example, Esther's children, so that she apparently did not have the guilt feelings I sensed in Esther. Esther, of course, also had the problem that her husband, Hymie, had a chronic illness.

At the same time, our different responses to the prison situation had undoubtedly a lot to do with differences of personality. Leslie tried to live life to the full wherever she was. She had a fine sense of her own identity and her motto tended to be: Don't live in the past, don't live in the future. Live now. Deal with your situation, as it is here and now.

Violet also, I think, lived a great deal in the gaol situation but it was more difficult to tell with her because a couple of weeks after she arrived she suffered an immense tragedy. The thing that could hit Violet the hardest, the death of her son, happened soon after she arrived.

It was wonderful to have Leslie and Violet join us. Not only were they two extra personalities but they brought us news from the outside world. They also brought some disturbing political information: how Bram had been captured, news of the terrible torture of detainees that was going on, Issy Heymann's attempted suicide – he had cut his wrists while being held for interrogation. Fred Carneson had been made to stand for days and had had epileptic fits. There was news of who had 'talked', who hadn't, who had turned traitor and given evidence, who had held out. Violet and Leslie described how Johannesburg was changing.

We liked all the details. However, when we thought there were too many changes, we began to feel insecure. It was often difficult for us to remember that life was continuing outside. Some people we had known had got married or had an extra child, and so on. With us, in many ways, time stood still and we had unconsciously believed that it stood still outside too.

Mark Weinberg dies

VIOLET AND LESLIE INJECTED new life into the group. Yet in prison – and I am thinking especially of a prison in apartheid South Africa – death is around the corner. This time, though, death came from an unexpected quarter.

Violet had been trying to obtain permission for a special visit from Sheila ever since her arrival. There were all sorts of family matters to sort out, particularly as the father of the family was also in gaol. Then one day Violet was told that she was getting a visit. For a few hours there was pleasure and excitement on her face as she got ready, ironed a clean blue uniform and had Ann 'do' her hair.

Violet had suffered a great deal in 180-day detention and after. The Security Police had used the sleep deprivation technique on her, together with all the other usual methods, such as threatening to pick up relatives and friends unless she talked. Importantly, they had threatened to pick up her son Mark. They told her that they had all the information they needed, and thus there would be no difficulties. Mark must have been about 24 years old at that time. He had been completely deaf from the age of thirteen as the result of a motor car accident; Violet had been driving. From that time a sense of guilt, on Violet's part, became an important part of their relationship. In this sort of situation, it becomes quite irrelevant whose fault the accident was.

I had begun to get to know Mark quite well before my arrest as, after some of the others had moved out, Mark and I were the only two left in the cottage in Orange Grove. After the initial difficulties, caused partly by my state of mind after the Rivonia arrests and partly by the difficulty in learning to communicate with him because of his deafness, I began to like and respect him. He was extremely intelligent. He had become a skilled lip-reader. What I particularly liked about him was his sense of humour and the down to earth way with which he dealt with the problems arising from his deafness, and all other problems he happened to come across. And he was kind. During the long months of the Rivonia trial, and we all wondered whether there would be death sentences, I often used to wake him up and chat to him through the night.

When news of the sentences came through, I had the radio on in the cottage. Mark, of course, could not listen to the radio but when I heard that it was 'life' and not death sentences, I went running with a rush of relief through to Mark's room at the other end of the passage to tell him. He smiled and said in his gentle way, 'That is good. They're very lucky.' I went out to see some friends and when I came back and opened the front door of the cottage, there he was with a pal, and he smiled again and commented, 'And she doesn't even come back drunk!' And I smiled too. His steadiness and matter-of-factness helped me at this time.

Mark was there, too, when the knock on the door came at dawn a couple of months later. I was woken by the loud knocks on the glass panel of the front door, and realised it must be 'them'. I got up, trying to think whether there was anything incriminating around that I could quickly dispose of. I made an effort to collect my thoughts as the loud knocking continued and the sound of men's deep voices. I slipped quickly through the little living room, across the small entrance hall and saw, through the frosted glass panel of the front door, hats on the heads of shadowy forms – it was 'them' all right – and I rushed over to Mark's room, shook him awake, and told him they were there.

The knocking got louder and a harsh voice said, 'Open up! Open up!' I went to the door and opened it. Four of them. They tramped in heavily and moved towards my bedroom. The SB knew which was my room because they had on another occasion raided the cottage when they came to pick up my (academic) material, taking it to headquarters in the centre of town. They started searching. I demanded to see a search warrant. The senior chap turned and said roughly and with irritation, 'We don't need a warrant. We're taking you in for 90 days.'

There was a scuffle in the living room and I moved quickly to my bedroom door to see what was happening. A hefty Security Branch man was engaged in a scuffle with Mark. Immediately I appeared he took his hands off Mark. Addressing me, he said, 'Tell him, we don't want him in here.' I ignored him, and mouthed to Mark, 'They're taking me for 90 days.' He understood immediately. Confirming that he had understood, he pointed at me and repeated, 'They're taking you for 90 days.' I nodded.

'Tell him to get out of here,' the Security Branch man who was leading the raid said. I mouthed what he had said to Mark. At first he did not go but then quietly wandered off somewhere in the cottage while the cops continued going through my things. 'You had better pack,' the leading cop said. I started packing slowly, trying to think of all the things I would need.

About half an hour later I said goodbye to Mark.

'Good luck,' he said quietly. We had recently acquired a dog and it had become attached to me. It seemed to realise I was going away and it began to howl most pitifully. A dog in apartheid South Africa. Mark had to lock it up in his room.

I went out of the front door to find Johanna sitting on a box in the rather unkempt plot of grass in front of the house. Johanna, of Khoi descent, lived in the room attached to the cottage at the back. As she saw me coming out, surrounded by four men, she realised immediately what was happening and started a very loud wail, more typical of funerals. There was an unbelievable noise, what with the dog howling and Johanna's wail. I thought, Good Lord, such a noise and so early in the morning! What will the neighbours think! Calling goodbye to Johanna, I walked the few steps to the car, with the four men around me. In the car was a fifth cop.

After that I saw Mark a few times at visits at the Fort while I was awaiting trial. We had mouthed conversations through the netting wire. It was quite a strain because it was difficult for him to see my mouth through the wire. Also, in a space a few feet square four other people were having visits so that I had to try and get Mark to shout so that I could hear.

Actually, these visits at the Fort while we were awaiting trial were real shouting matches. After many a visit I returned to the cell dry mouthed, with a sore throat, head aching and exhausted, knowing that I had not heard a great deal of what my visitor had said, but had pretended to hear, and wondering in turn whether my visitor had heard much of what I had said. While we were awaiting trial we could get two visits a week. Visiting days were hardly enjoyable – such a pity.

At Barberton I saw Mark twice when he came to visit Sheila. Once was through the window of the bathroom as he walked down the crunching grey gravel pathway and down the stone steps, round the gaol to the front entrance. He had obviously hitchhiked because he had a haversack on his back. The second time I saw him standing at the front of the gaol, smiling. He had realised that we were somewhere behind the cages. Of course this was all done behind the backs of the authorities. In the first months at Barberton when we were under such strict supervision, we would not have managed to peer out of the windows at all.

Sheila arrived at lunchtime lock-up for the visit. Violet had been waiting impatiently all morning, wondering whether, at the last moment, Sheila had not been able to come or the authorities had withdrawn their permission for a visit. I was in the single cell facing the mountains. Violet was next door to me, in the middle single cell. Leslie was in the third single cell on the other side of Violet.

I heard a car drive up and stop. I climbed up on my table and looked through the cage. Sheila was walking across the gravel driveway. She made no effort to look up at our windows. She went out of view, and I moved to the second window of my cell, overlooking the front steps. I was still standing on my table. Sheila, with head slightly down, went up the steps. I wondered why she was being so unfriendly. She knew, of course, where our cells were.

I was suddenly shocked by the sound of the central door of our section opening, and then the crash of the key in the lock of the central grille. I sprang quickly down from my table, sat down in my chair with my back to the portaal and pretended I was reading. Footsteps sounded on the concrete floor. They came closer. There was the sound of a grating key as a wardress opened Violet's grille.

'Your visit, Weinberg.'

I heard Violet mutter something. There were footsteps again across the portaal. The sound of keys in the central grille. And the door on the passage closing. Then silence.

I climbed back onto my table and looked towards the front steps. I couldn't hear anything from the visitors' room. But suddenly I heard Violet's powerful voice shouting, 'No, Sheila, no! You are not telling me the truth. Mark is not dead!' There was silence again. And then Violet's voice, hysterical and powerful. Violet had a powerful voice at the best of times.

I got down from my table and went to my grille. The others in the big cell across the portaal were standing at their grille, shocked, a question on their faces.

'Mark is dead,' I said.

'Mark is dead,' they whispered after me, shattered.

A few minutes later they brought Violet back, and we were unlocked. It was the end of lunchtime lock-up. We all went through to Violet, one by one. There was a tremendous silence in our section that whole afternoon, more silent then the usual silence. Such a stillness, as if life had stopped completely.

Life, such as it was, went on much as usual in our section the following day. To some extent, we had become resigned to suffering. We had come to terms with death. It had become so much a part of South African life. We had learned that, if you were in politics, there was always the possibility of death. People had died in detention. Sometimes these were friends, not just people out there whom you did not know. Friends, husbands and boyfriends had faced the possibility of death sentences in the courts. We had seen fellow prisoners in death cells. Many of us who had been held for interrogation had been confronted with the question: shall I commit suicide?

We did not ask Violet how Mark had died. We hardly discussed it amongst ourselves. We just knew the fact and accepted it. Later we heard that there had been a gas leak in the bathroom of the Weinbergs' house in Johannesburg. Mark had been bathing and died in the bath.

The Weinberg family consisted of four people. Violet and Eli both spent some years in gaol. Sheila had been held for interrogation and had served a six-month sentence. Mark had also been active in the movement, including in the Communist Party. They were a magnificent family, who had to come to terms with a personal tragedy, much like the Fischer family.

As it happened, it was Eli and Violet who had called me to their house, not far from me in Orange Grove, to inform me of the death of Molly Fischer, which occurred shortly after the Rivonia trialists had been moved to Robben Island in June 1964. Molly had died in a car accident on the way down to Cape Town where Bram planned, amongst other things, to visit the Rivonia prisoners. She had been delivering Kathy's letters to me from Pretoria during the Rivonia trial. Kathy, feeling guilty about endangering Bram, opening him up, amongst other things, to professional censure, had suggested that we put a stop to this correspondence. Bram later delivered a message from Molly that we should on no account cease corresponding. She liked being the link between us. I was – and still am – very grateful to Bram and Molly, and to Paul, their son, who also helped. Above all, for me it is an indication that communists in South Africa did not neglect the personal aspect of the anti-apartheid struggle. I wept when Eli told me about Molly's death.

The decade of the 1960s was a very hard one for people in the liberation movement. I suspect that the people of South Africa have tended to forget the sufferings of this decade.

The tortoise and I

AFTER THE MIDDLE OF September 1966, summer came back again, with heat and insects. And Arnoldus. He came out of hibernation and we got to know each other again. In fact, we got to know each other better. At least once a day I used to go out into the courtyard to say hello to him. I used to carry him, as Ann described it, 'like a sandwich' in my right hand, and talk to him. And he would stick his head out and his legs would hang out of his shell. Quite happy he was – although sometimes he would put his feet up to my hands and try and push himself off. And he would struggle. And there would be a blue angry look in his eyes. You wouldn't think that there would be different expressions in the eyes of a tortoise, especially a tortoise as small as Arnoldus, and, initially, I didn't really think such an ugly creature capable of changing expressions.

However, that second summer in Barberton, I got to know Arnoldus so well and used to watch him so intently that his different states of mind became quite obvious to me. When his eyes were looking particularly beady, with a little blue glint in them, I knew he did not want me to pick him up. And, sure enough, when I did, he would struggle, stretching his long fleshy boneless neck, with his head curved just a little bit down, and those feet that could push against my hands came up and tried to open my grip, while the other legs struggled in the air. Other days I would pick him up and I could feel how relaxed his body was. His head and legs would hang limp and relaxed. And there was such a soft, relaxed expression in his eyes.

One day I responded to the aggressiveness in his eyes by putting him back down on the concrete of the courtyard, and made a fist of my right hand and pushed my fist in towards his head. The normal tortoise fighting apparatus at the front had gone but Arnoldus pushed back with his body and tried to pin my fist against the courtyard wall. And his back legs stretched out behind him, with the feet clinging to the concrete, the legs so stretched that I could see the section of his legs that were fleshy and without scales. After this Arnoldus and I often used to have mock fights and he obviously enjoyed them.

I felt sorry for Arnoldus. In a way, I suppose I identified with him. I used to feel so pained when I saw him in the early months of the year, pacing the walls of the courtyard, desperate to get out. And I felt guilty about keeping him there, not sending him out with the wardress, out into the outside world. And so I tried to introduce some variety into not only my life but his also. I hoped the mock fights would make him feel more alive.

I used to kiss Arnoldus affectionately, too, as I talked to him, as though he were my best pal. And he learned to kiss me back. It seems crazy when I think of it now but then it did not seem crazy. My fellow prisoners would joke with me about him but then they accepted that he was a pal of mine, and they would ask me, quite seriously, how he was. Some of them became very fond of him.

I can't remember how it was that I first started feeding Arnoldus on pieces of bread. I think it may have been because I saw him eating bits of dry sand off the concrete. After I had discovered that he liked bread, I would give him a little piece every day. I used to go out into the courtyard about nine or ten in the morning, before the heat of the day so as to avoid the concrete when it was white and blinding, and try to find him. Sometimes he would be hidden under a canna or the mullein but usually on a hot summer day he would be very active, moving around the courtyard, though he never moved as fast as when he first came in to us.

Once we started feeding him bread, he began to wait for it in the morning. He'd wander around the courtyard, purposely getting in everyone's way, as they went out to hang a newly washed uniform on the line or a towel or a nightdress. Sometimes, when I had forgotten about him because Matron Bester was on the warpath or there was great excitement because a visitor was coming that day, Esther would come and tell me that Arnoldus was out, wanting his bread. And then I would quickly run to the plastic bag in which we kept the bread that came in each morning when the central grille was unlocked at six, and break off a little piece. I would remove the crust because we had found that too much bread gave Arnoldus diarrhoea and I concluded that the crust in particular could not be good for him.

Sometimes I went out into the courtyard, with shadow still on the concrete on two sides of the yard, and I would call him. Sometimes I would whistle. We became convinced, however, that Arnoldus could not hear us because he did not respond to our calls. What he did seem to respond to sometimes, though, were vibrations of the ground just next to him; often as I came close up to him, he would turn and come moving at high speed across the concrete or the grass, head and neck stretched out, eyes enlarged with excitement. But it could be that he had caught sight of a moving object out of the corner of an eye. As he got close to the bread, he opened his mouth wide and closed his beak on it, while some crumbs hung un-neatly around his beak. And then there would be some movement of his jaw and the soft skin under his head and at his throat. And often he would open his beak again. Some of the bread would have disappeared while some still lay in his mouth. And he would take another bite. It seemed to me that he got the bread down by having it pushed down by more bread but I never really worked out exactly how he swallowed. Later I put a little marmalade on the bread. At Christmastime I gave him a little dried fruit, a piece of dried pear or peach. He seemed to like these, but I was very careful about this as I feared it might give him bad diarrhoea.

Some of the wardresses were slightly amused by my relationship with Arnoldus, but on the whole – this was, no doubt, inevitable because they spent so much of their lives locked in there with us – they accepted it as part of the local scene.

One Sunday Brigadier Pretorius came round with another officer, for Sunday morning parade. Before they came in, we lined up in the portaal, feet apart, hands behind our backs. The Brigadier entered, with his stupid pompous look, his big paunch, wide flapping khaki trousers, and the brown wooden baton held importantly under one arm. There was the usual officious look around the place before he turned to us. I don't think he used to see much when he looked around. It was mainly done to create what he thought was the right impression, to make it clear that he was in charge. And then his eyes would turn from observing our cells and our table, laid ready for lunch, to us, standing quietly there, still at attention, waiting dead-eyed (fish-eyed?) for the Sunday morning clowning to be over so we could get on with what we had been doing.

'Môre, mense.' Deep voice. And he would look deep into somebody's eyes (although never mine).

'Môre, Brigadier,' would come back our mumbled reply.

'En hoe gaan dit vandag?'

Feeling sure of himself, he played his kind, patronising role. One of us probably mumbled some reply, although the Brigadier wouldn't have noticed. His attention was focused rather on his own style, pleased with it. The officer with him stood in the background, also mumbling 'Môre' and nodding. Then he stared into space, waiting for the Brigadier to finish his performance.

Matron Taljaard was on duty with us that Sunday and, as the Brigadier came in through our central grille, she had stuck her chest a little further out, put a smug smile on her pink and white plump face, and smartly saluted him.

'Môre, Matrone,' he had responded.

She had decided the Brigadier was in a good mood, and so, to my horror, I heard her telling him about 'Neame' and the tortoise. The Brigadier turned his eyes on me for a moment and there was a little flash of cold hardness but he kept the friendly look on the rest of his face, and, turning back to Matron Taljaard, he asked to see 'Neame' together with the tortoise.

'Kom, Neame,' Matron Taljaard beckoned me towards the courtyard.

Prison regulations required that I obey the Brigadier's orders. I moved out of the line of our parade across the shining concrete of the portaal and watched the ungainly figure of the Brigadier, followed by the other officer, lead the way into the courtyard. I felt the degraded prisoner feeling rise in me a little. I attempted to ignore it, trying to avoid seeing myself through the Brigadier's eyes, a prisoner in blue uniform and brown army shoes, going onto my haunches on the concrete and waiting for Arnoldus to come after the piece of bread I held out for him in my right hand. Arnoldus was next to the canna, his back partly to me, but I felt he should catch sight of me. He didn't move. I felt embarrassed. I was down there on my haunches, conscious of the two pairs of trousered legs standing there, watching silently. There were patches of blue uniform and brown shoes too; the others had come out to watch.

Although I experienced the situation as somewhat undignified, I longed for Arnoldus to move so that the performance could be a success. Should he not do so, I was likely to feel even more unhappy. I moved my hand with the bread a little in order to attract his attention, saying softly but urgently, 'Come on, Arnoldus, come on.' With relief, I saw him put his front legs firmly onto the ground and twist, as he turned his body round towards me. And he came at tremendous speed in my direction, head stretched out eagerly, shell swinging sideways a little in a flowing movement as he moved first one front leg and then the other in quick succession. This is definitely a success, I thought.

I backed a little on my haunches towards the courtyard wall so that Arnoldus would have to come further. I felt a further twinge of embarrassment as I did it. Arnoldus moved, if possible, even faster. He stretched his head out even more eagerly, came up to my hand, opened his beak wide and closed onto the bread. I heard Matron Taljaard laughing, a little patronisingly – 'Ag, Neame' – but also partly identifying with me because she felt a little that it was also her performance since she had suggested the idea to the Brigadier.

Arnoldus had finished the bread. I got off my haunches. I caught in flashes the sight of my blue uniform and my army shoes. The Brigadier might have mumbled something but he certainly did not say anything to me. Nor did he even smile patronisingly at me. He could not do that because he did not have the officer-prisoner relationship with me. It had never been like that. I made him feel uneasy. So he turned away from me and, together with the other officer, walked a few steps across the courtyard and up the little step. Then he disappeared into the portaal.

I picked Arnoldus up and talked to him, and Matron Taljaard stood next to me beside the canna, saying, 'Ag, Neame, Arnoldus is mooi.'

I said nothing.

Imprisoned

I put Arnoldus down on the reddish soil next to the canna and went inside to wash my hands.

We had never really known whether Arnoldus was male or female but it seemed natural for us to assume that he was male. I had called him 'Arnoldus' without even putting the question of his gender to myself. I think it was sometime before Christmas that a wardress brought a second tortoise into our section. All I know is that it was definitely after Violet and Leslie came in August because Leslie adopted the new tortoise. At first we didn't know what to call the new arrival. He looked very different to Arnoldus, much bigger, about three times the size, and had a much lighter shell. The shell was a bit squashed in on top. It looked as though the tortoise had been run over by a car.

At first we all thought him very ugly, particularly his shell. But Leslie later made us see that it was really rather beautiful. It had the most subtle colours, rather like an antique. At first I thought we should call the new tortoise 'Hudson', because he looked to me like an old and much battered Hudson car, parked as he was, near the mullein. But Leslie decided after she had discovered the 'antique' qualities of his shell that we should call him Rameses, after the Ancient Egyptian pharaoh. And so he became Rameses.

The first afternoon he was brought in, he seemed to me rather sullen. He refused to put his head out, and remained solidly and heavily on the soil next to the mullein. But he got used to us much more quickly than Arnoldus had. This was largely due to the fact that he saw Arnoldus was not afraid of us. I would feed Arnoldus bread in front of Rameses and within a few days Rameses was eating bread from Leslie's hand. Each morning, round about nine, we would go out together into the courtyard to give the tortoises their bread.

Early on in the year, when I had first got friendly with Arnoldus, I had hoped that we might get a mate for him, to make his life there a little more bearable. And so we wondered when Rameses came in whether he was male or female. But one of the wardresses told us he was definitely male because his shell underneath was slightly concave. Evidently there is a hollow there so that the male can climb more easily up onto the back of the female.

The tortoise and I

After Rameses came in, I used to sit quietly on the concrete watching to see how the two would respond to each other. One afternoon – it might even have been the day after he arrived – Rameses started making approaches to Arnoldus. And Arnoldus showed obvious excitement. She used to go up right in front of him so that he had his head facing onto her back. She would then start moving off, with Rameses following. That afternoon on the soil, under a geranium, Rameses climbed up onto the back of Arnoldus. In the days after that we'd find them side by side under a geranium or a canna. And one day I did a drawing of them together in the courtyard.

But we decided that their love affair never came to fruition. Arnoldus never produced any little tortoises and, within a few days, they seemed to lose interest in each other. I think their sizes were too disparate.

Birdwatching

LESLIE BROUGHT NEW LIFE into our section. She was full of bounce and initiative. She was constantly thinking of new things for us to do. Some of us had been doing bits and pieces of yoga ever since we had been in gaol but Leslie, who actually taught yoga as a profession, organised a programme to suit the needs of each of us. And from the time she came we were all more disciplined. We did our yoga regularly and concentrated more on it.

Birdwatching

She had been for many months in solitary for interrogation purposes under the 180-day law and then she had been for a couple of months with ordinary criminal prisoners at the Fort. There had been almost nothing for her to do there, other than to study during the long lock-up periods, and there was no one with whom she felt she could really communicate. Certainly there was nobody with whom she could discuss her studies. So to come to Barberton to join us was a big event for her, and a great relief.

I think it was just after the middle of November that I moved into the front big cell with Ann and Leslie. I was glad to have another chance there after Matron Bester and the Brigadier had ordered me out of this cell earlier in the year, following the accusations about the damaged wall.

Towards the end of the year, 1966, I began to take in as much as I could of the sights and sounds outside our barred windows and incorporate them into my world and my sense of myself. Just as I tried to increase my experiences and sensations within our four walls, so I now approached that part of the outside world that I could see and hear. My world no longer stretched as far as our bars and cages. It stretched as far as the mountains in the west and up to the top of the hills towards Swaziland behind our prison. It reached the hills and trees in the east where I now knew, without doubt, the sun rose. I had come to know, too, with certainty, that the sun set over the mountains across the valley to the west of us.

Despite the fact that we used to study until 10.30 and sometimes 11 at night, we would be up at 3.30 or 4 in the morning. We would turn on the light so that we could get some study in before the sun rose. As soon as there was enough light, we would be eagerly at the windows, peering through our cages to see if there were any birds in sight. If there were none, we would go back to our tables to study, with our ears pricked for any sounds outside.

In the evenings and in the mornings we often heard the stuttering sound of guinea fowl. Up from our desks and to the windows, and we would see them either on the red gravel road to our left, seemingly gliding, quick feet moving on the gravel, one supposed, or there they were on the golf course in the longish grass, moving like a peculiar flock of small sheep.

Leslie standing up next to me on the narrow red windowsill, with her right hand clinging to a white-painted bar, blonde hair, blue uniform,

Imprisoned

and excitement in her movements: 'Look, there they go.'

And Ann, down below, on a bed, trying to see, too: 'Where? Where? I can't see them.'

'There ... can't you see? ... Look, down there on the gravel road ... Look, there they go, in front of those trees near the grass.'

Ann, with despair and irritation in her voice: 'Where? I can't see them!'

'Come up here,' I said, jumping down from the windowsill. 'Perhaps you can't see them from there.'

Ann struggled up onto the sill. 'Oh, there they are!' she said triumphantly and relieved.

'Where?' asked Leslie. 'I've lost them again.'

'There,' said Ann, 'just above the sisal lands ... Gosh, they do move in a strange way, don't they?'

I was now trying to see from the bed. I caught sight of them now and again. 'I'm going back to my book,' I said. 'Call me if anything interesting happens ... I wonder whether the hamerkops will come today?'

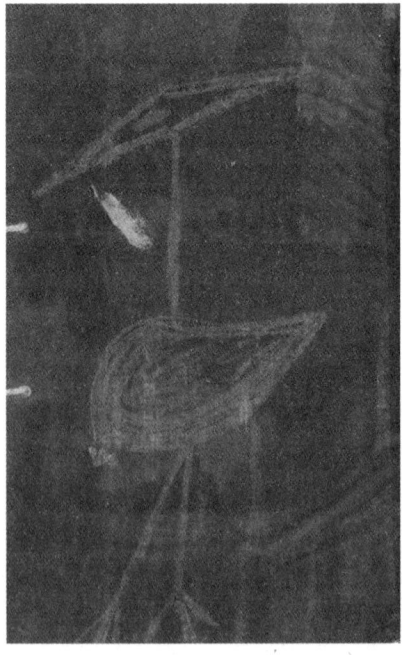

Above: Drawing by Ann on wrapping paper.

Several times we had seen one or two hamerkops, orangey brown birds with strange heads, shaped rather like hammers. They used to come sometimes to the edge of the pond, right in front of the gaol, slightly to the left of the left-hand window in our big cell. They would stand on the round stones on the edge of the pond, looking frustratedly at the netting wire that was stretched over the top of the pond. They couldn't even get their beaks through to the water. Sometimes we saw them near the little dam, just below one of the lookout posts where there was often a warder in khaki with a rifle.

We sometimes saw the guinea fowl there too. They glided and waddled down below the dam, appearing here, disappearing, coming into sight again. And we tried to count them. But we were often not sure if the one that had appeared wasn't the same bird as the one that had shortly before disappeared behind a piece of wall or a small tree.

One day I caught sight of a bit of bright yellow in one of the trees across from our cell, over on the other side of the gravel driveway. It was during a lunchtime lock-up, just after midday. The sun was bright, making the leaves of the tree yellow-green. There must have been a slight breeze because little pieces of shadow were partly erratically, partly rhythmically moving around in the yellow greenness. We weren't getting any breeze in the cell. I was leaning on the sill of our right-hand window, trying to see through the spiralling little rectangles of the cage. It was fairly difficult to see any smallish object beyond the cage, especially if it moved, and the fact that the wire was of the twisted type produced little flashes of silver and then shadow, which tended to divert one's eyes from an object beyond the cage. And if one were too conscious of the cage, it would superimpose itself on everything else. However, I seemed to have good enough eyes and sufficiently good concentration on outside objects to be able, to a large extent, to ignore the cage that was so firmly placed between me and the outside world.

There again I caught sight of a little yellow rounded object. It must have been a bird. Without taking my eyes off the object, I half whispered, 'Hey, you two, there is a bright yellow bird in that tree over there.'

I could always depend on Ann and Leslie for an eager response. They were there beside me in a couple of seconds, with excited voices, 'Where? Where?' I indicated the tree to them, tried to point to two main branches between which it seemed to me there was a bright yellow bird. 'You see that greyish-brown branch going up there diagonally ... to the right from the main trunk. Can you see it? ... There.' I drew the branch in the air with my right hand. 'Do you see? Can you see?'

'Ye-e-es ...' said Ann, a little dubiously. 'I think I know which one you mean.'

'Well, between that branch and the branch going off it, in the same direction ... Do you see right in the middle of that clump of leaves?'

'No,' said Ann firmly, 'I can't see anything there.'

I turned to her. 'You can't be looking in the right place then.' I looked at her eyes to see whether they were looking in the right direction. I moved my fingers from her eyes and, turning, pointed them towards the clump of leaves, where I could still see the yellow bird. 'It's got a bright yellow breast,' I said. 'Yes ... and, look, a black face ... I think ...'

Suddenly Leslie said, 'Yes. I can see it.'

I felt a rush of relief. It was so frustrating when other people could not see the things I saw outside. 'You see, it's got a little rounded bright yellow body.' And then Ann saw it too. That was marvellous.

'I wonder what it is?' Leslie said thoughtfully.

'Its body is rather like that of the robin,' Ann commented. 'Let's look it up in the Roberts.'

We moved away from the window and sat side by side on my bed. Leslie went through the Austin Roberts' *Birds of South Africa* page by page, running her fingers down the shiny pages of plates. Austin Roberts happened to be a relative of mine and my brother Graham had sent the book in to us. The Brigadier had told me the prison was only loaning it to me as my brother had donated it to the library. Needless to say, there wasn't really a prison library. When we first arrived at Barberton, there were no books at all. After we had made many complaints, they sent in some old, filthy and quite unreadable books from Pretoria Central. After more complaints, we were able, in the second half of 1966, to obtain a few books from the Barberton village library. The Roberts became a firm friend of ours.

On this particular day – the yellow bird day – we went through the book plate by plate but, although we came across many birds with that kind of shape and we discovered that it was, indeed, a typically robin shape, none of the birds in the book had the same colour. The yellow bird remained a mystery to us.

Another bird that we did not ever find in the Roberts was one that often flew close to our cages. It sometimes went up onto the brown gutter to our right above the level of the cage. On occasion it even settled on one of our cages. It had either a black or blue-black body. And it had a forked tail. We saw it several times quite clearly but, although we went carefully through all the plates in the Roberts and read the description of any bird that looked a bit like it, we did not ever find what could be a description of that particular bird.

Ever since I had been at Barberton I had heard off and on the bird with the bubbling noise in its throat. In several places in the course of my diary I noted that I had heard 'that bird' or the 'bubbling-throated bird' again. I do not know whether it really makes a mournful sound but it sounded very mournful to me. I can still remember lying on my bed in my single cell in those early months at Barberton and hearing that sound break the tremendous silence just for a moment. And then such still, still silence again. And then the bubbling noise. Echoing. I could hardly believe that it was really a bird. It was such an unearthly sound, as unreal as were our lives there.

Then one day we heard it on a record of bird calls Graham had sent in to us – this was after we had managed to get a record player in the second half of January 1967. We had the record player in our front big cell, and we placed it close to our grille so that the others could hear from their cells. Incredibly, I heard that bubbling sound echoing in our portaal. It was real after all! It may have been a coucal but since it was after darkness I guess more likely a nightjar. In October '66 I have an entry in my diary:

A Jacky-Hangman is sitting on the cage of my window, the sunrise reflected on the left side of its white breast.

In the second half of 1966 as our lives became less regimented, our exercise period became less of a ritual. We did not rush out at 11 in the morning, immediately 'Oefening' was announced, and march two by two around the courtyard until the wardress called out that we had had our half hour. Earlier we had often tried to get in that 'one more round' before we went in. Now things were a little more relaxed and, instead of always tramping, tramping, with our heads down looking unseeing at the concrete, and never stopping for one moment, some of us would pause sometimes to say hello to Arnoldus or Rameses. Or Mollie would stop to see how the few petunias she had planted were doing and Leslie might be in a yoga position on the grass.

On occasion a few of us would be lying on the little patch of grass staring up at the blue sky. So big the sky was, stretching and stretching and stretching. And sometimes there were little patches of white cloud and your eye would go round them, inside them, seeing the intricacies of one white cloud. And often there were swallows, a big flock of them, so very high up, wheeling, swooping a little, and then up and going higher so that each dark object which was a swallow became smaller and smaller … and then down again, gliding silently in the stretching-out blueness … and then swoop and gliding over what, I thought, must be a valley on the other side of the prison.

I always imagined that it was a valley with thick jungle-like undergrowth, lying below part of the mountains on the edge of Swaziland. On occasion I saw up in the sky what looked like some bird of prey hovering, waiting to plunge down onto some animal in my imagined thick undergrowth. Sometimes the swallows would wheel out of sight, beyond that section of stretching-out sky that we could see from our courtyard. It could be that only a part would disappear and we would wonder whether they had gone from our sight forever or whether they would come gliding gently back into that space above us. Time stood still with the blue sky and the effortless movement of the swallows.

Often from our cells we heard the loud cries of birds. And from the time I began to look out of the window without a thick mist in front of my eyes and a strange pain in my heart, I would see a flock of big dark birds flying over the sisal lands. They used to fly over most evenings, making what I thought were loud vulture sounds. Sometimes in the evening, from the front big cell, we would see them flying westwards across the sisal lands, as noisy as ever, and then a bit later we would hear them again. Back we would be at the windows and there they would be flying in the opposite direction, eastwards, above the sisal lands.

It seemed natural to me that they should be vultures for this seemed to fit into our gaol environment and they did have a very harsh and loud, almost frightening, call. Later I found out from Mollie that they were hadedas. She had known all the time because they had them on the farm. But it was only towards the end of 1966 that I had thought to ask what they were. At first when Mollie told me they were not vultures, I thought she must be wrong, so Ann, Leslie and I looked it up in the Roberts, and sure enough, there they were, and a description of their sound. Then I began to look at them with a different eye and different feelings as they flew over the sisal lands when the sky was pink in the west where the sun had just disappeared behind the layer of mountains across the plains to the north-west of our cell.

Preparing for the art exhibition

TOWARDS THE END OF THE 1966 we started getting ready for the art exhibition we had planned in July–August. We decided we would have it in mid-January 1967. Apart from the history of art, our art classes had been devoted to life drawing. To make the exhibition a success, we realised we would have to add different artwork to it; otherwise it would be dull. What we particularly wanted was colour. In addition, we realised that the authorities would probably not allow us to take the life drawings out with us on our release, and so it turned out – 'Kaal mense is nie opbouend nie.' Naked people are not edifying! In my last months at Barberton, I started doing still life.

Ann's history of art classes had gone very well. She really wanted to make our gaol experience a creative one. She was determined to keep classes going. And she did. Every week there she was, well prepared, with her heavy art books.

This keeping-things-going was an indication of what was going on in Ann herself. It is so easy in prison to sink into lethargy, into the nothingness of the whole prison situation, into the emotional aridity of it. It is so easy, too, to dismiss all your feelings and reactions and say Oh, it's because I'm in gaol, and then try and forget about them. You're feeling dead and arid: that is because you are in gaol. You feel aggressive and hate everyone else: that is because you are in gaol. That was largely Jean's response.

But some of us wanted to take it further than that. We did not want to lose these years – in a creative sense. Life was so short and we hoped to use every minute of it, perhaps one can say in very general terms in the pursuit

Preparing for the art exhibition

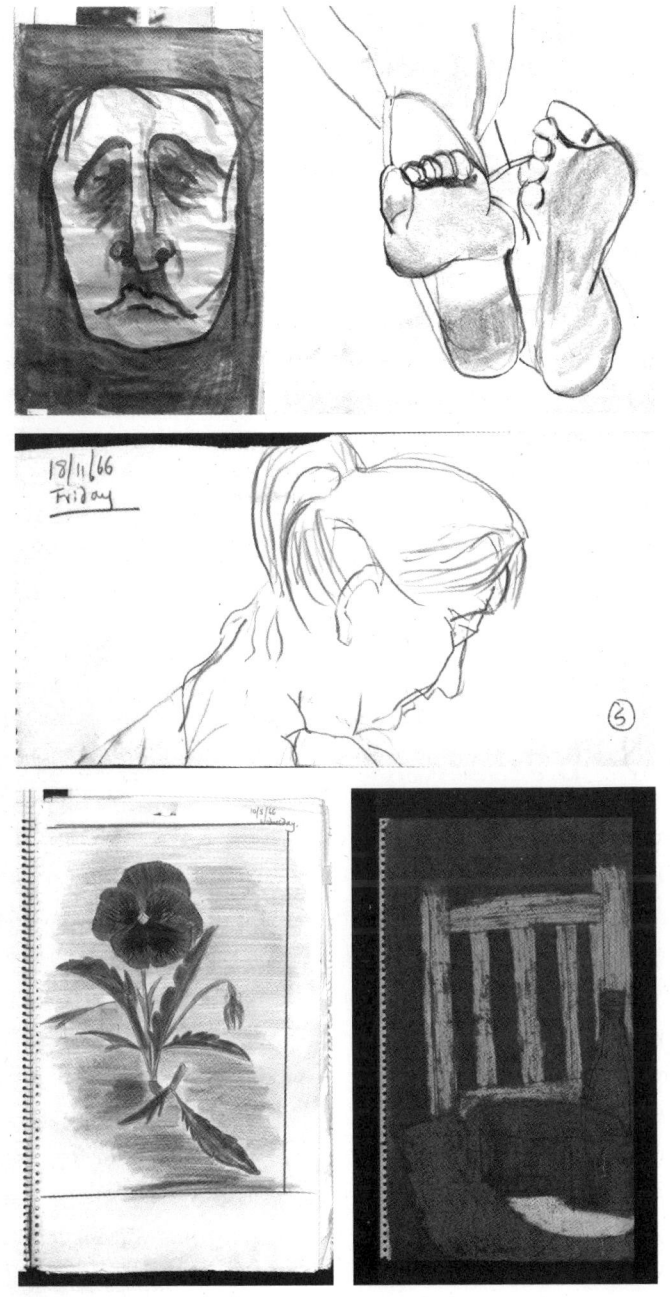

ABOVE: *All drawings by me except for the first one, which is by Ann. The central image is a portrait of Jean.*

of knowledge. In relation to our personal development there might even be some positive results for us from the prison experience, including in a personality sense. I, in particular, was interested to find out what gaol did to prisoners psychologically. I wanted to understand this in a general sense but also, specifically, in regard to what was happening to us because of our particular conditions in that section at the end of the passage in Barberton Prison. If that was especially my concern, the others came to participate, amongst other things, by using the art of parody.

Ann, in a way like myself and like Leslie, came to face the situation head on; she faced it and tried to look at it and at herself without any lies, any bluffing of herself. So Ann, too, fought the devil in that place. This is one of the poems she wrote a few months before I left:

'Shining eyes,
Or eyes of glass they say.
But not to see through.
They will find there,
Not a mirror of my mind,
But a picture of their own.

Deformed, like some sea-snail,
My thoughts confined,
Spiral in their fragile shell,
Contorting into unfamiliar shapes,
Shining through, a dim translucent grey.
And they say,
How pretty, or, how dull!
And that is all they know.
And that is all I know of them,
Clamped tight as frightened oysters.
In our disenchanted hoarding
We desolately bear our bitter self-protection.

And so we must take our knives
And lift and ease,

Preparing for the art exhibition

And gently prise each other.
And of the very few who cry
That this is all a silly bother,
Do they have so very much to offer?'

> New Year 67.
>
> Shining eyes,
> Or eyes of glass, they say.
> But not to see through.
> They will find there,
> Not a mirror of my mind,
> But a picture of their own.
>
> Deformed, like some sea-snail,
> My thoughts, confined,
> Spiral in their fragile shell
> Contorting into unfamiliar shapes
> Shining through, a dim translucent grey.
> And they say,
> How pretty, or how dull!
> And that is all they know.
> And that is all I know of them
> Clamped tight as frightened oysters.
> In our disenchanted hoarding
> We desolately bear our bitter self-protection.
>
> And so we must take our knives
> And lift and ease,
> And gently prise each other.
> And of the very few who cry
> That this is all a silly bother,
> Do they have so very much to offer?
>
> (written by Ann Nicholson)

Imprisoned

It was Ann and Leslie who did almost all the preparation for the exhibition. They asked everyone to give them all the work they had done and Ann then chose the pieces that would actually go on the exhibition. She framed all the pictures, rudimentary as it was. And she drew up a catalogue, a copy of which she gave to each of us. She worked on her own exhibits, painting with coloured inks, producing big coloured pictures to give the exhibition some variety. There was a tremendous sadness and suffering in the two big ones she did – one of a man and one of a woman. She did the paintings in a few minutes with ink on cotton wool.

The woman I called 'Ophelia'. I don't remember whether it was the name she gave it for the exhibition (probably not). I think she meant to make it a gay, colourful picture. Or not? She would never talk about it. She would not even react when I told her it looked liked Ophelia. She was on the floor in the yoga kneeling position, a position she got into quite unconsciously. She clearly found it especially comfortable. There, with a big sheet of brown paper in front of her, she held in her right hand a piece of cotton wool with intermingling colours on it, reds and browns, blues and blacks. I was at my table busy with the next issue of the *Barberton Bladsy*. I turned round and said, 'That's Ophelia,' and she didn't even look up.

The day of the exhibition I worked on a big coloured picture of a section of the courtyard. I used a sheet of white cartridge paper. I had told the Front that I needed it for maps for my history studies. I painted very quickly. My chief aim was just to get something colourful to put on the exhibition. I had always had a thing about the courtyard, at least from the time I started really looking at our section. I hated the cold, hygienic, nameless, atmosphere-less quality of our whole section and so I tried to build up in my mind a picture that meant something to me emotionally. In this context the courtyard played a special role.

This was the picture in my mind: It was a prison specifically in South Africa and it was a peculiarly South African prison, this in romanticised terms. It was hot there. And there were mosquitoes and insects and frogs and tortoises, rabbits and chameleons. Outside were wide open spaces, the long valley to the mountains, the huge trees, the birds, the heat, the humidity. The sun shone on dry gravel dusty roads and on brittle, pale green grass. And in the evening the red hot orange sun set across the valley.

In my mind not far from my courtyard was the Kruger National Park, the big South African game reserve with the wild animals of Africa, the lion, leopard, cheetah, rhinoceros, hippopotamus, elephant, giraffe, buffalo, African wild dog, jackal and varieties of buck. True, I had never seen it in real life, yet for me at that moment it was a very real experience.

All this contrasted with the inside where the rabbits, the chameleons, the tortoises hardly survived. Inside there was cold, hygienic concrete and inhumanity. And the mosquitoes and insects were there to torture us, to take our sleep away at night. In the courtyard itself the plants struggled to survive. There were a few nasturtiums, a small number of geraniums, elephant-ears, a mullein, a few violas, cannas and balsam plants, but they all grew separately. One here and then a bit of dreary sand; another there and then another expanse of sand to the next measly plant, struggling to stay alive in our desert, surrounded by brick walls. The elephant-ears, however much we nurtured them, never flourished. Their leaves were often looking torn and turning yellow in patches.

When I drew the picture of a section of the courtyard for the exhibition, I tried, as accurately as possible, to depict what I saw. I did this with black ink and wax crayons (which I had also claimed I needed for my history maps!). Finally, in order to draw it altogether and to transform the courtyard into my idealised picture of a prison in 'sunny South Africa', a tourist attraction, I washed the whole picture with deep red ink.

Ann said she thought it was one of the best things I had done. I can't say I thought so. But I think she liked it because she recognised in it an attempt to deal with a deprived situation. It was a child's drawing, meant to be so, an attempt to make a magic world out of aridity, out of lovelessness and not quite succeeding because the reality pushed itself stubbornly through and because the child did not want to lie too much to herself.

When I did a still life, Ann often set up something for me. I drew the rough outlines of it in pencil, and then started working with the wax crayons and the ink. I had a tremendous desire for colour, for very bright colour, the brightest I could find, for pure, unadulterated colour. And I knew that I wanted to put one particular colour next to another. I knew, for instance, that I wanted to put the brightest orange I could get next to the starkest purple. And I knew that that was quite right. Something in me told me that that was how it should be. It could be no other way. I must have that particular expanse of orange there and that particular expanse of purple there. And a small section of the purest yellow here, in this corner.

I used sometimes to ask myself why I felt this. How was I so certain that I was doing it exactly as it should be? I used to feel the excitement rising in me and I would mutter to myself, 'Yes, that is right, absolutely right.'

In my second run under the 90-day law, July–August 1964, I had, as I have indicated, been in a cell in the Fordsburg police station. It had largely black walls. My life there had been arid and empty, again with just a Bible to read and the small playing cards I had made out of cardboard. And my freedom songs. There, too, I had had a tremendous desire for colour. I used to sit on the edge of my mattress on the concrete floor and think, Today I am going to send a message out to Betty Neame [my aunt, Bunny's wife] to send me one pair of yellow socks, one pair of red socks, one pair of blue socks, and one pair of green socks. As it happened, I did send that message out but they probably just thought I was going mad. At any rate, my brightly coloured socks never came and subsequently they made no reference to my request. I waited and waited. There was no response at all. But then they had never been imprisoned. Or perhaps they thought it was a kind of secret message in code?

Preparing for the art exhibition

I had a bath towel in that black-walled cell with me. It was mainly black but there were also strips of very bright colour, bright blue, and reds and oranges. For hours, I used to sit on the edge of my mattress and imagine that towel up against the black wall, against the far wall so that I could see it clearly from where I sat on my mattress. I tried to solve the problem as to how I could hang it but I had nothing there in that cell that would enable me to accomplish the task. I had to content myself with just imagining it hanging up there on the black wall. And then I would go back to wondering when they would send in my red socks, my yellow socks, my blue socks and my green socks, and I would imagine looking at my feet with pleasure during the long hours of the day, each day a different colour.

I did have some red tights, which I wore under my slacks, so that, as I looked down at my feet I could see two red patches stretching from the bottom of my slacks up to the point where they disappeared into my brown suede shoes. One of the problems was that I couldn't see the redness of my red tights so clearly in my cell because the light was so bad, and so I used to look forward to my exercise time out in the yard where the sunlight made the red very red.

As I walked round and round the courtyard, I held my head down and watched with delight the two patches of red colour between my shoes and my slacks. I was certain that Ivan Schermbrucker, who was, for a time, in the cell next door to mine in the Fordsburg police station, had climbed up to the small window above his door and was watching me. For him that was something to pass away one of the many hours of the day and, although we could not speak to each other or even mention to a policeman that we were aware of each other's presence in that police station, this watching gave us a feeling of some contact. I felt sure Ivan would also have felt satisfied with the redness of my socks!

A bit later I managed with a spoon to increase what had been a hole in the wall between our two cells and we were able to communicate directly now and again. One day Ivan, returning from an interrogation, told me that at the next session he was going to throw himself out of the window of the room in the Grays where they were questioning him. In a voice, husky with exhaustion, he told me that they were making him stand for long hours and he feared he wouldn't be able to hold out.

Ivan did not throw himself out of the window. I was unable to find out the details of what had happened at his next round of interrogation because a policeman discovered the hole in the wall and it was closed up. Unfortunately, in my eagerness to be able to actually see Ivan while we were communicating, I had made the hole bigger and bigger. Madness! I was really annoyed with myself. At some stage Ivan disappeared from the Fordsburg police station. The next time I saw him was in court. He was one of my fellow trialists and was alleged to have been on the Central Committee of the Communist Party.

For a whole week at Barberton, from one art class to another, I wanted to do a still life with a blue chair. I knew that the chair must be a bright blue. I had done yellow chairs in some of my other pictures but this time I wanted it blue. I think some of the others thought I was going insane because I went around saying – this was in all seriousness – that I just could not wait for the next art class because I wanted to produce a picture with a blue chair. Ann was probably the only person who understood my deep need for a blue chair.

As it turned out, I did do the blue chair at the next art class. At first it took up quite a prominent position in my picture. However, later, in order to improve the whole composition, I cut away a great deal of it, so that anyone looking at the picture would hardly be immediately struck by the blueness of the chair. But to me, it is still 'Composition with a blue chair', or, just simply, 'The blue chair'. I left this still life behind for Leslie. When I left, it was up on the side of a locker so that she could see it from her table where she worked.

That was the first still life I did where I did not just use ink as a wash over the whole picture after I had worked mainly with wax crayon. This time I actually did a bit of painting with cotton wool, dipped in ink. Some of the nasturtiums I painted in red and blue, and I painted the white water bottle in blue too. Wax crayon, although it can give some interesting textures and lovely bright colour, is a rather inflexible medium. Painting with cotton wool and ink made me feel freer. That picture certainly has more life than any of the others I did. It was the last picture I did in Barberton Prison.

With life drawing, too, I often had a feeling of excitement when I knew that I had analysed, say, a particular section of the arm or the breast or a triangle of hips and legs in an interesting way. I don't think I had the same feeling that it was right and could be done no other way as I had with colour but I did feel excited when I felt I had done something interesting, that I had revealed a potential that wasn't immediately obvious. I felt as I used my pencil and, for instance, broke a finger down into its many angles, analysed it minutely, that I was actually making statements about ... What? The finger? That particular finger and bit of hand and arm? Or all this in general? At any rate, it was definitely only that which I saw before me that I was saying something about. At least I think so.

What interested and surprised me was that I felt I was definitely *saying* something and that this 'statement' would be communicated to anybody who came to look at the picture. And it often happened that Ann would come to my table, after looking at everyone else's work and suggesting improvements and telling them what she liked and what she did not like, and immediately pick out the section that had interested me or described what I had done in exactly the language I felt when I drew it. Communication at the level of the fine arts was, at least for me, a phenomenon difficult to explain.

Objectivity, subjectivity – and Rev. Canon Langley

ONE OF THE GREAT DEPRIVATIONS in our life in prison had been the absence of pleasant sounds or even, at times, any sound. The silence inside and outside the prison became almost a physical pain. I remember on one occasion how I perked up when I heard a leaf outside, moving along the concrete, being driven by a breeze, click, clickety click.

Music was clearly a great help, not only in terms of sound per se but as an emotional outlet. It could soothe and pull together the bits of one's life. Yet it could also provoke a feeling of intense suffering.

The first time we heard recorded music in almost two years – I am including the time when we were at the Fort and I was in Port Elizabeth – was when Canon Langley brought us a tape-recording of a church service that had taken place in his little church in the village of Barberton. His choir sang hymns to the accompaniment of an organ. In a way, it was a shock to our systems. I think, without exception, we all cried silently. There was also something distinctly out of place about the sound of church music on an organ in that space in Barberton Prison, a space echoing with the screams of Matron Bester.

Langley had forgotten to bring an adaptor with him and the plug of his tape recorder did not fit into the socket in the wall of the portaal so he had asked the wardress on duty whether she could find one. Matron Bester had then come through and been extremely unpleasant, as she always was when Langley was anywhere around. She had sighed and pouted and sulked and stamped her feet and shrugged and spoken rudely and abruptly to the world in general. It appeared to be a principle with her not to address herself directly to Langley if she could possibly help it. Langley looked more and more unhappy but said nothing.

Eventually the required device was sent to us from the Front and Langley had put on the tape. At the end of it all, we had been most enthusiastic and had thanked him profusely. I wonder if it looked like a lot of painful clowning to him? I watched us from the outside, at the same time keeping a constant smile on my face and making murmurs of 'thank you' off and on. I saw Mollie trying so hard. Was she being genuine? Did *he* think she was being genuine?

Naturally, we were pleased about the tape but at the same time there was something forced in our pleasure. Langley must have sensed how tired and dead inside we were. We were keenly aware of the rather unsatisfactory situation but tried so hard to overcome it. We felt intensely that he came from the outside world, and, therefore, should be treated according to its rules but somehow they conflicted with the whole atmosphere and routine in our gaol.

Had we the right, was it fitting, did it not look incongruous to treat him as though he were our guest? Was he our guest? Did this section belong to us? I remember when he came into the portaal through the central grille that I had wondered whether I should offer him a chair with a 'Please sit down'. Wouldn't it have seemed ludicrous, an act quite out of context? Nothing belonged to us, certainly not the chairs, not the space itself. Everything belonged to the Front, finally to the government, an *apartheid* government. Or at least most things did. Even we ourselves as human beings – were we human beings? – had no independence, no separate identity. As individuals we had ceased to exist. We were simply prisoners, convicts. The matter ended there. And if we as separate persons did not have an identity, did our group have one? Was Langley actually visiting us? Was he not rather simply visiting a prison, a prison space?

In prison our only certain freedom was the freedom to think. If the physical space was not ours, at least we had our own minds. The authorities, of course, even tried to take our minds, mould us according to their own outlook and rules. Yet for all of us, I think, this was one area where we finally felt that we were the masters. They might limit the impressions, what we saw with our eyes, the sounds we could hear, our experiences in general, but they could not control what we did with those we did perceive. They were our perceptions, not theirs.

Amongst other things, we were able to create a picture of the members of the Front, each of them, and those officials who visited the gaol. And we could make judgements despite the fact that a prisoner is, in principle, not allowed to judge. Simultaneously we created, to a growing degree, a picture of ourselves, one that was truly ours, not theirs.

Langley was the kind of person who normally found it difficult to communicate with other people. He seemed to be unused to the ways of the world in a kind of English, upper-class way. He was clearly used to keeping his distance as a priest, maybe even talking down to the members of his congregation. Dealing with people who saw life rather differently from himself and had their own minds was evidently not quite what he was used to.

So although Langley clearly gave us some thought and asked himself how he could help us, he never really tried to get to know us. At various times we thought he might make the attempt and were amazed that he did not; that, by and large, he cut himself off. Was it not his bounden duty as a priest to communicate with us as individuals, we asked ourselves.

Perhaps he decided the barrier was impenetrable or simply too risky to push aside. Apart from anything else, we were not male prisoners but women prisoners and he almost certainly suspected that there were certain dangers for him in that situation. Perhaps more important was that we were sure he had received strong warnings from the Front as to what he was allowed to do and not do, how to handle prisoners, and, finally, political ('security') prisoners. He did not want to make a mistake. To my mind, though, he was also a cautious type of person by nature.

There was a big gap in opinions and, indeed, in how we approached problems. Langley basically rejected our intellectual approach. Our relationship with him was difficult, not alone because of our leftist background but because this background and, perhaps more so, the situation we were in, had nurtured our concern with facts. In many key ways we lived on a different planet. In general, however, we were careful to maintain our good manners and to make clear that we were grateful for his visits and for the effort he made to make us feel not completely alone.

Set in a no man's land, in a way with no past and no future, in a place where time stood still, a place where I suffered intensely, I wanted to be honest, brutally honest if need be. I had to face everything head on, no hypocrisies, no romanticising, including in regard to our own political role and that of the political movement we belonged to. In a way, surprising though it may seem since many people think that running away from the facts is a sensible way of dealing with unbearable reality, facing facts without any cushioning was actually my technique of survival.

Though this may not be immediately apparent, my concern with objectivity was a moral position. In the most immediate sense, this had to do with the fact that I knew the authorities were trying to brainwash us and make us adopt their ideology of racism, an ideology which went together necessarily with a subjectivist outlook.

No doubt long-term personality factors also contributed to the way in which I dealt with the situation. I had early on in my childhood come to depend on my own mind, on my own capacity for observation, and this went together with a strong inclination to empathy and compassion, in particular in relation to a person who was being discriminated against or was being victimised for one reason or another, whose human dignity was being violated. That was why I had gravitated, quite independently, in my teens against racism, if initially I had seen only separate aspects of the apartheid system.

When I reached adulthood and became politically involved, more especially in left politics, I came to the conclusion that we, as political people, had necessarily to look at things as they really were. Apart from anything else, how else could we work out realistic policies? And I can hardly think of another country in the world where care in weighing up the possibilities is so necessary as in South Africa, in the first place in view of the relation of forces in the country and the multi-racial character of its population.

Absolutely crucial in my political and philosophical outlook was a strong desire for objectivity. I have found that 'liberal' ('First World'?) intellectual circles are inclined to have deep reservations about, even a fear of, objectivity, seeing it often as something immoral, almost evil, as geared against emotion, against the individual and the revolutionary traditions of the Western world, above all its tradition of human rights.

My belief, on the other hand, is that empathy and compassion – are these not part of the emotional sphere? – are promoted precisely by the capacity for observation and, in the end result, objectivity. My deep differences in this respect with so many people has been an important thread in my intellectual and personal development.

Subjectivism in political movements around the world has often been combined with an overestimation of the worth of particular nations/national entities. I have found that a narrow nationalist outlook is often closely linked to subjectivism, which pervades the intellectual, including the philosophical, sphere. German fascist thinking – I made some study of this in Barberton as a part of my history course – became for me the epitome of a subjectivist outlook. At any rate, to one degree or another, my concern with subjectivity/objectivity became intertwined with my rejection of racism and, in the personal sphere, my rejection of extreme egocentrism. My prison experience, not least to the extent that it promoted attention to detail, was one more building block along this path, and I think in the end an important one.

The prison board comes

THE PRISON BOARD CAME eventually. I think it was in October 1966.

By this time our uniforms were in tatters. There were holes under my arms, across my chest, the colour had almost faded out completely, my belt had disintegrated to the point where I could no longer get it around my waist, and the material on my seat had worn so thin that it had begun to tear. I had sewn together the splits across my chest so often that there was no longer sufficient material to sew it together again, and so my bra showed through. The uniforms of all of us were in much the same condition.

When we realised the board had arrived we felt a combination of anger – because they were so late – triumph, and, of course, unbearable excitement. We were kept separated as usual. Those who came back from the Front were locked in their cells so that they could have no communication with the rest of us. We all had our little notebooks where, for many months, about seven in fact, we had been noting down complaints and suggestions to make to the board. Despite our excitement, we admitted to ourselves that the whole thing was likely to be the usual farce. We felt a little foolish about our contradictory response but what could we do? It was a big break in the routine of our lives.

Jean had a bounce in her step. The usual pallor of her face was gone; the deadness had gone out of her eyes. Her tendency to stare into space had simply flown. She pulled at the sides of her uniform just below the belt, neatening it up, and paraded the large red gaol stamp across the back of her skirt. We could not miss the look of triumph in her eyes. We could imagine her before the staid members of the board, with a look of hurt dignity on her face and a bit of a swing in her step, as she turned round and demonstrated the ugly red stain on her skirt. We knew Jean would handle our complaint about the state of our uniforms with a punch and at the same time with great coolness, maturity and dignity.

As usual, the Front did not inform us of the arrival of the board. A wardress merely came to the entrance grille, unlocked it with a flourish and called somebody's name. And that person went through with a faint look of surprise on her face. As it happened, we knew that the board was there because one of us had seen the car draw up at the front of the gaol and had recognised one of the elderly ladies but we were not going to let the Front know we were aware of their presence.

'Neame!' the wardress shouted. 'Kom!' I went through the doorway, past the store on the left to the next room on the left. The board was not sitting in Matron Bester's office but in the room where we sometimes received our medicine. As I reached the entrance I saw on the far side to the right a small table with flowers, especially for the board. I moved to the left, hands behind my back, acutely aware of the indignity of my torn uniform, and was faced with a more substantial table, behind which were sitting two large-bosomed ladies, wearing two unbelieveably ugly hats. Viljoen was there and he said in a friendly way, 'Hullo, Sylvia.'

There was a chair on my side of the table. I wondered whether I should seat myself but the large ladies ignored my questioning look and my 'Good afternoon' greeting. Perhaps it was not usual to greet a prisoner or even necessarily to acknowledge the presence of one. At any rate, they simply muttered over some papers and files they had in front of them, apparently trying to sort something out.

Viljoen told me to take the seat. He opened proceedings by telling me that they were the board and that they had been waiting for the male member but he had been held up at another gaol. He said they had a report on me before them. According to the report my behaviour was good. I felt a mixture of pride, triumph and foolishness.

This whole business was undignified. One didn't know quite how to react when one was treated like a potentially naughty schoolchild. It was a constant problem in prison. How should one behave in such a situation? Should one react as they expected one to do in view of the fact that one was a woman prisoner – simper and look coy? Should one remain expressionless? Should one nod in a matter-of-fact, slightly irritated way as if one were tired of the stupidity of the whole business? Should one laugh cynically as one would in the face of an attempted blackmail by the enemy?

A confusion of conflicting attitudes fought for dominance in me and, as a result, my mouth was immobilised. What happened to the expression on my face I am not sure. Whether it reflected all of these feelings, I do not know. I may simply have looked impassive. I had so often felt like this in prison when faced with this kind of impossible situation. Often, of course, the authorities had been, to one degree or another, hostile or at least antipathetic. This was particularly the case with Aucamp and, to a lesser extent, Brigadier Pretorius. Anyway, I doubt the members of the board had an inkling of my contradictory feelings, particularly how undignified and even childish I found it all.

Viljoen informed me that I had been given symbols for various things, such as work, general behaviour and discipline, and dress. He asked me if I had anything to say. I opened up my notebook, starting with the state of my uniform. One of the women came in on this. She said they had noted the state of our uniforms. Something would be done about them immediately. They looked highly embarrassed. They would send a telegram right away to Pretoria. I pointed out that we had been asking for suitable uniforms for many months. The woman said she did not know how this could have happened but something would be done about it immediately.

I stressed that one of the prison regulations insisted that prisoners should not be exposed to indignities, that we had been told that the aim of the Prisons Department was to rehabilitate us. I told them about the other problems we had had with clothes, amongst other things that some of us had walked around without underclothing for many months. They assured me that the problem had been raised by other prisoners from our section and they would see what could be done.

I went through the usual requests and complaints: why were we not entitled to remission and parole? When were the authorities going to supply us with a gramophone? They had reclassified us to B but this meant very little as we had no gramophone, were shown no films, were not allowed musical instruments (to which we were entitled by the regulations), and for a long time could not buy books. I complained about the lack of library facilities. I complained about our work. We were still doing hard labour. According to the prison regulations, we should be given work suitable to our previous experience and aptitudes; the aim of the Prisons Department, from what we could understand from the regulations, was that we should be given training to equip us for the outside world. Was their aim to train us to be washerwomen?

Viljoen pointed out that they did not have the facilities at Barberton. We could not expect them to put in special facilities for us. This prison did not usually have white women. The Prisons Department did not have the money.

As so often before, we got onto the endless problem of whether the board was responsible for us, as, according to the prison regulations, it was supposed to be. They said, Oh yes, they were responsible for us. I pointed out that we had been told often enough that they were not. On their last visit they had said that they could not consider the question as to whether we should be granted remission and parole as was their function in relation to most prisoners according to the regulations because in our case they were not responsible for this. And it had certainly seemed that they were not responsible for deciding our conditions as prisoners, nor the type of work we should do, although this was their duty in regard to prisoners according to the regulations.

All this had happened so many, many times before. The hypocritical poses, the mass of evasions, the contradictions, the lies. The only thing that changed from time to time were the arguments. I was tired of it all and I decided to leave. My fighting spirit was at an especially low level that day. Viljoen was being extra pleasant to me, with 'Sylvia this' and 'Sylvia that', obviously trying to impress the two ladies with his good relations with us. He finished up on an excessively kindly note, holding that I was patient with the wardresses and the authorities, and was behaving myself.

The others had much the same kind of experience. Jean's uniform suitably embarrassed the two ladies. We kept them busy for many hours. They had to stay much longer at the gaol than they had expected. They had to return again the following day, for the 'bandiete'. (This was the

Afrikaans word used to refer to the black prisoners, essentially meaning 'convicts'.)

Round about November that year, some of us decided that we were not going to continue washing. We felt the authorities would find it difficult to take any strong action against us because they did not have much of a leg to stand on. The prison regulations were clearly against them, and we knew they would not be keen to do anything drastic at this stage, particularly as Flo and I were due to go out soon.

About three of us stopped washing and informed the authorities of this. I told Brigadier Pretorius that, in any case, I did not really feel strong enough to continue washing because I was in a thoroughly exhausted state. About that time, I was feeling really worn out. As we had suspected, the authorities quietly gave in. That very week and the following week some darning was sent in for us and thereafter we were put onto ironing sheets. That was the sort of work we did until I left Barberton. This work wasn't suitable either, it goes without saying, and we started complaining. We demanded that we be allowed to make clothing on sewing machines in order that we might be trained in something. By the time I left, though, nothing had come of this.

Cultural concerns

As B prisoners we should have been allowed to have a record player. But the authorities were not prepared to supply us with one as they did for other prisoners. They told us quite clearly that they were not prepared to spend the money on us. So it was that from 9 August, the date we became Bs, until, I think it was, 19 January, we did without one. We were told that if we wanted a gramophone, we must obtain it ourselves.

Over Christmas for a few days we hired one from a shop in the village, together with a few records. It was of poor quality and so were the records but it whet our appetites. Once we had heard music, we felt we just had to buy a gramophone somehow. After five months of campaigning we realised the authorities were not going to supply one. Eventually, Leslie's daughter, Jill, managed to send one in to us.

After the middle of January, Ann moved out of the front big cell into a single cell. Leslie and I had the gramophone in our cell with two speakers. We plugged it into a socket in the portaal, just outside the cell. Usually the wardress who locked us up pushed the plug in when we passed the flex through the grille. And, before we were locked up, we put the two speakers in different positions out on the concrete floor of the portaal so that the people in the other cells could hear the music too.

I can't remember what we played the first night. Each of us took turns choosing records for evening lock-up – three or four sides. We usually had about an hour in the evening. Lunchtime lock-up we often had something too, something shorter.

I remember lying on the floor in the cell with our rust-coloured curtain drawn on the left-hand window. There was a green venetian blind on the right-hand window, which we lowered. It had taken us a long time to get these. Indeed, it was only a few months before I went out that our campaign met with success. We also obtained curtains for the three windows overlooking our laundry basins. These were yellow.

It was a hot February day. The sun was still blinding on the other side of the curtain. I could see a bright yellow line of light on one side where the curtain did not quite cover the whole window. The sun was particularly bright because as it moved slowly down towards the mountains in the west, it fell directly onto our cell. There were lines of light showing, too, between the pale green strips of the venetian blind. The mosquitoes hadn't started yet so I was comfortable on the floor. Leslie was lying on her bed under the left window.

It was my record night. I had chosen Stravinsky's 'Petrushka' as my first record. Before I put it on, I had announced through our grille into the portaal so that the people in the other cells could hear me, what I was going to play and had then read some extracts from the record cover. Later, I bought the *Oxford Dictionary of Music*, ostensibly for 'study purposes', and we would read relevant extracts from there, too, before we started.

> (319)
>
> Female Prison,
> Barberton.
> E. Transvaal.
> 20th February, 1967.
>
> Messrs. van Schaiks,
> Box 724,
> Pretoria.
>
> Dear Sirs,
> I enclose R9.76 as payment for The Oxford Companion to Music, including postage.
> I am,
> Yours faithfully,
> SBNeame
>
> [This] S.B. Neame.

From the first sounds of the flute, I loved 'Petrushka'. I enjoyed the clear sounds of the instruments, the different techniques, the fragmentation of themes, just a little bit of a theme that is broken off by something else and that sometimes comes back later and is developed further. I particularly liked the wind instruments – the flute, the oboe, the clarinet – and how Stravinsky uses them with transparency and precision. And then how, dramatically or good humouredly, he breaks it all up. It is cheeky, humorous and full of pathos.

The people are all out there in the streets with their little tunes and dances, the organ grinder and various street musicians, the showman and his puppets, a peasant, a bear, a goat, a pig, a drunken merchant, gypsy girls, the coachmen. Stravinsky uses each instrument so that it can be savoured for itself. There is purity and innocence but he moulds all this into something more. I like its halting, analytical quality. At the same time, it has a romantic aspect.

I think this was the first time I enjoyed anything in prison. Maybe I would not have enjoyed it as much if I hadn't known that soon I would be out of there. For the first time the nightmare quality lifted from the cell. I was not locked between four walls. The cell could almost have been a room anywhere. I was conscious of the yellow light outside and filtering through into the room.

Petrushka – the sorrowful puppet. The humour and the sadness of his trumpet fanfare.

The second record I chose that evening was Shostakovich's 1st Concerto for Piano and Trumpet. These two records I was to choose almost every time my turn came round, although there were 70 odd records at various times, sent in by relatives and friends. Shostakovich was, I felt, genuinely, honestly trying to work something out. A mind was working there. He was sensitively analytical so that there was a kind of purity, almost naivety, in his analysis, never over-sophisticated and yet a sophistication of fine feeling. And there was the clarity of his use of individual instruments, the piano and trumpet. The precision of his statements. What he said he said definitely.

I felt that both Stravinsky and Shostakovich suggested problems, solved some, left many suspended and left one feeling that that was not quite the end of the journey. No thumping crescendos at the end. There was still open-endedness, potential for a new day. The road to knowledge was infinite. Moreover, they did not press life into the shape they wanted it to be. They waited for life to come to them.

A question that came up was as to how often we should have our gramophone sessions, whether twice a day and, indeed, every day. Some of us found the music very exhausting. I remember in this respect particularly Esther and myself. I started having intense analytical dreams about music. Eventually, we decided to cut down. About two evenings a week we had no music at all as well as during some of the lunch hour lock-ups.

We had continued with our regular poetry discussions. In four of our get-togethers we discussed TS Eliot's 'Gerontion' and 'The Love Song of J Alfred Prufrock', Wordsworth's 'Tintern Abbey' and Walt Whitman's 'Sparkles from the Wheel'.

I wrote the following about the Eliot poem:

Eliot, in 'The Love Song of J Alfred Prufrock', rejects the city by painting it as squalid, its people insincere and taken up with meaningless social rituals. I think that it is a fantastic poem. It is one of his earlier works, and in it he has a flexibility which he seemed to have lost in at least some of his later work in the cold precision of his symbols. In Prufrock, one feels, he is looking around at the real world. Prufrock feels uneasy about the sordidness and ordinariness of modern life, of himself and human beings in general. It is self-deprecating, in part a kind of recognition of the modern human condition.

'And indeed there will be time
  To wonder, 'Do I dare?' And, 'Do I dare?'
  Time to turn back and descend the stair,
  With a bald spot in the middle of my hair –
And later:

'And I have known the eyes already, known them all –
  The eyes that fix you in a formulated phrase,
  And when I am formulated, sprawling on a pin,

Imprisoned

When I am pinned and wriggling on the wall,
Then how should I begin
To spit out all the butt-ends of my days and ways?
And how should I presume?

What interested me, too, in this poem is that he used many different techniques to convey, at a particular moment, a particular thought. The thought, the impression dictates the form. He changes the rhythm and uses rhyme or repetition or whatever, as he finds it useful. The poem has a flexibility but also a unity of vision.'

'Petrushka', Shostakovich's first concerto, and 'Prufrock' were an important part of my experience at Barberton, and I suppose my response to each reflected, most immediately, my rejection of the narrow vision, imposed on us by our prison conditions. I wished to escape the narrowness of our space and experience. I wanted life in all its complexity and contradictoriness, its disjunctures, its sorrows and personal uncertainties, its open questions.

At the same time – was this a contradiction? – what I liked in gaol in the field of art or music was precision, clarity of line when drawing, clarity of sound in music, intelligence to analyse, flexibility, simplicity and humility, humour, pathos, a will to accuracy, and essentially compassion in relation to the human condition. The pencil must analyse. Music must analyse. The word must analyse, too.

I wanted detail, yes, but detail not confined to a still space somewhere in no man's land but placed in the framework of and, more, shot through with, the large contradictory world. My view was that in the end, at least, our focus should not be on the still space, indeed the need to analyse what was happening to us there, was, of course, an integral part of our efforts to *understand*, and, thereby, to place us intellectually in the wider world. It was a part of my search to understand the total human condition, including with respect to our place in the animal and the natural world as a whole.

I would like to have written sentences short, precise, accurate, one after the other. Drops of distilled water. But I felt that I dared not stop there. That is why I admired so much what Tolstoy had done in *War and Peace*. This was the last book I read just before I left Barberton. He had organised a mass of material into a rich sense of life. There were individuals not acting life out of context but deeply embedded in their social backgrounds, with the vast expanse of Russia always there, and individuals being made by history and yet retaining their individuality. I thought, in spite of, and probably partly because of, its loose form, *War and Peace* was the greatest novel I had ever read or was likely to read.

An aspect that is striking, and which made us very different, it seems, from the Robben Island prisoners, was our limited political interchanges. We were more concerned with the arts than with politics. True the prisoners on the Island were also concerned with cultural things. The difference seems to be that we at Barberton were more or less solely concerned with cultural matters. This was certainly, in part at least, imposed upon us by our circumstances. We could not keep any discussions we might have had, that is those involving all of us, from the authorities and, in order to ensure that we might have an intellectual life which we shared with one another, we chose the kind of themes we felt would be more acceptable to them – starting with our Bible study class.

At the same time, it does seem that we found the arts a sphere that better reflected our emotional needs in that stark situation. A more general factor was that, integral to the outlook of what I have designated the 'Sharpeville generation' of left white activists, political ideology did not play quite such a crucial role for us as it did amongst the older generation. True, this may have been more the case with women. Important for the outlook of younger members of the left at this time were Kruschev's exposures of Stalin in 1956. The fact that we came from the middle class was also a factor in our outlook.

To the extent that ideology did play a role, it tended to be subsumed under the head of Weltanschauung, a world view, and, to this degree, had a strong philosophical-cum-moral ingredient. This was very much the case as far as my own intellectual endeavours were concerned. Largely these were confined to study hours in my cell. One could argue that our studies remained very much an individual concern, except perhaps for somebody like Ann, who shared her history of art syllabus with us. Moreover, we did share ideas in Bible study, and we adopted similar, largely historical, positions. On occasion one of us would place excerpts from study material in our Barberton newspaper; and there were our poetry sessions where, as I have indicated, at least initially, our views often clashed.

That a lot of our thinking was confined to the cells where we did our studying is perhaps suggested by what Leslie said to me soon after her arrival. 'Sylvia, why don't you let people know what is going on in your head? There is so much going on in your mind but you keep it to yourself.' I must say I had not been aware of this situation at all and I don't know what provoked her comment. Now, when I think about what she said, I ask myself whether this might have had something to do with the fact that women are often brought up to hide their intellectual concerns for such an interest is considered unwomanly.

Our chief aim in pursuing our various intellectual and cultural activities had much to do with our desire to widen our horizons. Intellectual things, together with aspects connected more immediately with the senses, intertwined with each other in a complex pattern. We hung onto as many impressions as we could – from new ideas to the scent of 'honeysuckle' which penetrated through to our section that last summer (and we afterwards found was the scent of magnolia flowers) to that yellow bird in the yellow-green tree and the stuttering of the guinea fowl down in the sisal lands. There was Prufrock, descending the stair with a bald spot in the middle of his hair, the sadness and frustration of the puppet Petrushka, a still life drawn by one of us, a life drawing, the mental and emotional responses evoked by a concerto or a symphony. And we must not forget our concern with Arnoldus hibernating under a plant in the courtyard and with our frog with squeaking feet on the linoleum.

The tempest

THAT NIGHT, JUST BEFORE I put on the Shostakovich, I heard the mosquitoes tuning up. A high whine coming from you knew not exactly where but could make a pretty good guess – in the dark corners of the portaal, in the lockers, under the beds in our cells. By the time Shostakovich was finished, we could see the creatures, almost as big as flies, legs hanging down, flying between the bars of our grille from the portaal and into the cell. They began to whine around my ears and brush the side of my cheeks where I lay on the floor. I got up and lay on my bed next to our right-hand window until the record was finished. Then I pulled the plugs of the two speakers out of the record player, throwing the flexes out of the way into the portaal. They slid along the softly gleaming grey concrete. And then I closed the grey metal door of our cell in order to keep out as many mosquitoes as we could. I pulled on the white string which pulled up the venetian blind and Leslie closed the curtain above her bed.

It was warm and still outside. An occasional sound came from a frog somewhere – sometimes the frogs made such a noise at night we had difficulty sleeping. There was also the sound of crickets, and thousands of insects scratching their legs. And the call of the guinea fowl on the gravel road above the sisal lands. It was a few minutes before real darkness.

It looked as though there was going to be a storm for the mountains across the valley to the north-west – the top left corner of our world – were steel grey and well defined, the different ranges emerging more clearly than usual. I could discern what appeared to be a little valley between two ranges of mountains. The plain itself was dark green, mixed with steel grey, the contours especially sharp, the bushes green-black. The tall trees around the farm gaol were clearly defined as well as a bit of the roof of the gaol, the lines of sisal in the rectangle below. There was a strange greyish yellow light in the sky.

'There's going to be a ghastly storm,' I commented.

We could hear thunder in the distance. There were shivering flashes of sheet lightning. And then in the little valley in the far distance between the two ranges of mountains, we saw a moving mass of grey that came in a kind of funnel across the plain and up towards us. And the trees, 50 yards from our cell, started tossing their heads, and the noises of the insects and the guinea fowl were drowned by a swishing sound. Then the wind, with some rain, hit the prison.

It was dark now outside our cages, except for the artificial yellow light of the floodlights, one to our left and one a little to our right, and some light from another further away. The wind tore at the trees, whined around the prison in enormous gusts. It seemed to get caught somehow against the high hills behind the gaol and came whirling back again, spiralling in huge gusts against the walls.

Large flashes of forked lightning were followed by crashes of thunder. They echoed in the valley and, thrown against the hills, came deafeningly back at us. I quickly backed from the windows as another flash of lightning lit up the cages. The wind was literally screaming around the gaol; the leaves of the trees swished, and then bounced with a harder hiss. Lightning flashed, illuminating our cell every now and again.

'Do you think they've got a lightning conductor on the gaol?' I enquired. I asked the same question every time we had a storm. I added, not expecting an answer, 'I've never been able to see one, you know ... but they must have one.'

If I could only move more freely out into the portaal, that would be something. I imagined myself moving in the portaal, taking large swinging steps. If I could only move my body like that I would feel more in control of the situation. There wasn't enough room in the cell. I was cornered, a terrified animal in a dreadful storm.

I remembered the storms I had experienced during my first 90-

day detention when I had been in that little cell in Pretoria Central, in the hall with the fourteen unoccupied cells. In the late afternoon the storms would come crashing down into my precarious physical and mental balance. I had tried not to think about how close the walls were surrounding me, how cornered I was.

I did not directly think about the electric torture that some detainees were undergoing. I had gathered from a newspaper that had somehow come in to me that the Branch was engaging in electric torture. The paper had apparently come from Caroline but I guessed the Branch had put it with the food sent in in order to put me in a panic. They would never have allowed me to have a newspaper. It was reported that a first detainee, Looksmart Ngudle, had died under this kind of torture in the very same gaol I was in and perpetrated by my main interrogator, Swanepoel. I had known Looksmart while I was living in Cape Town. Indeed I had worked with him politically – this was in open political activity. I pushed the prospect of electric torture into the back of my mind. I decided I would face it when it came. None the less, it was not something one could completely forget.

The terrible crashes of thunder that penetrated that Pretoria cell splintered me into a thousand fragments. Then came the rain on the corrugated-iron roof, drumming, drumming so hard that I thought the rain must break through. Or was that the sound of hailstones? The noise cut me off completely from the rest of the prison. When there was no storm I could at least hear some sounds coming from a part of the female gaol below. I also heard something from the gaol on the other side of my window which looked over onto the men's section. This window was behind the gauze frame which slanted in from the bottom of the window into my tiny cell so that I could not actually touch the extremely dusty windowpanes behind and which it was difficult to see through.

These sounds – like the sound of tin plates and mugs – had become an important link to the world beyond my cell. They told me that I was not entirely alone. And then there was a strange scraping noise during the day coming from the men's gaol. It sounded like a spade scraping backwards and forwards on concrete, and then a short pause. And then the same scraping noise. I imagined a prisoner with a spade in his hand making cement and scraping the spade on the rough concrete surface of a section of a yard. But why did it go on and on, rhythmically, all day? That I couldn't decide. None the less I retained this picture in my mind because I had no means of checking. From the same direction came the sound of tiles falling together onto concrete. What were they doing with tiles, I wondered.

Sometimes I heard men's voices, rough men's voices. They seemed to be talking in Afrikaans but I could not make out what they said. Sometimes I would hear the voice of an African woman prisoner from down below in my prison. But more often the shouting voice of a wardress. At night the women used to sing a gloomy hymn over and over again. Maybe this was depressing but sounds were my lifeline. I knew that somewhere there were other human beings. Moreover, they were human beings who were not being tortured.

Then there was the sound of trains. There was something comforting about a train. Ordinary human beings, living ordinary everyday lives, were in those trains, if, of course, I reminded myself, they were not a Mrs Rheeder being brought up under escort by train to Pretoria to occupy that death cell down the way from me, later to be taken to the trapdoor next door in Pretoria Central.

But when the afternoon storms came I was completely alone. To me, locked up in my cell, with the thunder crashing and the rain thundering on the corrugated-iron, it seemed I was the only human being in the world. I would feel the hysteria mounting in my chest. I wondered whether I should shout for somebody, then realised I would not be heard. And, anyway, if Matron Britz did come, I knew she would get that look of amusement and sadism in her eyes when she saw my fear. She would look at me as she'd done when she saw the hysteria rising in me at the sound of the cat's wild meows as it tried to get out of my cell. She would discover my weak points and that was a danger. 'They' must know as little about me as possible. They must not know about my fears for they would only use them against me.

At least here in Barberton Prison I was not alone and there was in the communal cell more space to move in than in that single cell in Pretoria. The storm did not seem to be directly overhead anymore. My

The tempest

ears strained to pick up all sounds so that I could make an assessment of the situation. I knew from experience at Barberton that one or two or three gentle bits of thunder did not mean that there might not be another almighty crash. I felt myself tensing again. There was a moment of ominous silence outside, then a swish of the wind in the trees began, then a flash of lightning, and almost simultaneously a sharp deafening crash.

'God's truth,' I muttered, 'it's just above the prison.' I could see from Leslie's shadowy figure that she hadn't been so pleased about that one either. I heard Ann's voice across the portaal. And then Flo's.

The wind was at the trees again. There were fluttering yellow flashes, with no thunder. Yellow flashes fluttering in the sky, down in the plain, lighting up our cell for a moment, and then the darkness, except for the floodlights outside. Another erratic flutter of light. And then an enormous crash straight into the ground, sharp, precise. A pause. And then once more 'GUNG' into the ground. And again thunder crashing and echoing wildly against the hills and in the valley.

Would it ever stop? Surely, surely, there couldn't be another one like that?

I seemed to remember from storms I had experienced in the past – in Port Elizabeth and Cape Town, Durban – that they usually came to a climax with a ghastly crash. After one terrible crash, or two, the storm would move gradually further and further away, the time gap between the lightning and the thunder getting longer until the forked lightning turned back into sheet lightning and the thunder gurgled and rumbled in a friendly way some distance away.

But storms in Barberton did not seem so predictable. While they might have followed the usual pattern of starting with fluttering sheet lightning and low murmurs of thunder in the distance, there was no relief after the first enormous crash or series of crashes. There would often be one crash after another immediately overhead, with the flash of lightning and the thunder almost simultaneous. Then there would be some more gentle sheet lightning and thunder, and then, without warning, another crackle of lightning and crash!

I listened intently to all the sounds. It must be over now. It must be over. Yes, it was. I felt myself relax a little. I breathed more evenly, and also stopped inhibiting my sight and hearing. I looked out of the window, through our cages, lit up erratically by the floodlights. The wind was still there but not so violent as it had been. And the whine around the gaol had stopped. I no longer feared that the prison was going to crumble in a whirlwind or be picked up by an enormous gust and deposited in the valley below.

Just as I was beginning to feel so much better, our cell was lit by the next flash, and almost simultaneously there was a crash that seared through my body. When I recovered a little from that one, I found I had my fingers over my ears. Leslie laughed at me. I laughed, too, and felt a sense of relief.

The storm did gradually subside until there were just friendly bits of lightning in the little valley between the two ranges of mountain in the left-hand corner of our world. The trees across the grey gravel were no longer black and bouncing like monsters. They were just trees now, still mostly dark but some were lit up in parts by the lights.

I wondered how the guard had enjoyed the storm. He walked quietly below, with his rifle. Crunch, crunch, on the gravel. He was talking to himself, acting out some part, it appeared. Laughing, talking, swinging his hips. Then silent, as he readjusted his rifle against his shoulder. Deep in thought. He was quite unaware of me there watching him.

We turned on the light in our cell. It was late. Time for me to do my yoga. It took me 40 minutes. Just as I was finishing off, the nine o'clock siren sounded and, with it, the barking of dogs. I wondered how they had got through the storm.

The psychologically complex question of escape

I THINK IT WAS ABOUT AUGUST 1966 that there suddenly seemed to be a great many dogs in the area of the prison. We were told by Brigadier Pretorius at some point that if we ever tried to escape we would have Alsatian dogs after us. I do not know whether there were special police dogs, attached to the gaol, when we arrived. As it was designated a Maximum Security Prison, that might have been the case. But my impression is that it was only at a later stage that there were large dogs constantly on the prison property and I wondered whether there had been an escape at another gaol. Certainly, there had been no barking when the nine o'clock siren went off in the first few months I was at Barberton.

We had made acquaintance with police dogs for the first time during our Johannesburg trial when our large prison van was escorted, back and forth to the magistrate's court in the centre of town, by a car (cars?) with uniformed policemen with dogs and at least one rifle. And on my way to and from Humansdorp during my eastern Cape trial, those 58 miles, I had been escorted by a car with a huge Alsatian and a uniformed cop with a Sten gun.

The man with the Sten gun stood a few feet behind me in the court during the first two or three days of my trial in Humansdorp, until this fact received some newspaper publicity and my lawyer made an objection and the Sten gun was withdrawn from the court. The situation was most unusual. Not even in the Rivonia trial were Sten guns in court – at least not to my knowledge.

At Barberton we occasionally saw officers with Alsatians on leads.

Those dogs reminded us that we were convicts, as did the presence of the guard with the rifle. Not that we could ever really forget. But sometimes we ceased to bear in mind that there was always a life-and-death potential in our relationship with the authorities. We were taken up with the details of living from day to day, with seeing that we had our cleaning and other work duties properly organised, that we planned our 'complaints and requests' carefully and any campaign we might decide on, that we had successful group activities, such as our art classes or discussions of poetry, a table tennis tournament, an art exhibition, the bringing out of our newspaper and so on.

Especially after we had been classified to B category, what with extra visits and letters and magazines to read, we tended to forget who we were, who they were. And then suddenly we would be brought up against something that reminded us that, if we tried to get out of that situation, if we tried to make a break out of that no man's land, if we tried to escape from there, they could shoot and kill us. We were, in the final analysis, enemies.

The escape siren used to be tested at 11.30 every Saturday morning. This became to us, to a large extent, just a part of gaol routine. As the siren went off, we merely tended to think, It's half past eleven. We've got an hour and a half to unlock at one. On the other hand, when the escape siren went off at any other time, then you felt that flush of excitement and fear and unease; 'unease' because prisoners, I think, tend to have all sorts of contradictory feelings about escape.

I had an escape attempt behind me, if it certainly made a big difference that it had not been an escape attempt from a prison. More about that below. At any rate, escape was undoubtedly an especially sensitive issue for me and I never entertained another attempt. I was pretty certain that a second time would be used by them to shoot and, even if I survived physically undamaged, they would have used it to make my life utterly intolerable.

To get out of there was our constant wish and so the escape of another prisoner made us feel a rush of relief and almost unbearable excitement. For a moment, we felt that we, ourselves, had broken out of those four walls. We hoped against hope that the prisoner would get away.

The psychologically complex question of escape

One day, not long before my release from Barberton, we heard a great commotion and activity in the front of the prison. Somebody had escaped. Somebody was on the run. One of us. I rushed to the single cell with the west-facing window, and climbed up onto the table. Matron Bester and Matron Taljaard were standing out there with some African wardresses and some women prisoners.

The two matrons were obviously highly excited. They were talking and shouting and pointing in the direction of the sisal lands. Taljaard was swinging her large hips, with her khaki skirt drawn tight across her buttocks. Her pink and white plump face was full of excited smiles. She looked as though the side she was backing in a local rugby match had just scored a try. The African women prisoners seemed, to some extent, to enjoy the atmosphere of excitement that exuded from Taljaard and even from Matron Bester, who was smiling and pointing and walking backwards and forwards on the grass on the other side of the grey gravel pathway, above the sisal lands. The sisal had just been cut so that the lines of sisal were clear and the lines between the sisal.

I was trying to work out whether it was one of the women prisoners who had escaped. The relaxed attitude of the women prisoners down below and, indeed, of Taljaard and Matron Bester indicated that it was probably a male prisoner. And suddenly I saw an African male prisoner, in khaki shirt and off-white shorts (the type of shorts we had washed so often), running at terrific speed down through the centre of the sisal lands and out to the bush and trees and grass on the other side. Nobody seemed to be chasing after him and he disappeared from sight.

As we watched the performance outside, we remembered that prisoners had been shot dead the previous Good Friday. Maybe they would shoot in this case too. I looked out of the window into the warm summer day. I think it was near noon for the sun was high in the sky, and hot. The sky was clear and blue.

I felt uneasy. I was excited. I identified with the escaping prisoner, but, at the same time, I had a hunted feeling. In trying to escape, the prisoner breaks the tacit peace agreement between prisoners and the authorities. By the very nature of the situation, the authorities are your enemies. They lock you up against your will. They submit you to the torture of physical confinement and sensory and emotional deprivation. They treat you as non-human.

At the same time, most prisoners, in order to survive, have to keep the aggressions and hatred which naturally arise in this situation well in hand, even to bury them so deep that they do not know they exist, except when, on occasion, they fly out of control. Most prisoners are continually trying to convince the warders and wardresses that they have nothing to fear, that there is a normal working relationship between them. Above all, prisoners want to retain an atmosphere of normality in an abnormal situation, at least until on occasion the reality of incarceration rears its ugly head.

On the side of the authorities, when prisoners try to escape, they in turn recognise them as their enemy. Their job is to keep the prisoner in their gaol. And when prisoners try to escape, their role is undermined. It even seems to go further than this: the escape of a prisoner appears to give rise to all sorts of conflictual feelings. I do not really understand the feelings of the authorities fully since I was on the other side of the divide, and I found it difficult to identify myself with them. However, there is one thing I did feel in our relationship and that was, just as much as we feared what they could do to us – and they had power to do almost anything – they feared prisoners because they sensed the enormous well of hatred that lies below the surface in every prisoner.

Once or twice I saw a sudden look of panic in the eyes of a wardress when she felt that prisoners were beginning to get out of control – there were many of them, only one or two wardresses. They knew that prisoners could tear them to pieces and they probably sensed that that was exactly what their natural instinct inclined them to do.

So the prison authorities, almost instinctively, use all sorts of techniques to divide prisoners, playing one against another. They develop an army of trusties so that, amongst other things, they can pursue a policy of divide and rule and, moreover, seemingly bridge the emotional divide between themselves and the incarcerated.

Prison authorities fear escape, not only because they may be charged with negligence but because escape exposes, symbolises, clarifies, the relationship between the gaoled and the gaoler. And this, they feel, can snowball. It can bring all sorts of suppressed, and perhaps repressed, feelings to the surface. And that could cause an explosion, a prison riot, perhaps. I think when the authorities began to realise the sort of people we politicals were, that we were highly disciplined people, with high standards of behaviour in the face of the most trying circumstances, they felt, in a way, 'safe' with us, as they did not feel with other prisoners. But this was only after they learned to know us. They first had to overcome the lies they had been told.

The matrons and wardresses made it clear when we first arrived in Barberton that they assumed that we were not simply immoral but aggressive and our behaviour unpredictable. By Christmas 1966, that is, after we had been in Barberton 20 months, Matron Bester admitted that we were principled people and she respected us for this and for our courage in standing up for those principles, even though she did not share them. From a woman like her, this was quite an admission.

My own attempt at escape

I CAME UP AGAINST ALL THE complex feelings associated with escape for the first time when I tried myself to escape. For me to take such a step was quite traumatic. I had recently come out of my second 90-day detention, had been charged with membership of the South African Communist Party and, having been refused bail, I was, with the other accused, an awaiting-trial prisoner at the Fort.

In a way, it was a relief to come out of detention into a situation where I was not isolated from other prisoners and where I had contact with the world through visitors, whom we saw twice a week, and also through lawyers. Court appearances were also a relief after the trauma of isolation. In detention, in the normal run of events, there was no contact with other prisoners or with the outside world, no access to lawyers or the courts, no protection from society whatsoever. We were completely at the mercy of the police and we knew the police were prepared to use all kinds of torture techniques, both psychological and physical, to make us talk. The hatred they showed, partly genuine and partly, one assumes, an interrogration method, was absolutely terrifying. This hatred indicated that they were prepared to do anything to make us talk.

I was fully aware that if I tried to escape and was caught, I would lose my feeling of comparative safety. Not only might I again be faced with the Security Police but the relationship between the prison authorities and myself would be exposed for what it was – we were enemies. As it turned out, the latter did not occur as the Officer-Commanding at the Fort decided that the escape had had nothing to do with her prison because it had occurred outside its precincts. I attempted to contribute to this picture by holding that my escape had not been directed against the prison but against the Security Police – they had been transporting me to the dentist at the time.

It was during October 1964 that I decided I might try my luck, if the opportunity arose. At the time a feeling had been growing that the political movement should cease operating in a situation whereby (known) political people did conspiratorial work while carrying on with their normal lives. In more general terms, there was a sense that we should adopt a more thorough underground/conspiratorial culture, an attitude which appeared soon to be confirmed when Bram Fischer turned his back on the court proceedings and went underground. I should, at the same time, make clear that I had discussed my plans with no one else, not even with my own cell mates.

At the same time, my action had a strong personal aspect. It had something to do with the sentencing to life imprisonment of the Rivonia trialists, just a few months before. I was driven by the almost subliminal idea that I was a fugitive in the widest sense from the apartheid state and its legal system. It was not just my political views that were in question but my whole life as a human being.

Before his arrest at Rivonia Kathy had approached Walter Sisulu, whom he regarded as a kind of political father, concerning his relationship with me. He had asked whether it was Walter's view that we should bring it to an end in the interests of the political movement. After careful consideration, Walter had responded that the Immorality and Mixed Marriages acts were an integral part of the legal system of apartheid and that the ANC could only regard them as unjust laws. In this sense, a defiance of these laws could not be regarded by the movement as something to be criticised. As long as we remained vigilant, it was his opinion that we should not break off our relationship. The approach of Bram and Molly Fischer to the issue of ensuring that Kathy and I could correspond during his detention and trial underlined Walter's point.

I had an appointment with the dentist one afternoon. I was due to have a crown placed on one of my front teeth. Two Security Branch men escorted me from the Fort. One drove the car. The other sat next to the driver in the passenger seat. I was seated at the back. The driver was probably in his late thirties or forties. The other Branch man was grey-haired, probably late fifties, I thought.

The car pulled off from the front of the gaol and moved up Kotze Street into the centre of Hillbrow. Hillbrow was the (small) Manhattan of Johannesburg, lots of tall blocks of flats and quite cosmopolitan (minus black people, of course). Kotze Street was largely a shopping area. The pavements were thick with people, the streets packed with cars and buses. At both ends of almost every block there were robots where the cars and buses tended to build up. There was lots of noise.

As I looked out of the window of the car, I thought, with a sinking feeling in my stomach, because in a way I had hoped that this would not be the case, This is an ideal situation to attempt an escape. I could quietly slip open the door. In all the noise they might not even hear me go. I could attempt it at almost any time, either when the car had pulled up at one of the robots or just as we were pulling off or when the car was forced to travel very slowly because it was caught behind a bus. Once on the pavement, it would be easy to get lost in the crowd and, also important, the Branch would not be able to shoot – there were too many people around. They would not risk killing somebody else, I felt sure.

I was relieved that it was these two particular Branch men, for, as far as I knew, they were by no means the most vicious. Another Branch man, Erasmus, a young chap who, other detainees told me, was a vicious interrogator, keen to use his fists and boot, and fascist to the core, informed me later that he certainly would not have bothered to chase after me. He would have used his gun.

In my wildest dreams I could not have imagined so suitable an environment for an attempt at escape. I looked at the back of the heads of the two men in front. They were chatting to each other, completely relaxed. They seemed almost to have forgotten that I was there behind them. I wondered whether the driver could see me in his rear-view mirror. I examined the back of his head and the part of his face that I could see from the back seat. He was relaxed, not on the watch. I moved slightly closer to the left back door – it is to be borne in mind that South Africa has left-moving traffic – and kept my left hand ready to push the handle down when the car slowed down at the robots. I tried to assume a nonchalant pose but I felt enormous tension in my body and in my face.

I was amazed that those Branch men seemed so utterly unaware of that bundle of tension on the back seat.

There was a perfect opportunity at the first robot. The car pulled up in the left stream of traffic. There were lots of cars, a couple of buses and people on the pavements. And considerable noise. I felt my whole body stretched and tense, ready to move. But I just couldn't do it. My courage failed me.

The car pulled off as the lights changed to green. It was moving very slowly because of all the traffic. I could still do it but I decided I would leave it to the next robot. Perhaps there everything would be dead right as it had been at the last robot.

But at the next one, the car had moved to the right-hand stream of traffic. It wouldn't be so easy to get lost as would be possible should I step out onto the pavement. I might get myself run over into the bargain.

I must do it before I get to the dentist, rather than after, I thought. After an injection, I might not be able to run so fast.

The car turned right as the lights turned orange. We were in a street running at right angles to Kotze Street. The driver swung the car to the left and parked it. We were obviously at the dentist already. I got out of the car and, with the Branch some yards behind, I walked towards a shop window and had a look. They were still very relaxed about me. I wondered whether I should try it now. But I thought that would be irresponsible. Why choose the worst opportunity, instead of the best? There weren't so many people on this pavement, and the Branch would see me go since they were right behind me. Escaping to get caught would be irresponsible.

We went up some steps to the dentist, through a door on the left and into a fairly plush waiting room. One of the cops went over to the reception desk where he muttered something. The receptionist likewise muttered something and gave a quick look in my direction. I sat down on a chair, with the two Branch men next to me. I picked up a magazine and started to read a large article on Nikita Krushchev, who had just been removed from power in the Soviet Union. I tried to concentrate because I wanted to take the tension out of my body and the look of escape out of my eyes. Surely they could see it there? It was an article I never completely forgot, including the large photographs.

I wondered whether I would be left alone while the dentist was treating me and whether, if I was, I could just get up and try and slip out, or even ask him to help me.

The receptionist took me through to one of the surgeries. The dentist was there, young and friendly. I found it very difficult to be friendly back because of the thought of escape, making me so tense. One of the Branch men took a seat near the door with a magazine. This was about the only precaution they had taken thus far. I climbed up into the dentist's chair and he rubbed anaesthetic onto my gums above my two front teeth. He took the syringe. 'This is going to be a bit nasty,' he said.

'Yes, yes,' I said, bemused, 'I know, I've had it before.'

He pushed the needle in, up somewhere towards my nose. My eyes started watering. 'That's it,' he said, taking the needle out, and pressing his finger onto the gum. 'We'll just wait a few minutes.' And he walked out of the room, probably, I thought, to attend to another patient in another surgery.

The Branch man remained seated near the door, flicking over the pages of the magazine. There was a window directly in front of me and I could see a tall white building. There were several storeys, with windows behind which there were people working. It must be an office block, I thought. They can probably see me too. Bet they don't know I'm a prisoner.

I was very aware of Hillbrow out there. I knew the area so well. I had lived very close to Kotze Street for a time, and I had done my shopping there. I had often eaten in Hillbrow's many restaurants and cafés and for some time our Communist Party cell would meet at Jean Middleton's flat in the same area. Maybe I will not see Hillbrow again for six years, maybe more ... Or perhaps never again, I thought.

The young dentist came back again. 'Well, how is it?' he enquired in a friendly manner.

'I think it's all right,' I replied, trying to respond to his friendliness but failing.

'Well, let's give it a try,' he said. He got his drill ready, came towards me, and clutched my head so it was lying against his shoulder. He started drilling. The taste or smell of burning and the water in my mouth and the high whining sound. I felt the highly unpleasant response of a nerve.

'Ugh,' I struggled.

He stopped drilling. 'It's still hurting,' I informed him, indicating that the injection had not yet numbed the nerve sufficiently. This was always the problem with my front teeth. I usually needed at least two injections before I could bear the drilling.

'Well, let's leave it a few minutes,' he said. 'Maybe it hasn't taken yet.' He left the room again and I looked towards the office block and found myself counting the windows, from left to right and from right to left. From the top right-hand corner down to the bottom right-hand corner. I could only see half a window at the bottom. I added that in too.

As I started to count from the top left corner, the dentist came back. 'Well, how is it?' he asked, still friendly and relaxed.

'I don't know,' I replied. In fact I felt the injection was probably wearing off.

'Well, we'll give it another try. If it hurts, we'll give you another injection.'

It did hurt. He gave me another injection. I wondered whether the Branch man behind me was enjoying my discomfort. I felt a twinge of embarrassment that he should see me in this situation, just a twinge because my mind and body were still concentrated on escaping.

One of the problems of introducing into one's mind the idea of escape was that, once there, it was difficult to eradicate. And I found later that, once you had tried it, there always seemed to be something in you, putting you under pressure to try it again. I felt I could understand Gerrie van Rensburg doing it again and again, however much she suffered for it and in spite of the many years it added to her sentence. Once escape was in your blood, it was there for good.

I had to have a third injection. Was it because of my tension that my pain threshold was so low?

As I had the third, I realised how silly I was being. It would have been better to have borne the pain. Injections always stepped up my heartbeat, and that wouldn't be so good for my running if I decided to give it a go on the way back to the gaol. The problem was that, if he didn't deaden the nerve sufficiently, I would jump and then he was likely to send the drill through my top lip. I felt I had to have the third injection. Anyway,

I was so nervous, I wasn't really thinking very clearly.

The dentist finished off the drilling and started preparing the porcelain powder or whatever it was, to put onto the front surface of the tooth. He came back towards me and, as he did, a car exhaust in one of the streets below made an exploding sound. I jumped.

God! He must think I'm neurotic, I thought. Or perhaps he thinks I just can't take gaol. I tried to see myself through his eyes. He may think gaol and 90-day detention would make anyone tense. Maybe he even feels sorry for me.

He saw me from the outside. For me the situation was rather different. I was a prisoner. That was my life. So I couldn't feel like he imagined it was. He was a young dentist, doing well in Hillbrow. He saw his working life from the point of view of Hillbrow whereas I saw Hillbrow and his life from the point of view of prison. Even here as I sat in the dentist's chair and looked out at the tall office block ahead of me, I saw it all as an outsider. I did not belong here. I belonged there, down Kotze Street, behind the high red-brick wall of the Fort.

I wondered what he would think if he knew I had escape on my mind, in my body. Escape was the act of a prisoner, breaking down the walls of the prison, but not coming back into the world. I might run through Hillbrow away from the police, away from the Fort, the red-brick and the bars, and the degradation. But I would not become a part of the life of Hillbrow. I would not enter into his world at all. I would be a fugitive. I would have to hide from the world. I would have to hide from all those people walking in the streets down below. I would lead a hunted life, not a prisoner behind bars but a prisoner all the same. If I escaped, I would not be able to enter the outside world as myself. Therefore, I would not be free as he was free here in his dentist's surgery.

He would probably be very worried if he knew I was going to try to escape, I thought. He would probably feel some anxiety, fear of the police, because I would have tainted him, involved him somehow in my crime. The Branch might even suspect him of collusion. He finished off my tooth. 'That should be all right,' he concluded.

I spoke to him from far away, aware that there must be some anxiety in my eyes. 'Will it last for six years?' I asked. 'It will have to last for six years.'

My own attempt at escape

At this stage I thought I would get that number of years in our Communist Party trial. I saw him wince. He ignored the question. I didn't like him thinking of me like that. He was probably feeling sorry for me. That would be an insult. Did he not realise that I had chosen my life? There was always the possibility that I would go to gaol.

'I think it will be all right,' he said.

'They're always breaking,' I said. 'I often have to have them redone.'

'Well, that shouldn't happen,' he said, 'and I think this one will be all right.' He paused. 'If it isn't, come back to me.'

I muttered goodbye. He did not respond. I'm not sure why. He had always been friendly. He had examined my teeth at the Fort. I walked out of the surgery into the waiting room, the Branch man behind me. The other one had obviously spent the time in the waiting room. He looked in my direction and then at the other man. The man with me nodded the okay to him. We could go. I didn't know whether to say goodbye to the receptionist or not. Did prisoners speak to receptionists, I wondered.

One of the Branch men turned to her, 'Dankie ... dankie ...'

I walked towards the door. I made no attempt to open it myself. Prisoners do not open doors. One of the men opened it, and let me pass through. Then they followed after me. Out on the pavement I walked straight towards the car. I tried to look firm and nonchalant at the same time, perhaps firm and 'resigned' is a better description. I tried to make my walk look as though I was saying to myself: I've got to go back to prison, so that is that. I have accepted that I am a prisoner. I have accepted my fate ...

I went up to the back door of the car and waited there. A prisoner does not open car doors. The grey-haired cop opened. I climbed in. They got into the front of the car. Same driver, the grey-haired one in the passenger seat.

I can't remember how we returned to Kotze Street, but what probably happened is that the driver backed the car out, and turned across the road and up to the lights at the intersection between the road we were in and Kotze Street. I thought, God, will there be a chance or won't there be? And if there is a good one, should I take it? I hated the dilemma. It would be so nice just to sink back into the back seat, give up the whole idea, give up the whole responsibility of it, and just go quietly back to the Fort where I'd join the others in our cell.

I felt myself relax.

Thank goodness, I've decided not to do it.

The tension went out of my body. I thought of the others in our cell at the Fort. I imagined myself getting back there. It would probably be about lock-up time or just after. I saw the prisoners standing informally at attention behind their grilles, with Mrs Lubbe going from cell to cell, locking the wooden door and then the grille. She would be making some gently sarcastic comment about some prisoner, perhaps Irene.

The soft-spoken, white-haired Irene, well into her seventies, a pensioner with very little money, was doing a 'nine to fifteen' for repeated shoplifting, always small, relatively inexpensive items. The last article she'd 'lifted' was a woollen cardigan and the result was that she was stepped up from her previous sentence, which had been a 'five to eight', to a 'nine to fifteen'. Obviously she suffered from kleptomania. She should never have been in prison at all, let alone for nine to fifteen years. Apparently she had spent a great deal of her adult life in gaol.

Saying goodnight, Mrs Lubbe finished locking the 'hard labour' cell and the single cells which were on the other side of the wall from our cell, and then she came through the surgery to our cell. We were standing there at attention, smiling at Mrs Lubbe, and she was asking with a straight face whether Middleton was sure she had matches for the night and Jean, with her hands behind her back, opening her eyes innocently, asked, 'Matches, Mrs Lubbe?' And Mrs Lubbe responding, 'Yes, matches, Middleton. You wouldn't be able to survive the night if you didn't have your cigarettes.' Saying 'Goodnight' to us, she would lock the door, the grille would go 'gung', there would be another rattle of keys and another day at the Fort would be over.

I leaned back against the car seat with this picture in my mind. It was comforting in its ordinariness, one to which Mrs Lubbe contributed with her basic humaneness, her sense of humour, so different from her sister, the lieutenant. The day-to-day life of an ordinary white woman prisoner at the Fort. If I tried to escape that would be gone. It would be a declaration of war between me and them.

The idea of escape came back into my mind. Once there, it clung like

My own attempt at escape

an octopus to a rock and wouldn't let go. My body tensed again. I no longer felt the comfort of the seat behind me. I was straining forward. The lights turned green at the intersection, the car turned to the left and up towards the next robot. It was in the left line of traffic. A good position for me. On my left the pavements were packed with people. Lots of noise of people and traffic. I sat close to the left door. I looked at the backs of my escorts' heads – the driver's neck and head narrow, his hair reddish; the other man short, sitting low in his seat, with grey curly hair. I was absolutely amazed that they were so unaware of me. I got my left hand ready to lift up to the handle.

I still hadn't definitely decided to do it. In fact, I felt I probably wouldn't. The car was on the way back to the Fort. I looked at the people on the pavements, some with brightly coloured shopping bags. White people and black people. I wondered whether they knew I was a prisoner. Very unlikely. In fact, impossible. Just two men in plain clothes in the front and me sitting at the back. I wondered whether it didn't look strange for the woman to be sitting in the back, with two men in front.

Shop windows on my left. My top lip and part of my nose were still numb from the injections. I tried to move my face a bit but I still didn't have control over the muscles in that part of my face. I wouldn't be able to talk properly. Escape hadn't left my mind but there was room for other thoughts.

The robot was red. The car stopped. Oh God, here is the opportunity. The idea of escape took over. I had to do it. The chance might not be quite as good as it had been on the way to the dentist. There might not be quite as many people here on the pavement. But it was certainly a good one. The robot turned green. The driver got ready to pull off. Just before he did, I put my left hand on the handle, pushed it down, stepped out, and pushed the car door closed behind me. I did not slam it shut.

And then I ran: round the block and down the pavement, past people who hardly seemed to notice me. My heart seemed to be beating at enormous speed. I was not breathing very evenly. I had a red shirt over my jersey. I was wearing slacks and flat shoes, clothes suitable for an attempted escape. I turned left at the corner of the block and down the pavement. Were they behind me? Did they know I had gone? Thoughts flitted through my head. I wondered whether I should try and disappear into a shop where I could get lost among the crowds but the shops I was then passing were small, jewellers, that sort of thing. If I had still been on Kotze Street, it would have been possible to disappear into a big department store. There were lots of people on the pavement here but they would thin out at the next road. That worried me.

I felt the numbness in my thighs from running. Probably numb because my body was so tense. I decided to pull my red shirt off. It was far too obvious and if they were not directly behind at the moment, and, therefore, did not have me in sight, they might still look around for a red shirt. As I ran, I pulled it off, and dropped it behind me. And on I went.

Gosh, I thought, they must have lost me … Where are they? It was terrible not being able to turn round and look but I thought that would slow me down too much.

I reached a corner. Which way should I go? Should I turn right and go round the block? Should I cross the road – it was a side street – to the other side and run up the pavement to the right, turn left and down the steep hill? Yes, I thought, I know that area. I will be able to move with more certainty … perhaps I can even stay put for a bit in one of the garages of a block of flats round here, even do something about changing how I look.

I hesitated at the corner and looked left and right to see that no car was coming. I was far too careful but I didn't want to get run over. I stepped down from the pavement and ran across the road. I would slip between the two cars parked on the other side of the road and get onto the pavement. I was across the road, moving in towards one of the cars, then I was in the space between the two parked cars. I felt arms grip me around the legs. They've got me! I thought. I swung around in the air and fell half onto the bonnet of the second car. As I fell, I felt my head jar, hurting my neck.

I remained there calmly. The grey-haired security policeman had his arms firmly around me. I did not try to struggle. I thought, Well, you've got me. I tried to communicate my resignation to him so that he wouldn't start bashing me up. The other chap came across the road towards us.

The one who was holding me got up and took me firmly and roughly by the elbow. The other one did the same on my other side. They gripped me, handling me as I had on occasion seen the police handle Africans who had been picked up on the streets for pass offences. Neither of them had said a single word. Neither had I.

They took me back across the road, up along the pavement down which I had come. Some of the people on the pavement looked at me. Most didn't. I wondered why. It must have been rather a strange sight in Hillbrow to see a young white woman being gripped firmly at each elbow by two men. Maybe, I thought, they think I am ill or maybe they think I'm a political who has been caught painting slogans or something, and they don't want to take too much notice because they prefer not to think about it. That young people were involved in sabotage and in left politics, they well knew, for it was all over the newspapers at that time. More likely, they thought I was a shoplifter.

I moved my feet up the pavement. Passive. I saw a young woman coming towards me with my red shirt. She looked at me sympathetically, ignoring the two men. She handed it to me, not to them. I took it without a word. Prisoners don't talk to members of the public.

We went up along the pavement, through the crowds. There was a feeling of chill in me. In the back of my mind I wondered what they would do to me. I could not face that thought fully. We turned left at the corner and up along the pavement, passed the shop window I had noticed on my way down. I felt numbed, hardly knew where I was going. My neck was hurting. And my head felt peculiar. I realised I had almost knocked myself out on the bonnet of that car. I probably had for a few moments.

The two men steered me to the right side of the pavement, towards their car. It was further up the street from where I had got out. I found out later that the driver had got caught in the traffic, and had moved the car a bit while the other one jumped out. That was why he had come onto the scene of my capture somewhat delayed.

One of them opened the back door for me and shoved me in, shutting the door firmly behind me. The grey-haired one went round the back of the car to the other back door and climbed in beside me. He gripped my arm, hurting me, and swore at me – 'You bitch!' together with some other choice Afrikaans swear words. I said nothing. I felt he was trying to get me to say something, to commit myself. I must be careful. There would probably be some sort of case, and they could use anything I said against me. I turned firmly from him and stared ahead. My right arm was aching from his grip.

The driver drove up towards the Fort. The door was opened. I got out, and went up the steps towards the large wooden door of the Fort, with the large black bolts and black hinges, and the little window on the right that was lifted when somebody knocked or rang the bell. The African wardress on duty on the other side of the door was talking to a man through the 'window'. She must have seen us because I heard the key turning in the lock. The door opened and I walked into the front near the Lieutenant's office.

Black prisoners in red headscarves, brown overalls and bare feet were to be found there – they were the trusties, the prisoners who worked in the 'Front', doing various things for the Lieutenant. And there was a short line of prisoners in private clothes, barefoot, with their shoes lying on the floor in front of them, hands behind their backs. They were waiting to be booked in. There was that peculiar prison hush. Figures, like ghosts, moving silently on bare feet. The only loud, precise sound was the Lieutenant's military tones emanating from her office to the right. Everything else was cushioned. Dream-like. Apart from life.

It was this atmosphere at the front of the Fort that filled me with horror. There was a different atmosphere in our cell section. I had relived the experience every time we returned from the magistrate's court. As we stood in a line in that passage between two huge doors and on the opposite side of the passage from the Lieutenant's office, I used to get a sinking feeling, a kind of mixture of depression and anxiety, in the pit of my stomach.

One of the Branch men told me roughly, almost viciously, to stand outside the Lieutenant's office. I stood there, next to the other prisoners, feet apart, hands behind my back, but, as a white prisoner, with my shoes still on. I watched the Branch men go into the Lieutenant's office. One of them said something to her. She did not change her expression, except for a subtle hardening of the military look on her face. She did not look towards me. The Branch left her office and walked down the short passage to the door, heads down. They did not look at me.

The Lieutenant called for Matron Huiseman, her second-in-command. 'Yes, Lieutenant.' Matron Huiseman appeared from the Record Office, which was on the same small passage, and walked to the door of the Lieutenant's office. She saluted smartly and went into the room. The Lieutenant said something quietly to her. Matron Huiseman saluted once more and came out into the passage. Without looking at me, she said, 'Kom, Neame.'

I had seen them treating prisoners like this before. They were firm, almost brutal in their matter-of-factness. What they were attempting to convey was that the state was somehow an impartial instance and prison officers were simply acting as its instrument. What they did, how they acted, seemed to have a kind of inevitability about it. The Lieutenant had apparently attempted to polish this tone in her prison to perfection. At least she had succeeded at the Front. And she was proud of it. In her immediate vicinity there was no space for individuality.

The African wardress opened the grille at the end of the passage, the grille between 'the Front' and the rest of the gaol where the cells were. The Front at the Fort was the administrative section, where only the 'trusties' could spend their day. The rest of us were in the prison proper. Matron Huiseman and I passed through. The wardress locked the grille behind us. I followed the matron to the right along a path, to a red step. We went through a wooden door. This was usually locked too.

ABOVE: *Image from the Fort, just outside our cell where we were awaiting trial.*

To the right, across a bit of grass and a small concrete veranda was our cell where my comrades were. But Matron Huiseman did not take me in that direction. She turned left up a gravel path between the square of grass in front of our cell and the surgery on the right and the red brick wall of the 'hospital' section on the left (for black prisoners – mainly pregnancies and TB). A bit further we went up and round behind the single-cell section to the right. We came to the end of the single-cell section. Turned right again. Then sharp right again onto the concrete veranda in front of the single-cell section. So I was going to be separated from the others. I was to go into a single cell.

Matron Huiseman called a prisoner and told her to remove the bed from one of the single cells. Two prisoners took the bedclothes off the bed, exposing the grimy, uneven mattress. They took the bedclothes to another single cell. Then they folded up the black metal bed and carried it out onto the veranda. They left the mattress on the floor.

'Teresa!' Matron Huiseman called. Teresa was the trusty who worked in the surgery with Mrs Lubbe. Teresa came, and Matron Huiseman said something to her which I did not hear.

'Go into that cell, Neame,' Matron Huiseman ordered me quietly, indicating the cell with the mattress on the floor. Teresa returned with my bedclothes and my pyjamas from our communal cell on the other side.

'Take your clothes off, Neame,' Matron Huiseman said shortly, not looking at me.

I undressed, handing each article to Matron Huiseman. She looked at everything, shook it, put her hands up the sleeves of my jersey and looked inside my shoes.

'Put your pyjamas on ... Only the top ... Give me the trousers.'

So, I thought, they're only going to leave me with my pyjama top. It was short and came just below my navel.

'Right, Neame, give me all your clothes.' I handed them over to her. She backed out of my cell, and stood on the veranda, just outside my door. 'Stand to attention, Neame.' I stood next to the mattress, feet apart, hands behind my back, my bare feet cold on the concrete. I was conscious of my pyjama top coming just below my navel. I must look ridiculous, I thought. It would be better to have nothing on at all.

I was cold, and shaking a bit, partly, I suppose, from the strain of the previous hours and also the three injections I'd had at the dentist's. My head and neck were aching and I still felt a bit stunned. My mouth was dry and my chin and lips began to tremble, apart from anything else because I wanted to cry.

Matron Huiseman was clearly enjoying my discomfort, standing there to attention, with my pyjama top just below my navel. 'Jump, Neame!'

'What is that, Matron?' I asked. I was so taken by surprise that I couldn't hear clearly. I struggled to hear what she said. Yes, she did say 'jump'. But how did she mean? How must I jump? Why must I jump?

'Jump for me, Neame, with your legs apart.'

Oh, that was it. She wanted me to 'tausa', as it was called in prison jargon. I jumped. Crouched on the concrete, she looked attentively in the direction of my private parts. That done, she turned without a word, stepped out onto the red-floored passage in front of the cells of the single-cell section and shut the door of my cell. I heard the key turn in the lock. The grille went 'gung'. Again the noise of a key turning.

I stood staring at the closed grey door. I was freezing. I made up my bed and climbed in. They had put in some food for me and some coffee, which was cold. I couldn't face the food. It was pretty revolting at the best of times and cold it was utterly repulsive. I drank the cold coffee, not that it tasted or smelled like coffee but they told us that that was what it was. I had nothing to read so I just lay on my back staring at the cream-coloured ceiling, probably metal for I could see nuts and bolts in it.

There was a large gap under the door and an icy draught came from there, increasing the pain in my head and neck. I had such a headache I felt as though I were going to vomit. Apart from my fall onto the bonnet of the car, my headache probably came from the typical concrete chill I had experienced in winter in other cells – Marshall Square, for instance, or the cell in the Bloemfontein police station – at zero temperatures. The cold from concrete causes a very particular sensation in the head. Even very cold weather with ice and snow in the absence of the concrete does not lead to this sensation. I found it painful to move my eyes for there was a chill pain somewhere behind them.

My body began to ache. I had to lie in a curled-up position to try and keep warm but this meant that the thigh I was lying on was pressed hard against the mattress and thus was pressed closer to the concrete, and it began to ache horribly. So I had to turn, and curl up on my other side. The same process would begin on that side and so I had constantly to shift my position; and each time I moved I felt colder than ever. It would have been worse on the conrete floor, of course, had I only had a felt mat, as had been the case in the Bloemfontein police station. Yet it was almost as bad with the draught coming from under the door into my narrow cell.

The trouble with many of the mattresses at the Fort was that every so often the coir was taken out of them to wash, and then was put back again. And the coir was often packed back in very loosely and thinly. Sometimes a part of it was so revolting that it had to be thrown away, and this made the mattress that much thinner. Sometimes we found dead rats and mice in the coir.

I was fairly used to this sort of life on concrete and so it didn't worry me particularly, except that I thought it would have been quite nice to be with the others across on the other side of the wall. I wondered whether they knew what had happened. I did not really regret having tried to get away. I had tried and been caught and that was that. And here I was lying in a single cell, closer to the concrete floor than usual. Yet it wasn't as bad as I had thought it might be. It wasn't the unknown. I just wondered what the authorities would do with me. I was used to that kind of question too.

During the night I had my first experience with the rodents which we had heard infested the other side of the gaol. I never actually saw one. They came through the ample gap under the door of my single cell or through my open window. When I first heard my metal cup and tin plate clinking I was just coming out of a doze; I wondered what it was but simply turned over onto my other side, with my back to the sound of activity. I must have slept for a half hour or so when I was woken by something running over my face. It still did not strike me that it was a rodent. While I was serving my two-month sentence for escape – at this time I had a bed – I would wake up to hear similar sounds from the top of my little locker where I had my mug, and sometimes there was again something running over my face.

That first night in my single cell after the attempted escape I must have slept, all in all, about an hour. After some days (or was it weeks?) I was tried in the magistrate's court. George Bizos was the lawyer defending me. At some stage during the short trial I burst into tears. I was tired. It had been a long road. I was found guilty of attempted escape and served two months as a hard-labour prisoner. As I remember, it was by and large uneventful except for the mice that ran over my face at night. And Aucamp did come on a visit. All I can remember is the cold hatred in his eyes.

The festive season, 1966

MY THIRD CHRISTMAS IN Barberton Prison came along. We hoped very much that we would have our second chance of 'contact' with the other prisoners. If only we could manage to go through again to the other side to hear them sing, as we'd done the year before. Our excitement at this prospect rose as Christmas drew near.

We feared, though, that Matron Bester may have become aware of what had happened the previous year. Perhaps a prisoner had said something. At some stage in the course of the year, I, myself, in arguing some point for the improvement of our conditions, had made the slip of mentioning that there were some 200 black women in the gaol and had also mentioned something about the size of their courtyard. Matron Bester had taken the pout off her face for a moment and thrown the question at me: 'And how do you know how many *bandiete* there are in this gaol? And how do you know about the courtyard?'

Realising my mistake, I was thinking about a reply when Matron Bester had swung round to Matron Taljaard, who was standing beside her. 'En hoe weet Neame hierdie?' How does Neame know this? And Matron Taljaard had said from her pink and white smug face, 'Ek weet nie, Matrone. Ek weet nie.'

I used that interval to consider what I should say. 'It is usual for there to be about 200 black women prisoners in each prison, Matron. There were about 200 at the Fort. And this prison is built just like the one at Nylstroom and Doyle has described that prison to us.' Matron Bester's suspicious face relaxed a little. Remembering, she commented, 'O ja, Doyle.'

I had managed to manoeuvre myself out of that tight corner but another prisoner might easily have made a similar slip. And, of course,

The festive season, 1966

there were always 'naaks', prisoners who gave information to the authorities to their own advantage. At any rate, we suspected that this year we might not be as lucky as we had been the previous year.

Early Christmas Day came again but there was no singing this time, except for a little which started and which was then shouted down by a wardress somewhere along a passage. We were surprised. Evidently their attitude to the singing had changed. The previous year it seemed to have been regarded as an accepted 'privilege' at Christmas-time. The gaol was altogether much quieter this time. Possibly this might have been because Matron Bester was on duty. We were to find that there was also little singing at New Year, similarly at Easter.

It did seem that most of the best singers amongst them had gone out on the amnesty. Indeed, we found that the hymn singing in the morning was of a poor quality. However, Spokie was still there. We could not understand her silence. We thought that either they had been ordered not to sing, and it did seem from the shouts of the wardress that it was being discouraged; or maybe Spokie did not enjoy singing without other good singers with her (though this seemed unlikely); or, we thought, maybe Spokie was again in one of her spells in isolation, without sufficient food and feeling weak and worn out with her ulcer.

It appears that the authorities had decided that their bringing together of the black prisoners with us white political prisoners (and this had included Brigadier Pretorius bringing through black prisoners to sing for us in our section the previous New Year) had involved a dangerous softening up on their part. Moreover, it is not at all unlikely that the Front had been warned, even by Aucamp, that singing could be used to communicate political messages.

Christmas Day 1966 passed quietly. In the evening Leslie, Ann and I – at that time Ann had still been with us in the front big cell – decided that we must attempt some contact with the other prisoners so we climbed up on the little red windowsill beneath the window that overlooked the passage. We sang various freedom songs, 'Shosholoza', 'Mandela o'yeza', 'Vukani Nonke' and 'Kim bumby m'Lord, kim bumby' which we used to hear the other women singing occasionally in the morning, as a hymn. We also sang 'Where Have All the Flowers Gone?'

We had sung the latter, as well as 'Shosholoza', a great deal when we were in the cell underneath the magistrate's court in Johannesburg so that all the other prisoners could hear, including the ARM prisoners, who often passed by as they were taken to their separate cell underneath the court. We also sang these songs in the cramped compartment at the front of the prison van as we were driven back to the Fort. This Christmas evening we, sang, too, 'We Shall Overcome'. We did not get a response from the other prisoners. We did not know why. And so Christmas evening and night went by uneventfully.

Between Christmas and New Year we discussed amongst ourselves methods of contact with the other prisoners over this 'festive season' and one of us – I think it was Ann – came up with the really good suggestion that we should paint messages with ink on toilet rolls and then during the day throw them over the courtyard wall that separated us from the courtyard of the other prisoners. We decided not to write any political messages but to stick to Christmas and New Year greetings so that the authorities would find it more difficult to take steps against us. We painted several toilet rolls with different messages, such as 'Happy Christmas', 'Go Well in the New Year', 'Hope you will be out of gaol in the New Year', 'Best Wishes', and others of the same sort.

On the afternoon of New Year's Day, while the wardress was elsewhere in our section, we walked nonchalantly up to the back wall of our courtyard and flung the toilet rolls over the top. We had attached different coloured streamers through the centre of each roll. These gave them a lift and the rolls flew over the wall looking rather like decorative kites, with the streamers flowing behind them in the air against the blue sky. They dropped out of sight somewhere on the other side.

We were never able to find out whether the other prisoners had managed to read any of the messages or whether they had even seen the rolls flying through the air from our side of the prison to theirs, and thus realise that we were trying to communicate with them.

Matron Taljaard appeared in our section about fifteen minutes later with the kind of look on her face that we knew too well might mean possible trouble for us. We had envisaged that our little escapade might mean our being locked up in solitary 'with meals' for a few days, but we

The festive season, 1966

had thought it worth it. Matron Taljaard, with an important but slightly embarrassed look on her face, asked who had thrown the rolls. We either did not reply or told her that we had all participated. I cannot remember exactly. And she withdrew.

The authorities had obviously had a look at the messages and, finding that they were not political, had decided to take no action. They may even have felt that the throwing of the rolls with goodwill messages at the festive season was a sharp reminder of the tremendous isolation in which we lived. Possibly, too, they had felt that by our action we had paid tribute to a Christian festivity so they could hardly complain. About the only thing they might have done was ask us to pay for the toilet rolls we had used. They did not even do that.

Gate-fever

FLO AND I WERE DUE TO GO out in a matter of months and so we were particularly conscious of the possible disastrous effects of the isolation on us. We asked ourselves how we might respond to the outside world. We requested the authorities to move us somewhere less isolated as a prelude to our release so that we could recuperate to some extent. And we approached the doctor. He indicated, with something like fear in his eyes, yet allowed himself a little sneer about the authorities, that he could do nothing with 'them'. At some stage we had begun to refer to him as 'Luke'. Perhaps he was not so bad, only intimidated.

What is striking in retrospect is that we women political prisoners in Barberton had been able to obtain tranquillisers from the doctor, more or less as much as we wanted. (I don't think this was from the start; it must have begun at a later stage but exactly when I cannot remember.) One wonders whether this was allowed by the authorities, although it must have been since they were paying our medical expenses. At any rate, it appears to have been an admission that our conditions in Barberton Prison were intolerable. It cannot be excluded that the doctor, himself, had made this point to them and warned that, if he were not allowed to prescribe tranquillisers, he would not be able to take responsibility for our health.

At the same time, the point should be made that, with perhaps one exception, we were very careful to ensure that we did not become dependent on drugs. I myself, except for the bad patch I had had, only took a tranquilliser now and again in order especially to get a good sleep. That appeared to be the general approach amongst us. Most of us, I think, had come to the conclusion that we should live our lives there in a self-conscious way. Finally I think we managed very well.

Gate-fever

Off and on, we felt anxious about the possibility that we would not be able to cope with the outside world. I went on a conscious programme of attempting to broaden the framework of my life there. I had been doing this, of course, right back to at least the beginning of 1966. It was now the beginning of 1967. I had done some of this for myself individually, collecting experiences, perceptions from my immediate environment, enriching my intellectual life, filling out my world view. I had, in addition, made a contribution to our activities as a group. These activities had started with our Bible study class. Then had followed our poetry and art classes, our newspaper, later our music sessions, and even our birdwatching. And finally there was the discussion of problems that arose amongst ourselves.

Our classes were not just important in themselves, that is, as a contribution to our further education, they went much further than this. Every poem was an experience, in fact, a whole complex of experiences. Prufrock in Eliot's poem was a real personality to me, and the rhythm of the words with which the poet described him became a rhythm in my mind. The humour and the suffering of Stravinsky's Petrushka, the clown, belonged to me. And so on.

There were the sounds and smells from within the gaol, even the smell of Brigadier Viljoen's tobacco, the sounds that came on occasion from the side of the gaol where our black fellow prisoners were housed, and the sense of companionship we felt with the various animals that came from time to time into our section. I have described all this, and more.

As the time came closer to my going out, I attempted to add as many impressions as I could from what we could see from our windows.

All these experiences and impressions were, in a way – I am not sure whether this is the right way to describe it – rather intellectual, rational, very neat and clear and precise in my mind. No doubt because I had so few of them to deal with, my conscious mind could be fully aware of everything I was experiencing. I would give them my full attention. In a way, I suppose it was very mental, as though I had become nothing but mind ... and eyes.

Yet, if there was a downside, I think my naturally active mind, my inclination to observe, if in Barberton Prison it was in a kind of disembodied manner, to investigate all things around me as well as to extract knowledge from the most searing experience enabled me to come through my incarceration with some degree 'of sound mind', as it is sometimes formulated. Despite all, I had retained a sense of myself. Indeed had I not, at least in part, actually sharpened that sense as also my capacity for observation, my capacity to focus?

Flo and I asked ourselves whether it would be possible to bridge the gap between the inside and the outside. Was there a link between the two worlds? How can I make that leap, that leap from one universe to another? A voice said: There is nothing to be frightened of. It is so simple. That was the physical side, however. The mental aspect was quite different. That would be like breaking the sound barrier. Would it not?

The prisoner is, by force, confined to a small space, whether that be larger or smaller. It is perhaps one of the crudest types of force that can be used. And what seems strange and almost incredible is that this force is used as the result of a bureaucratic stroke of a pen. It might be human beings, in the form of wardresses and warders, who lock and unlock doors and grilles, but it is the state, that anonymous entity, which gives them the power to do so.

Matron Bester and Brigadier Pretorius and perhaps more so the Lieutenant at the Fort behaved as though they were the incarnation of an institution, the state, and, in part, of course they were. We were 'security prisoners', we were told, which appeared to mean that we were essentially enemies of the state. Once one of us in our section dropped a knife and it broke on the concrete floor and the wardress had screamed, 'Weet jy, dis die goewerment se goed!' ('Do you know that's the property of the government!') She seemed to be suggesting that it was close to an act of sabotage. What else, she evidently thought, could be expected from convicted communists?

The prison board on another visit

THE PRISON BOARD CAME once again, this time with its male member. It was during March, I think, some weeks before Flo and I were due to go out. The same method of separating those who had already gone to the Front from the rest was used. This time, however, we had on fairly new uniforms which had arrived at the prison shortly after the board's previous visit.

I went through to the same room as the board had been in on the previous occasion. Its male member, in khaki uniform, sat at one end of the table that had been placed in the room for the occasion. He had on large dark glasses, which he never once removed during the whole interview. I believe he kept them on during the interviews with the others as well.

I looked at him after I had entered, expecting him to remove his glasses and greet me with a 'Good afternoon' or even just a polite nod. He did neither and I sensed some hostility in his attitude towards me.

As I had received no greeting from him, I turned to the two ladies – who were once again sporting large and hideous hats. They, however, were busy discussing, in Afrikaans, some reports they had in front of them. I cannot remember which wardress was escorting me. Whoever it was, she did not say 'This is Neame' or anything of that sort. I had noticed that there was a chair on my side of the table but nobody indicated that I should sit down. I said 'Good afternoon' in an attempt at some contact with those present but received no answer. One of the behatted ladies merely addressed some comment in Afrikaans to the male member of the board, whom she addressed as 'Kolonel'.

I stood, with hands behind my back, waiting for something to happen. At least I thought it would have been proper for my presence to have been acknowledged in some way. I wondered whether I should take a seat of my own accord and decided against it. They would probably think I was being impertinent.

The colonel seemed to turn towards me – I was not really sure as I could not see his eyes behind the dark glasses. I wondered why his face was so red. Too much sun? Drink? Irritation? High blood pressure? He said, with a touch of impatience, more like a command than a polite invitation: 'Sit down.' I decided that he was, without doubt, being rude and hostile, although controlled. I was genuinely surprised. What had I done to deserve this treatment? This was more like the Aucamp-Brigadier Pretorius treatment than that of the Prison Board.

I took the seat on my side of the table and drew it a little closer to the side where the colonel was sitting as he appeared to be in control of the proceedings. He had a pile of files on the table in front of him. He took one, holding the brown cover between his thumb and index finger. I tried to see what was written there. I supposed there were symbols for my behaviour and various activities.

'You are going out soon,' he commented, 'so I do not think there is much for us to say, except to hope that you have learned something in prison …' He stopped. His tone was a mixture of hostility and indifference. He made it quite clear that he wanted to cut the whole business short. No doubt he has been told how long it took last time, I thought. And what a lot of complaints we had and requests for improvements.

'As you are going out so soon, you won't have any complaints?' he noted, in a mixture of an observation and a query. 'The best thing is just to accept your sentence as part of your past – I am sure it was not a pleasant experience – and put it behind you. All the Prisons hope is that you will not be back again … Well, well, I think that is all we have to say.'

I was trying to choose the right moment to produce my little green notebook. I did not want to appear rude or as deliberately attempting to go against his wishes. An unsympathetic audience in prison (maybe anywhere, but I particularly noticed this in prison, perhaps because there the audience was usually particularly unsympathetic), I found, was very difficult to deal with. One had to try hard to get a reasonable tone into one's voice. A natural response was for one's voice to rise somewhat and perhaps to be too emphatic. Having learned extraordinary discipline, I waited for him to give me some opening so that it would not appear that I was barging in.

The colonel was closing my file and making as if to put it aside, and getting another ready. I realised that he was determined to give me no opening whatsoever. I would simply have to go ahead.

'No ...' I said, hesitating (should I have used that word, as though I were giving him an instruction?). I was also not sure whether I should call him 'Colonel' as he had not been introduced to me and maybe he wasn't a colonel at all. How was I to know? So I left out the colonel and said, 'There *are* some things I would like to raise.'

I hesitated again, fumbling. I took a quick look down my list, wondering which would be the best to start with. The list was rather long. I found myself already mentally cutting out some of the points, deciding to raise just a few of them. I thought it a good idea to take up the issue of my release since he had mentioned that. Maybe I would raise only that and leave everything else out. Anyway, I would see how it went.

These thoughts flitted fragmentarily through my mind as I hesitated, trying to find a tone and a subject best suited to the situation. I had a strong desire just to give up, leave, escape the situation. At the same time, I thought: I must raise some of these. It is in the interests of those of us who remain behind that we should have some improvements. Moreover, political prisoners putting up a fight could be good for all of them. And did we not have a message about prison conditions in general?

Prison was so generally unpleasant and the authorities spoke so often with a disapproving, even threatening manner that there was always a strong desire simply not to raise anything at all. Of course, prison officials knew this and the unpleasantness was deliberate. Many a prisoner, more specifically in the case of female prisoners, felt it was better perhaps simply to simper like a half-child and raise nothing.

An important reason why it had always been necessary to resist such a response was that the authorities wanted to break us because, amongst other things, there was the constant desire of the Security Branch for more information and for state witnesses. The designation 'security prisoners' fitted nicely into the latter framework. So the visits of Captain Broodryk.

I decided to start with at least one of my 'complaints'. At the same time, I hesitated to start because I did not know what to call him, and I could not bear speaking to somebody without addressing the person by name. It was ingrained in me since my childhood. 'I am afraid I do not know who you are …?' I began. I looked at him, hoping he would understand that it was a matter of manners.

'What was that?' he asked abruptly.

'I do not know your name,' I said, 'nor the name of these ladies. Do you not think it possible to introduce yourselves? I find it difficult to address you if I do not know your names.'

Despite the dark glasses, I could sense his hostility and suspicion. 'Why do you want to know our names?' he demanded. He had obviously concluded that I wanted to know their names so that I could use such information in the future; the Harold Strachan case and other cases were probably going through his head and he was very aware, I now understood, that I was to be in the outside world very soon.

'Because it makes it easier for me to address you,' I explained. 'Surely it is not unreasonable for me to ask for an introduction?'

'No!' he said loudly and abruptly. 'We will *not* tell you our names. It is not necessary for you to know who we are. You know that we are the Prison Board. That is enough.'

'Very well,' I said quietly. I thought that I had better get started. 'You know that I am due to go out soon so I would like to speak to you about the conditions under which I am living here. I have raised this matter several times with various officials but nothing has been done about it. I would like to know if you can help. I believe that, according to the regulations, you are, that is the Prison Board is, responsible for the conditions under which a prisoner is held.'

I looked up at him for confirmation of this since we had been told so many contradictory stories about our position, but he made no attempt to either confirm or deny their responsibility in this connection. So I continued: 'I want to say that the whole manner in which I have been held here has been breaking me down. We have been living in enormous isolation, in a very confined space. I do not see how any human being could come through such an experience without it having disastrous effects on their mental and psychological health. We have been told that the aim of the Prisons Department is to rehabilitate us, whereas all I have seen is that they have been breaking us down.'

One of the plump ladies interrupted: 'But they have been trying to rehabilitate you. The aim of the department is that you should never again repeat the crime for which you were convicted.'

I said, 'We are given worse conditions here than for any other prisoner. We have been deliberately isolated from other prisoners. It is normal to have a larger area to live in. Usually we are not even allowed to come down the passage to this office from that grille down there' – and I indicated the grille to our section. 'As political prisoners, we are not even given remission or parole, as are ordinary prisoners.'

'You must remember that you have been convicted of a very serious crime,' one of the fat ladies intervened. 'You seem to forget that. And we cannot ensure that you do not go out and commit the same offence again.'

'That is the same with all prisoners,' I responded.

The colonel, clearly irritated by the interchange, indicated that the discussion should come to a close. 'What is it you want to raise?' he asked.

'I want to ask you to take steps to see that I am held for a time in such conditions that I will be able to recuperate somewhat before my release. For instance, I would suggest that I am moved for my last few weeks to another prison, where the inmates are not so isolated and where conditions are better.'

The colonel gave a little impatient shrug. 'What else?'

I went on to raise other issues, including how we were treated in public, but I decided to cut short what I had planned to say. The atmosphere was forbidding, not quite what I had expected from the board, which usually handled matters rather differently from the prison authorities and, indeed, Aucamp. I stood up, withdrawing rather hurriedly from the hostility exuding from the colonel. I backed out of the room with my hands behind my back. 'Thank you.' I nodded politely and formally to the colonel and then to the two plump ladies. Out in the passage, I breathed a sigh of relief and hurried towards our entrance grille, with the wardress close on my heels. There was another wardress guarding the grille.

'Volgende een! Duncan, jy's die volgende.' Duncan, you're next.

I was locked up in a cell so that I could have no contact with those of us who had not yet been through to the Front. I saw Flo moving fast across the portaal and disappear from sight. I wondered what her reception would be like. We were, of course, due to be released at the same time.

Flo had a more interesting time with the board than I had had. She told us that one of its members, evidently in a friendly fashion, had asked her how she had enjoyed her sentence. Flo had then let fly about how we had been treated when we first came to Barberton. She noted that instructions had obviously been given for us to be treated in a particular manner. She did not know whether these instructions had come from the board. She said that she knew from the prison regulations that it was the Prison Board that was supposed to be responsible for our conditions and method of treatment, and for the type of work we did. Flo warned them: 'I shall never forget how I was treated when I first came here. *You must remember that I have a memory!*'

Evidently, they were so impressed by her strong feelings and obvious sincerity and probably also because she had a good record that they had asked her for details of her treatment. And so she told them everything. She told them how we were not allowed to speak to each other for months, whether during work, at meals, or after lock-up at night. She told them how they had been refused all exercise and that, when they had demanded exercise, they had been given fifteen minutes a week, on a Sunday.

She told them how we had been constantly screamed at, how we had spent long hours locked up in our cells, how we had been made to do the laundry for long hours, the constant inconsistency of behaviour and instructions, the continual rudeness. She said that there seemed to be a pattern here, for we had heard that other political prisoners had received similar treatment. She told them that, when she had raised the matter with Colonel Aucamp, he had said that we were being treated in this manner on his instructions.

The board seemed utterly shocked by the treatment Flo described.

The prison board on another visit

One of the women turned to Wardress Taljaard and asked whether it was true. Taljaard had responded that she had actually been present when Colonel Aucamp had said this to Flo.

Flo noted that even if our conditions had improved – though there was still much to be desired – the way we had been treated at the beginning was part of her experience and had left a permanent mark on her. She would not forget it, she said. The board denied having given any such instructions. This was the first time they had heard of it, they maintained.

The prospect of release

EVEN THOUGH OUR CONDITIONS had improved, the pressures to try and break us were still there. Every now and again the screws were turned on. The attempts to confuse us also continued. Brigadier Pretorius, as I have noted, had suggested to Esther that he had a 'date', and that date, he had told her, was to be 'April 67'. It was precisely the same date that Matron Bester had suggested earlier.

The pressures on us to give information remained too. The access of the Security Police to already convicted prisoners was, of course, a very frightening aspect. It had been used, and that not without success, in connection with my Humansdorp trial in order to obtain witnesses for the state. Convicted prisoners were especially susceptible to pressures to give the kind of evidence that would be satisfactory to the police.

Captain Broodryk, the investigating officer in our Johannesburg trial, arrived again at Barberton about a month or two before Flo and I were due for release. He was there just to check up 'whether we had not changed our minds', an invitation, of course, to offer the Branch information in order to be able to bring cases against other persons. He also wanted to know where we were going to stay on our release.

One of the things he said to me on this visit, and he said it with a certain pride, as though it was their own achievement, was: 'You have changed, Sylvia.' And, perhaps ironically, I knew what he meant. He was referring to the tremendous discipline I had managed to develop, the care with which I tried to assess difficult situations, and the, not unrelated, ability to seek compromises.

There were other aspects of which I only became really aware very much later, aspects related to the whole character of my thinking, my mental processes and my response to sensory experiences. These were undoubtedly a reflection of earlier tendencies in my character but I think my years in prison brought them to the fore. This was not the achievement of the prison authorities, if one can designate it an achievement at all. It had to do with *how* I had dealt with that situation.

Our release was coming ever nearer. Almost everything Flo and I said was prefaced by our saying, 'When we go out ...' At the same time, we both made an effort to act as calmly as we could so as not to upset the others. It was, in fact, a really trying time.

Although I referred to the prospect of my release in conversation, in letters, in my diary, it was most of the time a word without real content for it was not possible to conceive of it in any meaningful terms. Here on this side of the bars in my cell was my life, or my existence, or whatever the most suitable word was. It was an environment that had become intensely mine, even more so than other environments because I had struggled with it, tried to mould it so that it was bearable, so that I and my comrades could survive.

Here were my fellow prisoners. Not all of them would necessarily have been close friends of mine outside. Indeed, in some ways, although this is an over-simplification, we had been thrown together by fate. I had only come to know even the members of my Communist Party cell not much more than a year before our arrest in July 1964. Since then we had developed bonds of struggle and common suffering.

Crucial was, I'm sure, that I had managed to assume in Barberton Prison a meaningful social role. Suddenly I was to be deprived of it. Not long before my release, as I felt the eyes of the others on me, I had a sudden sense that I was like a doll from which the stuffing had been removed. I was empty, exposed, unsure of myself as well as guilty because I was simply going and leaving them behind. Was going out, leaving them behind, not actually immoral?

I remember sitting in my cell a few weeks before I was due to go out. This was the front big cell overlooking the sisal lands, and I thought: I am sitting here in this cell. There are the cages on the windows. There are the bars. Here is the sanitary bucket. There is the grille. One day within a few weeks I will be out of here. This will no longer be my cell, my sanitary bucket, my blue uniform, my army shoes. I will no longer see these cages and the bars. I will no longer hear the stuttering of guinea fowl down on the gravel above the sisal lands. I will no longer hear the squeak of the frog's feet on the linoleum. There will no longer be that grille, the shiny concrete of the portaal, the voices of wardresses shouting at the other end of the gaol, the voice of one of us throwing a joke across the portaal at night … Yet one day I will remember this moment when I am outside. I will remember sitting here. I shall then be on the outside, looking at the inside and that is likely to be as unreal as looking in the other direction.

Sitting there, I remembered a conversation Jean had had with one of the doctors at the Fort. We were just due to be sentenced in our Johannesburg trial and Jean and the doctor had been discussing this prospect. He, evidently trying to salve his conscience because in some way he had felt partly responsible for what was happening to us, had told her that prison was not such a bad place, that many prisoners did not want to leave when their time was up. Jean had responded that, if they felt like that, they must be sick and that it was, no doubt, prison that had made them sick.

I myself had come to realise that imprisonment was a very effective technique of breaking down the human being. In a way it actually served as a method of severely weakening the ability of 'the convict' to survive in the outside world. The world is a highly complex place. It makes enormous demands on our sensory perceptions and ability to make decisions and it is precisely these which suffer behind walls, more so when the space is so small and isolated as ours was.

One of the points, often made by released prisoners, is that, once out, they found they couldn't cross roads or drive cars. Their eyes and brain functions had adjusted to the space in which they had served their

---

ABOVE: *Embroidered bookmark, a present from Leslie.*

sentences. Such symptoms were only the most obvious ones. We were told by a prison official at some stage that, beyond eighteen months, there were long-term personality changes in a prisoner. I could imagine how our brain functions had been influenced by our incarceration.

The fact that we constituted a very small group and one which was in a prison of some geographical isolation, in particular in terms of its distance from the big urban centres of the country, had assisted the authorities in constructing a very effective psychological hell. It is true that they had been able to mould this hell from the main structural elements that go to make up a prison. At the same time, their experience of how detainees reacted to the conditions of solitary confinement under the detention laws certainly fed into the kind of strategies they adopted in relation to us.

I had a mass of conflicted feelings about going out. I suffered from 'gate-fever', a 'normal' response of at least a long-term prisoner, facing the prospect of release. But 'gate-fever' or not, I was simply desperate to get out, away from between those walls that bore down on me. And no consideration for the others could halt this drive.

Sitting there in my cell, I imagined Matron Bester coming and opening the grille and saying, 'Neame, you can go now, if you like, or you can stay if you like.' And I felt myself pushing rudely past her at tremendous speed, through the grille that separated our portaal from the passage, down the passage as fast as I could, through the grille at the bottom of the corridor, past the other side of the visitors' grille, through the wooden door and the grille at the front of the prison and out onto the steps—

My vision of release stopped there, at the top of the steps, at the verge of the outside world.

What lay on the other side of that last grille had little meaning for me. Of course I made reference to my release in letters and during visits. However, this was, more or less, a purely mental consideration. Though I had plans for my life once outside, these were rather like architectural plans or a kind of scaffolding for a projected building. It was a structural conception with no real content. At its best it was like a small landscape hanging on a wall, a landscape over the details of which my eyes had wandered so often or like the details of a Beethoven piano sonata to which I have listened many a time. It was a sensory experience, eyes and ears, little more.

The prisoner's problem of space and location

ONE OF THE KEY PROBLEMS for a prisoner because one's location is so dependent on the decisions of other people turns on the need to find out about the space one is in or to envisage in some detail the space to which one is being taken. My history of having been moved by the apartheid authorities on several occasions without knowing my destination and the specific space to which I was being taken seems to have put an indelible mark on my psychology, amongst other things on my method of thinking about destinations.

The deliberate policy, pursued by the authorities, of leaving one in the dark, a policy carried out under the aegis of Colonel Aucamp, certainly aimed to make the prisoner feel extremely anxious, though no doubt they would have hypocritically justified their policy purely in terms of security needs. On the other hand, the response of the prisoner, I believe, has a lot to do with the acute sense of space which arises out of the innate drive to survive, characterising members of the animal world to which the human being belongs.

I remember how I had felt on the way down from Johannesburg to Port Elizabeth after the end of the Communist Party trial. I was cramped alone in the small front compartment of a large prison van. At this stage I did not even have the information that I was to face a second trial (my Humansdorp trial). When I was collected at the Fort, a few days after our sentencing, I had no idea where they were taking me or what for.

In the back of the prison van were white male prisoners, separated from me by a metal divide. Soon I was to find my feet in a puddle of liquid which, after a time, I guessed must be urine, its source at the back of the van. I spoke to the men through the metal partition about my problem and they pushed a large handkerchief through the crevice at floor level so that I could mop up at least some of the liquid. It seemed they had no sanitary bucket or perhaps only one.

On the way in a southerly direction, I was deposited in the Free State province at the Kroonstad Prison. I was to become acquainted once again with Kroonstad on my way back, this time in a northerly direction. I spent the night in that gaol; the men from the back of the van were apparently to be left there.

I discovered that we were to pick up a group of ANC women. We left Kroonstad at three in the morning, and I knew that we must stop at some prison for the coming night. I had still not been told where I was being taken or for what reason, but I believed I had heard Colonel Aucamp say early in the morning in a comment to the matron at the Kroonstad Prison – Aucamp was accompanying the prison van in his car – that we would be stopping at Port Elizabeth that night. Had he, I wondered, deliberately let me hear him say that? Extremely likely.

Everything Aucamp did in relation to prisoners was carefully calculated. He certainly knew how to make our lives decidedly unpleasant. Whether he had had training in psychological manipulation (warfare) I do not know. What I do know is that he would have been aware that the news that I was being taken hundreds of miles to the south of the country, especially in the absence of any information as to the reason, would fill me with intense anxiety.

Alone in the little compartment at the front of the van – the African women had replaced the white men in the large compartment at the back – travelling, by and large, into the unknown, I spent quite a lot of time peering out through the little gap on the side of the van to my left. It was a few inches across, with small cream-coloured bars and covered with a piece of chicken wire. I wanted to have a more certain picture of exactly where they were taking me.

I had come to the conclusion that it was the intention of the authorities that I should spend my whole sentence in solitary somewhere in the south of the country. That appeared to be the only explanation for what seemed to be an almost inexplicable decision to separate me from my fellow trialists and take me across South Africa. On no account did I envisage a new trial.

I also used the long hours, on my distinctly uncomfortable small wooden bench which just fitted into the compartment at the front of the van and wobbled backwards and forwards and sideways as the van moved along the roads, to try to construct a picture of the space in which I would spend, it appeared, at least a night. Although I had been born in Port Elizabeth, had gone to school there and finally left it when I was eighteen years old after the death of my mother – our house had been sold – I could not remember where the gaol was situated. A gaol would have played no role in my life at that time.

To have a picture of the space I was destined to occupy, if only for a night, was apparently a psychological necessity. I constructed a picture of a section with little cells. There must have been about five of them, all on the same side of a gloomy passage. The passage had a red, concrete floor. I saw the doors of the cells and the shiny brass around the large keyholes.

I assumed that I would stay there for quite a few days before I was moved on somewhere else, maybe to Worcester, about 500 miles to the west of Port Elizabeth where I knew there was a long-term prison, housing also white prisoners. There was a cold chill in me as I thought of being kept in solitary, first in a cell in Port Elizabeth. In the picture I was constructing there were no prisoners in the red-floored, concrete passage and all the cell doors, with their large keyholes, reinforced by brass, were closed. Inside one of those cells was me.

I was sitting on the end of my bed with a somewhat grubby charcoal-grey blanket and a light in the middle of the ceiling, grey and dirty, towards which my painful eyeballs continually moved and stared as I tried to rearrange the dirt on the globe into a new pattern in my mind. Me here, and the sounds out there. Could I not hear somebody in the passage outside? Could I not hear soft footsteps? No, not footsteps, the sound of material, like legs coming into contact with the material of a skirt as somebody moved. And soft breathing. And the sound of somebody's tongue lying not absolutely still in the mouth. Alone in my cell at Pretoria during 90 days I had come to know, very precisely, what human beings sounded like out there on the other side of my cell door.

The prison van was turning sharply. It must have been going round a corner because my wooden bench lurched dangerously. I put my hands up to clutch onto something but there was nothing to hold onto so I placed my palm flat against the metal surface of the left side of the compartment. The bench started lurching the other way as the van swung round another corner, now going in the opposite direction. Or maybe it was just straightening out. I brought my outstretched arm down and quickly put the other one up, placing the palm against the metal on the other side of the little compartment.

As the van came into some sort of balance, I looked down at the floor. It was not a completely smooth metal floor. It had little ridges running probably about two and a half inches apart down the floor of the van, that is from the back to the front. And between these ridges and sometimes even flowing over them, I saw the streams of urine moving fast towards me. I lifted my feet in their high-heeled shoes up into the air a little, and tried, at the same time, to take up the ends of my open dark silver-coloured woven coat but that was no longer much use. The ends were already wet from the urine.

After the van had been steady for some time, the little streams drifted back under the metal partition that separated my compartment from the larger one at the back, with the ANC women. Small puddles were left behind. I put my feet down onto the metal floor. I was unable to miss some of the pools of liquid. I told myself I would simply have to bear with it.

My mind returned to the picture I was constructing of the gaol at the other end of my journey, initially in Port Elizabeth. There was a prisoner in the passage outside my cell, a prisoner in khaki uniform with a little faded green collar, and little faded green facings on two pockets on the front of the skirt. White buttons ran down the front. A gloomy figure with a slightly bent back and slightly hunched shoulders, like many long-term prisoners have.

My inside and my outside separated out as I watched the prisoner. The panic went. Instead there was gloom, and smells. A sanitary bucket clanged. The prisoner in the passage had taken the bucket from somewhere and placed it to one side of her. There was water in it. Gloomy water, with a bit of grey dirt mixed with some soapy froth on the surface and a grey dirt line forming just above the surface of the water, around the inside of the bucket.

She rolled down her thick stockings to her ankles, just above her heavy brown leather shoes – she was a white prisoner. She moved very slowly, in an endless dream. She took a cloth from one of her pockets, a rather dirty rag, dipped it in the water in the sanitary bucket, wrung it out a little and went down on her knees on the concrete and slowly washed the floor, getting up on her hauches now and again as she rinsed the cloth in the sanitary bucket, and then down onto her knees once more.

Meanwhile the tone of the engine of the prison van in which I was travelling had deepened and our pace was slowing down. We were obviously pulling up a steep hill. I stood up carefully from my bench, trying to keep my shoes out of the deeper puddles of urine and peered through the gap with the chicken wire. Outside, on either side of a pale grey tarred road, were steep hills, almost like cliffs, with thick dark bush. This is eastern Cape bush, I thought. We were just moving towards the crest of a very steep hill. This climbing of hills, with the deep struggling sound of the engine of the prison van, went on for miles. There was a constant changing of gears and a shuddering sensation. It was a landscape not well known to me.

Later, however, when we had left behind the steep-hilled country, I realised that we were travelling in that part of the eastern Cape I did know. This was the country of my childhood and youth. I had passed along here many a time by car with my mother and sister, later in my own car when I was at the university in Grahamstown, a small university town about 70 miles from Port Elizabeth.

I was not sure whether we had passed Grahamstown yet. I recognised the countryside but could not exactly place where we were. Was it just to the north of the town or rather to the south of it, towards Port Elizabeth? At least I knew vaguely where I was. We were indeed on our way to Port Elizabeth. Aucamp wouldn't be pleased if he knew that this area is familiar to me, I thought. He probably thinks he is bringing me to somewhere completely unknown to me. Instead he is in a way bringing me home ... And then the thought struck me that he was almost certainly very well aware that Port Elizabeth was my home town and this thought gave him sadistic satisfaction.

It was very strange to be going into prison in my own home town. Little had I dreamed of such a possibility when I lived there in a large comfortable home in an upper middle-class suburb. However, there seemed to be a kind of logic in it all. The seeds of my later opposition to the apartheid system were sown in young years. It had initially been a very personal response, relating to individuals who worked in our house, our nursemaid, the cook, the gardener. Our gardener came from Zimbabwe. These people were an important part of my life, of my upbringing. They looked after me, were apparently concerned for my welfare. The nursemaid played hide-and-seek with my sister and me and taught us sentences in isiXhosa. As I reached adolescence they were people with whom I empathised. Moreover, I tended to look up to them as adults. I was a child.

I sat down again on the little wooden bench in my metal space. I went back to the picture I was constructing: I must sort it out. I must have a picture in my mind of where I am going. I may be going to my home town but I will not see it. I will not live in that town. I will live in a gaol which is a world on its own.

My thoughts were interrupted again, for a few moments, as the prison van swung around a corner and I had to put up a hand to balance myself against the metal side of my compartment. The van straightened out and it was slowing down; there was a slight jerk, and the tone of the engine changed. The driver was changing down into a lower gear. I got up and peered again through the chicken wire. No, we were not climbing a hill. So why had he changed gear? The van seemed to be travelling in the centre of the road. Then it pulled again to the left-hand side. I realised that it must have been passing some vehicle. I sat down again on my bench, went back to my picture.

I asked myself if, because that white prisoner was there in the passage, busy with her bucket, I might be together with other prisoners. It was a gloomy thought but at least I would not be in solitary.

One of the things that worried me was the scale of my mental picture of the prison, I mean that part I was in. It was too small in scale. Why was it that I could not make it bigger? Maybe only buildings I had actually seen in real life, if I recreated them from my memory, would appear to correct scale?

The prison van was gathering speed. The tone of the engine was low and steady. And it sounded as though we were out in the open. Not the same engine noise as when we travelled between steep cliffs. Then the sound was enclosed, deep and loud. The puddles of urine on the floor were fairly steady. I decided that we were travelling on the level, out in the open. Flat, open land.

I peered again through the little rectangle of chicken wire. Yes, I knew this area well. The flat stretch of land before we got to the Zwartkops bridge. We were only a few miles away from Port Elizabeth now. Flat land on either side of the worn, and therefore light-grey, tarred road. There were little bits of low green-grey scrub. Bare, dry land. Typical eastern Cape countryside of the really bare, dry variety. I caught sight of a few sheep on the other side of wire fences. I knew that a few miles to the left there was the sea but I could not see it from where I was inside the van.

I sat down again on my bench. I returned to my picture.

As I was not, according to the picture in my mind at least, to be in solitary, I thought, I had better have the door of my cell open. Moreover, I would go out there into the passage, maybe whispering to the prisoner as I did, and go down on my knees onto the concrete floor, with my stockings rolled down to my ankles and dip my rag in the water of the sanitary bucket to the left of me. I would then see the wet patch spread on the floor with a little bit of light with bars across it reflected there. And the movement of my right arm, up and down and sideways. Slow motion.

I found the sense of gloom oppressive. I had a strong desire to escape from it, to get out of there, away from a demoralised prisoner in khaki uniform with dull, straggly hair and a pale face with dark shadows under the eyes. But what was the alternative? I knew the only alternative was solitary.

Here was Port Elizabeth, my home town. For the rest of the journey, I peered through the chicken wire in my little metal compartment. We had already bounced across the narrow Zwartkops bridge which could only take one car at a time so that other cars had to wait their turn. I had a fairly bumpy and jerky passage from now on. The surface of the road was uneven and the van kept on pulling up behind what I assumed must be other vehicles.

The result was that the urine went backwards and forwards under the metal partition that separated me from the larger compartment at the rear. It had splashed up onto my shoes so often by then that I decided that I was wasting precious time avoiding it. That precious time I could better use by trying to see whether I could recognise anything through the chicken wire.

I did recognise bits and pieces, a building here, a bit of railway there, a shed or a warehouse. But I couldn't remember exactly where it all was, except that it was at the north end of the town, the industrial area, with warehouses and motor car assembly plants.

Eventually the van pulled up. Was this the prison? I peered out through the chicken wire but all I could see was a concrete roadway, or something of that sort, and part of a grey, concrete structure which I thought might be part of the gaol. A metal door was opened at the side of my compartment and there was a warder and my female escort – she had been travelling in Aucamp's car – indicating to me that I should get out. So we *were* stopping at Port Elizabeth! I wondered for how long.

I must try and slip in a question, I said to myself. It is always worth a go, even if I don't manage to get any information. I felt panic rise in me at the uncertainty of it.

'Do you know whether we will be going to Worcester tomorrow?' I asked the escort. Since Worcester was about 500 miles to the west of Port Elizabeth, there was, if we were indeed going there, still quite a long trip ahead of us. I tried to get the question in quickly because I saw Colonel Aucamp climbing out of his car and coming towards us. He would not like me to know where I was going. Anyway, I didn't want to see the triumph in his cold, hostile, blue eyes when he sensed the anxiety that lay in my question. The escort, realising a little how I felt, laughed with amusement. 'I don't know where you are going,' she said, 'but I am stopping here.'

They hurried me out of the van and through a door. I was inside North End Prison, as I was later told. Nobody will know where I am, I thought anxiously. I turned to Colonel Aucamp.

'I would like a visit as soon as possible,' I said. 'My pre-classification visit.'

Aucamp responded with obvious satisfaction: 'You have already been classified.' He paused, savouring the moment. 'You have been classified a "D" prisoner.'

I knew, of course, that that meant only one visit and one letter in six months. I turned away from his blue triumphant eyes. I could be lost to the world for months.

'Kom.'

Inside the gaol a wardress took me up red polished concrete steps and then quite a way along a corridor to a cell on the left. Shortly before it on the same side was what appeared to be a kitchen. Up to this point there had been no cells along the passage. So I *am* to be in solitary! My cell was very different from the picture I had had in my mind in the prison van. It was relatively large. Moreover, it had a parquet floor. Probably

The prisoner's problem of space and location

the hospital section, I concluded, otherwise the floor would be concrete. And this was apparently confirmed by the fact that there was next door a bathroom and a toilet.

Other than the stairway, the passage and my section I knew nothing of the prison. Something that struck me, however, was the great hum of voices of what seemed to be hundreds of prisoners. As I knew now what my new space looked like, my task was to build up a picture of the gaol I was in. And, as it turned out, I spent many hours of that night working on a picture of the gaol on the basis of what I heard. I listened very closely. The cells, with the hum of voices, were apparently down the stairs I had come up and I concluded that they were big communal cells and with black female prisoners.

I was involved in rather a different thinking process from that I had been engaged in while in the prison van. For a start, it was all much bigger in my mind and I did not have the same difficulties with scale as I had had in my imagination in the prison van. It was a real space, part of which I had seen, and I was receiving auditory impressions which my brain sorted with great intensity.

Yet I felt constantly uncertain about my conclusions and in many ways I knew that what I constructed in my mind was merely an act of imagination and that things could be rather different. Indeed, in a way, the uncertainty in a real situation in a real prison represented a new type of mental torture. The attempt to use the senses to establish my surroundings was much more concentrated. I strained to gather as many impressions as I could.

What I had feared had come to pass.

I was alone.

And I did not know why I was there nor for how long.

Two years after my arrival in the Port Elizabeth Prison I was facing the prospect of release into the outside world. To a degree, a similar process started, only now I was straining to gain a picture of the outside from the inside. I tried to imagine the world I would be going out to.

It was more or less an impossible task. How could I put together two quite different worlds? There was no bridge between here and there. I looked at the soft fluffy white clouds in the sky above our courtyard in Barberton Prison and thought: The sky is the same inside as outside. If I were standing out there, beyond the front door of the prison, I would see the same clouds, would I not?

I did not answer that question.

Author's note

I DID NOT QUITE COMPLETE THE manuscript I had written in the house of Sonia and Brian Bunting in London after I left South Africa in April 1967.

I had started it about ten days after I came out of prison. At the start of the British academic year I began a thesis at Oxford University on the English revolution of the 17th century. It was the study of Christopher Hill, which I had read in Barberton, that had whet my appetite and, as it happened, Christopher Hill was to be one of those who supported my entry into Oxford. He was then Master of Balliol, a male Oxford college. I had obtained a fellowship for Southern Africans from the United Nations.

Until the year 2017, 50 years later, I was too busy in my profession as a historian to return to the manuscript. Moreover, in my spare time, I was concerned with other things, chiefly German history and culture. After a few years in England, I had moved to Germany, where I was to spend over 40 years.

I had written in one of my letters from Barberton Prison that I wanted to go to Germany because I was interested in the problem of subjectivism in German philosophy, which I suspected was closely related to narrow nationalism. That I went to East rather than West Germany was effectively to make little difference on that score and, after the fall of the wall in November 1989, a historic process which I was to capture in my 'German Diary', I was to find myself in a reunited Germany, where I lived almost 25 years until I returned to South Africa in 2014.

What intensified my search for answers about German philosophy and history was my marriage to a German citizen who had been brought up during Hitler times. As it happened, he, himself, was looking for answers, in particular in relation to the Hitler phase of German history. This was more especially in order to make sense of his own childhood and youth – it was shortly before his fifteenth birthday that defeat of the Third Reich was consummated. For decades he simply devoured books on the subject. We made a point, too, of watching the many documentaries on German television on the period. I found this all very instructive. The 40 or so years I spent in Germany were to prove to be a key phase in my pursuit of knowledge.

In 1967 I had intended to end this manuscript with something about my response to the outside world, starting with the drive from Barberton to Johannesburg – Flo and I were taken back to the Fort to be released from there a few days thereafter. Although the time factor played a role in my not having done so, there is no doubt that I had considerable resistance to completing it.

What would completion have actually meant? The outside world was too complicated to describe. How could I tie down my responses to the mass of impressions? More to the point, was there any meaningful connection between the two worlds? As I had sensed, there was no possible process of transition from the inside to the outside and this was not only in a psychological but also a literary sense.

Sylvia Neame
May 2018

Author's note

ABOVE: My exit permit with a gaol photo.

Above: Demonstration, London, soon after release, with me in a mini. Photo supplied by the Naidoo family. The child is Natalya Dinat.

Index

A

African National Congress 9–11, 18, 102, 103, 161, 165, 419, 455, 457

All Saint's Church, Barberton 213

Anderson, Ewald 179

Anderson-Doyle, Mollie 39, 40, 68, 74, 102, 103–4, 139, 140, 169, 178, 179, 192, 198, 214, 236, 288–9, 291, 294, 309–10, 313, 329, 378–9, 391

Armed Resistance Movement (ARM) 99, 135, 145, 305–6, 438

Aucamp, Colonel 1, 15, 22–6, 27–30, 32, 34–5, 37–8, 42, 48, 56, 59, 68, 89, 99–100, 112, 123, 142–3, 147, 161–2, 174–5, 205, 279, 291, 305, 308, 313–21, 323, 324, 345–7, 350, 352, 354, 397, 435, 437, 444, 447, 448–9, 454–5, 458, 462

Aucamp, Mrs 27–8, 34–5, 37

B

Barberton Bladsy 231, 309, 384

Barberton Maximum Security Prison, Eastern Transvaal 1, 5, 22, 24, 34, 37, 41, 42, 48, 50, 52, 58, 60, 61, 63, 65, 66, 67, 68–73, 76–9, 84, 86, 88–92, 93–5, 103, 111, 114, 116, 119, 120, 121, 128, 133, 137, 138, 147, 152–4, 169, 180, 186, 196, 207, 210, 212–3, 219, 222–3, 226–7, 228, 252–5, 268, 281, 289, 306, 308, 357, 376, 382, 388, 390, 398, 410, 417, 436, 440, 441, 448, 464

Barlow, Maude ('Anna') 329, 355

Barnard, Wardress 55, 56, 150–1, 184, 222, 224–5, 255

Barsel, Esther 40, 68, 103–4, 116, 167, 174, 179, 193, 204, 237, 259–60, 272, 305, 306, 310, 312, 326, 336, 358, 366, 403, 450

Barsel, Hymie 306

Benjamin, Pixie 5

Bester, Matron 49–53, 61–4, 70, 76, 82, 91–2, 98, 100, 105–9, 111–5, 116, 126–7, 152–3, 160, 161, 163, 165, 170, 183, 194, 198, 202, 215–6, 224, 226, 229–31, 235, 254, 257–8, 270, 276–83, 284–5, 288–91, 295, 297–9, 302–3, 304–5, 308–10, 313–21, 322–7, 328, 335–9, 346–7, 349, 366, 373, 390, 396, 415, 417, 436–7, 442, 450, 453

Bezuidenhout, Meneer 153, 159–60, 222–6

Bijl, Val (née Hutchinson) 220

Bizos, George 435

Bloemfontein police station 123, 433–4

Bloemfontein prison 123, 433-4

Bosch, Joey 65

Bonhoeffer, Dietrich 81, 236, 267

Boshoff, Judge Victor 161–9, 237, 284, 293, 341

Botha, Matron 126, 153, 159–60

Briggs, CP 27

Britz, Matron (Lieutenant) 1, 7, 11–13, 22, 24–6, 174, 190, 410

Bronkhorst, Wardress 69

Broodryk, Captain 142–8, 304–5, 347,

469

446, 450
Brookes, Alan 143
Bunting, Brian 465
Bunting, Sonia 465

C
Cajee, Amien 170
Cajee, Ayesha 170
Caledon Square police station 155, 219
Carneson, Fred 143–4, 358
Chiba, Laloo 135
Cilliers, JL 18
Colesberg Prison 1
Communist Party 1, 5, 29, 67, 68, 71, 77, 102, 135, 144, 161, 165, 235, 341, 354, 363, 388, 418, 422, 425, 451, 454
Congress Movement 171
Congress of Democrats 18
Cross, Sholto 143
Cullinan, Patrick 177
Cullinan, Wendy 177

D
Dinat, Natalya 468
De Crespigny, Caroline 86–7, 124, 142–3, 145, 170, 355, 357, 409
Defence and Aid Fund 205
De Melker, Daisy 6, 20
Doyle, Mollie *see* Anderson-Doyle, Mollie
Du Preez, Sergeant Jonathan 9, 10, 15, 23, 24, 29–30, 33, 37, 62, 144–5
Duncan, Florence (Flo) 40, 68, 104–6, 109–10, 115, 116, 119, 134, 150, 174, 231, 259–60, 268, 272, 293, 301–2, 305, 310–1, 335, 399, 411, 440, 442, 443, 448–9, 450–1, 466
Durrant, Geoffrey (Geoff) 186

E
Eastern Cape 2, 9, 18, 30, 42, 86–7, 206, 458, 460
Eastern Cape trials 2, 9, 114, 144, 413
Erasmus, Officer (security Branch) 420
Evening Post 205

F
First, Ruth 3
Fischer, Abram (Bram) 5, 77–8, 142, 162, 170, 174, 234, 289, 290, 306, 342, 354, 358, 364, 419
Fischer, Molly 364, 419
Focus 143–4, 147
Fordsburg, Johannesburg 5
Fordsburg police station 5, 145, 270, 386–9
Fort *see* Johannesburg Prison
Freud, Sigmund 262

G
Gandar, Laurence 147
Gazidis, Costa 235
Groote Schuur Hospital 82

H
Hanson, Harold Joseph, QC 199
Harris, John 17, 135–6
Hayman, Ruth 60, 204–5
Heymann, Issy 358
Hiemstra, Judge Victor 292–3
Hill, Christopher 82, 465
Hitler Germany 236, 326, 465
Huiseman, Matron 174, 430–3
Humansdorp 20, 10–1, 18, 23, 29–31, 33, 60, 72, 86–7, 113, 136, 142, 171, 195, 205, 413, 450, 454

I
International Defence & Aid 205

J
Jessop, Jill 155, 157
Jewell, Gillian 17, 19, 87, 155, 158, 220
Johannesburg Prison (the Fort) 5, 9, 21, 31–2, 36, 43, 52, 65, 70, 77, 99, 113, 135, 138, 142, 152–3, 164, 174, 212, 315, 361, 373, 390, 418–9, 424–7, 430–1, 434, 436, 438, 442, 452, 454
Joseph, Adelaide 120

K
Kathrada, Ahmed (Kathy) 3, 15, 18, 119,

Index

127, 140, 170–2, 186, 190, 208–9, 234, 364, 419
Kemp, Stephanie 40, 56, 59, 68, 96, 99, 104, 106, 108–9, 111, 254, 305–6
Khayinga, Wilson 9
Kotze, PJ 18
Kroonstad Prison 1, 34, 65, 66, 134, 230, 286, 316, 343, 455
Kruschev, Nikita 421
Kuny, Denis 31
Kuper, Justice Simon Meyer 136–7

L

Langley, Reverend Canon 212–7, 236, 272, 330, 333, 390–4
Liberal Party, South African 18, 135
Liberal Party's sit-in campaign 20, 32, 155, 219–20
Liliesleaf Farm, Rivonia 30, 208
Louw, Matron 22
Lubbe, Mrs 174, 426, 432
Ludi, Gerard 68, 136, 144–5, 161, 234–5, 343
Ludorf, Judge JF 284–7, 288, 290–1, 293, 294, 323–4
Lydenburg Prison 177, 227

M

Makwabe, Terrance 18
Mandela, Nelson 3, 249
Mandela, Winnie 119
Marshall Square 433
Mati, Winnard 18
Mbeki, Govan 18, 30, 171–2
Middleton(-Strachan), Jean 36, 38, 40, 45, 49, 50, 53, 68–, 84, 89, 116–7, 120, 142–3, 148, 149, 165, 167, 186, 188–9, 193, 195, 228, 231, 234–8, 265, 267–8, 271, 276, 280–1, 287, 292, 301–2, 311, 331, 356, 380, 381, 395–6, 398, 422, 426, 452
Mini, Vuyisile 9, 15, 17
MK *see* Umkhonto we Sizwe
Mkaba, Zinakile 9
Mountain View, Johannesburg 30, 120, 208

Mpendu, Zibia 114
Muil, Lieutenant 318

N

Naidoo family 468
Naidu, Savathrey (Savi) 177
National Union of South African Students (NUSAS) 99
Neame, Betty 204, 386
Neame, Graham 124, 142, 170, 175, 177, 199, 205, 357, 376, 377
Neame, Jennifer 329
Neame, JR (Bunny) 147, 204
Neame, Peter 175–8, 205, 357
Nel, Matron 6–8, 24
Nelspruit Prison 235
Ngudle, Looksmart 135, 147, 409
Nicholson, Ann 40, 52, 68–70, 94, 96, 102, 103, 108–10, 116, 119, 127, 134, 138, 143, 145, 148, 149, 168, 174, 183–4, 187, 192–4, 259–61, 266–72, 273–5, 287, 288–91, 292, 294–5, 300, 303, 304–6, 310–1, 323–4, 329, 331, 336, 344, 349, 359, 365, 373–6, 379, 380–9, 400, 406, 411, 437–8
North End Prison, Port Elizabeth 1, 2, 6, 7, 10, 12, 17, 20, 23, 24, 29, 32, 34, 37, 42–44, 52, 61, 75–6, 86, 100, 113–4, 134, 136, 150, 164, 209, 236, 315, 318, 462, 463

P

Pan-Africanist Congress 11
Pietersburg Prison 198
Pogrund, Benjamin 75
Port Elizabeth Prison *see* North End Prison, Port Elizabeth
Pretoria Central Prison 1, 2, 3, 5, 6–7, 20, 25, 34, 52, 145, 150–1, 153, 169, 174, 207, 208, 316, 328, 342, 376, 409, 410
Pretorius, Brigadier 64, 149, 290, 294–5, 305–6, 312, 315, 346–7, 350, 367, 397, 399, 413, 437, 442, 444, 450
Prison Board 100, 202, 227, 230, 344–8, 352, 395, 443–4, 446, 448

Progressive Party 342

R
Rand Daily Mail 29, 75, 147, 204, 205, 213
Rheeder, Margaret 6
Rhodes University, Grahamstown 18, 19, 329
Rivonia 30, 119, 135, 170, 208, 359
Rivonia Trial 2, 135, 170, 171, 328, 360, 364, 413, 419
Robben Island 18–9, 134, 140, 171, 172, 364, 405
Roberts, Austin 376
Roeland Street Prison 32, 219, 220, 326

S
Saloojee, Babla 135, 147, 233, 234
Schermbrucker, Ivan 358, 387–8
Schermbrucker, Jill 358, 400
Schermbrucker, Leslie 183, 5 338–9, 354–8, 359, 362, 370, 372–4, 375–6, 378–9, 382, 384, 388, 400–1, 406, 407, 411–2, 437, 452
Scholz, Doctor 152, 158–9
Schoon, Di 100, 103–10, 116–7, 326, 335, 342, 354
Security Branch 3, 9–11, 15, 23, 29, 68, 112, 120, 123, 134, 135, 140, 143–5, 153, 176, 190, 208, 233, 234, 329, 346, 347, 352, 361, 409, 419, 420–5, 430, 445, 450
Sisulu, Walter 208, 419
Soggot, David 10–1, 28, 33, 42, 49, 60, 62–3, 121, 171, 205
South African Prisons Department 6, 18, 23, 32, 59, 63, 64, 85, 112, 150, 231, 306, 315, 346, 349, 397–8, 447
Stalin, Joseph 405
Steyn, General JC 59–60, 64, 98, 109, 213
Strachan, Harold 12, 75, 98, 106, 204, 342, 446
Supreme Court 43, 121, 292

Suzman, Helen 135, 162, 342
Swanepoel, Captain Theunis 147, 234, 409
Symington, Major 89, 209, 315

T
Taljaard, Matron 47, 49, 55, 59, 61, 62, 64, 66, 83–4, 91, 92, 104, 111, 140, 153, 170, 187–9, 191, 214, 223, 226, 231, 281, 297, 305, 332, 340, 368–9, 415, 436, 438–9, 449

U
Umkhonto we Sizwe 11, 167
University of Natal, Pietermaritzburg 186
University of South Africa (UNISA) 123, 232, 236, 267

V
Van Rensburg, Gerrie 65–6, 423
Van Rensburg, Nic 145
Van Wyk, Colonel 22, 29
Van Zyl, Sergeant CJ 147
Vassen, Tommy 208
Viljoen, Brigadier 64, 149–50, 294–300, 301, 305, 307, 309, 331, 344–53, 396–8, 441
Vorster, Minister BJ 1, 99, 167, 174, 296, 300, 309, 310–1, 323
Vorster, Mrs 296, 348

W
Weinberg, Eli 161, 342, 363–4
Weinberg, Mark 359–64
Weinberg, Sheila 161–2, 173–4, 184, 194, 235–6, 238, 252, 259, 261, 267–8, 276, 280, 284, 287, 293, 308, 313, 320–1, 322, 342, 354, 359, 362–3
Weinberg, Violet 161, 338, 342, 354–8, 359, 362–3, 370
Wilkin, Wardress 125–6, 301–3, 313
Worcester Prison 34, 254, 456, 462